A Redlight Woman
Who Knows How to Sing the Blues

My Life in White Institutions

D1468600

MARY F. SISNEY

ISBN: 148270725X
ISBN-13: 978-1482707250

For My Favorite Students, especially Paulette Fonches

ACKNOWLEDGMENTS

Thanks to my first readers/responders, all but one of whom (my brother) were English majors and all but one of whom (guess who) appreciated my unique interpretation of <u>Great Gatsby</u>. In chronological order, they are: Bill McAdams, Paulette Fonches, Richard Sisney, Lindy Olson, Karen McGuire, and Celest Martin. Thanks also to my patient CreateSpace team, team 4. In alphabetical order, they are: Adam, Ashley, Carina, Colleen, Donovan, Jonny, Lance, Martin, Megan, Molly, Sarah G, Sarah J.

PROLOGUE
Why I Sing the Blues

While teaching freshman composition during the late seventies, I read (and subsequently taught) an essay by Joan Didion that helped me form what has become a kind of philosophy of life. The essay, titled "On Self-Respect," described how Ms. Didion felt when she didn't make Phi Beta Kappa. She said she understood at that point that lights wouldn't always turn green for her, and she became depressed. I realized as I read that statement that I never expected lights to turn green for me, and so I never became depressed. I was often angry, occasionally disgusted or bitter, but never depressed. People who don't expect lights to turn green for them are not disappointed when they see a red light. And on those rare occasions when lights do turn green, they are delighted. I shared my thoughts with the freshmen, pointing out (I don't remember now if I actually had evidence or if I was just blowing smoke) that working class and/or nonwhite people were less likely to commit suicide because they were too busy trying to survive to think about dying. Most students bought that argument, but one rebellious critical thinker argued that there was more than one way to commit suicide, and when working class and/or nonwhite people took drugs, drank too much, ate too much, ate the wrong food, or joined gangs, they were committing a different kind of suicide. Touche. That's why I loved teaching. I could learn so much from students, often students who weren't smart in the usual book-learning way, the "A" students, but those who could think and didn't just buy what the teacher was selling or weren't just there to take in information needed to pass the test, to earn the "A," to make Phi Beta Kappa, and get on with their lives.

As the years passed, I developed my redlight philosophy to include something I call the power of negative thinking. It's part superstition and part belief based on experience. I believe that the best way to avoid being surprised by trouble is to expect it. I try to borrow a little trouble to avoid finding myself in big trouble. Most of the time this braking for the red light instead of hoping for the green light method works. I'm most likely to encounter major problems when I'm cruising through the green lights, thinking that all is well. When I expect trouble, it's less likely to arrive

Although my borrowing trouble, expecting the worst and hoping for less than the best approach to life might make me less carefree, I am convinced that my recognition from childhood that life would not be easy helped me handle the many barriers, burdens, trials, and tribulations that I have faced throughout my now lengthy life. Being born a black female in almost exactly the middle of the twentieth century (1949) in a town (Henderson, Kentucky) where the South began (there are many of these towns; this one was separated from the North by the Ohio River) to parents who were too young (my mother had turned 21 twenty days earlier; my father was 24; I was their second child), not well educated (my mother graduated from high school; my father finished tenth grade), and not really suited to raising children (one being an alcoholic, the other being a high-strung, verbally abusive drama queen) in a two-room bungalow/shack with an outhouse, suggests that I should have ended up married to a batterer or (given my personality) in jail for killing the batterer. Instead I earned a Ph.D. and taught English at two universities, one private (Tufts) and one public (Cal Poly Pomona), for thirty years. That I became an English professor is especially remarkable since my maternal grandmother, with whom I lived when I was four and five and again when I was thirteen and fourteen, was illiterate, not just functionally illiterate, but literally illiterate, unable to read and able to write only her name until I somehow taught her to write, even though I was the only person who could read her writing. She was, in fact, my first student. When I left my grandmother's house not quite three months after my fifteenth birthday, I certainly had no reason to expect that fifteen years later I would earn a Ph.D. in English.

Just because I didn't expect life to be easy doesn't mean that I stoically accepted the hard times. I complained often and loudly. In her book about blues singers, Angela Davis distinguishes between blues songs that are complaints and blues songs that are protests. Although I'm often mistaken for a singer because of my husky, apparently somewhat melodic, speaking voice, I can't carry a tune well. But in my own way I sang the blues, and my concerts included both kinds of blues songs. I complained about the small things and protested the more important ones. I complained, for instance, about some of the stupid rules that Cal State professors had to follow, like how many office hours we should keep during finals week (unlike many of my colleagues, who ignored the rules, I followed them while complaining), but I protested when the CSU system introduced merit pay to try to make the state schools more like private schools. I complained about all of the papers I had to grade and how large some of my classes were, but I protested when, during the RTP (retention, tenure, promotion) process, I was ranked second behind my white male colleague, who taught one or two classes per quarter while I taught three. Whether complaining or protesting, I loved to sing the blues. It was one of my hobbies. Sometimes people assumed that my complaints were protests and would try to suggest solutions, but I would let them know that I was just complaining because I liked to complain. I believe that my willingness and ability to sing the blues, along with my ability to laugh, helped me overcome and survive many of the obstacles that I faced.

Starting my educational career in an all-black institution also gave me a head start toward success. Timing may not be everything, but it's often helpful. And I guess I was lucky to be born before Brown vs. Board of Education. I was five in 1954, but integration didn't come to Henderson, Kentucky, until after I started school in 1955. All of the black children my age attended first and second grades at all-black Alves Street Elementary School. It wasn't until third grade that those blacks who lived "on the other end of town" and those parents with the most nerve and/or the most prestige in the community sent their children to what whites called "integrated" and we called "white" schools. I didn't go to the white school until the seventh grade, and I went then because there was no black junior high school in Henderson.

The black teachers at Alves Street Elementary School weren't as well educated (only the principal and one teacher had the B.A.; the rest had A.A.'s) as the white teachers at Barrett Junior High and the two main elementary schools in our town, but they could teach as well as, and in some cases better than, those other teachers. And they provided something the often racist, Southern white teachers of the late fifties and early sixties could not have provided--a strong sense of identity and the self-esteem that I needed to survive the racism I would face when I moved into the white world. The black teachers knew me and knew my parents. At least one of them had taught both of my parents, and another younger one had been a classmate of my mother's. Alves Street was also my neighborhood school; we lived in three different homes during the time I went there, and all three were within three or four blocks of the school. I felt at home in that school. I was with my people.

After I left Alves Street, I entered a new world, where I was definitely not at home. From the seventh grade until I completed my Ph.D., I had only one black classroom teacher, an Education professor at Northwestern. At University of Southern California (USC) I took a directed study in black literature with a black professor, and I had an Asian professor for a linguistics course. All of my other teachers/professors were white. Once I entered this new world, I started singing a new song, call it "These White Folks Blues." Often when I sang that song, especially in later years when I was a professor and my white colleagues got on my nerves, I would remind myself that I was not at Fisk or Howard. I had chosen to spend my life in white institutions. Once I graduated from high school, I could have attended black colleges, but I was living in Evanston, Illinois, at the time, and I didn't think about taking a train or subway to Chicago, where I might have found at least a blacker school than Northwestern. Once I earned my Ph.D. at USC (don't ask!), I could have tried to find a teaching job at a black college. But I wasn't aware of any black colleges in Southern California, and that's where I wanted to live. Besides, having been born and mostly raised in the Jim Crow South, I saw integration as a good thing. Had I been from the generation born after the civil rights era, I might have felt a need to get in touch with, or stay in touch with, my black roots. But having spent my early years immersed in a black community, a black church, and a black school, I felt quite rooted in my blackness, maybe too rooted there, which is why I had trouble in white institutions.

Several times when I taught graduate seminars, I talked about reading from the inside versus reading from the outside. I explained that I read Toni Morrison and Richard Wright's books from the inside; I identified with their characters and the experiences that they described. But I read books by such writers as Joan Didion, Edith Wharton, and F. Scott Fitzgerald, who focused on upper-class white folks, from the outside. I enjoyed some of those books as much as I enjoyed Wright's books, but I just read them differently. I had that same kind of outside/inside experience in white institutions. When I retired in 2009 at the age of sixty, I had spent forty-eight years in white institutions, starting in 1961 when I was a seventh grader. But to revise my hometown motto ("on the Ohio but never in it"), I was in the white institutions but never of them. No matter how long I stayed in white institutions, I never became an insider.

Now that I'm finally "free at last! free at last!" as I jokingly shouted at my last department meeting, I am ready to tell the story of how I survived and occasionally thrived, despite being a stranger in what often seemed the strange land of white folks. As I look back on those forty-eight years, I am not only happy to be free but also mostly satisfied with what I have accomplished. I like to believe I changed a few attitudes and behaviors in those white institutions, and I know I changed some minds. Following are the blues notes of a redlight woman, looking back with few regrets, occasional anger and bitterness, but also considerable satisfaction at having survived the white institutions while remaining mostly black.

CHAPTER ONE

Nobody Knows the Trouble I've Seen

D uring the early nineties, a student I didn't know interviewed me for a class in Ethnic Studies. She wanted to interview a black woman, and I guess the pickings were slim at Cal Poly, so her instructor, who knew me, sent her to my office. The student gave me a copy of the paper that she wrote based on that interview. At one point in the paper, she reported that I had lived with my grandmother in Kentucky while my mother worked in Illinois and commented that the situation must have been difficult for me. I thought about that statement; it didn't seem difficult at the time. I loved my maternal grandmother, and she adored me. And living with a grandmother while the mother works up North or even lives in the same town is typical in the black community. Ask Oprah Winfrey, Maya Angelou, and Jamie Foxx.

I guess if I just list the details of my childhood it will sound sad, tragic, pitiful. Like most black babies born in the South in the forties, I was born at home (on the ides of March), which was that two-room bungalow with the outhouse. My twenty-one year old mother already had my brother, who wouldn't turn two until late July, but I was the last child she had. My father was somewhere drunk when I was born, so he missed the excitement. I caught pneumonia at some point during my first couple of years living in that shack, and it developed into tuberculosis, but the old black doctor who delivered me and treated the black folks in Henderson didn't recognize it, so he just treated what he thought were persistent colds. When I had my tonsils and adenoids removed at seven, a younger black doctor, who had just arrived in town, discovered the spot on my lungs but said it had healed. I didn't have to go to a sanatorium, but I did have to take cod liver oil for years. Possibly because of the TB, I was a weak, sickly looking child with long bony limbs and big feet, thanks to my father, whose nickname was Foots. But I was clearly already a survivor, having fought off TB without the help of a doctor or any real medicine.

Foots was a drunk. I don't have to explain what that means for a family. Others have written books about living with alcoholics. Read Suzanne Sommers' first book, and you'll get the picture. But I had it easier than some children of drunks because Foots had the decency to become a rolling stone. Since I moved in with my grandmother before my fourth birthday (and stayed with my parents only on the weekend), and since Foots left for Baltimore to be with his army buddy (they were the only two in

2

their unit to survive some hideous battle in World War II) right around the time I was losing my tonsils and discovering I had TB and stayed for almost a year, returning sober, I remember only his drunken antics when he fell off the wagon after four years. I figured out before my mother did that he was drinking because he came home from work (as a shipping clerk at a department store in Evansville, Indiana) and went straight to the bathroom to gargle. Hello! Soon he was coming home sloppy drunk. I was in sixth grade at the time. My favorite scene from that year of living with a drunk occurred when he was talking to some friend of his, who wasn't actually there, and said, "They said make ourselves at home, so let's make ourselves at home" and then peed on the rug in my parents' bedroom. Did I mention that my mother was a neat freak, one of the cleanest women in Henderson? Another time a friend of the family found him in the street, the gutter, my mother said, in Evansville and drove him home, where he promptly messed in his pants. He was embarrassed when he sobered up that day, and I felt sorry for him. But again, he had the decency to give us a break. Just before my thirteenth Christmas, he was supposed to go to court in Evansville because he had been caught in a raid (gambling, maybe), but he went instead to Cleveland where he found a soul mate, a fellow drunk, and lived with her and her mother and children until she and the mother died. I saw him only three times after he left Henderson in 1961, the same year that I entered Barrett Junior High: once around 1963 or 64 when he came home to see about his mother after she had a stroke; the second time in 1969, when we both returned to Henderson to attend the funeral of his older brother,

Uncle James; and the last time in 1992 when he and my mother had both returned to Henderson to live (not together, although he had high hopes), and I visited her and saw him at his sister's house.

Soon after my father deserted in 1961, my mother also left Henderson (in early 1962) because she lost her job at the segregated hosiery mill. The company closed the black mill and sent most of the workers to the white mill but decided that my mother, who was probably the best worker among the young women and often assisted the foreman, the only man working in the mill, was too mouthy. They said she was too old, but she was thirty-three at the time, not exactly ancient. She tried to find work as a maid, but there were not enough rich white people in Henderson to provide her with sufficient income to pay for the house that she and my father had bought in the summer of 1958 and to support her two children. So she moved to Highland Park, Illinois, to work as a live-in maid.

Thus began a journey that took me to six different households (seven, counting the original household with my mother, father, and brother) in a little over two years. Here we go: First, from late January, 1962, to May of that year, I lived with my paternal grandmother, the original Mary Sisney, her daughter, my Aunt Mary Belle Harvey, her husband, Uncle John, and his nephew, Bernard, whom they were raising as their son. I slept in the bed with my grandmother. Then my brother (who was living with my paternal uncle while I lived with my grandmother and aunt) and I moved to Evanston to live with our maternal second cousin, his wife, three children, and their "maid" (don't ask). We had to

4

live in Evanston because my mother was living "on the place." She was living with the white folks for whom she worked, and those folks don't usually have room for children. I slept in the room with my two male third cousins. I was in the twin bed of the younger cousin while he slept in the same bed as his brother, except that one time when he left his bed, came and crawled into mine (or actually it was his) and peed. Meantime, my brother slept in the basement because, of course, "the maid" had to have her own room. At some point that summer, it became clear that Second Cousin didn't have room for two teenage children, so I moved in with my mother on the place in Highland Park. I slept in the bed with my mother, just off the kitchen while the white folks all slept at the other end of the house. It was a fairly spectacular house with lots of glass, but I didn't really enjoy my stay the month or so that I lived there. My mother realized that it wasn't a good idea for me to stay in Highland Park, where I would be the only black child in the school and would be in the same class as the white folks' son, who unfortunately didn't have my, or apparently any, academic gifts. She also saw that my brother wasn't in a good place in Evanston, so we went back to live with my maternal grandmother in Henderson. Initially, I slept in the bed with that grandmother while my brother slept on the rollaway bed in the kitchen. He lasted there about two months before she threw him out one night. At fifteen, my brother was a normal child who liked to have fun and go out, so he was better off living where I had started with my paternal grandmother and aunt. He shared the room with Bernard. I stayed with Mother, my maternal grandmother, for the next two school years. But in the summer of 1963, I had a job working as a junior live-in maid, called a "mother's helper," in Highland Park, around the corner from where my mother now lived (she and the family she worked for had moved out of the glass house into a larger but less spectacular house, and my brother stayed with them for the summer, sleeping in the room with their academically challenged son). I had a bed to myself for the first time since I left the house that my parents bought, but the bed was in the basement, down the hall from the laundry room. The Rs' house was also fairly spectacular. It was a split-level house with a dishwasher in the fancy kitchen and modern, expensive-looking furniture in the rest of the house. Finally, my mother married my stepfather in May, 1964, and when school ended in Henderson, my brother and I moved to Evanston (again), where he shared a room with my stepbrother, another not quite adopted child, my stepfather's great nephew whom he had raised. I shared a room with my stepfather's younger sister when I was at home, but mostly that first summer I was back in Highland Park, working for the Rs and sleeping in the basement. By the time school started in Evanston, the younger sister, as well as another sister and her children, were out of my stepfather's house, and I had my own room for the first time, unless you count that room in the white folks' basement, and I don't; it wasn't mine.

When I summarize my life during those two tumultuous years, I have the same impression as the student interviewer. It must have been difficult. It certainly should have been difficult, especially considering that I had just started through puberty when my journey through these very different households began.

I can remember exactly when puberty started for me because it happened on Christmas Day. I had a red Christmas in 1961, and probably less than a month later, I was moving into the first of six new households. But at the time, I found the moves more exciting than traumatic. My brother and I stayed at my paternal grandmother and aunt's house during our summer vacation days while my mother worked at the nearby hosiery mill. We stopped going there when I was ten or eleven, and I kind of missed being with them. They were good cooks, and my aunt and grandmother were both funny. (However, I discovered during my brief stay in their home that they were not as much fun to live with as they were to visit.) Moving up North seemed like a great adventure to me at thirteen, although I admit that I was happy to move back to Kentucky after spending a month or so in the white folks' house.

All of that moving from place to place and from family to family taught me to adjust to my surroundings quickly and easily. When one of my graduate school friends who now lives in Pasadena and I traveled together in the summer of 1984, she noticed how quickly I made myself at home in motel rooms in Berkeley, Lake Tahoe, and San Luis Obispo. I explained that I had experience moving into new places and finding a spot to settle when I was a child. My Pasadena friend and I made good travel buddies and are still good telephone friends because we have similar personalities. We like to read and think and are both rooted in our homes, although not necessarily in families, being single ladies. We are also not that into traveling (We were escaping the L.A. Olympics in 1984). But while Pasadena Friend (I will occasionally use real names but will mostly use fake names to protect the innocent and the guilty) didn't leave her parents' house until she was twenty-nine and then just moved to an apartment a few blocks from her parents and down the street from her uncle and aunt, I moved from Evanston to L.A. when I was twenty-three and then from L.A. to Boston when I was thirty, leaving behind my mother and stepfather, who had followed me from Evanston to L.A. And while Pasadena Friend has never taken a trip alone by bus, plane, or train and never driven alone farther than probably a couple of hours from home, I've traveled to New York City (twice alone, once with my mother) as well as to New Orleans, and took several trips to and from Chicago alone. In my youth, I boldly walked the streets of Chicago, New York City, and L.A., looking for jobs, for landmarks (The Empire State Building), for well-known restaurants (Tad's Steakhouse), and just exploring the cities, seeing what I could see. I suspect that I would not have been so adventurous if I had not had such a peripatetic childhood.

My childhood gave me other tools. Because my maternal grandmother couldn't count (she used quarters to measure money: "How many quarters are in $2.55?" she would ask), I handled the weekly allowance that my mother sent to support me. So at thirteen and fourteen, I bought my food, paid for my beautician, and paid my church dues out of the money my mother sent. It's not surprising, therefore, that I have been a fairly good money manager as an adult.

I also learned to devalue material things because of my early experiences. I moved back and forth between my grandmother's old rundown house and the mansions of the white folks two years in a row. Guess which house I preferred? A passage from my favorite novel, Toni Morrison's Song of Solomon, describes how I felt about my grandmother's house: "the only one [Pilate's house] he knew that achieved comfort without one article of comfort in it." The white folks' houses had matching curtains and bedspreads while my grandmother's house had homemade quilts on the beds with no bedspreads and those brown pull up-and-down blinds on the windows. She also had sticks in the windows to hold them up in the summer. The white folks had at least one color television in their houses, but my grandmother had no television, and she played her radio only on Sunday when she listened to Oral Roberts (since I was her favorite grandchild, she did allow me to play it for an hour on Saturday to hear the top ten hits). The white folks had dishwashers, washers and dryers, and, of course, showers and bathtubs. My grandmother did not have hot water; we had to boil water on the stove, and we took baths in a round aluminum tub. She was very proud, however, of her indoor toilet, and she had a refrigerator, which she still called an icebox. The white folks had multi-level or multi-wing houses with four to five bedrooms, multiple bathrooms, and attached garages. Mother had a shotgun house, with the front room, where her roomer, Miss Martha, slept, the middle room, where she and I slept, and the back room, which was the kitchen, but had that extra roll- away bed for emergency sleepovers. She had added a side room, which contained a place to do the washing with one of those washboards and that aluminum tub, and her indoor frost proof toilet of which she was so proud. Of course, that added room was not heated, so in the winter she and Miss Martha used their chamber pots if they needed to go to the bathroom during the night while I just threw on a sweater and tried to do my business quickly.

I didn't think much about the differences in the living conditions when I stayed with the white folks in the summer and my grandmother in the winter. I guess if I thought about it, I would have seen it as the difference between living in the North and living in the South and/or living with blacks and living with whites. I also knew, of course, that my maternal grandmother's house was unusually primitive for the sixties, even for a Southern black widow's house. My other black relatives, both in the North and the South, had more modern homes. Everyone else I knew had bathtubs, hot running water, and televisions. Still, I preferred Mother's house because in Mother's house I was the Queen of the World. She thought I was the most wonderful person who ever lived, and so as Milkman felt in Pilate's house, I felt very comfortable in my grandmother's home.

One of my colleagues, noticing my self-assurance and probably wondering how a black woman looking like me (I'm not exactly a great beauty) could be so confident, asked for the source of my self-esteem. She wondered if my mother had given it to me. I said, "Nope, my grandmother. I lived with her for a total of four years." My white colleague said, "That's all it takes." And she's probably right. Four years of being worshipped and adored should be more than enough to build the confidence needed to survive years of being demeaned and diminished. In fact, it was probably good for me to have the experience of working for the white folks to balance my Queen of the World experience with my grandmother. If I hadn't lived with the Js, my mother's white folks, for a month or so and not dealt with Mrs. J's annoyance when I answered her question about missing her two dogs with a sincere (she'd probably say sullen) and astounded "No," then I might have thought that I was a really important person whose feelings mattered more than some boring dogs (although the basset hound did have an interesting face and at least made himself useful by mouthing the paper and bringing it into the house). I was a thirteen-year-old girl, leaving my mother behind, and Mrs. J was offended that I wasn't going to miss her smelly (The basset hound also had gas) dogs? If I hadn't had to hear at fourteen, my white employer, Mrs. R, tell a racist joke to calm her two children's nerves during an especially violent late afternoon storm, I might have thought that I truly was one of the most important people in the world and expected to be treated with respect at all times. My mother, God bless her bold, fearless, get-her-out-of-Kentucky-before-they-lynch-her soul, had to explain to Mrs. R that her little joke about Mary's being so scared that she turned white wasn't funny and that she probably shouldn't tell such jokes to any black folks, no matter what their age.

I didn't laugh at Mrs. R's racist joke, but Mother kept me laughing all the time. She was effortlessly funny, and what made her especially funny is that she wasn't trying to be funny and didn't realize that she was funny. I would never call either of my grandmothers a clown or fool to her face and usually used those terms derisively, but I once used Ralph Ellison's distinction between the fool and the clown (in <u>Invisible Man</u>) to explain the difference between them. The clown, as Ellison suggests, wears a mask and tries to be funny. The fool is not aware that he or she is funny. Grandma, my paternal grandmother, was a clown. She told jokes and was deliberately funny. Mother was the fool. She was not an obnoxious fool, but a delightful fool, who didn't understand the modern world and couldn't figure out why I found her cluelessness funny. I still tell stories about Mother, who died in 1981. I like to tell the story of the time she was talking on the telephone and kept saying "yes ma'am," "yes ma'am" and then started frowning. Finally, she slammed down the telephone. When I asked her what was wrong, she said, "That white woman kep' sayin' the same thang over and over." I think the white woman was saying something like, "The number is not in service at this time." When I told Mother that she was talking to a recording, she said, "A what?" In response to my howls of laughter, she shook her head and said, "You sure is nervous. You jus' laugh all the time."

Another favorite Mother story was such a hit that it was used as part of my retirement party roast. I was going with my "play" boyfriend to Audubon Park to look for insects for a biology project during my freshman year in high school. When Mother heard my plans, she warned me to keep my dress down while I was around "that boy." When I said that I was wearing shorts, she said, "Well, keep'em down." Of course, I started laughing, and Mother shook her head and talked about how nervous I was. Actually, I was probably less nervous living with Mother than at any other time in my life. Certainly I had less trouble with her than I did with the other adults with whom I lived. And because I lived so peacefully with Mother, I can now tolerate living with her lookalike daughter, my mother.

When I left Mother's house in May, 1964, I moved to Evanston (spending the summer and then weekends during the school year with the Rs in Highland Park) to live with my mother and stepfather. My stepfather had an aristocratic sounding name, Dexter D. Weathersby, and when he visited Henderson a few months before he and my mother married, he described his house, which seemed worthy of a man with that name. According to him, this palatial house had four bedrooms and two full baths, with a toilet and sink in the full basement. There were several televisions in the house as well. What Dexter didn't mention was how many people lived in the house at that point. Let's see: there were his half sister and her two little boys, his youngest (half) sister, who was not quite two months younger than I, his and his sisters' father, and his not quite adopted son/great nephew. It wasn't a house; it was a freaking hotel.

When my brother and I arrived there, we were surprised to see all of the furniture from our house in Henderson (it had been in storage) in the living room and three of the four bedrooms. Only the dining room set and one bedroom suite were different. His youngest sister and my stepbrother talked about how impressed they initially were with the Henderson furniture, making me wonder what the original furniture in the house looked like. Fortunately, I was working at the Rs that summer, so I didn't spend much time in the too crowded house. By the time my summer job ended, the one sister had married and moved with her two sons to her husband's apartment, the father had moved in with another of his twenty-two children (by three or four women, two of whom he married), and the youngest sister had moved in with one of her other siblings. That left Dexter and my mother, my stepbrother, John Lee, my brother, and me. Then the next year my brother went to college, and my stepbrother joined the air force, leaving only three of us, plus our roomer, Melva. We had roomers several times, but in the last few years that I lived in Evanston, my mother, Dexter, and I were the only permanent residents in that four-bedroom house.

Unlike my father, Dexter was not a drunk, but he had other problems. He liked to control everybody's money, which would have been okay if he had been a good money manager. He was not. His first wife had been a few years older than he and not well educated, so he handled all of their money badly. One of the first stories John Lee told my brother and me was about how he paid for his car, a 1958 Pontiac, twice; he gave Dexter the money to pay, he thought, for the car, but when it was time for John to take possession of the car, the money was gone. Dexter had been very generous to some of his other family members, not requiring sufficient rent from the sister who had two children, for instance, to cover her share of the expenses, and he constantly borrowed to cover his bills, so shortly after he married my mother, she discovered that he was so behind in his house payments that he was about to lose the house. She had to help him pay the house note.

Most men would have been a little wary of marrying a woman with two teenagers, but when Dexter saw my brother and me, he didn't see potential trouble; he saw two more checks that he could control. Forget it, Dexter! My mother, brother, and I weren't having it, especially after we heard John Lee's story. My mother was a much better manager of money, and eventually (after maybe seven years of marriage) Dexter figured that out, but until he did, there were often arguments whenever money came into the house, and he couldn't get his hands on it. When I found a summer job in the federal Youth Opportunity Program, Dexter planned for me to pay the mortgage on the house in Henderson, which was temporarily without a tenant. I suggested that maybe I couldn't work after all, at which point my mother said that I would just work to buy my own clothes and wouldn't have to pay any mortgages.

After a few times of being rebuffed when he tried to take money he hadn't earned, Dexter tried to be more subtle. It didn't work. After two summers of working at Fort Sheridan in the Youth Opportunity Program, I took the civil service test so I could make more money. After I passed the test, I was invited to work during the Christmas break of my senior year of high school. Dexter volunteered to give me the money to pay the woman who drove me and several other federal workers (all adults) to Fort Sheridan from Evanston. I could have paid for the ride myself since I had a babysitting job, but I took Dexter's gift. I wasn't fooled, however. I told my mother that Dexter was giving me the six dollars for transportation, hoping that I would be so grateful that when I was paid, I would give him most of my check. My mother accused me of being hateful and ungrateful. Maybe I was, but I was also right. As soon as I picked up my check and didn't give any of it to Dexter, he had a fit. He talked about how I should at least offer to pay back the money he had "given" me. Why would I pay back money that he gave me? I didn't borrow it. I can't remember how that argument ended. I may have paid back the six dollars, but he didn't get any other money from me. I used the rest of that money to pay for my class ring and to save for other graduation expenses.

When I turned eighteen, Dexter decided to have a little talk with me. My relationship with him had become so strained that I played a game of seeing how long I could avoid encountering him outside of the required dinner table meetings, and I tried to talk to him as little as possible. In fact, from January, after I received my check for the two weeks of employment at Fort Sheridan, until our makeup meeting on my birthday in March, my "conversations" with Dexter consisted on my part of one or two words: "Hi," "Bye," "uh, huh," unh,unh (that's "no), "okay." So Dexter was going to clear the air. Or so he thought. He also thought he was going to lecture me on how to behave. But I actually lectured him; I wouldn't count him as one of my students as I did my maternal grandmother. But I think Dexter got schooled on the day I turned eighteen.

I don't remember exactly what he said, but it had something to do with my becoming an adult and needing to act like an adult by being responsible. When it was my turn to speak, I pointed out that he had never known me when I didn't have a job, that I always worked. He wanted to know how that helped him. Well, I told him. "You carry me as a dependent, right? You get more money in your paycheck because you say you're taking care of me. But you have never bought my lunch for school, bought my books, paid for me to get my hair fixed, or paid for my clothes to be cleaned. I give Mama money in the summer to help with the household expenses, and that helps you. You should not want to take the money of a child that you didn't know when she wasn't making any money," I said. Dexter was astounded, mainly because I said so much at once. I think he had forgotten that I could talk in complete sentences. But he also knew that he had lost the argument because Dexter was no fool.

Still, he made one last attempt to persuade me to give him money directly before he gave up. Because during my freshman year my mother worked for Northwestern as a maid in one of the freshman dorms, I paid only 50% of the tuition. And because I had both an Illinois State Scholarship and a scholarship from Northwestern, I received a stipend every quarter. The stipend could be used to buy books and pay living expenses. Now as an official adult, I didn't mind helping with the household expenses. After all, one reason I received the maximum amount given for the Illinois State Scholarship is that my parents' salaries were fairly low. But I planned to give any extra money to my mother, the person who knew how to manage money, and the one who had taken care of me financially before I had a job. I also worked part time at Montgomery Ward during my freshman year, so I had money to spare, but not for Dexter to spend lavishly on God Knows What so that he could come back looking for more money. When he needed money for God Knows What, he started raving about "that scholarship money." My mother just quieted him down while I made noises about living in the dorm. Eventually, Dexter shut up and learned to appreciate the money that I gave my mother. And when I graduated and worked full time, I actually paid rent, which he appreciated even more.

In one of my graduate African American Novel seminars, we discussed why there were so many interesting portraits of the black mother, even in texts written by black male writers such as Langston Hughes and Richard Wright, and so few black father figures portrayed. We decided that it was because the black father was often absent or weak. My story seems to support that argument. My mother was the dominant figure in my life, partly because she didn't disappear but also because she made more money than my father, even when he was sober and working. And she made more sense than my stepfather, especially when it came to understanding how to handle money.

Still, Dexter and Foots were not complete losers. When he was sober, Foots was funny, smart, and much calmer than his wife, a better parent in some ways than she was. And Dexter, while a lousy money manager, was also very smart in many ways. Although he didn't finish high school and what little education he received was in the segregated schools in small town Mississippi at the beginning of the twentieth century (he was born in 1911), he was a very literate man, who loved to read the Bible and the newspaper and could pronounce words that gave me trouble. When he wasn't getting on my nerves trying to take my hard-earned money, he and I had fun speaking French to each other. Dexter's French accent was probably better than mine, so I guess he was one of my early students, since I taught him French as I was learning it. He would crack me up saying, "Merci beaucoup" when I passed the bread or the butter during dinner. He was also an excellent chauffeur, who drove me from Chicago to Los Angeles when I started graduate school (my mother and I couldn't drive at that point), partly because he did it for a living after he resigned as a Pullman porter, but also because he was great with directions. Unlike his stepdaughter, who always turns left when she should turn right or vice versa, Dexter was rarely lost, and if he went to a place once, he could find it again.

I wonder what these two men would have been like if they had been born white or a generation later. They probably would have gone to college and been successful. Foots might have still had problems with alcoholism since his mother was an alcoholic, was, in fact, drunk when he was born. But maybe he would have entered a rehab facility and become a manager of a Burger King, McDonald's, Arby's, or Dunkin Donuts, all jobs his son held. And Dexter could have gone to college and maybe become an airline pilot instead of a Pullman porter and chauffeur.

I'm not mad at my two poor excuses for father figures because I realize now that they gave me a wonderful gift. If they had been the kind of daddies that every little girl hopes to have, I might be with that wife batterer now, scared to leave because I need him to take care of me. Or I might have just stayed home with my parents, reading books in my room until a handsome or not so handsome man found me there and took me away to live with him. But by the time I was eighteen, I knew that I would have to take care of myself. I knew there would be no Knight in Shining Armor or Prince Charming to rescue me. Even if I married, I expected to work and to take care of myself.

I also knew by eighteen what kind of work I didn't want to do. I didn't want to be a maid, nor did I want to work in an office. I knew that because I had already done those jobs. I worked for the Rs during my fourteenth and fifteenth summers. I also worked for them every weekend during my sophomore year, my first year at Evanston Township High School. I left school at 3:30 every Friday, rushed home, caught a ride with Dexter when he was in town, or caught a cab to downtown Evanston and took the train to Highland Park when he was on one of his Pullman porter runs. I babysat the two children on Friday and Saturday nights, loaded the dishwasher on Friday, cooked breakfast for the children on Saturday and Sunday, made the beds, cleaned the bathrooms, ironed clothes, and ran the sweeper in the living room area on Saturday, made the beds again on Sunday, and then went home. I didn't like that job and not just because I didn't especially like Mrs. R or her children, nor because I couldn't enjoy my weekends, going to the movies or attending football or basketball games. I didn't like being a maid because I don't like to clean houses. My mother and my maternal grandmother both liked cleaning; my mother, at eighty-three, still does most of the cleaning in our house. But I prefer to read a good book; let someone else dust and vacuum.

When Mrs. R became pregnant with her third child, she decided that she needed a full-time maid, so that freed me to find more suitable work (or so I thought) the summer that I was sixteen. My connected friend (her father was an optometrist, her mother a teacher) and future locker partner, Colette, heard about the Youth Opportunity Program that was hiring young people to work for the federal government. So she, her boyfriend, and I drove (well, he drove) to Fort Sheridan to apply. Fortunately, I took typing during my sophomore year, preparing for a backup job as secretary in case I couldn't earn scholarships to college.

Colette and her boyfriend couldn't type, so I was hired. I worked at Fort Sheridan four summers in a row (and one Christmas break). I worked in the Finance Department the first two summers and in two other not especially memorable departments the other two summers. The work was easy but deadly dull. I preferred being busy to having nothing to do because the time moved so slowly. Work started at 7:30 a.m. and ended at 4:30 p.m. We had two fifteen-minute breaks and, I think, a half hour (maybe it was an hour) for lunch. During those summer days, I lived from break to lunch to break to the end of the day. I would try to take my afternoon break late so I wouldn't have long to wait for the end of the day.

During those long summer days, I encountered the kind of single working woman that I didn't want to be. Actually, I encountered one of those women at Fort Sheridan and the other one at Northwestern during my few months of working in the Investment Department there before I moved on to teaching high school. These women were wedded to their jobs. The one at Fort Sheridan had been in the army before she became a civil servant (I like that word for obvious reasons; we English majors are punny). She was my last supervisor at Fort Sheridan during the summer between my freshman and sophomore years at Northwestern. After that summer, I became a work study employee and soon landed a dream job working for Dean Black (his too appropriate real name), the dean of black students. I felt that job, which I held for two summers until I graduated and moved to the Investment Department, was payment for the torture I endured working for that woman in whatever department she was

21

running. This woman was very concerned with the appearance of the letters that I typed. She wanted the margins to be perfect and ordered me (I suspect she had been a drill sergeant in the army) to retype a letter if it weren't spaced appropriately. She really got on my nerves until I figured out a sneaky way to pay her back. Ms. Sergeant couldn't spell to save her soul, so instead of correcting her spelling without commenting as I did at first, I began to take the handwritten letters back to her desk, show her the spelling errors and ask as sweetly as I could (I have trouble even faking sweetness): "Do you want me to spell it like this or spell it correctly?" By the end of the summer, I was having less trouble with Ms. Sergeant. In fact, I didn't have to do as much typing for her.

Ms. Sergeant's twin at Northwestern, Ms. Head of the Investment Department Secretarial Pool, was not as abrasive as her sister spinster, but she was much more demanding and controlling. I had been warned by the employment agent who sent me on the interview that there was a problem in that office because he had sent another young woman to the same job, and she lasted only a week. But I was tired of waiting for substitute teaching jobs, so I went to the interview and was hired by Ms. Head, who seemed quite gentle and nice. Because I took the bus and would either have to arrive early or rush in at the last minute at best and at worse be late, I arrived at work about twenty minutes early. Ms. Head was the only person already there. We greeted each other, and I sat at my assigned desk, opened my book and started to read, since it was not yet time to work. Ms. Head immediately left her glassed-in office and scurried to my desk. She stood beside me with her hands folded and said in a condescending tone, "Now, Mary, when you arrive in the morning, take the cover off of your typewriter immediately because you know you're going to use it at some point during the day." I know what you're thinking. What difference did it make if I took the cover off the typewriter when I arrived in the office or if I took if off when I was about to use it? That's exactly what I was thinking. In fact, it made more sense to me to leave the typewriter covered until I was ready to use it. The purpose of the cover was to protect the typewriter. Why not keep it protected? But I took the cover off the typewriter and tried not to look annoyed. Things went downhill from there, though. And inevitably Ms. Head and I had a confrontation. I had to tell her about my Northwestern GPA (3.74) and how I was not stupid and didn't appreciate being treated like an idiot, and she complained that I mocked her. Well, yeah, I did because she acted like a damn fool. After the confrontation we agreed that we both needed to respect each other, and, fortunately, I knew I was leaving soon for a teaching job. But I left with the vow that whether I was married or not, I would never behave on a job the way Ms. Head and her predecessor, Ms. Sergeant, behaved. I would have a life outside my job and recognize that my coworkers also had lives outside their jobs.

As I've told my stories about my childhood to various friends and colleagues, I've come to appreciate how much I benefited from facing hardships as a very young person and being able to cope with them. Of course, my early hard-luck life has made me a bit hard. While I'm a champion of the underdog in many ways, I am not a fan of what I call whiners (not to be confused with complainers/blues singers; the difference is tonal). Some of my colleagues have supplemented their English professor salaries by working as therapists. I've told them that I would not be good at that job because I would want to scream at my patients, "Stop whining." And, after conversations with my more privileged friends, I know I would respond to some clients' whines about their troubled childhoods by listing my own troubles. When one white friend blamed her lack of self-esteem on her ugly duckling childhood, I listened for a few minutes and then asked, "Did you have to ride in the back of the bus or go in back doors because you were short, wore glasses, and had buck teeth?" I mean, I was dark-skinned, had the kind of Negroid features that the Michael Jacksons of the world pay good money to alter, had naturally yellow buck teeth because I used to suck my bottom lip, had long skinny limbs that led to my "friends" calling me Spider, and had very long, narrow (women's size 11AAAA when I was eleven) clown feet. But those physical oddities were not my primary problems. Had I been a rich white child, I might have worried about my feet, my legs, and my teeth, but I had more important things to worry about at eleven and twelve.

I do, however, have sympathy for people who have suffered truly traumatic childhood experiences, people (like my father, aunt, and uncles) who had alcoholic mothers, for instance. If I had to have an alcoholic parent, I'd prefer it be the father and prefer that he disappear as Foots graciously did. I also am sympathetic to people who were physically and sexually abused. Like most people my age, race, and class, I was whipped as a child but never excessively (although always unnecessarily), and I should thank all of the men (and the women) with whom I lived for not sexually abusing me. I had some close encounters with molesters in public places but never in any of the homes where I lived. Childhood sexual or physical abuse is a trauma that is hard to overcome. It can kill the spirit. The struggles that I had were the kind that can build spirits and make weak children strong adults.

As I entered adulthood, first, at eighteen, when I left high school for college and then, at twenty-three, when I left my parents' house for graduate school and a home of my own, I wasn't exactly singing "glory hallelujah," but I was ready to be an adult. And I have enjoyed being an adult. After all, I was working as a child and taking on many other adult responsibilities without having the freedom and autonomy of an adult.

A few years ago, one of my white friends was bragging, for some reason, about her wonderful childhood. It was an odd conversation for her to have with me since she had heard many of my stories and knew my childhood was not so wonderful. Because she knew my stories, she probably thought I was being defensive when I pointed out that childhood doesn't last long. If we're lucky, we will be adults four or five times longer than we were children. (I was not being defensive; if I were being defensive, I might have pointed out that children have little control over childhood experiences; parents, grandparents or whoever else raised us can take the credit or the blame for our relative happiness as children.) So, given the choice, I prefer to have had a not so wonderful, even unhappy, childhood, so long as it prepared me for a successful life as an adult. My childhood did that, and for that reason, I'm grateful to have lived and survived a hard knocks early life.

CHAPTER TWO
Don't Know Much about Algebra

I t's not surprising that when I picked a career, after rejecting those early options of maid and secretary, I chose to be a teacher. Being a teacher allowed me to spend my life in school, and school was where I was most successful. As a child I was physically and socially awkward. I didn't talk much in my early years and was so physically challenged that I didn't learn to tie my very big shoes until I was nine. But I was a star in school. Even though I started first grade behind most of my classmates because I had not attended kindergarten, had instead been living with my illiterate grandmother, I quickly caught up and passed most of them. My only problem in elementary school, in fact, was my messy handwriting, the result of my lack of physical coordination.

One story that I related in angry detail to that Cal Poly student interviewer involved my Evanston Township High School counselor's telling me that I was an overachiever because my I.Q. was average, and my grades were very high. He warned me that I shouldn't expect to do as well in college as I was doing in high school. I really blasted that counselor in the interview. I talked about how old he was and ironically pointed out with disdain that he lived with his mother. Now that I'm at least as old as he was, and my mother and I live together, I realize that his mother was probably living with him, not the other way around, and he was probably a nice enough man when he wasn't counseling Southern black girls with average I.Q.s. But my bitterness toward him decades later illustrates how much students take to heart comments made by their teachers and counselors. Had I been a different type of personality, I might have become a victim of the self-fulfilling prophecy. I might have failed in college because I believed that I wasn't smart enough to succeed. But I didn't buy what the old white man was selling. I quietly decided that I would show him who was overachieving. I would do well in college. That would fix his old white ass. I became a defiant high achiever. Overachieve this Ph.D., old white man!

When I first started telling the I.Q. test story, I framed it as an example of how "those kinds of tests" (aptitude tests) are culturally biased, how they don't accurately measure black people's intelligence or ability to succeed in school or life. I compared my performances on the SAT and National Merit tests, both aptitude tests, to my performance on the ACT test, which was an achievement test. I scored well on the ACT test, helping me to earn the Illinois State Scholarship, but did just okay on the other two (although I was a National Achievement Finalist, based on my National Merit test scores and GPA). As the years passed, and my bitterness toward that old counselor faded, however, I started to rethink my I.Q. score. I actually didn't remember taking the I.Q. test, which means I must have taken it in my primary school years. If I took the I.Q. test in first or even second grade, it might have reflected my slow start and the absence of a kindergarten education. In fact, that white counselor was not the first educator to underestimate me. My black first grade teacher told my mother that I was not as smart as my brother. (Fortunately, my mother didn't mention that woman's doubts to me until I was making better grades than my brother was; I'm not sure I would have been so defiant when I was six and when the doubter was a black woman.) The I.Q. test might also reflect what I call my idiot savant nature. I'm either really smart in an area or really slow, which could lead to an average score. I have trouble with geographical directions, with pronunciation, and, unless I'm in a car, with left and right. I did well in all subjects in school, but I had trouble with math. I suspect that math is something like music, art, or writing; some of us have a talent for it, and some of us don't. I was one who didn't. I had no trouble with arithmetic, as we called it in elementary school, but when I took algebra my freshman year in high school, I thought it would destroy me. It took me so long to understand those stupid formulas that I would occasionally fail the quizzes but always somehow figured out what the hell was going on just in time to ace the tests. One of my favorite movie lines is from Peggy Sue Got Married; Kathleen Turner says something like, "I happen to know that I won't need algebra in my adult life."

29

Right on, Peggy Sue! Still, among my proudest academic achievements were the "A's" I earned in algebra.

My lack of talent for math cost me some class ranking points when I moved from Henderson High School to Evanston High (ETHS). ETHS was a "track" school, meaning that students were placed in classes according to ability. There were English, science, history, and math classes for "A" students (honors), for "B" students (team taught), for "C" students (regular), and for "D" and "F" students (basic). I guess because of this system, I had to take tests to see what "track" I would be placed in. My freshman grades should have placed me in sophomore honors classes, but I guess they didn't trust those country teachers from Kentucky. I remember whoever was talking to me (a counselor or teacher) telling me that ETHS was the number two public school. I thought this person meant number two in the nation (nearby New Trier was number one), but maybe she meant just in Illinois. Anyway, she was letting me know (like that old counselor) as subtly as she could that I should not expect to do as well at ETHS as I did in my little small town Southern school. I don't remember my brother having to take the tests. Maybe his grades matched his I.Q. and pigmentation better than mine did.

The tests were given one hot summer day. I had to climb to the fourth floor to take the tests and had an adventure when I finished that I turned into a funny story for my Speech for Teachers class during my freshman year of college. Henderson High School had only two floors, so when I reached the third floor after four hours of testing, I looked for the exit. I saw the stairs leading down, but Henderson High had a basement, so I assumed that those stairs led to the basement. I walked through the hallways for at least twenty minutes, passing several stairways as I looked for the elusive door. Finally, tired of walking in circles and passing the same open doorway, where I saw the same summer school students staring out at me, I decided to go to the basement to see if I could find an exit down there. As I started down the stairs, I looked out the window. That's when I realized I was on the third floor, not the first. If the tests had been examining whether I could find my way out of the building quickly, I would have failed.

Fortunately, I was tested only in subjects I could pass, and I did quite well on the written tests, except, of course, for the math. Because of my math scores, the counselor/teacher didn't know what to do with me since I had already taken algebra and done well in it. I couldn't take basic math after acing algebra, so what to do? She decided to assign me to basic earth science and regular geometry. Now my science scores were fine, but the counselor/teacher was trying to help me succeed in this difficult school, and assigning me to basic earth science, she felt, would do that. For English, history, and social science, I was assigned to the "B" team-teaching classes, and I added typing as my sixth class.

After school started, I learned pretty quickly that I was misplaced in basic earth science. The teacher basically read the book to us. I missed exactly one question on the many exams and quizzes during the year. At one point, that same old white counselor who told me I was an overachiever advised me to move to regular earth science, but that class had a lab, which meant I would miss study hall once or twice a week, so I decided to stay where I was. I wasn't thinking about class ranking points or college at that point. I just didn't want to give up the study hall where I could do homework. And, of course, my parents didn't know that they should encourage me to take more advanced courses, so I just sat in earth science with the slow and/or trifling students, bored, but happy to earn easy "A's."

Ironically, the one class (other than p.e.) that I had trouble with my first year at ETHS was not geometry, but typing. Probably for the same reason that I had trouble learning to tie my shoes, I had trouble typing. It looked as if I might fail at one point, but I worked hard, practicing on my little manual typewriter, and earned "B's." I also earned "B's" in geometry, but I excelled in English and history, moving up to honors in my junior year. That year I also took French, and despite my problems with the accent (I explained to Monsieur DuBois, or *mon sewer* as I called him, that I was from Southern France), I was moved up to Honors French my senior year. That year I also took chemistry and impressed some of my black friends by acing it. But I was not in any college level courses that last year of high school, only honors. I didn't understand the significance of that slight until years later. I probably should have been in college English and history, which would have meant that I could have tested out of those freshman classes when I attended college. I also would have had a better class ranking since points were given for honors and college (and taken away for basic). Now my ranking was not bad. I graduated 24 out of about 1000 students and was pleased with that ranking. I was easily the highest ranked black student, but if either my parents or I had known how to play the system or advocate for my rights, I could have been ranked at least in the top 20, if not the top 10.

Not having parents to advocate for me was a problem in one way, but in another way, it was a blessing. My parents also did not pressure me. I was a self-motivated over- achiever. Although I disagree with many of Richard Rodriguez' arguments in <u>Hunger of Memory</u> and taught that book mainly to attack it, I identify with his description of what he calls the "scholarship boy." I was a scholarship girl. I like to say that I worked my way through college when I was in high school and worked my way through graduate school when I was in college. In other words, I made the grades that helped me earn scholarships for college when I was in high school and earned the grades that helped me win a Ford Fellowship when I was in college. I knew that my parents couldn't afford to pay for my college tuition, so I had to do well enough to receive financial aid. I brag that I went to two expensive private schools and didn't pay one penny of tuition; I also didn't have to borrow money. When I earned my Ph.D. at thirty, I was broke, but not in debt.

If my willingness to work hard, to overachieve, was my great-est asset as a student, probably the second biggest asset was my love of reading. Luckily, I learned to read before my family bought a television, and I fell in love with the printed word. I don't remember being read to by anyone in my family. I'm certain that my parents never read to me, and my maternal grandmother couldn't read. That is probably why today I still prefer silent read-ing, reading to myself. I'm not a fan of books on tape or hearing someone else read aloud. Just hand me a book (I haven't yet tried the new Kindle or the Nook), a magazine, or a newspaper, and shut up so that I can read.

My ability to concentrate was another great asset. I was the kind of child who could sit still for hours, reading a book, putting together a jigsaw puzzle, or just staring at the cars driving down the street. Once when I was about ten, I was sitting on the porch of my old Kentucky home when a bird flew into me. It scared the hell out of me, and vice versa I'm sure. My father, sober at the time, said that the bird probably thought I was a statue. Well, statues make focused students, who have no trouble paying attention in class, even when the teacher and the subject are dull (although I did sleep through several large lectures when I was an undergraduate).

A fourth great asset was my sharp memory. I was best in those classes that required memorization. In fact, English was actually harder for me than history because it involved less memorization and more creativity. But I was an avid reader, who often read a couple of novels a week for fun, so that made me enjoy English more, which is why I chose it as my major. I not only read novels for pleasure, I also read a list of books that were supposed to help me do well in college. The one long, difficult book that I remember from that collection or maybe it was more than one book (multiple volumes) was Carl Sandburg's biography of Abraham Lincoln. I really don't think that book or any of the others that I read helped me succeed in college, but it proved how disciplined and determined to succeed I was. Too young and inexperienced to understand most of the books I read from that list, I certainly wasn't thinking about the content much as I read them, but I was completing a goal, reading the books and checking them off the list.

My success in school was taken for granted at Alves Street Elementary School. My brother had done well there, and my first cousin Ricardo, the first college graduate in our family, had apparently also been an excellent student. After that brief slow start in first grade, I remember sailing through those first six years with little trouble (although I hated my really mean fourth grade teacher and cried and screamed in her class occasionally just because she got on my nerves) and not that much fanfare. But when I moved to the white school, things became interesting. My play boyfriend and I were the stars in our reading class, which clearly freaked out the very racist teacher. But the teacher who was most impressed with me was the geography teacher. I think it's ironic that I was such a star in my seventh grade geography class because I have so much trouble with geography in real life, suggesting how little connection there can be between school and life. Geography must have required memorization, my specialty. But because I was the only black student in this guy's class, and he acted as if he had never dealt with any other black people, I blew his mind. He couldn't get over how well I did, that I was the best student in the class. He was so impressed that when I had passed to the eighth grade, and he saw me sitting in a science class soon after the school year started, he came in and told the man teaching that class (who was apparently his friend) that I would scare or intimidate him. I liked that man's response; he looked at me with a smirk and a wink and said he thought he could handle it. I mean I was just an eighth grader. What was so scary? Still, I liked that I had freaked out the creepy geography teacher with my academic performance. And I looked forward to impressing more white teachers. I also had landed on the honor roll toward the end of seventh grade, and I liked how that felt.

Most of the other junior high school teachers (like the science guy) seemed to take my performance in stride. Some were pleasantly surprised or quietly supportive, but most just acted as if a black student making good grades was normal. The eighth grade history teacher was interesting because he returned the exam papers according to the grades, with the exam receiving the highest grade given back first and the lowest last. Believe me, I was happy that I did well in history and felt sorry for the person who received his or her exam last. Occasionally, the last one to receive the exam was one of my black friends, a pretty and sweet, but not very smart, girl. I was not always the first to receive my exam, but I was usually one of the first three, and when I was the first, the teacher gave me a little nod, which I interpreted as a "way to go" affirmation. This guy was mean and very big, probably six-five. He had even scared my brother, which was hard to do (although my brother didn't enter the white school until eighth grade, so maybe that's why he was intimidated). Earning a slight nod from this big dude was a big thing and not just because he had a really big head.

By the time I left junior high for high school, I was fairly comfortable in the white school, used to being the only black child in at least some of my classes, and confident in my ability to perform well in all classes. That was until I encountered algebra. But even that course didn't stop me from making the high honor roll, probably the highlight of my academic career in Henderson. First of all, the names of the students who made the honor roll in high school were listed in the paper, so everyone who read the <u>Henderson Gleaner and Journal</u> knew that I made the high honor roll at Henderson High. Then there was a special assembly near the end of the year when the honor roll students from each class stood on stage to be applauded. Play Boyfriend had made the low honor roll, and I had made the high honor roll. We were the only blacks to make the honor roll. He stood on stage first with the other freshmen who made the low honor roll, and then it was my turn. I was slightly embarrassed by the attention but also very proud. I was also proud to see my picture in the yearbook with the other high honor roll freshmen.

Had I not been a star student, most people in Henderson, black or white, would not remember me. I was a relatively quiet, not especially interesting child. People who bothered to get to know me discovered that I had a sense of humor, but why would anyone want to know a quiet, homely, working-class black child? However, once my academic achievements were publicized, I became more popular. Other black students at Henderson High were not jealous of me; they were proud. I remember a mature acting occasional girlfriend of my brother's telling me at that high school assembly how proud she was of me. Contrary to the myths of the abused and mistreated nerd, I was treated with affection and fondness by the black students and also had quite a few white middle- to upper-class friends/acquaintances. The black girls more likely to be beaten up and tortured in my day, especially in the South, were the fair-skinned ones with the long, "good" hair. So maybe my dark skin, Negroid features, and long and thick, but kinky, hair actually saved me. If I had been pretty <u>and</u> smart, I might have been killed.

There was another benefit to my being such a good student during my days of living in the South. I became a star actress in the church Christmas play because I was the one young church member who could be counted on to memorize the lines. I wasn't playing a young girl, though. At twelve, thirteen, and fourteen, I played a middle-aged woman who needed to learn what Christmas meant. I had about ten times more lines than anyone else in the play. My brother, who also could and would memorize quite a few lines, had the second biggest role, which was, get ready, my husband. We performed the play three times, and each time, the church audience laughed inappropriately at my brother's line, "That's my wife." (Maybe that's why I never married.)

My star dimmed a bit when I left Henderson for Evanston, but it didn't take long for the black students at ETHS to discover my academic gifts, and they had the same reaction as the Henderson High students. The first day of my sophomore year, two friendly black girls, who I learned later were not popular, approached me, introduced themselves, and welcomed me to the school. One of those girls became my locker partner that first year, and the other one became my best friend during the three years I was there, even though she and I never had classes together, and she actually didn't graduate on time. The smarter, more popular girls, an upper-middle-class high achiever named Colette, for instance, didn't notice me during those first weeks. That changed when I landed on the honor roll. Colette became my friend, and we were locker partners our junior and senior years.

I would never have been welcomed into the cool, pretty, middle-class black girl clique if I had not been a good student. I didn't look cool, didn't act cool, didn't dress cool with my dark-colored, matching sweaters, skirts, and wool over-the-knee socks (one friend saw me dressed all in brown and declared that I looked like a tree), didn't sound cool with my Southern accent, but being smart was cool to these suburban black students in the mid to late sixties. So even when I did foolish things, I didn't lose my place at the cool girls' lunch table. I made better grades than all the other cool girls, so I could be as country as I wanted to be, and I was still cool. Probably my least cool moment occurred in the locker room when we were taking swimming lessons in our sophomore p.e. class. Colette and a few other black girls were in that class. Of course, we had hair issues because in 1965 the Afro was still a few years away. I needed to put my thick, kinky hair into a pony tail but didn't have the appropriate equipment, so I asked if anyone had a "rubber." Sorry, but that's what we called rubber bands in Henderson, "rubbers." I didn't even know why all of the girls were laughing until my brother explained what a rubber was and why boys used them. Even after that blunder, the cool girls kept me in their clique.

Most of my humiliating high school moments happened in p.e. class, usually not because of what I said, but because of what I couldn't do. Because of my long legs and big feet, I could handle some of the traditional sports, like track, kickball, and basketball. But I was terrible at any activities that required even a little bit of grace, not only modern dance and gymnastics, but even tennis and bowling. And I was worse at swimming. I couldn't even float. Decades after I left high school, some semi-celebrity was criticized for saying that blacks couldn't swim well because they weren't buoyant. Hey, I agree with that guy. He could have used me as Exhibit A in his defense against the racism charge. I was definitely not buoyant. I thought at the time that my big feet were the problem. Or maybe I was too skinny to float. Whatever the reason, I was such a pathetic floater that one day when the whole class was waiting for me to float from one side of the pool to the other, one student, tired of waiting, grabbed my arm and pulled me across the pool.

The one slick move I made in high school (in fact, in my entire academic career) was to ask the family doctor, for whom my stepfather worked as a handy/cleaning man to supplement his Pullman porter income, to write a note saying that I caught colds too easily so should be excused from swimming my senior year. It was true that I caught colds very easily, a problem caused perhaps by the early TB, and it was also true that I looked very ugly during the six weeks that I took swimming because of the hair problem, but mainly I needed to avoid swimming my senior year so that I wouldn't have to swim in the deep end of the pool, a requirement for graduation. Can you imagine an honor student, the #24 ranked student in the senior class, not being able to graduate because she couldn't swim? I had to take modern dance again, and that was no fun, but I was happy to look clumsy for six more weeks, so I could graduate on time. And fortunately, grades in p.e. courses didn't count in the GPA.

My problems with p.e. continued even into college, but I was finished with physical activity after my freshman year and could focus on doing well in the "real" courses. Despite that old counselor's warning, I had no trouble succeeding at Northwestern. ETHS was actually a junior Northwestern; their athletic teams were even called the Wildkits while the Northwestern teams were Wildcats. My freshman English classes especially seemed redundant since we read many of the same books that I read during my senior year at ETHS. My freshman grades reflected my comfort level, and I was inducted into the Alpha Lambda Delta Honorary Society for freshmen earning a 3.5 GPA or higher. The following year I received the Pan-Hellenic Scholarship Award for having the highest GPA of any sophomore woman in the School of Education. That award was given in a special ceremony near the end of the year, and I walked up to the stage to great applause. I wasn't as impressed with myself, however, as the audience was because the woman receiving the award in the College of Arts had earned a 4.00 GPA, while I had a measly 3.57. Still, I beat the woman in one of the mostly male schools (probably engineering or science) who had a 3.00 GPA. I wonder how many women were in that school. Maybe she was the only one, and I also wonder now why they had a separate award for sophomore women. Why not just the highest GPA for any sophomore in each school?

Probably because of those two early honors, I became very competitive in college. I needed high grades to hold onto my scholarships, but a 3:00 GPA would have been sufficient. I also didn't need to be the smartest person in each class in order to keep the scholarships. But I suddenly wanted to be the smartest person in the room, to make the highest grades on the tests. I remember my junior year going to the psychology professor's door to find my posted final exam score. When I saw that the score was very high, I spent several minutes looking at all of the other scores to see if anyone had a higher score or tied my score. Now I wasn't a psychology major, and I had clearly made an "A" in the class, so what difference did it make if I earned the highest "A" or the lowest "A"? There were probably 200 people in that psychology class, but I stood there looking at all of the scores until I found one that tied mine and then slinked off, disappointed because someone I didn't know had done as well on the test as I did. As part of my job working for the dean of black students, I had access to all the other black students' GPAs. We even conducted a study comparing the GPAs to the SAT scores to see how predictive of academic success the scores were (the answer was not at all, at least not for black students). I was pleased to see that I had a higher GPA than any of the other black students. But when one of those students bragged about his scores on the exam to enter law school (LSAT?), I asked if the scores were good, and when he said "good for a black student," I was very dismissive of him and his obviously not that good scores. At that point in my academic career, I wanted to be the best student, not just the best black student.

In pursuit of high grades, I worked hard and stayed focused. One of my black friends who was in the physical geography (phys g) class with me my freshman year shared a joke going around the dorms the night before an exam. One of the phys g students said that if the group that was pulling an all-nighter to prepare for the exam were me they would be asleep, and someone responded, "yeah, but if she was us, she'd be awake, trying to cram all of this boring shit into her head at the last minute." Well, I stayed up late the night before the phys g exams also, but I was just reviewing the material I had already crammed into my head. And here is how I was different from 95% of the phys g students. I went to the lectures. The first time we had an exam in that class during Fall Quarter, I was shocked to see how many students were in the class. I knew that the lectures were held in a large auditorium, but I didn't know how many discussion classes there were (there were about fifteen or twenty students in my discussion class). There were probably more students in that class than in my psychology class, but only about twenty or thirty of us regularly showed up for lectures.

I missed a total of four classes during the almost four years (I graduated a quarter early) that I attended Northwestern. One of those classes was that psychology class, and I missed it because the streets of Evanston were covered in ice on the day of the lecture. That class was the only one I had that day; the rest of the day I was supposed to observe an elementary school class as part of the work for my Education units. Of course, I tried to make it to class, and the buses were running, but I fell twice as I walked the two blocks to the bus stop, and the bus took off just as I arrived at the back door. Only then did I give up and go home to write my humorous report on why I didn't observe the elementary school class. I missed another class because I had to go to the Health Center with a 103 degree temperature, and then I had a mild case of senioritis and decided to skip two classes that I was taking pass-fail during the quarter before I student taught.

Although I did fall asleep occasionally in the large lecture halls, especially when the instructor and the material (the phys g teacher wrote the textbook and simply repeated everything he'd said in the book during his lectures, reminding me of the earth science teacher in high school) were dull, I didn't just show up for class. I was an attentive student, taking copious notes, which I studied carefully before each test. I also read and reread all of my books before tests so that I knew the material thoroughly. During Spring Quarter of my freshman year, our composition teacher focused on the theme of love, and one of the texts that we read was Shakespeare's <u>Antony and Cleopatra</u>. I read the same play again during the second quarter of my sophomore year when we focused on the Renaissance in the required two-year sequence for English majors. Then a couple of quarters later, I read the play again for my upper-division Shakespeare course. By that time, I could recite passages from the play because I had read it so many times. We read a play a week in the Shakespeare class; my approach was to read the play once before the professor lectured on it and then read it again during the week that he lectured. I used that strategy with <u>Antony and Cleopatra</u> even though I had already studied it twice. It took me years to forget key passages from that play.

My hard work paid off with good grades and a high GPA, later helping me earn a Ford Fellowship. But, like Joan Didion, I didn't make Phi Beta Kappa because I was in the School of Education, which had a different honor society. I was invited to join that one but declined. Why would such a competitive student decline an invitation to an honor society? She was still angry about not receiving an invitation to the Alpha Lambda Delta Honorary Society dinner or ceremony or whatever it was they had. My mother found out about the event when she was cleaning rooms in the freshman dorm. She and I both complained, and the student head of the organization actually brought the invitation to my house, but I refused to attend. I was still holding a grudge about that seeming slight and didn't see any reason to put myself in a position to be slighted again. Only later did I realize that I denied myself an opportunity to be honored when I graduated.

My original plan was to continue my education and earn the M.A. while I was still in the mood to study. I applied and was accepted into the graduate English program at Northwestern but was not given financial aid. Say what? When I talked to the graduate advisor, he focused more on my performance at ETHS than on my grades in the English Department at Northwestern. He had children who attended the high school and knew it was difficult to make high grades there. I kept trying to focus him on how well I had done in the department where I was now planning to earn the M.A. if he would just make sure I received the financial aid that I had earned by working so hard as an undergraduate. He wasn't buying it. Apparently, most graduate students who received financial aid were working on the Ph.D.; he also seemed unimpressed with the fact that I was in the School of Education. Of course, I was not advised by that old counselor or any of the college representatives who talked to us in high school that an undergraduate degree in the School of Education might be harder to sell to graduate schools. I was planning to be a teacher, so, of course, I applied to the School of Education.

I did not plan to pay for my M.A., so I moved to Plan B, finding a job, first in the Investment Department at Northwestern and then teaching seniors and sophomores at ETHS. But I had been teaching only a few weeks when I knew that high school teaching was not for me. If I were going to teach, I would have to teach college, so I applied for a Ford Fellowship and to three graduate schools. I was accepted at all three, offered a fellowship at the University of Illinois, Urbana (I'd been offered a scholarship there when I applied for the undergraduate program but decided not to go there when someone else's acceptance letter was sent to me; I was intimidated by the school's size). I decided to go to USC because I wanted to live in Southern California, and when I earned the Ford Fellowship, I was on my way.

I had a couple of interesting moments during the Ford Fellowship interview, held in New York City. If I remember correctly (the interview took place in February or March, 1972), there were three interviewers. One was a black woman who wondered why I wanted to go to USC. That should have been a hint that I had picked the wrong school. I mentioned that the English Department offered courses in African American literature, but she didn't seem impressed. I also remember that one of the interviewers, possibly the same woman, asked what would happen if I married. I stated very firmly that I would still complete my degree, and the black woman definitely was the one who said that she believed me. Of course, now they probably couldn't ask a woman about marrying. I also remember the panel of interviewers warning me that the fellowship would last only five years, which I thought was much longer than it would take me to complete a degree. After all, as an undergraduate, I had graduated a quarter early without going to summer school and while working. Little did I know that it would take me seven years to earn my M.A. and Ph.D. During those seven years, I took three major tests, passing two of them, and wrote a dissertation. I also took and audited more classes than were required. As usual, I stayed focused and was always over prepared. But for the first time since my problems with high school algebra and typing, I had trouble in school.

The first indication I had that there might be problems with USC was the discovery after I arrived that the two African American literature courses that had attracted me to that school no longer existed. Now, I had said in my application that I was interested in studying African American literature, but no one bothered to warn me when I was accepted that the courses would disappear. The African American professor who taught the courses was still in our department, but only temporarily. He moved to comparative literature the year after I arrived. I had taken a directed study with him during my first semester, and we didn't really like each other (he apparently preferred flirtatious, pretty women, and I didn't respond well to dismissive, hostile teachers, whatever their race or gender), so I decided not to follow him into a new department. I was stuck studying American literature with the white professors.

My second problem was with the first graduate coordinator. He was a well-known eighteenth century British literature scholar, and I'm sure that his work was interesting, but he was a terrible advisor. He was so shy or weird that he didn't speak to people he knew. Shortly after I started at USC, I encountered the coordinator on an elevator in the library. He and I were the only two people on the elevator; I spoke to him since we had met in his office and talked about my schedule. His response was a throat-clearing harrumph and a fixed stare at the ceiling. Now here's the problem: black people are paranoid, so if they see a white person who is their advisor and speak to him, and he doesn't speak, they assume he's prejudiced. Dr. Harrumph may or may not have been prejudiced. But he didn't speak to anyone. His response to me was neither personal, racist, nor sexist. It was just weird.

That first semester I took a course in Research Methods. The professor was a nice guy who was trying to help us succeed in graduate school. Early that semester, perhaps even the first day, he told us that we needed to attach ourselves to one of the well-known scholars and work with him. He even named the well-known scholars. Dr. Harrumph was one of them. I don't remember if I said something, shook my head, or just looked angry at the suggestion. But he focused on me and tried to convince me that I really needed to be someone's apprentice; it was the only way to ensure success. I thought he was out of his mind. I wasn't going to be a brown-nosing, apple-polishing Aunt Chloe (Uncle Tom's wife for those of you who've forgotten or didn't read Stowe's novel). I would do what I always did, work hard. But, of course, Professor Research was right, except he may not have realized that the apprentice method worked only for white men. A black woman could have brown nosed and apple polished until her nose and fingers fell off, and she still would not become one of these renowned scholars' (all of them white and male) favorite students.

At first, my usual method of over preparing worked fine. Another course that I took that first semester was Chaucer, a requirement for the M.A. I didn't really like Chaucer; the only two tales I enjoyed were "The Wife of Bath's Tale" and "The Miller's Tale," but I studied each tale very carefully. I first read each tale in Middle English, then read a modern English translation, and then reread the tale in Middle English. The medievalist apparently was not one of those renowned scholars looking for apple-polishing disciples. He appreciated the students who did the work. So, of course, he appreciated me. Dr. Medievalist also had a good sense of humor, which I guess is useful for a Chaucer scholar, and would joke about how his students tried to avoid making eye contact with him when he asked a question. Everyone would pretend to be busy looking at the book. One day, desperate for someone to answer his difficult question, he turned to me, one of the more faithful responders, and said, "Miss Sisney, you always know the tales really well. What do you think?" From then on, I had to hear from several students that he really liked me, and I was his favorite, blah, blah, blah. I didn't think his comment showed that he really liked me; it showed he was aware which students knew the tales and which ones didn't. Doctor Medievalist wasn't expressing a preference; he was stating a fact. I knew the tales well because I read them <u>three</u> times.

Another professor who was impressed with me that first year was a female guest lecturer, who taught Early American literature during the summer. She liked my writing style as well as my readings of specific passages and made a point of saying so in class. One of my classmates, a future well-known American literature scholar and UC professor, expressed surprise to me after this female professor praised one of my papers; he claimed only half-jokingly that he hadn't been that impressed with me when we took another American literature class together in the spring. That class demonstrated how my yet to be articulated redlight philosophy worked for me. The professor, we'll call him Dr. Penny because that's not his name, was kind, but he didn't like to give grades. We turned work in, and he returned it ungraded. Now, I knew that he would give me a grade at the end of the semester, so I wanted to know what my final grade would be. He tried to reassure me that I was doing fine, but I wouldn't leave his office until he let me know what grade I was earning. He made a deal with me to give me an "A" if I did well on a paper or an exam. I don't remember the details now, but I received an "A" in that class. Other students, who just went along with Dr. Penny's I-don't-like-to-grade-until-I-have-to policy, assuming that they would earn "A's" were screwed. I don't remember if the future UC professor was one of those people, but I was not. I assumed that Dr. Penny avoided giving grades because he wanted to give some of us "B's" but didn't want to deal with our complaints during the class; I made sure I wouldn't be blindsided by that "B."

I didn't recognize it at the time, but the redlight philosophy was at work again when I took the M.A. comprehensive exam and then a few months later the Ph.D. screening exam. I worried about the M.A. exam because I had never taken that kind of comprehensive exam before. It was a four-hour exam covering ten books. The exam was scheduled for late in the Spring Semester, probably May. By that time I had read all ten books multiple times. One of the books was by John Stuart Mill. I still feel sleepy when I think of that book and of Mill. I could pick up that book immediately after waking up from a good night's sleep and still fall asleep within minutes of starting to read. I had the hardest time reading and studying that dull book. I pity anyone who is a John Stuart Mill scholar. The other books were easier to read, and as usual I over prepared, not only studying the texts but reading critical articles/books and even attending one of Dr. Harrumph's classes (uninvited) when he taught The Dunciad, another one of the ten texts. Toward the end of my preparation, I was suffering from impacted wisdom teeth, but I waited until I took the exam to have them extracted at the USC Dental School.

I thought I did okay on the test but wasn't sure how the three male examiners would determine who passed and who didn't. I was worried until Dr. Harrumph told me that I had passed and, in fact, wrote the best exam of the six people taking it. One person had failed, and another person, a middle-aged friend of mine named Helen, who had an M.A. in library science but was hoping to earn a Ph.D. in English, was told that her M.A. was terminal. She did not do well enough to be accepted into the Ph.D. program. I was told by Dr. Harrumph that my performance, while good, was not exceptional enough to let me move into the Ph.D. program without taking the screening exam in the fall. He let me know that it was unusual for someone to go straight into the Ph.D. program after taking the M.A. exam. It never occurred to me to question why the M.A. exam could not be used to screen me into the program since it screened Helen out of it. I accepted Harrumph's explanation and wasn't worried about taking another test. After all, I had done better than everyone else on this first test and had done quite well during my first year in graduate school.

The screening test covered only four books, and the most boring one, <u>The Education of Henry Adams</u>, was much more interesting than John Mill's book. I also preferred the Shakespeare play on the screening exam list, <u>Othello</u>, to the one on the M.A. exam list, <u>Corialanus</u>. So I wasn't worried about the screening exam, both before and after I took it. I felt I had done better on that exam than on the earlier one. There were only three of us taking the exam; the other two were new to the program. I tried to reassure them that we had probably all passed. Uh, wrong. Only one of us passed, and I was not that one. The woman who passed had come from UCLA after failing the qualifying exams there. In other words, she had completed the coursework in the graduate program at another school and so clearly knew more than the two of us, who were just starting the Ph.D. program at USC. I was shocked. This was a red light that I did not expect.

Naturally, I started singing the blues. I complained to everyone that I knew. One of the male students who had been in a few classes with me advised me to keep quiet; he said that I could overcome the problem, so I shouldn't let anyone know what had happened. But I wanted everyone to know that those fools had failed me. Who the hell were those clowns? The problem was that there were three different white men evaluating the screening exam. If the men who had evaluated the M.A. exam had been the examiners for this second test, I clearly would have passed. Of course, on the other hand, if the clowns who had evaluated the screening exam had been the examiners for the M.A. exam, all six of us might have failed. That's just how arbitrary these judgments were. And to make matters worse, I was later told that the problem was with my still not very legible handwriting. These guys didn't want to waste time trying to read my handwriting, so if they didn't understand what I was saying, they just assumed that it wasn't worth reading.

My male student friend was correct; I had too many supporters among the faculty, including the three men who had evaluated the M.A. exams, after a year of doing really well, to be told that I wasn't good enough to succeed in the program. So I passed the screening "procedure," as they renamed it, and from then on, they decided that people who had a strong pass on the M.A. exam would not have to take the screening exam. The other person who failed was just told to go because he didn't have any supporters. Before he left, he and I sang a loud blues duet about the foolishness of accepting people into a program and then making them take a test to prove that they belong there, which was especially stupid when one of the people had already taken many classes in the program and done well. But that failed exam clearly made a difference in how I was perceived. Unfortunately, I was taking two of the examiners for two-semester courses that year. One of them was the renowned American literature professor, we'll call him Dr. Harry Potter (obviously not his name). Dr. Potter really liked me because he earned his Ph.D. from Northwestern and because he was one of those liberals who liked to believe that he wasn't a racist. He loved to joke with me about William Faulkner's racism. It looked like I was on my way to an "A" in Dr. Potter's class until after I failed the screening exam or was failed by him and his colleagues. Suddenly, I earned a "B" in his class, and somehow I made "B's" or "B+'s" in all of my classes that semester. Hmm.

The problem with English is there is an element of subjectivity to any evaluation of writing. Some people like Faulkner's style, for instance, while others like Hemingway's. So a professor can always find a reason to criticize a student's style if he doesn't want to give her an "A." When my fellow black Kentuckian Gloria Watkins, later known as bell hooks, showed up a few years after me and earned "B's" on some of her papers, she said, "B for black." But I had earned "A's" before the screening exam results, and I was always black, so my "B's" were for bad exam. However, as I told my friends and a couple of the faculty, it was too late for anyone to try to convince me that I was not capable of succeeding in the graduate program. I had moved from a black school to a white school, from a small Southern school to a large, highly ranked Northern suburban high school and from high school to college and did well each time. I had even done well when I entered graduate school, so I was not the problem. I was also now capable of evaluating my competition. I knew that I was not the best student in all of my classes, but I was never anywhere near the worst. Only a few middle-aged women, including the one who passed the screening exam, seemed to know more and write better than I did.

Even before I had trouble with the screening exam, I wasn't happy with the requirements for the Ph.D. in literature at USC. First of all, African American literature had disappeared from the curriculum (although bell hooks' boyfriend was hired a few years after I arrived, he wasn't teaching graduate courses in African American literature). Also, I had to take exams in three areas, one of which would be either Renaissance or Medieval. I chose Renaissance. A second exam would be in Victorian, and my main area would be American literature (that's all of American literature). Then the graduate professors decided to combine modern British and modern American and make early American a separate area. So I would have modern British and American as my major area. I had been looking at other universities and noticed that some allowed students to focus on a genre, the novel, for instance. After the exam, I started thinking about taking my fellowship and switching to one of those schools; a school that actually had African American literature as one of the options would be nice.

But there was a new program at USC that allowed students to study literature, linguistics, and rhetoric (RLL). I listened to the two women who were in that program, talked to the director (we'll use the name that my mother called him when she misunderstood my pronunciation of his last name--Dr. Willie Rose) and decided to switch to his program. That meant I could study modern British and American as my major area and rhetoric and linguistics as my minor areas. I preferred those subjects to Victorian and Renaissance literatures. Of course, some of my friends in the literature program thought I was being foolish, but I was actually preparing myself to be a better teacher.

I found some of the courses in the new RLL program difficult and a little strange. Classical rhetoric was more interesting than John Stuart Mill and easier to read than Chaucer, but it wasn't my favorite course. Still, I enjoyed the research and writing papers in my rhetoric courses more than I did most of my literature research and papers. I liked, for instance, writing a paper for Dr. Rose that focused on my composing process. I actually used notes from the paper to illustrate my points about how I wrote a paper. And probably my favorite graduate paper was written in a sociolinguistics class. That class and psycholinguistics were both taught by a female professor, a rarity in my academic career. The paper that I wrote for sociolinguistics focused on the studio audience at talk shows. I argued that the conversations on talk shows are odd because there are multiple audiences--the people participating in the conversation (the host and at least one guest), the studio audience, and the television audience. The studio audience could not participate in the conversation, but they could applaud, laugh, or boo. By its responses, the studio audience lets the television audience know how to react. To demonstrate, I analyzed a "Tonight Show" segment that featured Diahann Carroll and Ronald Reagan. Reagan was no longer governor but was thinking of running for President (around 1975). At one point, he told a politically charged joke that the audience was supposed to laugh at, and they didn't laugh. Reagan's rhythm was thrown off, and Johnny Carson pointed out that Reagan had said that his comments would be controversial. I taped the show to present my findings to the class, and everyone noticed the long silence after the joke, as Reagan and Carson waited for the audience to respond, and how uncomfortable Reagan became when the audience didn't provide the proper feedback. It was a fun paper to research and write.

I did well in my classes again after I switched to the RLL program and eventually took the qualifying exams. As usual I over prepared, studying for more than a year. Still, those exams made the M.A. and screening exams look like quizzes. I took four four-hour exams (two in literature, one in linguistics, and one in rhetoric) in about a week. I was much more nervous about these exams than I would have been if I hadn't experienced the screening exam fiasco. And then I didn't do that well on the rhetoric exam and had to redeem myself on the oral. The hour that I spent in the oral exam was the longest of my life. I didn't realize that I was shaking (despite taking half of an over-the-counter pill for my nerves) until one of my examiners commented on it later. As I stood in the hallway, waiting for them to decide my fate, I considered running. But Dr. Potter came out mercifully quickly and said I had passed.

Next, I had to pick a dissertation topic, form a committee, and write a proposal. I had chosen a topic while I was studying for the exams. But I had trouble finding someone to direct my dissertation because I wanted to compare black and white American writers. I was comparing Faulkner and Styron, two writers who wrote about black characters, who in fact had black characters as their protagonists, to black writers Richard Wright, Ralph Ellison, and John Williams. The American lit scholars all begged off because they didn't really know black literature, so Dr. Moore, the British literature professor, agreed to direct the dissertation, joined by a relatively new rhetoric professor, Dr. Greene, and Dr. June Brown, a black Social Work professor who was my outside reader. After my three readers approved the proposal, it had to be accepted by the graduate committee. There were problems again because some of these scholars didn't think my topic was worth doing. One made fun of my discussion of black and white (they were probably also amused by the readers' colorful names--Brown and Greene) in the proposal by saying it would be typed on white paper in black ink. One well-known female scholar, who was new to the school and so didn't know my work, didn't like the idea of my using rhetorical strategies to analyze the five novels. She thought rhetoric was some kind of fad or gimmick. She ended her evaluation by suggesting that some people should just be satisfied with the ABD (All But the Dissertation) and not try to write a dissertation. Again, I pointed out that it was too late for anyone to try to tell me that I wasn't capable of doing what some people who had been in classes with me and couldn't write as well as I could had already done or were being allowed to do. Eventually, my proposal was accepted.

It took me two years to write the dissertation. Part of the problem was that I grew tired of being poor and in the last year of my fellowship started T.A.ing at USC, and then when my five-year fellowship ended, I started teaching at Cal Poly Pomona. So I was teaching at two different schools and grading compositions while writing the dissertation. I was also riding the bus twice a week between Pomona and L.A. I wrote some of my dissertation and graded compositions on the bus. During the second year, I formed a dissertation support group with two of my friends, two women who had taken the qualifying exams before I did but were still working on their dissertations. We felt that if we met once every couple of weeks and had to report on our progress, we would progress. It worked for me better than it did for them since I finished a few years before they did. It also helped me that I had a job at Tufts by January, 1979. I knew I had to finish the dissertation by August to keep that job. I wanted to tell that famous woman scholar (infamous to me, she showed up at Cal Poly as a guest speaker at our Student Awards Banquet several years after I joined the full-time faculty, and I welcomed her with one of my famous or infamous stare-downs) that the sample chapters from my dissertation helped me land that job.

The other problem, of course, was that I had to type my dissertation. I'm no fan of technology, but as I sit here typing quickly on my laptop, watching it correct mistakes as I make them and being able to make changes without having to retype a whole page or whole chapters, I know that I could have finished that dissertation in a year if I had composed it on a computer. I still laugh every time I think about the undergraduates who lived next door to me during my last year at USC and who played their music so loud that it made my apartment vibrate (I named them the Rolling Stones), complaining about my typing.

I had one last redlight/greenlight moment before I left USC. My oral defense of the dissertation was scheduled for June 4, a little more than fifteen years after I left my grandmother's house in Henderson and exactly thirty years before I taught my last class at Cal Poly Pomona. I thought the dissertation defense would be just a nice conversation, so I didn't have the problems with nerves that I had during the oral exam. But my three usually very gentle readers grilled me. I decided later that they thought I was too calm this time, too relaxed, and they wanted to see me sweat one last time. I had to wait in the hallway again, but I wasn't really worried this time, despite the grilling. Soon enough, they were all shaking my hand and congratulating me. And I was at thirty finally finished with my education (or so I thought) and ready to educate. My first stop was Massachusetts.

CHAPTER THREE
The Places I've Been

Several days after I arrived in Cambridge, where I lived in a furnished second floor apartment while teaching at Tufts, I felt something strange but somehow familiar in the air. It wasn't the heat because L.A. was hotter. But the air seemed oppressive, energy sapping. I couldn't figure out what it was until it stormed. Then I knew; it was humidity. I hadn't felt humidity since I left Evanston in 1972. After seven years of living in L.A., I had to become reacquainted with some other feelings and experiences from my past, such as heavy overcoats, boots, snow, which I had forgotten falls silently, and overheated commercial buildings in the winter. But Cambridge turned out to be in many ways the perfect place for a newly minted Ph.D. to live. It was full of universities (Radcliffe and Harvard were both within walking distance of my apartment) and great bookstores. During the ten months I lived there, I attended lectures at M.I.T. and Harvard and met with other women scholars at Radcliffe.

There were other advantages to living in the Boston area, some I had experienced in the past, and others I hadn't. First, Boston, like Chicago and unlike L.A., had efficient public transportation. There were not only buses and taxis for those of us without cars, but also trains and subways. As a result, many Bostonians used public transportation, not just poor students, the working poor, and mentally ill derelicts, who were the bus riders in L.A. during the seventies. Cambridge was also a good place to live for those who liked to read newspapers and magazines. I enjoyed buying the Boston and New York papers at a famous newsstand (viewed briefly in the 1970 movie Love Story) in Harvard Square. I also occasionally bought the Washington papers on Sunday. And before there were so many cable channels, television viewers in the Boston area could choose between broadcast channels from New Hampshire and at least one other New England state, along with the Boston stations. Thus, I could usually catch "Edge of Night," the soap opera that I had become hooked on during the two months that I spent living with my mother and stepfather after I left my apartment in L.A., on the New Hampshire station because it played an hour later than on the Boston station. Even though I had to take two buses from my afternoon class in Medford to my apartment in Cambridge, I usually made it home by the New Hampshire air time, 4:00 p.m.

Of course, a blues singer can always find something to complain about in any town, and I found some problems with my new place of residence. First of all, Boston was a smaller city than

I had imagined. If I had come straight to Boston from Henderson, I probably would have been impressed and even intimidated by its size. But I had spent the last half of my thirty years living near the then second largest city in the country, Chicago, and in the then third largest city, L.A. And compared to those two cities, Boston (as I said to the chair of the English Department at USC to his amusement) seemed like a "country little town." And for some reason (I think they called it "blue laws"), the supermarkets were closed on Sunday and even on minor holidays like Columbus Day (which seemed less minor in the Boston area). I also was disturbed by the narrowness of the streets and the craziness of the drivers. During my first bus ride through Harvard Square, I saw a commercial van get its mirror stuck in the door of the bus. And it didn't take long for me to realize that pedestrians did not have the right of way in Boston. The Boston driver's law seemed to be if you are in my way, I'll run over you. I had not yet learned to drive and thought I might learn in Boston until I saw the narrow roads and the crazy driving.

There was also, of course, the winter weather, but the winter that I lived there was mild. The temperature never fell below 20 degrees, and there was only one significant snow storm. So it wasn't the weather that made me decide that Boston was definitely not my kind of town. It was the racial climate. If I had been a thirty-year-old white woman, I probably would have loved living in Cambridge and might not have noticed the problems with racism or at least not been as bothered by them. However, I had been in the Boston area only a few weeks when a young black boy was accidentally shot while playing football. Immediately the Mayor and other prominent political figures assumed that the shooting was racially motivated. If I remember correctly, it was eventually determined that the shooting was accidental. Someone shot a gun in the backyard, and the bullet traveled to the football field where the young black guy was playing. Later, some white students left school to protest something or other and attacked a black man in downtown Boston. One guy used the American flag in that attack. Now I knew that there had been protests against busing in South Boston, but I assumed that the racism was confined to that area; most cities have areas where blacks are less welcome. I remember hearing about Cicero when I lived in the Chicago area. And several sections of L.A. have over the many years that I have lived here been called unfriendly to blacks, including Fontana, called interestingly Fontucky by some Southern Californians, Glendora, and a whole county--Orange. But the racism seemed more widespread in the Boston area. And I was directly affected. Not long after I arrived, I was walking down a main street near my apartment when I heard the word that I hadn't heard shouted at me since I left Kentucky. Someone whom I couldn't see shouted, apparently from an apartment window, "Hey, nigger! Hey, Afro!" I had a large Afro in 1979, but I had been wearing that Afro since 1970, and it hadn't attracted that kind of attention in Evanston and L.A. Shortly after that incident, I was walking toward my bus in Harvard Square and saw some young white boys throwing water at pedestrians from the windows of a waiting bus. They seemed to be targeting blacks. And sure enough, as I passed their bus, I felt a few drops of water. I turned and considered entering the bus, but just then it took off with the boys laughing at me as they rode away. I was not amused.

Having to confront this kind of racism in 1979 in a place so far North of Kentucky shocked and enraged me. I couldn't believe it. I found myself walking around town with a chip on my shoulder, ready to do battle with any white person who even looked as if he or she wanted to say something racist to me. One morning I was rushing to the bus stop, a little late for my bus, and saw it arrive before I could cross the street. I was about to give up and just hope the next bus would allow me to reach Medford and my class on time when the driver caught my eye and waved for me to hurry. Relieved, I ran, hopped on the bus, and said thanks to the driver while I dug change out of my wallet. Unfortunately, another woman was talking to him at the same time, so he didn't hear my thanks. As I was walking away after paying, the driver said sarcastically, "You're welcome." I walked back to a seat, sat down, and got pissed. After a couple of minutes of silent steaming, I left my seat, walked up to the white bus driver, who had been nice enough to wait for me, and said, barely able to contain my rage, "I said 'thank you' when I got on the bus; maybe you didn't hear me because that lady was talking to you." The driver looked slightly shocked and said quietly, "Okay." He probably thought I was insane, not because of what I said, but because of the way I said it. Now I knew later (and probably even then) that the driver wasn't being racist, but he was white, and I was black, and that difference was enough to ignite me because of what I had seen and heard while trying to live peacefully in Cambridge.

Maybe I would have been less shocked by the racism if I had not chosen to come to the Boston area for what I thought would be its socially progressive political climate. When I applied for jobs, I focused more on where I wanted to live than on where I wanted to teach. After all, I knew I'd be living more than I would be teaching. Thus, I applied primarily to colleges and universities in California, especially Southern California, because that's where I wanted to live. I decided also to apply to a few schools in Southern Florida for the same reason I wanted to stay in California, the weather. Because I knew that I couldn't count on finding jobs in those two popular states, I chose two others with less desirable climates. Except for Florida, which I didn't really consider typically Southern, I made a point of not applying to schools in the South. I applied, instead, to universities in Illinois because I was already familiar with that state and had many family members living there, including my brother and his family, who at that time were in Chicago. Massachusetts was my fourth choice. I knew the weather there would be colder than I liked, and I knew only one person from Boston, a graduate school friend, who now lived in California. I chose Massachusetts because McGovern won there in 1972 and because my favorite rich white family, the liberal Kennedys, were from there. I'm serious. I thought Massachusetts was the most liberal state in the nation, so imagine my surprise when I encountered more racism there than I had in Illinois and California.

I should have been suspicious when the only job offers I received were from the Boston area. I applied to many more schools in California but didn't even get to second base with any of them.

Not one of the job search committees at those schools asked to see a chapter from my dissertation, much less scheduled an interview at the Modern Language Association (MLA) Convention. The same thing happened with the four or five schools that I applied to in Florida and Illinois. But I was scheduled for MLA interviews with two Boston area schools, Tufts and Northeastern, and was offered both jobs. I chose Tufts over Northeastern because the pay was better. I was paid $15,000 a year to teach four classes at Tufts while Northeastern first offered me $11,500 to teach nine courses and then raised it to $13,000. The people at Tufts were also willing to pay for me to come to the campus and be interviewed by the entire English Department faculty and by several administrators. So I actually had seen Boston, Medford, and even Harvard Square during the less than 24 hours I spent there the winter before I arrived for the job. That was clearly not enough time for me to discover the problems with race.

My coming to Boston because of its supposed liberalism and encountering racism was similar to my experience at USC. I wanted to go to a school in Southern California because of the warm weather, but I also assumed that schools in California were liberal. I had seen (on television) and read about (in newspapers) some of the political activities of Berkeley students but didn't really know anything about USC students. I assumed that they would be anti-war, pro-civil rights hippies. I didn't even know how important football was at USC, and I certainly wasn't aware of the dominance of fraternities and sororities at what turned out to be a politically conservative school.

I probably would not have been so eager to move to Southern California if the weather in the Chicago area had not been so, well, frightening. It snowed in Henderson, and occasionally the temperature dipped well below freezing, but compared to the Evanston blizzards, the winters in my hometown were mild. It was not unusual for the temperature to be below zero during the coldest months (December and January) of the year in Evanston, and that's not including the wind chill factor. The Chicago wind was so brutal that it had a name, the Hawk. And when the Hawk started whipping around corners and trying to tear open my coat as I trudged through snow in my heavy knee-high boots or slipped and slid on ice, trying (usually unsuccessfully) not to fall, I didn't think about spring and summer, I thought about moving. The spring before I moved to California, it snowed in April. As I walked home in what I hoped would be my last snow storm, I said out loud, "Go ahead and snow because this time next year I'll be in L.A."

The summer before I moved to L.A., I was working in the linen department (during the annual August white sale) at Marshall Fields in Old Orchard, a mall near Evanston, making a little extra money, when I met a woman who had just moved from L.A. I told her I was about to move there, and she warned me about earthquakes. I returned the favor, warning her about below zero temperatures, the wind, the snow, and the ice. But she seemed to think that earthquakes were worse than any cold weather because they were more dangerous. I said to that woman something that I still stand by, "I'd rather die in L.A. than live in Chicago." And

I could add Boston and Henderson to that list of cities where I don't want to live.

L.A. was dangerous for me, but not so much because of the earthquakes. USC, like several other major American universities, is in a low-income urban neighborhood. The combination of young, vulnerable, mostly white, often rich, temporary residents and poor, often nonwhite, more permanent residents can be toxic. Only a couple of weeks after I moved into my dorm room, I was walking down Exposition Boulevard with my new roommate (a pot-smoking, tall, thin, and beautiful white woman who was soon forced out of the building because she left some furniture and dishes in the hallway, too frightened to try to move all of that junk into the already furnished room with her mean-looking, black roommate). It was about eight-thirty in the evening, so it was dark out. A police car pulled over, and the officer asked how far we were going, then warned us that we had better hurry home. Now I had gotten off buses in Evanston as late as 10:00 p.m. and walked the two or three blocks home without anyone's worrying about my safety. And I used to walk the few blocks home in the dark from choir practice or Christmas play rehearsal at my church in Henderson when I was only thirteen and fourteen. Two tall women couldn't walk down the street after dark in L.A. when they were on or near a university campus? Now that was dangerous!

During the almost seven years that I lived in the USC area, three students were murdered in the neighborhood. One female student was kidnapped from the parking lot of the apartment building where I lived for two years. Her car, driven by the murderer, was found in some distant state, maybe Texas. A few years later, a young couple, members of a fraternity and a sorority, were killed near Fraternity Row. Rumor had it that the killing was a gang initiation.

There were also sexual crimes. I was standing in the English Department talking to one of the secretaries when a beautiful young white woman walked in and said that she would have to drop her English class because she had been sexually assaulted twice. The secretary and I were both startled and asked some questions. This young woman calmly explained that the rapist entered her apartment through the window. Later, one of my friends tried to persuade me to spend a few nights with the woman who had taken the screening exam with me. I assumed that she was ill, but whatever her problem, I couldn't stay with her because I had no transportation, and she didn't live near campus. I later found out that she had been raped while walking on or near campus.

Even I had a problem with a peeping Tom when I moved off campus. The apartment building had one of those communal porches. Our non-air-conditioned, hot-as-hell-in-the-summer building, which was on the corner of Adams and Hoover, faced another building. One morning a male tenant of the other building knocked on my door and told me that he had seen one of the men living in my building peeping through my window the night before. I kept the curtains drawn because I didn't want people walking by and looking in, but there was a gap between the two curtains in the kitchen. And this creep had probably walked by, saw me walking around my very hot kitchen in a blouse and panties, and stayed to watch the peep show. I figured out who the guy (a young black man) was later because he always called me sexy when I went by his apartment on my way to the laundry room.

Given all the crime that I had to contend with during my years of living in an urban environment, I didn't have that much time to worry about earthquakes. I experienced my first earthquake less than a year after I moved to L.A. I was living in an upper-class undergraduate and graduate women's dormitory on Exposition Boulevard. This dormitory was an old building; I was told that Pat Nixon had lived there. But it was also a noisy building when I lived there from the fall of 1972 to the summer of 1973. They were constructing a new architecture building in back of our dormitory, in fact, right behind my window. And Exposition Boulevard was a busy street, complete with a train running down the center of it. The day of the earthquake, I awakened, felt the ground rumbling, heard noise, and just assumed the train and the bull dozers or whatever they were using on the new building were running at the same time.

I've been in a tornado in Henderson and strong wind storms in Evanston and a couple of times even in the L.A. area. Those storms were more stressful and frightening than the earthquakes. In fact, I wasn't even mildly disturbed by an earthquake until the Whittier one in 1987, and what frightened me then was not the first earthquake but the almost equally strong aftershock a few minutes later. Earthquakes happen so quickly that by the time I realize that it's an earthquake and move into the doorway, the earthquake is usually over. If there are many aftershocks, and I'm near the epicenter, then my nerves can become rattled. But generally I'll take earthquakes over tornados, hurricanes, and blizzards any day.

The fires are, however, a different story. Since childhood when my then three-year old cousin was badly burned in a house fire, and a few years later I witnessed an apartment fire (near my grandmother's house) that killed one person, I've been paranoid about fires. And there are more fires in Southern California than there are earthquakes. Usually they happen somewhere else--Malibu, Laguna Beach--, but in October, 2003, the fire came within a couple of miles of my house. I went outside at midnight to see what was happening and could feel the heat from the fire. We breathed smoke and ashes for days. Still, I didn't consider leaving Southern California. Despite the fires, mudslides, earthquakes, and the long droughts followed by the torrential rains, Southern California is paradise to me.

I don't, however, consider myself a Southern Californian; although I've been living here for a total of thirty-eight years, more than twice as long as I lived anywhere else, I still talk about "these L.A. folks" or these "Southern Californians" as people very different from me. I see myself as an immigrant, an outsider. When I was still in L.A. and had been living there for at least six years, I was crossing the street at Hoover and Adams on my way to my apartment when a black woman with an accent jumped out of her car and asked hopefully, "Where are you from?" Back in those days when I had my big Afro, I was often mistaken for either a Nigerian or a Haitian. She probably was from one of those countries and thought she had spotted a home girl. I could have responded, "Here." But I said, "Kentucky." If someone asked me that question today, unless it was clear that they were asking where did I presently live, I would still say, "Kentucky."

I identify as Kentuckian, not because I'm proud to be from that state; I can't even be proud that I left since the decision was not mine; I was following my mother. Kentucky is the only state where I lived that voted against the first black President; Obama won in Illinois, Massachusetts, and California. And while Illinois has given us two black senators, Massachusetts has given us a black senator and a black governor, and California gave us a black mayor of its largest city, now led by a Mexican American mayor (not to mention the two female senators), Kentucky has given us Mitch McConnell, Rand Paul, and before Rand, some former baseball player who seemed to be mentally ill. So I'm no prouder to be a Kentuckian than I am to have long, narrow feet. A Kentuckian is just who I am.

I sometimes have trouble distinguishing my Southern traits from my black traits. I'll describe some behavior that I'll think is black, only to find out that Southern white folks act the same way. I'll use expressions like "what's the matter with you?" thinking I'm talking like black folks and realize later that Southern white folks use the same expression. And, of course, it's also hard to distinguish between soul food and Southern food. I even found one personality trait that might be Kentuckian. I always thought that my don't-mess-with-me hostile glare that held long enough turns into a stare was a black female thing until I encountered the husband of one of my officemates. He was about sixteen years older than I was and also came from Kentucky. One day he dropped by the office to pick up his wife and engaged in a stare-down with the tall, skinny white man in the office next door. That man was from Texas. My fellow Kentuckian bragged about how he stared down the Texan. Don't mess with Kentucky!

When I tell someone I'm from Henderson, Kentucky, and he or she looks blank, I say, "Have you heard of Evansville, Indiana?" Most people have heard of Evansville, so I explain that Henderson is eight miles from Evansville, just across the Ohio River. When I want to shock people with my clown feet stories, I tell them that my feet were so big when I was a child that I had to go to a different state to find shoes. I sometimes later admit that the other state was only a few miles away, and that we went there to buy most of our clothes.

But Indiana wasn't just another state; it was a northern state. And that meant that during the fifties the rules were different there. Until the buses were integrated, we could ride on any part of the bus in Indiana but had to move to the back in Kentucky. Since we usually took the bus only from Henderson to Evansville and back again, we always stayed in the back, but people coming from farther North would complain about having to move when the bus left Evansville for Henderson.

Many people who lived in Henderson worked in Evansville, and if we wanted to do anything interesting or fun (like see Santa Claus, for instance), we usually had to go to Evansville. Not much happened in Henderson. When I was still in elementary school, they built a swimming pool for blacks, called the W.C. Handy Pool. I obviously wasn't a swimmer or I wouldn't have had so much trouble at ETHS, but I went there with my brother and other neighborhood children to watch other black folks swim and to eat candy and listen to the jukebox. During my early childhood, the city also built low income housing, called "the projects," where my family and I lived for several years (after leaving the two room bungalow). The projects were initially segregated, so we blacks lived in one area while the whites lived in projects in another part of town. Our projects included a community center where we could hold wedding receptions and birthday and anniversary parties. Even when we no longer lived in the projects, we could rent the community center for parties.

But most of the social activities for black people in Henderson originated in the church. There were four black Baptist churches when I lived there. My family and I went to the one "on the other end of town," the end of town closest to Evansville. That church, which is still there, although in a different location, was called Seventh Street Baptist Church (for obvious reasons; it apparently is still on Seventh Street, just on a different corner). I'm not sure why, but my family members were very prominent at Seventh Street Church. My Aunt Mary Belle was the church organist, my mother one of the choir soloists, both my aunt and uncle (Uncle James) taught Sunday school, and several of the men in our family were deacons or trustees. My brother and I were also active members, singing in the junior choir and serving as junior ushers.

Since we now think of the fifties as a more innocent time and since Henderson was a small southern town, my childhood should have been quiet and peaceful. And in some ways it was. Foots disturbed the peace in our home occasionally, but the town seemed quieter than the other places I have lived. But when I think back to those early years in Henderson, I realize that beneath the quiet of that small town was a great deal of trauma, and I'm not referring to racial strife or my dysfunctional family. Henderson was certainly a safer town than L.A. or Pomona, and I don't ever remember anyone being raped, but I do remember two murders. My brother witnessed one of them. He was walking home with a friend from some event, maybe boy scouts or practicing for the band since he briefly played the clarinet, when he saw a man beating his very drunk wife. The wife died that night. The couple, whom I didn't know well, were attractive and had three cute children, all of whom were in grades below mine (I was probably in sixth grade) at Alves Street. When they came back to school, I thought I should say or do something, but I didn't know what to do or say.

The second murder happened when I lived with my grandmother after my mother moved North. One afternoon we heard a woman running up and down our street screaming, and Mother, who always wanted to know what was going on in her neighborhood (her daughter has the same instincts), went out on the porch to find out what was wrong. When the woman came down the street for the second time, Mother called to her, "Hey! What's wrong with you, gal?" and she said that someone had killed her son. We learned later that her son, who apparently was something of a bully, was stabbed to death.

There were other tragedies. Before the burning of my cousin and the apartment building, I attended the funeral of a young child who had died from being scalded by hot water. Because the funeral was held at Seventh Street Church, I was in the choir. I'm not sure how this child was scalded or if anyone was jailed for neglect or abuse, but I remember hearing the adults suggest that the child's mother should be punished. Even though I was older than the dead child, I worried about being scalded to death for several years after that funeral.

But the most troubling tragedy of my childhood involved a weird family that I didn't care about until after the incident. I always think of that family when I read Toni Morrison's <u>The Bluest Eye</u> because they were Henderson's version of the Breedloves. All of the family members seemed a little strange, and they were very homely, but the oddest one was the girl who was about a year older than I was. She had some kind of problem that made it difficult for her to walk up and down stairs. She held on tight to the railing, looking panicked and stepping very high. I thought about her when I read Rona Barrett's memoir years later, and she described her problems with stairs. Maybe this young girl had the same problem that Rona did. But back then we all thought she was just strange. One day the girl and her younger sister didn't come to school, and a few days later it was reported that her older sister, who was a student at the black high school, had died. But how she died was what freaked me out. She starved to death, and the whole family had been without food for days. I couldn't get over it. How could people starve to death? I mean, we weren't rolling in money, but we always had food. Even my maternal grandmother, who lived in a fairly rundown looking house, had plenty of food. I was haunted by that family for months. What were the parents doing? Why didn't the high school student try to find a job? Why didn't they go to the church or to their relatives or neighbors for help? I finally decided that they didn't eat, not because they were poor, but because they were weird. They didn't want to eat. I don't remember what happened to the two sisters of the dead girl. I don't think they returned to school.

Maybe one reason the starving episode bothered me so much is because eating was one of the favorite activities of the black people in Henderson. We ate in the community center, in each others' homes, and especially at church or during church-related activities. At Seventh Street, there were Sunday School picnics, Homecoming dinners, and bags of candy and other treats for children on Christmas Eve and Easter Sunday. Some of the more enterprising black folks had businesses based on eating. One woman had a little popcorn stand, and the black drugstore on the corner of Dixon (where the black projects were located) and Alves Street (a couple of blocks from the school) was known more for its ice cream cones than for its medicine. There was also a well-known, black-owned barbeque restaurant just outside of town. But we didn't always have to buy food because many of us raised fruits and vegetables in our yards. The white woman who lived next door to Mother had a very large garden, where she grew the best tomatoes I have ever tasted. Included in the backyard of the home that my parents bought were a grapevine, an apple tree, and several apricot trees. The backyard next to ours had cherry trees. The apricots weren't worth much, but we enjoyed the grapes, cherries, and apples, and my mother made preserves and even wine from the fruit.

Before a law was passed, intended (I assume) to make Henderson more of a town and less like the country, people also raised animals for food. The black woman who lived on the other side of Mother raised turkeys in her yard, and the woman who lived across the street from us when we lived on Dixon raised chickens in her house. One woman who lived near our church even had a horse (not for eating, of course) in her yard. Now I enjoyed all of the free fruit, and among my favorite childhood memories are the summer days when my brother and I joined the children next door in eating grapes and cherries. I always think of those summer days when I read Charles Chesnutt's famous story "The Goophered Grapevine." I can understand why a slave would risk being conjured to eat some sweet grapes. I wasn't, however, as fond of the animals. I didn't see why anyone would want to keep chickens in their home or turkeys in their back yard. Those turkeys next door to Mother terrorized me, and that was before my close encounter with the wayward bird. They gobbled so loudly and looked so mean that I was worried that one would jump the fence and attack me. Believe me, I was thrilled when they outlawed raising animals inside the city limits. I believed that people who wanted to raise animals should live on farms in the country, not in my hometown.

I thought of Henderson and its city-living chickens and turkeys when my traveling buddy, Pasadena Friend, and I were dropping resumes at various campuses in Southern California and arrived at Cal Poly Pomona. I saw the horses, the cows, and the rolling hills that the promoters of the school brag about in their brochures and sealed my fate by saying to Pasadena Friend: "Aw, hell, no, I'm not going to teach here. I didn't leave Kentucky to work at a country school like this, with cows and horses grazing."

I, of course, worked at Cal Poly for a total of 31 years, two years as a part-time lecturer and 29 as a full-time faculty member. After a few years, I didn't even notice the horses (and rarely passed the area where they kept the cows).

Pomona turned out to be not that much like my old Kentucky home, but when I first started teaching at Cal Poly, I felt as if I had traveled back in time and was stuck in the country. I had adjusted to seeing the orange, lemon, and lime trees (free fruit again) growing sometimes in the front yards of homes and even apartment buildings throughout the L.A. area, but I did not expect to have to look at animals. I also was bothered by how undeveloped Pomona looked from where I stood on the campus, waiting for the bus to take me back to my apartment in L.A. I looked toward what I now know is Diamond Bar and saw nothing. Temple Avenue, heading toward Diamond Bar Boulevard, which now has a hotel and other commercial buildings, was not yet developed. It was barren back in the late seventies. I thought, as I stood staring at the open space, that even Henderson had buildings. This place looked like a wasteland.

But when I found myself with job offers only in the Boston area, Pomona started to look better to me. As I rode the bus, I found places near Pomona that looked livable, not as country as Cal Poly and not as barren as the area around the campus. I could live in Walnut or Hacienda Heights. Then once, when I caught a ride with a friend, I discovered Covina and West Covina. So, before I left for Boston, I asked the English Department chair if he thought there would be any jobs at Cal Poly in the next year or two. I didn't exactly beg, but I'm sure I looked very eager to land a job at a place where two years earlier I had declared I would never teach. He claimed (and maybe believed) that there were no jobs on the horizon, so I went to Boston only to get a call a few months after my arrival, alerting me that there were two tenure-track job openings at Cal Poly for the 1980-81 school year. After my experiences with Boston's illiberal racism, I couldn't wait to move to Pomona.

And the Pomona that I found when I rented an apartment within walking distance of the campus was more like L.A. than like Henderson. When I was buying a television in the now defunct department store, Zody's, the clerk asked me where I was living, and when I answered, "Pomona," he volunteered that I had better buy theft insurance. I got the picture. Keep the doors locked and don't walk around the neighborhood in the dark.

The neighborhood may have been unsafe, but the apartment complex where I lived was fairly swanky. Like most apartment buildings in L.A., this one featured lush landscaping, but it also had two laundry rooms, a swimming pool, and an exercise room. And when I moved there, it was for adults only. Then a law was passed preventing landlords from discriminating against renters with children, and children were allowed to move in. I didn't have problems with the few children who lived there, though. My problem was with the adults.

The part of the complex where I lived had four apartments on each side, two on the second floor, and two on the first. I lived in one of the second-floor apartments and shared the stairs with the other second-floor residents. That other apartment was jinxed for couples. Three couples (two black, one white) in a row lived there,

81

and each ended their relationships and their stay in the apartment in a major fight. After the third battle, where the woman was screaming in her Haitian accent, "ou will have to kill me here tonight!" I went to the manager's office and asked that they put a single person in that apartment. So the last two years of the six years that I lived there, my next door neighbor was a sweet young man who was a student at Cal Poly. Unfortunately, during my last few months in the building, the apartment beneath me was occupied by a couple who were major partiers. They smoked pot and played their music almost as loud as my L.A. neighbors, the Rolling Stones. When he saw me moving out of my apartment, the man asked if they were the reason I was moving; I told him they weren't because I had been planning to move for a couple of years and had bought a townhouse. I was telling the truth, but I was also happy to leave Pomona for Claremont, mainly because of Ike and Tina, as I called my downstairs neighbors (although they at least didn't fight).

I initially resisted moving to Claremont. Ironically, I preferred Diamond Bar, which was slightly closer to Cal Poly, and which I discovered was not as barren and undeveloped as it had first appeared. But since I was now a driver, proximity to the campus was not as big a concern. I had another problem with the college town. I thought it was a pretentious little old town, with its streets named after colleges (three of the main streets are Harvard, Yale, and Dartmouth) and its fake Harvard Square. As I complained about the snobbishness of Claremont, I snobbishly pointed out that I had experienced the real Harvard Square while living in Cambridge. The town described itself as the city of "trees and

Ph.D.'s." I preferred Henderson's motto: "On the Ohio but never in it."

Unfortunately, I was still an associate professor when I was townhouse hunting, and so my funds were limited. The townhouse communities in Diamond Bar were too expensive, and for some reason the association fees were very hefty. The townhouses in this Northern Claremont Community surrounding the tennis club were cheaper, so I reluctantly moved there. Given my track record of choosing the wrong places to live, study, and/or work for the wrong reasons, USC for its hippies, Boston for its liberalism, and rejecting the right places for the wrong reasons, Cal Poly for its grazing livestock as if the cows and horses would appear in my classes, it should not be surprising that the once scorned Claremont became my favorite place to live. First of all, it was quieter and safer than Pomona, and although it was initially a little too white and too Republican for my taste, the population eventually became more diverse and, consequently, more liberal. I still think the college names for streets are ridiculous; in fact, I laugh every time I pass the street named after Northwestern; I guess I should have tried to find a house on that street. But I like the trees and the many parks. Claremont is a very green city, not necessarily in the energy saving connotation of that word but in the landscaping. The Claremont Club community included several parks, and even this smaller community where I live now has a small park.

Partly because of the parks and trees but also because of its mixture of very old and relatively new homes, Claremont is a great place to walk and run. Unlike parts of the area in Pomona where I lived, it has sidewalks. I especially love walking on the Claremont Colleges campuses. I no longer even mind the fake Harvard Square, which features some interesting little shops. When I started looking for a bigger place for my mother and me to share, I went to other nearby towns--Upland, La Verne, San Dimas, even Chino Hills and Glendora--but I kept circling back to Claremont. And just when we were giving up on finding a place here, this community of fifty houses was built within walking distance of my townhouse.

Of course, the houses weren't built as quickly as we hoped and the builders promised, so we actually had to leave our already sold townhouse and move to an apartment in San Dimas for seven weeks. During that brief period of exile, I described myself as a refugee. I clearly had found my home in Claremont, and we have now been in our not so new house for more than twelve years. We've had to deal with a fire coming near our home and an overly controlling association who not only want to tell homeowners when to paint but also what kind of locks we can place on our door. But I expect to remain here until I die.

When I think about the places where I have lived, studied, and worked, I realize that they include four major regions in America. I spent my childhood in the South, my adolescence in the Midwest, and my adulthood in the West, with a brief stay in the Northeast at thirty. I've also lived in three of the four major time zones (Central, Pacific, East). I've lived in a small town (Henderson), in the suburbs of major cities (Evanston, Cambridge, Pomona, Claremont), and in the inner city (Central L.A.). But more interesting than the differences between my places of residence are the similarities. With the exception of Henderson, which didn't even have a community college when I lived there, all of the places where I've lived have been either college towns or near colleges. Of course, L.A. is much more than a college town, but during the almost seven years that I lived there, I lived on or near the USC campus, and my Pomona apartment was around the corner from Cal Poly. I also often lived (or worked) on or near busy streets and/or freeways, even in the small towns. Cal Poly is just off the 10 freeway. The community where I live now is between the formerly very busy Baseline Road and the recently extended 210 freeway. My Pomona apartment complex was on Valley Boulevard, which became Holt in two blocks, next to the Corona Freeway off ramp.

Most interestingly, with the exception of Central L.A., I've lived near borders. Henderson was on the border of two states; the street where I lived in Evanston was two blocks from Skokie. I didn't live on a border in Cambridge, but the school where I taught, Tufts, was actually in two towns, Medford and Somerville. Even the places where I lived briefly followed this pattern; my parents' house in San Fernando, where I stayed briefly in the summer of 1979 before I moved to Cambridge, and again in the summer of 1980 before I moved to Pomona, was two blocks from Pacoima, and during the seven weeks that my mother and I lived in San Dimas, waiting for our new home to be built, we were on a street where one side (ours) was San Dimas and the other side was La Verne. My current hometown, Claremont, is on the border between L.A. County and San Bernardino County. In fact, both of my Claremont homes have been within walking distance of San Bernardino County.

Some of these similarities are probably coincidental, but it's appropriate that a person who spent her entire adult life either studying or teaching or both should live in college towns. And, of course, college towns usually have great bookstores and good libraries, and I love to read. But I'm more interested in the experience of living on the borders. Clearly, the North-South border between Kentucky and Indiana was the most significant because it actually affected how I was treated as a black person. And the sales taxes are cheaper in San Bernardino County, so my finances are mildly affected, based on whether I buy my groceries in Claremont or cross the border into Upland. I guess if I had been an alcoholic like my father, the Evanston/Skokie and Somerville/Medford borders would have been more important. One of each of those pairs of towns is (or was when I lived there) dry, which means that drinkers went to the other town to quench their thirst. When I was at Tufts, I was told (perhaps as a joke) that whether or not faculty social events could include liquor depended on which side of the campus they were held. I can't remember which of the towns was dry, but liquor was supposedly not allowed on the side of the campus in that town.

In some ways, I have spent my life on borders, on the border between the white and black worlds and on the border between the academy and the real world. Because I was never completely integrated into the institutions where I studied and worked, because I was always an outsider, I never moved into the center of those worlds. Even now that I'm retired, I cross borders very easily. I can have lunch with two retired English professors, talking in standard English about the state of education or politics or our psyches, and then return home to join my mother's complaint, her blues song, about the cancellation of two of her favorite soap operas, slipping effortlessly into dialect, saying with her, "Ain't it a shame." So even though I've settled into my little snobbish Claremont community, it's appropriate that I know that I don't have to go far to get out.

CHAPTER FOUR
I'm Black, and I'm Loud

The character Gallimard in David Hwang's play, M Butterfly, says at one point that we are all prisoners of our time and place. Indeed, where and when we live can have a major effect on how we live. But we are also prisoners of our class, gender, and most important, our race. And unlike time, which changes and can change us, and places, which we can always leave, race is something we can't escape. Clearly, we can move up or down in class. We can even change our gender now, but no matter how much bleach or spray tan we use on our skins, we cannot change our race.

I always say that black is my primary identity. Because I am dark-skinned, people seeing me from a distance know that I am black before they know my gender, age, or nationality. My race also affects how I view the world and how I am viewed by the world more than any other identity marker. My perspective is also affected, of course, by place and time. In my e-mail conversations with a former student, who is also a black female but from a different generation (X) and born and raised in Southern California, I see how my being a Southern-born baby boomer affects my perspective. She seems less sensitive to race issues, slightly less likely to call out the white folks. But while my gender, class, age, and profession may help shape my ideas, everything that I think, say, and do is colored by race. My race, for instance, helped determine where I lived and how I felt about where I lived. I avoided going to the South because I didn't want to deal with racism, and I didn't like living in the Boston area because of the racism I encountered there. Indeed, one reason that I initially resisted moving to Claremont is when I visited friends who lived here, I didn't see many black people.

Black people are probably more obsessed with race than any other ethnic group in America. Certainly we are more concerned about it than our white friends are. I first became aware of how differently from whites blacks view color when I was talking to a black friend at USC about her younger brother and his bird. The bird was always escaping its cage, and when it did, the younger brother yelled, "Get your blue ass back in that cage!" Now I thought the whole idea of someone talking about a bird's "blue ass" was hilarious, but I wondered if a white person would talk like that. I asked one of my white friends who didn't become nervous when I brought up race if she ever said anything like, "I have to get my white ass in the bed." After my friend stopped laughing, she claimed that she never had said anything like that, nor had she heard any other white person talk like that. But black people that I knew talked about their black asses or their black selves all of the time, and so did I. Even lighter skinned black folks weren't above talking about their black asses.

Decades later when I was teaching a black literature class in which about 50% of the students were black, some of the black students in the class and I were in a heated discussion about who was lighter, Vanessa Williams (that's beauty queen Vanessa Williams who starred in the movie <u>Soul Food</u>, not the darker skinned Vanessa Williams who starred in the "Soul Food" television series) or Halle Berry. I was with the group who thought Vanessa was lighter. The argument went on for several minutes before I caught the eye of one of the white students, looked around the room and realized that the nonblack students were all either laughing or staring at us as if we were crazy. I then stopped the discussion to explain why skin color was so important to black folks. Of course, it soon became clear why skin color was so important to us because the first two books that we read (<u>Autobiography of an Ex-Coloured Man</u> and <u>Passing</u>) in the class were about blacks light enough to pass for white.

Some white people try to convince blacks that color doesn't matter. Long before they started talking about a post-racial, or is it a post-racist, society, some whites wanted everyone to be colorblind. This attitude bugged me as much as (if not more than) the attitude of the whites who couldn't forget and couldn't let me forget that I was black. I remember two of my colleagues, whom I generally liked, playing the colorblind card on me when I asked about a student who talked to them when he claimed to have left a paper in my mailbox. These two gentlemen shared an office that was (in the old building; our department moved in 1990) next to the mailroom. The brown-skinned student had described the two of them perfectly. But when I asked them about him and described him as a young black man, they both pretended they didn't notice his color. Oh, come on, white men! He noticed they were white. These men were from my mother's generation; one was her age, and the other a year younger. One of them may have even been born in the South, so I don't believe that they could have seen a brown-skinned man and not noticed that he was black.

The writer Lucille Clifton gave a speech at Cal Poly, where she commented on white folks' trying to talk black people out of identifying themselves by race. She said that when white people told her that they didn't see her as black she asked them why they wanted to deny that essential part of her identity. Well, exactly. Did they not see her as a woman? Did they think it would be a compliment to say that they didn't think of her as a woman? I sometimes want to ask my white "friends" how they would respond if they were made to feel uncomfortable about discussing some part of their identity. How would married women feel if their single friends didn't want them to mention their husbands? How would women with children feel if their friends who had no children became restless and uncomfortable when they talked about their children? White people can afford to be colorblind because usually their color is not such an important identity marker. But blacks don't have that luxury.

Most black people, especially those of us born before the civil rights movement began, understand that, contrary to Ralph

Ellison's theory of black invisibility, our blackness, when we're in white institutions, makes us more visible. I was the only black person and, as far as I could determine, the only nonwhite person in the small English Department at Tufts. Cal Poly had a larger and more diverse department, which combined English with foreign languages, but while there were several other nonwhite faculty members, including an Egyptian man during the first few years I was in the department, there were only two blacks, both women. The other black woman, whom I will call Other Black, was light-skinned, about the same color as two of the Latinos and probably a bit lighter than the Egyptian. So I was easily the darkest person in the department.

I became aware of my visibility in my first year there. Probably like many universities, Cal Poly has a time period (it's now noon on Tuesday and Thursday) set aside for meetings. The problem is that many professors have conflicting meetings, and that was certainly true for me during my years as a junior faculty member. As chair of the department curriculum committee, I was a member of the College of Arts Curriculum Committee, for instance, and I served on other college and university committees. Usually when the department met at the same time as one of these committee meetings, I skipped the department meeting and attended the committee meeting. Every time I missed a department meeting, several of my colleagues greeted me in the hallway or walking across campus with, "Where were you during the department meeting?" There were more than thirty people in our department during this period, and most of them attended the meetings regularly. I certainly didn't notice every time a white person missed a meeting, and I doubt that others kept tabs on all of the whites, which is why the secretary took roll.

Of course, high visibility is not always bad. I was more memorable than the other faculty in our department because of my skin color. A few years before I retired, one of my colleagues, the chair of a search committee, was encouraging us to come to hear the candidates' presentations. He wanted us to know how important our presence was to the candidate, so he said that he still remembered where I sat during his presentation. Another newer faculty member said that I sat in the same seat during his presentation. Well, yes, I had favorite seats during department meetings. But I doubt that either of those gentlemen could remember where any of the white men sat. In fact, I challenged the chair of the search committee to tell me where any of the men sat. Of course, he couldn't do it and probably felt a little sheepish about remembering where I sat.

I was probably also more memorable to the students because of my race. For most of the time that I taught graduate classes, I was not just the only black but the only nonwhite female instructor. Other Black did not teach graduate courses, and the other nonwhite females taught Spanish (although one of them taught a few English graduate courses during the late nineties). After winning the Graduate Teaching Award two years in a row and an unprecedented third time, I did an Oprah (after her multiple Emmy wins) and refused to compete because I thought my race gave me an unfair advantage. I noticed that I won the first two times during the quarter when I taught African American Fiction. I thought maybe the students were giving me the award out of guilt. After reading about how much blacks had suffered, they might have decided to compensate me for my pain with the teaching award, a kind of reparation. When I won the award again after teaching 20th Century American Literature, I just decided that they picked me because I stood out from the graduate instructor crowd.

I initially learned the lesson of black visibility the first day that I attended Barrett Junior High School, my first day in a white institution. Because several of us who had continued to attend Alves Street decided to go to the "white" junior high, and because quite a few of our black former classmates had already been in one of the "white" elementary schools, there was a larger percentage of blacks among the seventh graders in 1961 than in previous years. The seventh grade reading teacher was an older woman (probably in her fifties) who lived across the street from the school. When she walked into our class of about thirty to forty students that first day, she stopped and very obviously, even dramatically, counted the black students. I counted with her; there were ten of us. The reading teacher left the room and came back several minutes later looking red in the face. We found out later from the mother of one of the black students in the class, a woman active in the NAACP, that the teacher had gone to the principal's office and asked him to remove some of the blacks (whom she probably called "nigras" and maybe even "niggers") from her classroom. He refused. She taught the class nervously at first and then with more assurance, but she died of a heart attack during the summer. I like to think that the fact that the two best readers in that class, Play Boyfriend and I, were dark-skinned blacks who had attended the all-black school through sixth grade helped her to her somewhat early grave. I know that having to face so many "nigras" in one class helped send her to her final reward a little early.

Another older teacher acted as if the black students were actually invisible. He was old enough to be retired and was substituting for the seventh grade English or history teacher. I can't remember which one now. He was telling some story and said, "You know how nigras are; they are always using big words and don't know what they mean." I couldn't believe those little words were coming out of his big mouth. I gasped. He looked at me curiously, as if he didn't understand what was wrong with me. There were three other black students in the class, all female, but, unlike me, they had spent several years in a white elementary school. I looked at each of them, moving in my seat, trying to catch their eyes, but they acted as if they hadn't heard him. I asked one of them about her response (or lack thereof) later, and she said that kind of thing happened all the time in her old school, and I should just get used to it. Well, that kind of thing never happened again in any of my classes, and I suspect if it had I would have said something or walked out, but since this was my first year of dealing with white folks, I didn't quite know what to do. After making as much noise as I could to try to remind the old white man that I was a "nigra" and didn't exactly love what he said, I followed the lead of the more experienced black girls and just sat very still.

But the teacher who made me most aware of my black skin during my first year in a white institution was that creepy geography teacher. He was not old, probably no more than thirty. Yet he seemed to be as disturbed by me, a single skinny black girl, as the reading teacher was by ten of us. If he had been a weird teacher, like Dr. Harrumph, a man who didn't like talking to any students, I would have had no problem with him. But this guy was a chatty, informal teacher, who clearly enjoyed the company of the other students. He was the kind of teacher that I would ordinarily like. First of all, I thought it was interesting that he was a man. There were no male teachers at Alves Street; only the principal was a man. And except for that old substitute, I think the geography guy was the only male teacher that I had in seventh grade (I had two in the eighth grade). He was also kind of a nice looking guy, tall, slim, and very erect. And he could be funny. But I clearly freaked him out. He never said one word to me all year, and when he handed back my quizzes or exams, he stood back and kind of dropped them really fast as if he were afraid I might touch him. He would say my name at least, although he seemed to have trouble with that, but he never talked to me and even tried to avoid making eye contact with me. Hell, even that older reading teacher was more comfortable in my presence than that jerk was.

The students in the geography class and in my other classes seemed to adapt to my blackness more easily than some of my teachers. I remember specifically a cute blonde girl in the geography class whose mother worked at the local A&P. She was very friendly. And there was another girl in my homeroom, a really beautiful girl named Vickie whose parents appeared to be wealthy. She and I formed a strange kind of friendship that blacks and whites had back then. We were friends at school but didn't hang out together when we left school. However, when I was in eighth grade, there was an end-of-the-year picnic that the whole school attended, and Vickie and her mother drove me to and from the site. It was one of the rare times when I was slightly embarrassed by the condition of my grandmother's house.

There were, however, a few young whites who did not appreciate being around blacks. In 1961 we were still transitioning from "separate but equal" facilities to everyone rides wherever they want in the bus and drinks from the same water fountain. In fact, there were still restaurants where blacks weren't allowed to eat. And some of the white students clearly thought blacks should stay in their place. I was once pushed away from a water fountain by an oversized white girl who hadn't heard or didn't accept the civil rights message. I decided not to attack her because she outweighed me by about one hundred pounds. She was even taller than I was. But when I was called a nigger in my ninth grade p.e. class by a white girl closer to my size, I had to punch her. I would have probably punched the big ass white girl if she had called me a nigger.

We were playing kickball the day Alice, the ninth grade white girl, decided to turn her rage on me. For some reason, all four black girls in the class were on the same team, and our team was winning. I was a relatively good kickball player, probably because of my big feet. But two of the other black girls were even better. They were also very good at signifying and catcalling the other team. At some point, Alice and one of her friends on the other team got into it with my black teammates. I was trying to be the peacemaker, suggesting that we just play. Probably seeing me, the skinny "A" student, as the weakest link among the black girls, Alice snarled, "Shut up, nigger!" Without thinking, I punched her. Down went Alice! Well, actually, she didn't go down, but she was shocked by my punch and clearly frightened. The teacher was not in the gym, so some of the other girls tried to cool us down. Before the teacher returned, I told Alice that I was going to meet her after school and beat her ass, and for some reason, I even threatened her mother, whom I didn't know. I guess I thought "I'll beat you and your mama" was the appropriate response to being called nigger.

Alice was frightened enough by the threat of an after school beating, which I never intended to administer, to report my threat, and I was called to the principal's office. I was warned that I would be suspended if I punched Alice again. During the next p.e. class, the teacher took me aside to counsel me. She told me that she had been called "white trash" when she was younger, and she learned to ignore those kinds of taunts. She complimented me on my academic achievements and predicted a great future for me but warned that I needed to control my temper. When she finished her little talk, she asked if I would handle the situation differently next time. I politely let her know that if anyone called me a nigger, I would punch that person. I gave her a look that clearly suggested that she was included among those anyone's who would be punched if they called me that name.

Fortunately, I left Henderson after my freshman year and moved to Evanston, where the racism was more subtle. I will always wonder if I would have been placed in remedial earth science if I were white. And I'm not sure if my "A's" from Henderson

High were taken less seriously because I was from the South, because I was black, or both. Would a white girl from Kentucky or a black girl from New York have been placed in honors classes immediately? I am fairly certain that the old counselor would not have warned a white girl that she was overachieving and shouldn't expect to do as well in college. But I also wonder if I would have received as much positive attention from some of the teachers if I had been white. In fact, I think I know the answer to that question. No, I wouldn't have. Two of my teachers called my parents to tell them how smart I was and to encourage them to be sure that I went to college. The number two ranked student in our class happened to sit near me in homeroom. I once asked her if teachers called her parents. She looked at me as if she were surprised at the question and said that they didn't. Although her parents were probably educated and knew how to advocate for their daughter (she went to either Harvard or Yale), I still was a bit troubled by these teachers who felt that they had to meddle in my business.

ETHS seemed much more progressive than Henderson High. There were black cheerleaders, for instance. But when one of those black cheerleaders became the first black Homecoming Queen during my senior year, the racism became more overt. I don't remember the exact taunts that were used, but I am sure that Toreen A, the 1966-67 ETHS Homecoming Queen, does. I think some graffiti about an African Queen appeared, and some white jerk said that he didn't dream of black girls when he thought about beautiful women or some such nonsense. We all survived the fuss, but it was just a reminder that racism didn't end at the North-South border.

Interestingly, the next year, during my freshman year in college, Northwestern had its first black Homecoming Queen, Daphne Maxwell (now Daphne Maxwell-Reid), who became an actress, starring, for instance, as the second Aunt Viv on "The Fresh Prince of Bel Air." She received more positive attention than Toreen did. I don't remember anyone's complaining about her selection, but there was an article in the college newspaper about how lonely she looked during the Homecoming Dance. I knew Daphne; she didn't strike me as the lonely-waif-standing-in-the-corner type.

The late sixties and early seventies, my college years, were a time of great change and upheaval in race relations; the word "revolution" was heard often during that period, and too often for my peace of mind the black students seemed to be leading the revolution at Northwestern. The night that Dr. Martin Luther King Junior was killed, I happened to be on the West side of Chicago with a busload of white Northwestern students who came to the ghetto to tutor blacks. I was in the group as part of my requirements for my Education degree, but most of the white students (and one black man) were there as volunteers. We enjoyed each other's company on the trip from Evanston to Chicago. But as we were listening to an administrator describing the program that we were joining, another officious-looking person came in and whispered something to him. There was a quick, quiet consultation among several people, and we were told that we needed to leave immediately because Dr. King had been shot. We all left quietly, in shock. Unfortunately, however, we arrived outside before the bus returned and had to stand for several tense minutes, waiting for it to reach us. Several blacks walked by, mumbling angrily to themselves while eying the innocent white students. I decided to stand slightly apart from the other students. If the blacks attacked, I was going to pretend that I was a local. I didn't know any of those white students well enough to die with them. Fortunately, the bus arrived before the riot started (and the riot did start later that night), but the trip back to Evanston was much quieter and sadder than the trip to Chicago. And we never returned to the West side. I fulfilled my Education assignment by tutoring at the local Evanston junior high school.

Shortly before or after Dr. King was killed, the black students occupied the bursar's office for several days. They made demands that led to the establishment of a Black House and the hiring of a black dean, for whom I worked for more than two years. The students who lived on campus also demanded separate black corridors in the dormitories, which seemed a little odd to me, a Southerner who had experienced segregation up close and too personal, but then I lived at home. Because I didn't live on campus and because I was focused more on making good grades and working at Montgomery Ward than campus politics, I didn't know anything about the sit-in until I saw it on the news. Still, I received more publicity from that occupation than some of the student leaders. I just happened to be at the right place at the right time, or the journalists looking for a story were at the wrong place and found me there.

On the Saturday after the sit-in, when I heard that the black students had occupied part of the administration building, I wanted to find out what they were trying to do, so I planned a trip to the campus to see what was happening. My mother, who was still working in one of the freshman dormitories at that time, went with me. It was raining that day, so we took our umbrellas. We were standing outside the building, talking to some of the black students through the window, when a photographer from the Evanston Review came to take our picture. He posed us with our umbrellas and with the students sticking their heads through the window. We've heard from a family friend that those pictures are still on the wall in the Black House.

A few days after the sit-in ended, I was sitting in the library, studying between classes, when a reporter from one of the Chicago newspapers (I am fairly certain it was the Tribune) came looking for black students. Now a smarter reporter might have realized that student activists would probably not be in the library. That's a place for nerdy scholarship girls. So, of course, he found me, and prominently displayed on top of my other books was a copy of Stokeley Carmichael's Black Power. I was writing a paper for my Education seminar on race and education. The reporter thought he had struck gold; he didn't seem too concerned that I wasn't actually in the administration building during the occupation. He interviewed me for several minutes. At one point, he asked me to compare the Northwestern protest to the Columbia one a little earlier in the year. Now I didn't know that much about the Columbia protest, but according to what I had read in the newspapers, they had been more rowdy, so I said something like, "We were more mature and responsible; they acted like brats." I don't now remember what else I said, but it doesn't matter because that quotation was the only one that appeared in the paper, along with a surprisingly large picture of me, sitting in the library with my copy of <u>Black Power</u> clearly visible. Sorry, Columbia students!

The next year the Black House was opened, and I was soon working there while those black students who preferred living together (and not all did) had their black corridors. But there was still more trouble for the relatively small number of black students enrolled at Northwestern at that time. Something happened between a white fraternity and some blacks, and then I guess some black male students retaliated and were suspended. And, of course, during this period (1968-69), young men, especially young black men, who weren't in college could be drafted and sent to Vietnam. To protest the suspension, several black students staged a hunger strike. They sat outside another administration building all day and night, drinking water, but not eating. This strike went on for days, and a few of the black students became ill. Those of us who were not on strike were told to go to the registrar's office and ask for paperwork for transferring in a failed attempt to scare the Northwestern administrators into believing that all of the blacks were leaving. I actually considered transferring just to escape all the conflict, but eventually the strike ended, and we went back to focusing on our courses. I don't remember whether the strikers won concessions or if they just gave up and let the suspended students take their punishment.

During my junior year, the blacks remained quiet, and I kept my fingers crossed that we would escape the year without turmoil.

Then students protested the war at Kent State, shots were fired by the National Guard, and there were four dead in Ohio. The whole Northwestern campus was shut down in protest, but except for classmate Eva Jefferson, a somewhat famous student leader, at least this time the black students weren't leading the revolt. I just went home and read two lengthy Victorian novels, George Eliot's Middlemarch and Charles Dickens' Little Dorrit. I returned to campus a few times to hear some of the speeches, but I was sick of revolutions. I just wanted to complete my education in peace. I wrote a paper that quarter about why those two novels I read while other students were protesting were relevant to what was happening in our culture. I don't remember what I said, but I earned an "A" on the paper and in the class.

But although my participation in this third revolution in three years was minimal, I again benefited from the activism of my fellow students. As part of the demands for ending the strike, the leaders of the protest asked that students be allowed to create and teach some upper-division classes. I wasn't interested in teaching a student-organized seminar, nor would I have taken one. However, I was required to complete a senior project before earning my B.S. in Education. My idea for a senior project was to make a case for an Education course in Teaching the Culturally Deprived (a term used frequently in the late sixties and early seventies to describe mostly nonwhite students whose parents were not well educated; in other words, students like me when I entered school). I assumed that I would just plan the course, list which books should be read, and suggest paper and presentation topics. But the director of the program I was in recommended that I actually teach the course, so during my last quarter at Northwestern, Winter Quarter, 1971, I taught to about a dozen students, most of them black and quite a few of them seniors like me, a course on "Teaching the Culturally Deprived."

I also student taught at ETHS that last quarter, and once I completed those two final requirements, I breathed a sigh of relief and left Northwestern, glad to escape what I was sure would be the final revolution of my undergraduate years. But maybe because I was no longer on campus, there were no student revolts during the Spring Quarter of my senior year. The 1970-71 school year ended peacefully.

While my classmates completed their education, I searched for jobs. Since my work study job ended with graduation, I needed a temporary job that would carry me to September when I hoped to have a teaching job. The temporary job in the Investment Department at Northwestern was a little easier to find than the permanent teaching job. The year that I graduated, 1971, was not a good year to find teaching jobs; there were too many graduates and not enough teaching positions. Before I started working in the Investment Department, I was interviewed by members of the English Department in one of the four schools that now made up ETHS. I had substitute taught at the high school a couple of times, and of course I both attended and student taught there, so many of the teachers and administrators were familiar with me. The interviewers gave me a good evaluation and said that I should be hired if a job became available. Before I heard from ETHS, I was contacted by the Northwestern job placement office and told that there was an opening in a high school on the

North side of Chicago. It was a job designed just for me because it was for a black English teacher. The school didn't have any black teachers, and I think there were a few black students planning to enroll there, or maybe a few black students were already there. At any rate, I would be the only black faculty member. Now I wanted a teaching job, and apparently this school was in a relatively prosperous section of the city and had a good reputation. But I was no more eager to be the only black faculty member in a high school at twenty-two than I was to be the only black student in the Highland Park junior high school at thirteen. Fortunately, just as I was deciding whether to take the job for a year until I could find something better or take my chances on finding a better teaching job that year, I was saved by receiving a contract from ETHS. Since I hadn't yet developed my redlight philosophy, I thought I was in heaven. I was even more excited when I discovered that I would teach mostly seniors.

When I came to ETHS as a student in 1964, there was only one black teacher, a man who taught history. And as far as I knew, when I left in 1967, there was only one other black teacher, another man who might also have taught history. But during the year that I student taught there, I saw several new black teachers. Most of them had gone, however, when I came back as a teacher the next year. I soon discovered why they left.

During the new faculty and administrators orientation, I met the only other new English teacher. He was a white man, twenty-eight years old, who had an M.A. from Harvard. The man tried to tell me that we had both been hired for the same job, and there had been a big battle in the department, but I didn't take the hint.

I asked him when he received his contract; he told me, and I said that I had signed mine a couple of months earlier. I thought that ended the discussion. But what the white man was trying to tell me was that the white folks who interviewed me and would now be working with me had never meant to hire me. They had said that I should be hired if there was a job because they assumed there would be no job. What they didn't count on was that the very clever assistant superintendent, who happened to be black, received the senior English teacher's resignation and immediately sent me a contract. He did not let the department members know what he was doing because he knew they would come up with some excuse not to hire me and hire a white person instead. When the white folks found out that there had been a resignation in their department, they didn't realize that the clever black man had already filled the position with the black woman they claimed they wanted to hire, so they happily searched for a new faculty member. They found this white man with the M.A. from Harvard and, of course, they were prepared to make the case that he was superior to me because his M.A. from Harvard trumped my B.S. from Northwestern. When the white man came into the assistant superintendent's office all cool and calm, thinking he had the job, the black man told him that I already had the job, had already signed the contract. That's when the battle began. The black man had hired another black female the year before (she was one of only two or three new black faculty members who were actually still there) by making her a permanent substitute (which is probably why I was called to substitute so infrequently). Since that black woman had found another teaching

108

position at ETHS for the 1971-72 school year, the white folks in my department argued that the white man should be given the permanent substitute position. And that's the mess I stepped into my first year of teaching.

I don't know why the black assistant superintendent didn't tell me I was entering hostile territory. Maybe he didn't want to scare or intimidate me. But he certainly should have warned me that the whites who would be my colleagues and supervisors were not happy that I was in the department. Since he was clever enough to know how to sabotage their plans to avoid hiring me, he should have been clever enough to know that they would try to sabotage me to prove that he had made "an administrative blunder" as the man who led the protest against my hiring called it during the inevitable blowup.

But here is the way some white folks behave. Before I arrived in September, this same man had done everything he could to try to prevent me from taking the position for which I had a contract. Another young woman who had been working in one of the other schools was transferred to the department I was joining. I learned, after we became friends, that this man had called her and told her what was going on, trying to enlist her in the fight against my hiring. But when I showed up, he acted as if he were my best friend. He had a good sense of humor, so I liked him. We also bonded because he too was originally from Kentucky, which should have been a warning to me. Interestingly, I initially didn't like the young transfer, whose name was Helen, because she looked so mean whenever the sneaky and fake Kentucky guy and I traded jokes. Of course, she was disgusted by his hypocrisy, but I just thought she didn't like him or me or either of us.

One way to sabotage a new instructor is to give her too much to do. The senior teachers were trying a new program where all students not in college level classes took mini-courses designed by the teachers. Each nine weeks, new courses were offered, and the students had to enroll in those classes. Clearly, the point was to mimic college, but some of these students weren't ready for college and didn't plan to attend college. We spent a few days before classes started organizing courses. I ended up teaching several sections of a course I created called "Comic Spirit," as well as a section of "Fiction and Fantasy." And I was assigned another course called "Beat and Black Poetry," which I team taught with the Harvard M.A., meaning that he taught the class unless he had to substitute for someone else. I'm not sure what he did the rest of the day when he wasn't substituting, maybe he was teaching sections for other senior teachers. I also, in what Oprah would call a "full circle moment," had a section of team-teaching Sophomore English, which was the course I took seven years earlier. And one of the teachers on the team with me was a woman who (while not my teacher) had been on the team when I was in the class; she was now also the chair of our department.

Because I was teaching so many courses with different preparations, it took me a few weeks to feel that I had my classes under control. I did not, however, always have the students under control. The sophomores were not a problem, but I hadn't considered how close in age the seniors and I would be, and I hadn't realized how many high school students were not happy to be

110

in class, even a fun sounding class like "Comic Spirit." Still, I was beginning to feel more comfortable in the classroom when the chair came to me with a proposition. I knew that there had been discussions about creating new Junior English classes for (I thought) the Harvard M.A. to teach. I heard the two women who taught Junior English planning which students they would send to the new classes. Of course, they were picking the worst students, which generally meant the discipline problems. I felt a bit sorry for the Harvard M.A., but I thought a man might have fewer problems with discipline. But then came the chair's proposition. She thought I should take the Junior English classes. She made one good point in her pitch. There would be basically one preparation for me because all juniors would read the same texts. As I understood it, these new classes would all have regular students, not honors or team teaching. The problem was, of course, that I had just finished preparing the senior classes, and I would have to start over with new students and a new preparation. And even more important, my biggest problem as a new teacher and very young woman was discipline, so the last thing I needed was to take on classes full of disciplinary rejects.

At this point I had to develop a strong backbone. I told the chair that I preferred to continue to teach the classes I had already taught for a few weeks. I knew the students, my courses were organized, and I didn't need to start over with difficult students. She suggested that I might be forced to move by the principal; I made some comments about my contract, when I signed it, and what I understood its terms to be. The Harvard M.A was given the newly formed junior classes. I had won the first battle, but I still didn't realize I was in a war. I noticed, however, a chill developing between the fake guy from Kentucky and me.

The next battle developed when we planned the courses for the next nine weeks. Someone, maybe Fake Guy, suggested I teach Bible as Literature. I resisted because I didn't think I was qualified to teach that class; during the discussion of why I wouldn't teach it, I pointed out how many different preparations I had, and the chair of the department started talking about how many different classes she taught when she first came to ETHS. She claimed to have taught two or three different subjects (math, history, English, whatever). I asked her when she came to the school, and she responded, "1947." I gave her a long look and then said in a voice that Ms. Head of the Investment Department at Northwestern would have called mocking, "I was born in 1949." My new friend Helen liked that verbal slap.

I don't remember now what caused the final blowup, but eventually Helen, the chair, Fake Guy, and I (there may have been a couple of other department members there too, but the details are thankfully less clear to me now than they were in the seventies) were in a meeting, where he uttered the "administrative blunder" crack. At some point before this meeting, Helen had filled me in on the details of Fake Guy's attempt to stop me from teaching in the department. By the end of the meeting, Helen and I were crying. I don't remember which of us started crying first, but I know that she left the room at one point. When we were reduced to tears, Fake Guy and the chair thought that they had won and so started condescendingly talking about how we were all going to just get along, and they would take care of us poor young women or whatever. I had pointed out that Fake Guy, who was in charge of the senior program, had refused to speak to me and had even very unprofessionally snapped at me in front of one of my classes, so they were reassuring us that the nasty, unprofessional behavior would end.

However, Helen and I were not finished. We called each other after the meeting and decided to write letters detailing our harsh treatment. Helen was primarily victimized by Fake Guy because he was angry that she didn't go along with his attempt to prevent me from teaching in the department. As we planned our letters that would be addressed to the superintendent and the assistant superintendent, Helen said that we should send copies to the teacher's union. I thought that was a good idea and decided also to copy in the black teacher and staff organization. That was one of my better decisions.

I had written two letters to the coordinator of the two-year English major sequence at Northwestern, and when I talked to him about the second letter, he said that he always enjoyed my letters as if I had written dozens. Maybe because of that compliment, I was confident as I composed my lengthy letter, detailing the unprofessional behavior of Fake Guy and the attempt by the chair to pressure me into taking new junior courses after I had spent many hours developing the senior courses. Those letters led to administrative reprimands for the chair and the school principal because the superintendent did not know that they had created those new junior classes. Harvard M.A. was supposed to be still serving as the permanent substitute, and the fact that he wasn't cost the school district money.

The people who really took charge of this battle, however, were the members of the black faculty and staff organization. They immediately sent a letter to the superintendent and assistant superintendent, saying that they would be watching what happened. It turns out that a new black faculty member from the previous school year had been sabotaged by the whites in her department and basically left because she couldn't handle the stress and pressure. One of the older blacks said that she should have done what I did, contact the two unions. Several of the black faculty and staff members complimented me on the letter. It wasn't so much that they were impressed with my writing. They knew I was an English teacher, so they expected me to write well. They liked the way I drew on my good memory (at least back then) for dates and times to show just what the chair and Fake Guy had done. I laid out my case like a lawyer.

But just as we black folks were planning our strategy, preparing to fight, the black assistant superintendent who had gotten me into the mess in the first place swooped in and tried to shut us down. He told the other blacks that he had everything under control, that he would take care of me. A few of the blacks were ready to give up the fight, but others, including one middle-aged woman, who was either a librarian or a counselor (definitely not a teacher), argued that he was doing what he always did, trying to protect himself. They said that we should continue with our plans and let him take care of himself. I think we even brought in the local head of the NAACP.

The battle ended with each of the department members involved in the incident going in to talk to the superintendent. On the advice of some of the black faculty and staff, I took an older staff or faculty member with me. He was a man whom I didn't really know; as I remember him, he wasn't especially large or intimidating, but he was very cool, Obama cool. And I needed a cool head to keep my hot head under control. My black colleagues and Helen had helped me determine what to say to the superintendent. I now remember only one of my complaints and demands. I pointed out that I was the only one involved in this conflict who was being evaluated, and I was being evaluated by the chair of the department, who, I believed, was now hostile toward me. So my demand was that the conflict not affect my evaluation. The superintendent agreed to that demand. I remember being relatively calm in that meeting because I had that cool black man sitting with me. I don't think he said a word; he just sat there, looking cool. When I felt myself tensing or choking up, I made eye contact with him, he gave me a "hold on" look, and I held on. I walked out of there, feeling that I had won that battle, but I now knew that I was in a war where the enemy had more lethal weapons.

The next battle involved the evaluations. The chair evaluated me just before those meetings, but she didn't show those evaluations to me until after she evaluated me a second time. I received both evaluations at the same time; the first set of evaluations was negative and harsh, giving specific details of what I did wrong and including a comment about my discussing department business outside of the department. The only favorable comments I remember from those first evaluations focused on my fashion sense. The second set of evaluations was positive and included vague comments about how I had improved, but with no specifics. By the time I received the evaluations, I knew that I was leaving ETHS. I had been accepted by three universities, including USC, and had been offered a fellowship at the University of Illinois (I can't remember whether I already had the Ford Fellowship at that point). I knew that I would not return to high school teaching, but I still would not let this woman sabotage my year of teaching under extraordinarily difficult conditions. I refused to sign the evaluations, and I didn't sign them until she eliminated the comment about discussing department business in the first evaluations and added specific details about how I had improved in the second ones. She also had to acknowledge that I had been put in a difficult political situation because of the hiring controversy. So I won another battle, and this one I won without the help of Helen, the other black faculty and staff, or the cool black man. For some reason, the old white chair never intimidated me, maybe because I didn't think much of her as a teacher or administrator.

Before I left the battlefield, I had two more interesting skirmishes. First, the department members decided to give me a farewell party. They went to Helen, my only real friend in the department, to ask her to organize it, but she assured them that I would not appreciate such a party. Because I will laugh at a funny joke even when the person telling the joke is a bigoted fake who tried to stab me in the back and needed to go back to Kentucky where he clearly belonged, the department members assumed that I was a nicer bitch than the more reserved Helen. Or maybe they just assumed that all black folks like to party, no matter who is throwing the party or for what reason. At any rate, the chair came to me with the party proposal. I told her that I wasn't interested. She couldn't understand why, so I told her. I pointed out that Helen was my only friend in the department, and she and I could say our goodbyes privately. Then I hit her with one of my patented verbal jabs: "The rest of you can party after I'm gone." The chair was shocked that I didn't think I had any other friends in the department; she didn't mention herself, Fake Guy, or even Harvard M.A., who was a friendly acquaintance, but she named the two Junior English teachers as other possible friends. Those two women, who were closer in age to me than the chair, were not my friends. In fact, one of them had twice gotten on my last nerve, first, asking me what my father did for a living because "I dressed so nice." I pointed out that I had a job, you know a teaching job; I reminded her that I was paid for teaching, just as she was. Then she responded to the news that I had been awarded a Ford Fellowship by declaring that she wished that she was black. I forget exactly how I told her that she was lying, but I let her know that she clearly did not want to be black, even if it did mean that she could possibly, if she were smart enough, which I doubted, win a fellowship. That white woman was definitely not my friend.

I rewarded the chair's generous offer of a farewell party with a little lecture on the difference between professional courtesy and friendship. I talked to her as if she were twenty-three, and I was the much older woman. I condescendingly explained that I was too polite and professional to treat other people the way I had been treated, refusing to speak to them the way Fake Guy had done me. But friendship means more than saying hello and making small talk with colleagues in the office or in the faculty dining room. The junior teachers were my colleagues, generally friendly colleagues, but Helen was my only friend.

Having set the chair straight, I next took on the superintendent. He called me into his office because he wanted to be sure that I wasn't being driven out of my job by my older white colleagues. He remembered that the black faculty and staff were monitoring this case and clearly didn't want any more trouble from them. The chair and the principal assured him that I had this great fellowship and was going off to earn my Ph.D. I was not leaving because of that "little incident" that happened earlier in the year. I was alone with the superintendent this time; the cool black man was not there. But I felt no fear or tension. I listened to him, then leaned back in my chair and let him know that yes, I had earned a fellowship, and yes, I decided that I preferred teaching college students, but that incident did have something to do with my decision to leave ETHS. I let him know that I had been treated unfairly and that my first year of teaching was made especially difficult because of department politics. I also pointed out that it didn't do any good for the administrators to recruit and hire black teachers if the white teachers ran them off. I mentioned that some of the new black teachers who were there a year earlier were no longer there, and I knew from talking to other black faculty that at least one of them had faced the same kind of harsh treatment that I had. He tried to defend the school's retention record for black faculty, but I wasn't really listening. I had made my point.

I'm not sure if my comments to the chair and the superintendent registered, but if they did, they may have learned more from me than did any of my high school students. I worked hard, prepared diligently, and taught to the best of my ability. But I was undermined by the white teachers who were determined to prove that the black assistant superintendent had made a mistake in hiring me. Besides, by the fourth week of school, I already had one foot out the door and my face turned toward the university. I was sending out applications, preparing to enter graduate school. Still, I may have taught at least one white student a good life lesson.

Something had happened, I believe a fight between the nearly all white New Trier and ETHS students at a football or basketball game, that made the administrators decide that we needed to talk about race relations. Since all students were required to take English, our classes were chosen as the places to conduct these discussions. One charming young white guy dominated the race relations conversation in one of my classes, telling us how he defended his girlfriend when some blacks attacked them (as I remember it, I was the only black person in this particular class) and commenting on how blacks seemed to travel in groups. When I asked why he and his girlfriend had been attacked, he claimed not to know; they were apparently attacked for no good reason. He then discussed a phenomenon that troubled me a bit too, the tendency of black students to gather in one place, away from whites (I talked about the black lunch tables when I was a student at the high school and about the Black House and black corridors in the dormitories at Northwestern). The gathering place for blacks, both when I was a student and a teacher at ETHS, was under a large hallway clock. Charmer talked about

119

how he felt as he came near the clock where the blacks were gathered. He said he could almost hear drums. That's when I stopped Charmer. I laughingly (because I liked him) said that I thought maybe I knew why the blacks beat his butt. That drum playing remark is the kind of comment, I said, that can get a white guy and his innocent white girlfriend beaten by a gang of blacks. I told him I had never played drums, didn't know any black people who played drums, and so I wondered why he "almost" heard drums when he saw black people. Charmer had the decency to look sheepish, and the rest of the class laughed. I hope he remembered that lesson; I hope they all did.

The only drums I heard during my year at ETHS were the ones drumming my black ass out of the all-white Michael School English department. I was happy to leave even though I landed at conservative, very white USC, where at least my color allowed me to blend safely into the surrounding neighborhood. I quickly learned that if I weren't carrying books, most locals assumed that I lived in the neighborhood, and so I was not a target, at least not for the nonwhite residents. But, of course, my color did not allow me to blend so easily into the English Department. Throughout my career as an English student and/or teacher, I was usually either the only black or one of only two in the department. When I first arrived at USC, there were no other black graduate students in the English Department, although there was one black female in the American Studies program.

At one point in my second year, my color and the fact that the surrounding neighborhood was both nonwhite and unsafe led to an insulting face-off with one of the American literature professors. This professor, let's call him Dr. Bigot, had a reputation for spending too much time in a nearby bar. But drunkenness does not excuse his reaction to me. I was working in the Social Work library during my second year in the program and had to be at my job by 8 a.m. One day on my way to the job, I dropped by the English Department to leave a library book in one of the T.A's boxes. As I was walking away from the mailboxes, Dr. Bigot came out of his office and said "hello" rather aggressively. Although I was a little surprised by his greeting since he had never spoken to me before, and I had not yet been (and would never be after this encounter) his student, I responded with a friendly "hello." He left his office and followed me to the door, saying to a white female, who was definitely not a graduate student, that he was going to lock the office door because "that's how typewriters get stolen." I wondered if I were hearing things. He thought I was there stealing typewriters? Now this man had seen me at special events held for the faculty and graduate students, where such scholars as Wayne Booth and Kenneth Burke or writers such as Joan Didion's husband, John Gregory Dunne, spoke. I was usually the only black person in these meetings. He had also passed me in the hallways of the department. He should have recognized me. But even if he didn't recognize me, why did he assume that I was stealing typewriters, and the white girl wasn't? I told that story for years. And I never saw that professor without giving him an evil look, which seemed to puzzle him.

The more celebrated (and sober) American literature professor, Dr. Potter, and I had a much better relationship. He seemed to love the fact that I was black. He called me "Sisney, honey" and talked about how lucky I was to be sitting in the class with the white folks. He loved discussing Faulkner's portraits of blacks and watching my reaction. When some of the white students suggested to me that he was out of line, I let them know that I didn't mind; I understood what he was doing. He wanted everyone to believe that he was one of those white liberals who was comfortable with blacks. I also wasn't bothered by his teasing because I knew that I would fire back sooner or later. I even knew what I would say if given the chance. Finally, I had my chance. Potter was going on about Faulkner's racism and said that anyone who would distinguish between a mulatto and an octoroon was clearly racist. When I laughed, he asked me was I completely black. I was ready with my jab. I said, as I looked at his suspiciously kinky hair, "I don't know, Dr. Potter, I might be a distant cousin of yours." Everyone laughed, and a white man who attracted my attention because he was amusing, and because his hair was blonde but his beard was black, chimed in with a comment about the hair. While Blackbeard and I looked at each other knowingly and continued to laugh, Potter mumbled something about his ancestors that I didn't hear. But I enjoyed seeing him grow nervous at the idea of being related to me. He didn't embarrass me, but I certainly embarrassed him.

Potter may have had the last laugh, however, because he joined several other white male faculty members in writing tepid letters of recommendation for my job placement file. Several of the male faculty told me that I could find a good teaching job because I was a black female. Not because I was a good student and not because I was in popular areas--20th Century American

Literature and Rhetoric/Composition--but because I was a black woman. But then some of these same men tried to handicap me by writing letters that said I would make a good two or four-year college instructor. At least Potter's letter wouldn't have prevented me from being hired at universities with graduate programs, but his was so short that it was clear that he didn't think much of me. Of course, I was to blame for even asking him for a letter in the first place and then insisting that he write one although he was clearly reluctant. He wrote what I told him to write, that I had done well on his section of the Ph.D. qualifying exams. Thanks, liberal white man.

Although I was smart enough after my dealings with Fake Guy at ETHS to have an open employment file, I had not yet read my letters when they were sent out to support my first job application. My resume dropping trip with Pasadena Friend provided me an opportunity to land a one-year replacement position at UC San Diego. The department flew me down for an interview, and all went well in the morning. I noticed a chill in the air and more pointed questions about my plans in the afternoon but wasn't sure what had happened. But then I heard from Department Chair Sherley Williams, the writer who later published the slave narrative <u>Dessa Rose</u>. She let me know what had happened. Because the placement file didn't arrive until the afternoon, the faculty saw me and liked what they saw until they read the letters. The letters cost me the job. Sherley's last words to me were, "Get those letters out of your file." So I did. I took out Potter's letter and had a couple of other faculty members, including Dr. Rose, rewrite their letters, taking out the "two- or four-year college" qualifier.

As I pointed out to Rose, I wasn't above teaching at a community college or a four-year college, but even those schools will probably be reluctant to hire a Ph.D. who is seen as not qualified to teach graduate students.

I often referred to my experience with the tepid letters when I served on job search and affirmative action committees at Cal Poly. It was interesting to see how often the argument for picking the white male candidate over the nonwhite and/or female candidate focused on letters of recommendation. It was also interesting to compare some of the candidates to their letters. When I served on the job search committee for a literary theory and composition position in 1982, the two white male members of the committee noticed that several of the white men who had outstanding letters of recommendation seemed dull and listless in person. There were no nonwhite candidates, but the women tended to be more impressive than we expected while the men were often disappointing. I understood, after going through the employment process from the other side, why I didn't book many interviews and why I landed both jobs when I was interviewed. It wasn't that I was so impressive in interviews; it was just that I was a better candidate than my letters (even after they were revised) indicated. People who wonder why the affirmative action and other diversity programs don't yield more nonwhite teachers need look no farther than the letters of recommendation. The white male faculty members write tepid letters, which are then evaluated by white males, who make the case that the white male candidates should be hired because their letters are stronger. And even when there is a loud-mouthed, blues singing black woman on one of the committees to point out what is going on, the white man is still usually hired. At one point (1985-87) during my years at Cal Poly, our department hired three white men in a row while some of the senior white men complained about how hard it was for white men to find jobs because of affirmative action.

Of course, sometimes the black woman lands the job, especially when she's competing with a smaller, quieter white woman. I was hired at Cal Poly without having to submit any letters of recommendation. After we drove past the grazing livestock and found the English Department, Pasadena Friend and I were interviewed by the assistant chair and left our resumes with him. Just before school started in the fall of 1977, not long after the UC San Diego fiasco, I received a call from the chair of the English Department at Cal Poly. He told me that I had been highly recommended by the assistant chair. When Pasadena Friend generously volunteered to drive me back to the campus for an interview with the chair, I took another copy of my resume, along with another copy of Pasadena Friend's since she still hoped to teach a class there. When I finished the interview, the chair handed back what he thought was the new copy of the resume, but was actually the one I left with the assistant chair earlier in the year. The assistant chair had written on that resume, "Mary is black and very personable." Pasadena Friend and I laughed all the way back to L.A. She was white and obviously not so personable, whatever that meant. Maybe the assistant chair added more details to his "high" recommendation when he talked to the chair, but I always assumed that I was hired at Cal Poly because I was "black and personable."

During the two years I served as a composition lecturer at Cal Poly, teaching only one class each quarter, usually in the late afternoon, I didn't witness anything or anybody that made me worry about dealing with racism. So, of course, when I had the opportunity to leave racist Boston (although I didn't have any problems with bigots at Tufts during the year that I was there), I didn't hesitate to take the position. But it wasn't long before I was dealing with what I eventually described in a letter to the then dean of the College of Arts, a black man, as "casual, but relentless, abuse."

That letter was written in January, 1991, a little more than ten years after I joined the English & Foreign Languages (EFL) faculty. The letter was written because I had received an accusatory and threatening letter from the then chair of the department, a man who had caught my attention when I was a lecturer by his response when he saw me wearing a dashiki. I wore the dashiki because I was broke, and it was cheap, but this future chair clearly had a similar attitude to Dr. Potter's about blacks. He loved to let blacks know that he knew that they were black, and he didn't mind at all (interestingly, he now has at least one half-black grandchild). When he saw me in my dashiki, he started using some kind of jive talking, black hip language and tried to walk like a cool black cat, what some of us black folks used to call "pimping." Now he looked like a fool, but his Superfly antics didn't bother me. I had dealt with fake liberals in the past and knew how to handle them.

But this attack at the beginning of Winter Quarter, 1991, was more serious. Someone complained to the black dean about something (I don't remember or care what) Superfly was doing as chair. I guess because the dean was black and I was black, Superfly assumed I was the sneaky faculty member who went behind his back to complain. Now, as I said in my letter, Superfly had known me long enough to know that I was not sneaky. He and I had exchanged lengthy memos (this was, of course, before e-mails) arguing about issues in the department. He had even complimented me on my courage, leading me to wonder why it took courage for one adult to debate department politics with another adult. I was a lot of things, but sneaky was not one of them. If I had a problem with the chair, I would have talked to him about it. If I wanted to complain to the dean, I would have written a letter and sent a copy to the chair as I did with that 1991 letter of complaint. In my letter I demanded a written apology, which I never received, but Superfly did admit in a department meeting that he had erroneously accused the wrong person, for which he apologized. He nodded in my direction but never called my name.

I thought of that episode a few months before my retirement when one of the white male lecturers told me that another white male lecturer, a man who had started as a lecturer around the same time as I did and had recently retired, accused me of telling the current chair that the senior lecturer didn't keep his office hours. No one had been more supportive of the lecturers than I had over the years. I even shared my one-person office with a lecturer for twenty years. And just a year before that conversation, I had driven to Cal Poly on a late Friday afternoon in a heavy rainstorm (I hate driving in the rain, but I also suspected that the meeting was scheduled on Friday afternoon partly because Friday was my one day off) to support the composition lecturers who were feeling besieged. And I didn't sit silent in the meeting; I spoke up loudly, criticizing the chair for not using the same diplomatic approach with the lecturers that she used with me and other tenured and tenure-track faculty members. In earlier years I had prevented Superfly from using his position as composition coordinator to secure a better position for his then girlfriend and future wife by overriding seniority and dismissing senior lecturers. The guy who supposedly accused me of tattling on him was one of the lecturers whose classroom I visited so I could write a strong support of his teaching, ending with the sentence, "Not only has Dr. Senior Lecturer (unlike most lecturers, this guy had a Ph.D.) taught well in this class, but he has taught well in many classes for many years." No one was less likely to make trouble for a lecturer than I was. And yet I was the one accused. Defending myself, I called this the Susan Smith (she left her two children in the car to drown and then blamed an unknown black man) phenomenon. Blame or frame the black person. I'm sure the white folks thought I was playing the race card when I angrily went there, but I thought the race card had played me.

In the new post-civil rights racism, white folks take the attitude that calling someone racist is as bad as being racist. I have had to set several white colleagues, including Superfly, straight on the difference between being oppressed by racism and being accused of racism. I have been accused of racism; I have even been accused by at least one black student of preferring whites, but that charge just made me laugh because I knew it was a lie.

When people like George Bush and some of my white colleagues become so upset over the charge of racism, one has to wonder if the shoe fits too tightly.

One of the many examples of the casual abuse that I referenced in the 1991 letter involved my colorblind friends from the office next to the mailroom. These two gentlemen, let's call them Ben and Jerry (for you MLA devotees, this is not the Ben that you knew; Ben is a pseudonym for this guy), usually were collegial and supportive of me. In fact, Jerry and I got along so well that I twice recruited him to serve on committees with me. And Ben and I found each other amusing. One reason I knew Ben was not colorblind is that he found what I'm sure he considered my black dialect very funny. Back then I would often use the phrase, "What's happening?" the way people today might use Wendy Williams' "How you doin'?" Some people responded to the question with "nothing" or "not much" while others simply told me what was going on, but Ben always laughed joyfully. He and I also enjoyed a race-based pun during one tense department meeting. The self-important chair of a committee was jabbering about something that he at least thought was important when he used the cliché, "call a spade a spade." Ben, who was sitting next to me, gasped and then gave me a shocked look. I whispered loudly enough for the committee chair to hear, "It's okay; don't worry about me." Ben and I cracked up while the committee chair fumed.

But the problem with interracial humor is there is a line which can't be crossed, and some whites have trouble recognizing that line. And, of course, the line differs for different blacks. Superfly's routine was not over the line for me. However, Ben crossed the line one day when he and I were taking the elevator. I was already on the elevator when I saw Ben approaching, so I asked him if he were going up. His response was, "Yes, Mary I'z be goin' up on de elevator." Now I don't know if my southern accent emerged when I said his name or if Ben just thought it would be funny to launch into a minstrel routine. Whatever was going on in his head, I was not amused. Without smiling, I asked, "Where are you getting that accent?" I'm sure my face showed how annoyed I was, but I did not curse him out or slap him upside the head. Still, Ben became instantly defensive and upset. He told me that I had to allow him to be himself, and he enjoyed southern humor. I said that he could be himself, but I also wanted to be myself, and my self wanted to know where he was getting that accent. By that time we had reached our destination, and we parted without anyone's being (physically) hurt. I was through with the discussion. I did not consider complaining to the chair, the dean, or the affirmative action officer. I hoped that Ben, who probably occasionally had black students in his classes, had learned that the minstrel act was not amusing to at least some blacks.

But the next day, I saw Jerry in the mailroom, spoke to him, and was ignored. I thought maybe his hearing was going or that he was so preoccupied that he didn't hear me. But later the same day we were walking toward each other in the hallway, and instead of breaking into a smile, which is how he usually greeted me, he glowered. I knew what had happened. Ben had complained about my response to his "southern humor," and Jerry was angry at me. My response to Jerry's anger was fury, so we passed each other without speaking, both of us looking like soldiers marching off to war. The next day I saw Ben walking toward me and gave him the same evil look that I had given Jerry. He stopped, looked worried, and asked me what was wrong. I said angrily, "Well, are you speaking? Your officemate isn't. I don't know why he would stop speaking to me. I haven't done a damn thing to him." Ben feigned ignorance and innocence. But soon Jerry was in my office apologizing and pretending that he had just been thinking about something when he walked past me, looking as if he wanted to shoot me. As he kept talking, however, he gave himself and Ben away because he told me that Ben was really hurt that I seemed to think he was racist. We all made up and moved on, but Ben and I never again shared racial jokes, and I'm not sure that he learned the lesson that he needed to learn, that his "Amos and Andy" humor wasn't acceptable during the Cosby age.

The racism was not always so obvious, and I was not always the target. During my years of serving as basic writing skills (the program for students not academically ready to take freshman composition) coordinator, I occasionally noticed a double standard in the way nonwhite tutors and instructors were treated. Students and teachers were more likely to complain to me about nonwhite tutors, and tutors were more likely to complain about nonwhite instructors. Once each quarter I invited the basic writing skills and English as Second Language (ESL) instructors to attend a tutor meeting so that they could confer with the tutors about specific students. Because most of the composition instructors were lecturers who often taught at other colleges, not all instructors could attend. During one meeting, I was talking to

131

two tutors; one was experienced, and the other was new. As we talked, the new tutor asked about the one (besides me) black basic writing skills instructor. When I told her that the black woman couldn't attend the meeting, the experienced tutor complained angrily about how this woman never came to the instructor-tutor conferences, and she never said in her comments on student essays what she wanted the tutors to do. She went on and on about how difficult it was to figure out what this woman wanted her to do with her students. When I finally turned to answer another tutor's question, I could hear the experienced tutor continuing to advise the new tutor. Another teacher's name was mentioned, a white woman. The experienced tutor said quite calmly that this white woman never came to the meetings, and she never gave the tutors any instructions. There was no anger, no condemnation, just the facts. Why so much anger toward the black woman?

The tutors had two supervisors. I hired and trained them, but there was a young white woman who supervised them in the writing center, where the tutoring took place. When tutors did not perform satisfactorily, this young woman contacted me so that I could either fire them or put the fear of Sisney into them. My one problem with this woman was that she was too kind, not strict enough. When she had to report on a rogue tutor, she usually began her comments by saying how much she liked the tutor, and if the tutor was a woman, she often called her a friend. But during one meeting, several tutors complained that this usually kind woman was being mean and grumpy. It certainly didn't sound like her, so I said I would find out what was happening. Initially, she claimed that all was well, but when

I said that some tutors had noticed a change in her attitude, she changed her tune. First, she complained about Lisa, the African American student I had recently recruited. When I said that Lisa had not complained, she then called the name of Lily, the Korean American student, also a new recruit. At that point, I saw what the problem was. I had recruited Lisa and Lily, two students in one of my black literature classes, because most of the students being tutored were nonwhite while at that point all of the tutors were white. I was always looking for new tutors in my classes because there was frequent turnover of student employees. There were never any problems between the writing center supervisor and the new recruits until Lisa and Lily arrived. After she called Lily's name, I said that Lily had complained, but so had several of the white tutors. Oops! The woman immediately realized that she had given herself away. Her complaints about Lily and Lisa were not as serious as some previous problems, like a tutor's consistently missing appointments, or, in one case, a tutor, called a friend by the supervisor, coming to her sessions drunk. So why the bad attitude toward Lisa and Lily? The woman soon left the job, I hope because she realized that she had exposed her perhaps previously unrecognized racism.

Had I been a white woman, I might have misread what was going on in this program. Being "colorblind," I might have assumed that the black instructor and the two nonwhite tutors were just not doing their jobs as well as the whites. I would have assumed that the anger of the tutor and supervisor was justified. But I knew what was happening. I had seen it many times before.

In fact, during my twenty-nine years as a full-time faculty member at Cal Poly, I saw so much racism, subtle and not so subtle, that I could write a whole book on the topic. But probably the episode that best illustrates how racism works in the post-civil rights era was the situation that I turned into a parable called "The Race" (See Appendix). It was based on my competition with a white man, called Charlie Blank in the parable, for retention, tenure, and promotion (RTP).

Charlie and I were hired at the same time and were the same age (I was not quite two months older). He was a graduate of UCLA and had been working as a remedial composition coordinator at one of the UC campuses. According to what I heard, when that school decided to make his temporary position permanent, Charlie applied for the position and was not hired. Apparently, a similar situation happened at Cal Poly where Charlie was hired instead of the lecturer serving as coordinator for our basic writing skills program.

I, of course, had taught at Cal Poly for two years while completing my dissertation and had earned excellent student evaluations. The assistant chair, a nonwhite man, called my apartment in Cambridge to invite me to apply for one of the two positions, the one that would replace the retiring American literature professor. While I was going through the application process for that job, I was also being evaluated for a three-year contract at Tufts. I passed that evaluation and spent a few tense weeks trying to make sure I had the contract from Cal Poly before I turned down the Tufts contract.

As far as I could tell, Charlie was an excellent instructor, and he was certainly a productive department member. But given that I had already worked in the department and was turning down a contract at a more prestigious college to come to Cal Poly, I would seem to have the upper hand in any competition or race. But here's the problem: I didn't realize that there was a race. Charlie apparently knew from the beginning that we would be ranked when we went up for promotion, and he was watching me and making sure that he could compete with anything I did. I didn't realize until about a year before the race would end with one of us ranked first and the other last that I was even in a race.

But what was worse, Charlie was given all kinds of advantages that would help him win the race. He received administrative re-leased time for his position as basic writing skills coordinator, meaning that he taught at most six classes a year while I taught nine. And he was piggybacked onto a grant-funded program that a senior faculty member had already secured when we ar-rived. Also, because he was the coordinator of the basic writing skills program, his composition load consisted primarily of basic writing courses, which at that time had a maximum of fifteen students while I was teaching larger freshman composition and Advanced Professional Writing courses.

Here's how I was welcomed into the department. For Fall Quarter, I was assigned three composition courses, two Advanced Professional Writing courses that had twenty-five students each and a third smaller freshman composition course (about eigh-teen students) designed for English majors. I was also named the curriculum chair, inheriting a mess created when the previous chair resigned over department politics. Mos Def's comment that Barack Obama would become President because they always hire a black man to clean up a mess should be amended to say unless they can hire a black woman. As one senior faculty member said in response to my application for promotion, the curriculum chair should be a senior faculty member. Now I probably wasn't the first and I certainly wasn't the last junior faculty member to be saddled with the difficult job of shepherding all of the department's curriculum changes through the College of Arts Curriculum Committee, but most new faculty at least didn't have to clean up the mess left by the previous committee chair. Also, because I was one of the few black members of the Cal Poly faculty, I served on numerous committees during those early years. I was on, for example, the College of Arts Affirmative Action Committee, the University Executive Grievance Panel, a department job search committee, and an Educational Opportunity Program (EOP) advisory committee. I was also often asked to write exam questions for students earning their M.A's. Although I was only thirty-one when I came to Cal Poly that first year, I was exhausted most of the time.

But then came a remarkable incident during the Spring Quarter of my second year. My old friend Ben had to leave his classes a few weeks early to have his gall bladder removed. The chair, called Mr. White in my parable, taught at least one of his literature classes, which seemed appropriate since the chair was teaching only one class that quarter. Someone else taught another literature class, perhaps the assistant chair (I'll call him Non White) since he taught only two classes, but they needed someone to teach a composition class. I was already teaching two composition classes and a graduate course in 20th Century American Literature. Charlie was teaching at most two classes, and remember, his composition classes were smaller than mine. Guess who they asked to take Ben's composition class? That's right; I was asked to teach a fourth class while Charlie was teaching two. Now since I liked Ben (this was before the minstrel incident), I was thinking about taking the assignment because I assumed that I would not be grading essays. Composition classes are actually easier to teach (at least for me) than literature courses, and of course when the students write in-class essays, the teacher can just sit in the class and read or grade papers. When I asked Non White how many in-class essays Ben had planned, he seemed nervous and said something like, "Oh, I'm sure not many." That's when I realized that I was expected to grade the essays on top of all of the other work I was doing. Ben would be hospitalized and ill; he couldn't grade essays. I was stunned. Were they kidding me? Were they crazy, or did they think I was crazy? Non White tried to use the RTP process to pressure me into taking the extra class. He sang a little RTP song, but I was unmoved. I knew that I didn't have to teach an extra class free to earn tenure and promotion, and I certainly didn't appreciate the attempt to force me to do more work than everyone else just because I was untenured, especially since my white male untenured counterpart was teaching fewer classes than many of the senior faculty. What made this attempt to pressure me into taking another composition class even more disturbing is that both the chair and assistant chair knew I was planning to teach two classes (one a composition class) during the summer. I needed the money to buy a car. So had I taken on that extra composition class for three weeks, graded all of those extra essays, and computed all of those extra final grades, I could not have recovered during the summer from the fatigue caused by all of that extra work. I don't believe Charlie Blank taught summer school classes that year.

When I refused to teach the class, the chair went to Plan B, which was to hire and pay a graduate student to teach it. But I never forgot those few days of having to fight off an attempt to overload me with work, probably because it reminded me of my teaching experience at ETHS. And, of course, when I was inevitably ranked second behind Charlie, I was even more angered. I realized I had been set up. I remembered the three composition classes my first quarter, the mess I inherited from the curriculum chair, and the way the chair always mentioned Blank's name in his report on work done in the department while somehow forgetting to mention mine when he discussed work done by the curriculum committee. I even remembered how I had been given two different composition classes to teach one quarter, thus erasing one of the advantages of teaching two composition courses, having fewer preparations.

The day that she earns tenure and is promoted to associate professor should be the highlight of a professor's career. In a way, I had been working toward that day at least since I started graduate school in 1972 and perhaps since I started college in 1967. But because of "the race," that day was devastating for me. I was so unhappy about what I perceived to be the unfair ranking that I felt trapped. I didn't want to go through another process like that at another university, so I was, as I said to several colleagues, friends, and family members, "stuck." When one friendly colleague dropped by my office to congratulate me, he was surprised to find me not delighted and proud but bitter and disgusted. He felt so bad for me that he and his wife invited me to dinner to try to lift my spirits.

Although I knew the ranking would not be changed, I protested the committee's decision, writing a detailed explanation of how the chair systematically made Blank's path to tenure and promotion easier and mine harder. I didn't include information that the tall Texan who had lost the staredown contest to my officemate's husband had shared with me. According to Tall Texan, I was hired, not so much because of my performance as a lecturer but because of my doubly affirmative race and gender. The department thought the College of Arts Affirmative Action Committee would accept white male Charlie Blank if they also hired me. In other words, while the Affirmative Action Committee members were smacking their lips over the black woman, they could slip the white man in through the back door. As Tall Texan saw it, Charlie was always their number 1 choice.

However, not everyone felt that Charlie should be ranked number 1; two members of the five-person RTP committee had supported me, and Non White, who had called me in Cambridge to invite me to apply for the job, was also a supporter. I appreciated their support at first, but after I talked to some other people about their rankings and how the RTP process had worked over the years, I had second thoughts about how much time, energy, and emotion I had invested in the race for a ranking. I realized that Non White and one of my supporters on the committee, a linguist, had been ranked number 1 when they were promoted, so they had a vested interest in making sure that every candidate took the ranking seriously. If I had not minded being ranked 2, then their number 1 ranking would not mean as much. I started slightly to resent Non White and Number 1 Linguist. And I also resented the RTP committee for not finding a way to undermine the unnecessary ranking. If not everyone could be promoted, ranking mattered. But since it was clear that both candidates had earned promotion and that there was enough money to promote all candidates going up for promotion in the university that year, the rankings were simply symbolic. Of course, as I pointed out to the Vice President of Faculty Affairs, English teachers deal in symbols, so naturally I took the symbolic ranking seriously. But the committee could have talked to both of us and offered to flip a coin or to let one of us be ranked 1 this time and the other one would be ranked first when we competed against each other for promotion to full professor, assuming that we were both still in the department. I would have accepted that deal and even let Charlie have the number 1 ranking first since his name came before mine alphabetically. But the RTP committee probably needed to feel important, and in a school and a department where almost all candidates are promoted eventually, if not as soon as they apply, the only power committee members have is to decide a rank for each candidate. I could tell that the woman supporting me wanted to see me sweat a bit. I wasn't worried about being promoted and tenured since I clearly met the criteria, but she wanted me to worry about something, and the ranking was all she had.

I took the power away from the next RTP committee that ranked Charlie and me by conceding the number 1 ranking to him. I didn't say I was conceding, so I let the committee members worry about what to do, but I did what I had to do to earn promotion and didn't worry about Charlie. When I was ranked number 2, I wasn't upset because I wasn't trying to be number 1. It probably also helped that at that point I had Charlie's old job, the basic writing skills coordinator, and was teaching even fewer classes than he had, three per year, because I was also an advisor in a program called the Intensive Learning Experience (ILE). It was fun to watch Non White and Number 1 Linguist look puzzled and then disappointed when they saw me walking around the department, perfectly content with my number 2 ranking. Anyone who asked me how I felt was quickly told that I didn't care because I would rank each of the RTP committee members number 3 out of 2. Who were they to rank me?

Still, the ranking race changed my attitude toward the department. Before I was put in my place, I had felt, for the first time, like an insider in this white institution. I attended many of the afterhours social events, ate lunch with many of the department members, and even organized a major retirement party for my first officemate the same year I was ranked 2. After the race, I was much more selective about which social events I attended and eventually stopped eating on campus.

Clearly, the perceived unfair treatment left a deep wound which made me less eager to socialize with colleagues, but I also came to realize how different I was from the nonblack folks in the department. My willingness to concede number 1 was different, for instance. I don't think most of my white colleagues would have done that. Also, most of them would not consider undermining the RTP process by flipping a coin or persuading the candidates to agree to take turns being ranked 1. I remember complaining to Charlie, before I realized we were in a race, about how foolish I thought the RTP procedures were, and he said something like, "That's how it's always been done, so we have to just get through it." But blacks don't think like that. If things were still done the way they had always been done, black folks would still be slaves. That's why we like change and moving forward, while white folks often prefer the status quo or going back.

Another quality that separated at least this black person from most whites was an overdeveloped sense of fair play. Being punny, I said I was the fairest of them all in the department because, of course, I was really the darkest. Several times I was surprised by how unfair my colleagues were willing to be. I remember being in one department meeting where there was discussion of eliminating one of the linguistics courses as a requirement for English majors. Although I didn't realize it, the department was moving toward a vote on the change when Number 1 Linguist said that he didn't think it would be fair for the majority of the department to vote to eliminate a course taught only by the three linguists in the department. I said naively, "Oh, we wouldn't do that." When Kentuckian's Wife and I reached our office, she said, "Mary, that's exactly what White and the others are planning to do." I was shocked, but she was right. Number 1 Linguist had to work hard to round up enough votes to keep White and his associates from eliminating that course.

Years later, when a foreign languages professor prepared to become chair of the department, White, Charlie, and several other faculty members argued for splitting the department into Literature/Rhetoric/Composition and Foreign Languages/Linguistics/ESL. Again, the Literature/Rhetoric/Composition group outnumbered the others, so it seemed to me that the majority would be voting the minority out of the department. I joined some other mostly outsider English professors to keep the Foreign Languages/Linguistics/ESL faculty in the department. I thought the attempt to kick them out, which is the way I saw it and the way they saw it, was motivated by the desire to prevent a foreign languages faculty member, who happened to be a woman, from being in charge of the department. I assumed that they thought it was okay for a foreign languages professor to be an assistant chair, but since the department was called "English and Foreign Languages," not "Foreign Languages and English," they felt the chair should always be an English faculty member. That seemed snobbish and territorial to me. What I didn't realize is that White and some of the other English faculty might have been worried that if the foreign languages faculty member became chair, she might favor her programs over the English programs in the same way that White (and perhaps other English chairs) had favored the English programs over foreign languages and linguistics. And they were right to worry because this chair certainly showed favoritism in her treatment of the lecturers, being much more protective of the foreign languages lecturers. And while she made plans to add new foreign languages to the curriculum, she kept increasing the number of students in composition courses. I never thought I would have to say that White was right, but he was. The department should not have been divided into two, but we may have needed co-chairs, one representing the English programs and one representing foreign languages.

My overdeveloped sense of fair play not only caused me to misread some departmental power plays, it also affected my teaching schedule. When I taught only three courses a year, I did not teach the two-quarter 20th Century American Literature graduate seminar because I didn't think it was fair for me to have two-thirds of my teaching load be graduate seminars. Very rarely, a professor taught two graduate courses in one quarter, but no professor had taught six graduate courses in a year. I also always taught at least one composition (out of the three) course a year, therefore limiting how many literature classes I could teach. For some reason, I foolishly assumed that all professors on administrative released time taught composition. When I discovered that they did not, I proposed and persuaded the department to support unanimously a "fair share of composition" rule, which meant that a person teaching a reduced load because of administrative released time must teach the same percentage of composition classes as those teaching a full load of nine classes. At the time the rule was established, most people teaching nine courses taught three composition courses a year (1/3 of their teaching load), so that meant a person teaching six classes was required to teach two composition courses a year while the person teaching three classes would teach one, which was what I had been doing.

Although the rule was intended to apply only to people blessed with administrative released time, it was somehow used to force people teaching nine courses always to teach one composition course a quarter, so the linguists were at one point hiring lecturers to teach one of their courses so that they could teach their "fair share" of composition while some people with released time still avoided composition. I finally gave up on trying to make people be fair as I watched two different faculty members (at different times) try to turn their one course a quarter teaching schedule into an all graduate course schedule. I don't know how these people convinced themselves that they deserved to teach only graduate classes while other faculty members, some senior to them, taught multiple sections of composition and 200-level literature courses.

Something else that might come easier to black folks is sacrifice for a cause or a higher good. As I once sanctimoniously pointed out when trying to rally my colleagues around the cause of not participating in the merit salary program when it was just a one-time $2500.00 check, black folks walked for over a year to end segregation on buses. I didn't mention the black and white folks who died so blacks could have equal rights. Our cause was less noble, but I initially convinced the department to vote unanimously to refuse to participate in the merit salary program, which we agreed was, along with the newly required post-tenure review, designed to undermine tenure. And Kentuckian's Wife joined me in drafting a department declaration, explaining our stance, a statement which was copied by a few other departments (I believe that the political science department was one of them).

After the department vote was taken, White cornered me to complain that some of the department members had been intimidated (he seemed to imply by me) into voting to support the boycott when they really wanted the money. Assuming that he was speaking primarily for himself, I dismissed his complaint with the contemptuous comment, "If people don't have the courage of their convictions, they don't deserve the money." I probably also said something about no one's putting a gun to department members' heads to force them to vote a certain way. But, of course, again White was right. Some of my colleagues wanted the money but didn't have the nerve to vote against my call for noble sacrifice. When other departments accepted the money, members of our department became competitive, and soon quite a few of them started applying for the money, some of them donating the prize to the department. Then when the merit salary money became a permanent raise that would affect not only the size of our monthly paychecks but our pensions, almost everybody else (only one other tenured faculty member declined to participate) joined the competition for merit salary. I still refused to participate.

My decision to opt out of all merit salary programs probably set me apart from the rest of the department members more than anything except my pigmentation. One man was so shocked by my decision that he asked only half-jokingly if I were independently wealthy. Well, no, I wasn't, but unlike him, I didn't have a son at Stanford whose tuition I had to pay. Because I lived fairly modestly and had no children to support, I could afford to turn up my nose at the extra money. But not everyone who competed for the merit salary money needed it to support their families. At least one department member was independently wealthy, and he joined the competition because, of course, it wasn't just about the money but about the need to be number one, the need to be seen as superior.

We all knew that the competition for the merit salary money was not fair, that it was based on subjective criteria, that what would earn a faculty member merit pay in one department might not in another department. We also knew that the merit salary competition was similar to the competition for tenure and promotion, that it was more about packaging and selling what one has achieved than it was about the actual achievement. As I pointed out in one of my post-tenure reviews, the person who succeeds under this system is the one who can make an insignificant, badly written article, published in an obscure journal, sound like a Nobel-prize-winning book. (Probably because of my negative personality rather than because of my race or gender, I was not good at packaging and selling myself, highlighting my strengths and hiding my weaknesses.) We knew these things, but when a few of my colleagues acquired significant merit salary raises, they suddenly started acting as if the merit salary raises were the best indicators of a teacher's performance. So a bad teacher couldn't really be bad if she earned a merit salary raise.

I always thought that the Faculty Teaching Award for graduate professors was a bad idea. I thought its only purpose was to make one graduate professor feel good while seven or eight others would feel bad. I felt that way before I won the award, and I still felt that way after I won it three times. In fact, the more times I won the award, the more it bothered me that the male professors couldn't seem to win. Two other women professors won twice while the men were overlooked. There was one very dynamic Renaissance professor who I knew was a good teacher because I had read his student evaluations when he moved through the RTP process and because students often quoted him or referred to his classes in my graduate seminars. According to one of the female faculty members, this man was really hurt that he had not won the award. He should not only have been hurt but pissed. He was being robbed; he deserved to win. When I won the award for the third time, I asked one of the students who had mentioned Dr. Renaissance in my most recent graduate seminar why he hadn't voted for him since I had won the year before. The student said that he had not realized that I had already won or he probably would have voted for Dr. Renaissance. That's when I decided to take my name off the ballot. The fact that Dr. Renaissance and my former competitor, Dr. Blank, had not yet won the award when I retired does not diminish them, it diminishes the award and the people who have won and want to feel good about it.

My thinking is so different from whites that I sometimes let them convince me that there are differences between us when there aren't. I saw through the colorblind lie, but White (I realize now that I talked and listened to that man too much in my early years, but in my defense he was the chair of the department when I arrived and a power player until he retired) once told me something I actually believed until I started watching him and the other white folks. I had been comparing my schedule with a colleague's when White told his lie. I don't remember complaining about my schedule, just suggesting that maybe I would prefer the schedule that my colleague had. When White told me that he never noticed anyone else's schedule, I shot him down with, "Well, if black folks hadn't noticed that white people were riding in the front of the bus (I probably focused on Montgomery a lot during those days because I rode the bus until 1982 and still thought about bus riding for years after that), they would still be riding in the back."

Then I became department scheduler and saw that White and some of the other white folks not only noticed other people's schedules, they were much more likely to battle over perceived slights than I was. They complained not just about assigned times and courses but even room assignments. The real story I realized was closer to a point made by a black comedian (I believe it was Eddie Murphy on "Saturday Night Live") who said that slavery would have ended much sooner if white folks had been slaves. They would not have stayed out in that hot sun picking cotton for generations.

The English Department was notorious for its chair battles; during my 29 years as a full-time faculty member in the department, there were six chairs, and three were overthrown during contentious battles (a fourth chair, my old competitor Blank, resigned). Each time the coup was orchestrated by white people. Although each chair who was forced out had attacked me and other nonwhites at least once, he was not tossed out until he got on the last nerve of one or more white people in the department. Number 1 Linguist and his good friend, a male Spanish professor, planned and carried out the coup that took out White. Dr. Renaissance was a major behind-the-scenes player in the overthrow of Superfly, the man who falsely accused me of sneaking behind his back to complain to the dean. And the final chair who was tossed out (or actually left under pressure), a man who appears in my parable "The Race" as Gray, was taken out by a posse of women. I was one of the women, but I was not the woman who planned the coup and drafted the other women.

In fact, another major difference between the white folks with whom I worked and me was their unwillingness to fight alone. I remember my second officemate, Kentuckian's Wife, saying to me after she had received an inappropriately bad RTP evaluation that she couldn't fight her battle with the committee alone. Remembering my experience at ETHS and how much help the older black faculty and staff were, I was sympathetic to her plea for assistance and joined another woman in supporting and defending her. But later, I realized that the white woman's situation and mine were quite different. At twenty-two and just out of college, I was a lightweight in every sense of that term. But my officemate, while physically unimposing, was in every other way a heavyweight. She was a mature woman in her early fifties; she had a Ph.D. and was as smart as, if not smarter than, anyone else in the department. Why did she need help? I didn't seek help from other department members when Superfly sent me his accusatory letter. At almost forty-two, having fought many battles and won some, I was more than able and willing to fight alone. I didn't need anyone to accompany me to the dean's office or to advise me on what to say and what to do. I knew exactly what to say and do. I was just sick and tired of having to defend myself.

But none of the other faculty seemed to want to be the Lone Ranger, and now that I think about it, he wasn't even so alone. After all, beneath that black mask (And why a mask? Couldn't he find a sheet?) he was white, so even the Lone Ranger needed Tonto. And in my department I was Tonto. I didn't start any of the coups, but I was usually one of the first soldiers recruited for the battle. Number 1 Linguist and the Spanish Professor had a special role for me to play in their coup, and Spanish Professor took me to lunch to prep me for my assignment. I accepted the job although I let him know I would play the role my way. But when Dr. Renaissance tried to draft me, I refused to join his army. I was dealing with some serious family issues during that time and didn't want to be drawn into another chair fight. At one point, as he encouraged me to join him in meeting with the black dean, I snapped, "Renaissance, you are not going to wrap yourself in my blackness; I'm not going to see the dean with you." My suspicions that Renaissance and others wanted me on their side because the dean was black, and so they thought he would support me, were borne out when the department finally met with the dean, and people on both sides (there were some Superfly defenders) kept mentioning my name. I had taken a vow of silence, but someone finally said something (I don't remember what, but the dean looked at me, clearly expecting a response) that made me have to speak. Meantime, Dr. Renaissance never said a word during that meeting.

Probably for every battle that I fought to defend myself, there were five or six in which I either joined a posse or defended someone else. I fought for colleagues, lecturers, students, but most of all for the other black woman. I was involved in so many Other Black battles that I created a very thick file labelled "Other's Mess."

Other Black and I were as different in personality and our behavior in the department as we were in physical appearance. She was a much more passive, less combative woman, but she also had many more problems with students and administrators than I did. Other Black had been hired in the early seventies, and like several faculty hired before 1980, she did not have her Ph.D. Most of the faculty initially hired with just the M.A. went back to graduate school, and, by the time I arrived, were Ph.D.'s. Other Black, who was a few years older than I, earned her Bachelors at the historically black Hampton College and was working on her Ph.D. at Claremont Graduate School when her dissertation director, a black man, was denied tenure, leaving her with no Ph.D. and no dissertation director. After she was hired at Cal Poly, the departmental RTP rules were changed, requiring faculty to have Ph.D.'s to be promoted to full professor, so Other Black was stuck at the associate professor level.

But not being promoted was the least of Other Black's problems. While I had an almost perfect attendance record, having taken only one sick day and three personal leave days (only one of which required me to cancel an already scheduled class) in twenty-nine years, Other Black had constant problems with attendance. She disappeared for whole quarters. Also, while I was not a fan of guest lecturers, preferring to teach my own classes (I did ask my friendly colleague who invited me to dinner after the RTP race fiasco to talk to several of my "Teaching Basic Writing" graduate seminars about using the computer in composition classes because I knew nothing about the subject), Other Black was accused of allowing a staff person and random students to take charge of her classes.

Although she clearly was a problem faculty member, Other Black was never accused (at least not while I was in the department) of having sex with any of her students. Yet she was treated as the proverbial black sheep of the department, the worst EFL professor ever, while one white man, who actually was temporarily demoted from full to associate professor for having sex with three different students, one (a top student and daughter of a Cal Poly professor from another department) a seventeen-year-old when the affair started, was later made assistant chair, replacing me. Apparently, all was forgiven for the white man who also bragged about taking drugs. But everyone remembered and continued to discuss Other Black's problems. New faculty barely arrived on campus before they started dissing Other Black. And at least one secretary was caught soliciting student complaints; when students called asking for Other Black's office hours or other information regarding her, this secretary told them what a terrible teacher she was and asked if there were problems in the class, telling them which administrator or faculty member to contact to register complaints.

Because I felt that Other Black was unfairly targeted, I rode to her rescue on many occasions. I let her know when the chair was trying to remove her from the computer rooms, where she liked to hold her classes. And I wrote memos defending her. After I became the literature coordinator, I assigned her two 200-level literature courses a quarter rather than two or three composition courses, which she had been teaching for many years. And as the RTP chair, I refused to go along with a plan by the department chair (Gray) and the white female (she replaced the black man) College of Arts dean to use the post-tenure review process to add a negative evaluation to her personnel file as a first step toward overturning tenure and firing her. I knew that they wanted to use me, another black woman, as a shield against Other Black's charges of racism and sexism. To their credit, three white men on the RTP committee, including Number 1 Linguist, stood with me against the chair and the dean.

Twice Other Black involved me in legal complaints against the department and the university. The first time, I simply had to be interviewed by telephone. The second time two lawyers (one representing the school) and a stenographer were in my home during Christmas break, asking me questions about the treatment of Other Black and whether or not I felt particular members of the department were racist. Since this was an official deposition, I had to swear to tell the truth. These three white people were in my house for more than three hours.

But probably the moment that most captured my relationship with Other Black was a Christmas break a couple of years earlier when she called me at 6:30 a.m. to report on her latest problems with department administrators. Like most people who don't have to go to work, I was asleep at that time. When I realized what time it was and saw that it was still dark outside, I wondered why my mother hadn't answered the telephone since she is always awake by five a.m. I assumed incorrectly that she wouldn't walk in the dark, so I asked Other Black to hold on while I went to check on my mother. I went down the hall, saw that my mother's bed was made and realized that she was indeed walking in the dark, headed back to my room, picked up the telephone, and suddenly felt very ill. I told Other Black to hold on again and then fainted, luckily landing on the bed. I didn't realize that I had fainted until the paramedics knocked on my door. Other Black had called 911 for me, but she never called me back to see if I was okay. When I asked her later (after we returned to school) why she didn't try to find out what had happened to me, she explained that she thought I had died, and she didn't know what she was going to do if I wasn't in the department to defend her. Oh!

And here is why some blacks have trouble overcoming oppression. I was Other Black's strongest (and often only) supporter in the department, but she was not mine. In fact, if I was on one side of an issue that didn't directly affect her, she was on the other side. During the period when Gray was pressuring the RTP committee to place the negative evaluation in her file, a time when Other Black and I were communicating frequently about how to fight the two administrators who were trying to fire her, Gray was also battling the graduate committee. Other Black didn't teach graduate classes, but she knew that I did and that I was on the committee. Still, when the department voted on an issue that pitted Gray against the graduate committee, she abstained. She didn't want to vote with Gray, but she still couldn't bring herself to support me.

Even after that slight, I continued to support her; in fact, both the deposition and the fainting spell happened after the abstention. But the year before I retired, Other Black finally went too far in her need to oppose me. I volunteered to serve on the chair evaluation committee because I wanted to be sure that the chair's problems with the composition lecturers were not whitewashed. I was not trying to have her removed because I didn't know who would replace her, and besides, I was leaving in a year and didn't really care who the department chair would be after I left. I just wanted to point out areas where she needed improvement. But because the whites in the department don't think like me or maybe don't realize that I don't think like them, they assumed that the only reason I would join the committee was to overthrow the chair. They thought I was planning a coup. Somehow Other Black, who often didn't know what was going on in the department because she rarely attended department meetings, heard that I was going after the chair. In response, she wrote a more positive evaluation of the chair than anyone in the department, including the chair's best friend. Interestingly, she made a point of saying that she had no evidence that this woman had been discriminatory. There was one problem, however. The chair had been one of the defendants in the Other Black lawsuit for which I gave a deposition. Since I swore to tell the truth, I assumed Other Black had as well. When Other Black came looking for me to see what I would say after she had sent in that ridiculously over the top praise of a woman that she had accused multiple times of discriminating against her, I faked concern about her welfare. "I hope they won't arrest you for perjury," I said as she followed me to my classroom, trying to explain what she meant to say in the chair evaluation when she told those outrageous lies.

Of course, I had the last laugh. I knew that before I retired, Other Black would be looking for me to defend her one more time. I didn't realize that it would happen within weeks. When she didn't like her schedule of courses for the fall, she sent me an e-mail, which I read and without replying, deleted. I also deleted Other Black from my list of people who deserved my support and protection.

I'm not sure why Other Black was so determined to oppose me in department battles where I wasn't defending her. I suspect it has something to do with what White supposedly told her after I accepted the tenure-track position. During my first year as a lecturer in the department, I shared a desk with the then elderly black writer, Lorenz Graham, also a part-time lecturer. One course that he taught was black literature. When Graham retired in 1978, I was at first asked to teach black literature while still a lecturer, but then I was told that there was a black woman in the department (Other Black) who had been there for several years and really wanted to teach the course. She taught black literature that year and the year that I was at Tufts; then I was assigned the course. According to Graham, who was filling me in on department gossip at a Christmas party (1980) he and his wife hosted, White told Other Black that I would be teaching the course because I had a Ph.D. in black literature (not true, my major area was 20th Century <u>American Literature</u>). When I found out about this decision, I told White that I would share the course with Other Black. But maybe the damage was done; the competitive fires were lit, and she always saw me as the junior faculty member who took her course.

White was capable of taking the course away from Other Black and giving it to me just to cause friction between the two black females in the department. But he might have also been trying to provide the students with the best teacher. During his tenure as chair, he moved at least one senior faculty member, a white male, out of the graduate classes because students complained about him. And after I temporarily replaced another white male as the English Education coordinator, supervising the student teachers while he was on sabbatical, White offered me the position. He thought I could do a better job than the older man. (I declined the offer to take someone else's job.) Although Other Black had some fans among the students, she had more detractors than most of us. She blamed most of her problems in the classroom on racism, but I had few problems with racism in my classes.

Indeed, the classroom was usually a refuge, a safe harbor from the racism I found in the department and the university. Occasionally, there was a clueless white student who made the kind of mistake that Charmer made, hearing drums when he saw blacks, but I could handle those situations with humor. If the students who put their white feet in their mouths happened to be in the black lit class, where they were usually outnumbered, I protected them. In fact, one white student, an English major whose name was also Mary, wrote a paper for her composition class (taught by a friend of mine, which was how I found out about the paper) about my diplomatic handling of controversial comments in the black lit class. There were, however, two classes where my diplomacy failed and where I felt under attack by students. One was a new graduate seminar that I taught several times subsequently with great success. The other was a linguistics class that I taught to help out the department and that I never taught again.

The graduate seminar focused on African American Fiction. I had developed a two-quarter Ethnic Literatures of the U.S. course in response to a request by students. I spent part of a sabbatical leave reading primary and secondary texts by and about Native American, Asian American, and Latino American writers to prepare to teach the first quarter of the course and looked forward to the second quarter because I knew much more about African American literature. During the first quarter, I noticed tension between several nonwhite female students and a few of the whites. Some of the tension was apparently carried over from White's 19th Century American Literature seminar, where they discussed Huckleberry Finn. One student who was in the 19th Century American Lit class and the first quarter of Ethnic Literatures of the U.S. refused to take the second quarter when she realized that one of the white women in White's class had registered for African American Fiction. She knew trouble was ahead.

For the most part the tension did not erupt into actual battles, but there was quite a bit of signifying during that seminar. I remember one white student's making a totally irrelevant comment about not wanting to go to Watts, causing the one black student in the class and me to challenge him. One indicator of the tension was the seating arrangement. The class was in a room with a table. I sat at one end of the table, and three of the four non-white students in the class sat nearest to me. Usually I would point out that kind of obvious self-segregation, but I decided to ignore it in this class. At one point, the bickering grew so bad that I found myself snapping at one student whom I generally liked that she needed to show more respect for me as the professor of the class. Because I liked to tease and debate, students occasionally stepped over the line between informal banter and disrespect, but I could usually push them back across that line without becoming angry. This class was clearly different. I was so exasperated with the atmosphere in the class that I considered asking an older American lit professor, who I knew had read the novels I was teaching, to switch classes with me. He would teach the African American Fiction graduate seminar, and I would teach his freshman composition class that met at the same time. The thought of announcing to the graduate students that I would teach a composition class and let this white man teach them amused me enough to get me through the quarter. And every subsequent African American Fiction seminar was a joy to teach. They were some of my favorite classes.

My least favorite class of all time, however, was "Language and Human Behavior." I taught it during Spring Quarter, 1989, as a favor to the department. The Egyptian man, who had taught the course, left for a more lucrative career in business, and no one else wanted to teach it. Since the course, a requirement for some English majors, had not been taught in a few years, there were seniors who needed it to graduate. The class was supposed to hold a maximum of thirty students, but I accepted an extra thirteen students because I was teaching only one class that quarter. Initially, the class went well. I knew some of the students because they were tutors in the basic writing skills program, and I was their supervisor. There was also one black woman in the class who had followed me from the black literature class she took the previous quarter. She enjoyed that class and liked the sound of this one.

The first two books that we discussed were typical sociolinguistics books. I don't remember the titles, but they were books assigned in the course in the past. However, the last book was my addition. This book, written by black (and often Black English using) scholar Geneva Smitherman, is titled <u>Discourse and Discrimination</u>. As the title suggests, it examines the intersection between language, race, gender, and class. The first day that we were to discuss the book, I pointed out that, unlike the other books we studied, this one had a clear point of view. One older white man in the class interrupted to say that he was offended by the book and thought it was racist. He had made other off-the-wall comments during our discussions, and the other students usually took him on, so I waited for someone to engage him in this debate. But no one spoke; instead I noticed that several of the students looked hostile and angry as if they agreed with the older man. As I looked around the room, noticing for the first time how many of the students had blue eyes, I realized quickly that this man was expressing the feelings of many of the students in the class. Instead of seeing red, I saw black and white. I told the students that one of my favorite writers was William Faulkner, who actually said that black folks smelled bad, and one of my favorite novels to teach was <u>Huckleberry Finn</u>, which some people thought should be banned because of its use of what we all agreed was the worst racial slur, "nigger." Just as I wound up for a full sermon, denouncing narrow-minded, ignorant people, it started storming outside, surprising all of us since it had been a sunny day when we entered the room. The almost too symbolic storm distracted us, and I cooled down. But I did something I had never done before and never did again. I stopped teaching that class. I took a personal leave day on the day that we were supposed to discuss Black English, turned another class meeting into a workshop for the final papers, and the rest of the time we listened to presentation panels on teaching, gender, and, yes, race. Because the class was so large, there were quite a few students on each panel, but ordinarily I would have limited how much time each student could speak so that I could teach. Instead I sat in the audience, let the students talk as long as they needed to (Thank God, there were some talkative women in that class), and then asked them questions until it was time to go. I stopped teaching the class that quarter and never taught it again.

It's too bad that those blue-eyed students in "Language and Human Behavior" didn't want to hear what Smitherman and I had to say about language and discrimination. They didn't recognize what the graduate students who kept giving me the teaching award probably understood. Being a black woman gave me a perspective that most of their other professors did not have. Just by walking into the classroom, I sometimes taught the students a lesson. Yes, black people do teach English. I could tell that they were learning that lesson because of the way they stared at me when I entered the room and wrote my name on the board. And I often taught them the kind of lessons that would later (I hope) prevent them from becoming birthers during the Obama administration. I taught more than one student (including several in the racist "Language and Human Behavior" class) that "white" and

"American," and "minority" or "colored" and "foreigner," are not synonyms. I even had to explain to one Mexican American that, except for the red Indians or Native Americans, all of our ancestors were immigrants, foreigners. I like to believe that none of my students would be birthers because they know that nonwhite people can be as all-American as whites. And even some of those students who thought they understood the immigrant experience had to be taught that not all of us came to America seeking the American Dream; some of us were brought here against our will, and what we found when we arrived here was a nightmare.

Unfortunately, too many faculty and administrators failed to recognize the value of my black perspective. I can think of only one time when several of my EFL colleagues hung onto every word I said. Ironically, at that moment, I was speaking to only one department member, or so I thought. It was at the end of a department meeting in 1992, a few days after the riot in response to the Rodney King verdict. That riot, which started in South Central L.A., spread to Pomona, causing the administrators to close the campus early on Thursday afternoon and cancel classes that Friday. I don't remember what I was saying to my liberal white female colleague as we left the meeting; I just remember noticing that several other whites stopped to listen intently to my analysis of the riot. I guess they wanted to hear their educated, civilized black colleague explain those wild blacks who were rioting.

But, unless I was helping them fight some battle they started, the whites in my department usually wanted me to be quiet, to shut up. I suspect if we had done a poll of the EFL department members, asking which member was the most talkative, I would be listed, if not first, certainly among the top three. However, while I was very vocal during some department meetings, such as some of the chair fights, I was also often quiet. I almost never, for instance, asked questions of the many candidates for new positions during their presentations. And yet the candidates noticed and remembered me. And when I talked, my talking seemed to bother people more than when others talked. After one meeting where I had spoken several times, a white man made a comment to a white woman (that I assume he didn't mean for me to overhear) suggesting that I had dominated the meeting. Replaying that meeting in my head, I realized that I was the fourth most talkative person in the meeting (not counting the chair), but that man seemed to think that I was the only one talking. And when I occasionally forgot my manners and whispered something to someone sitting near me, I was much more likely to attract attention than other whisperers. I was even occasionally shushed by people who themselves liked to whisper. Now perhaps I was an unusually loud whisperer, but I doubt it since sometimes the intended audience for my whispers couldn't hear me.

To be black is to be loud. Black is a loud color in white institutions. That's why I always seemed to be talking too much or too loudly. That's also why I was more likely to provoke a reaction to whatever I said or did.

And those reactions were more likely to be negative than positive. As I said in one of my numerous memos in defense of myself, given my performance as a teacher, advisor, and active member of the university community, my career as an English

164

professor would have been (and should have been) more pleasant and peaceful had I been a white man.

CHAPTER FIVE
A Man's World

When I visited the new affirmative action director, a black woman, in her office, mainly so I could meet her and let her know what my life at Cal Poly had been like before she arrived, I surprised her by saying that I thought my gender was more of a problem for me in the EFL Department than was my race. My reputation had preceded me since this woman was acquainted with one of my white male colleagues. The man who had sex with several students and consequently moved primarily into administration told her all about me. Student Screwer and I had known each other at USC. Although he started in the program a few years after I did, we were officemates when I became a T.A. While very bright, Student Screwer was almost pathologically shy and had very little charisma, a point not made in his glowing letters of recommendation.

I am sure his description of me made me sound like a meaner, louder, more militant Angela Davis.

The black woman let me know that she assumed my problems were primarily the result of racism. While I agreed that racism was at the root of quite a few of my problems, I felt that sexism played an even stronger role. I mentioned specific facts to make my case. I pointed out, for instance, that at that time our department still had not elected a female chair while most other departments, including p.e., had at least one. I mentioned that two EFL women had been assistant chairs. I was the second one, but neither of us lasted a year. And I thought it was interesting that of the faculty hired after me, only one man had left, an Italian-born gentleman hired to teach French, who left either because his wife had problems with her passport and couldn't come back across the Canadian border (his explanation) or because he didn't want to teach French to mostly Vietnamese students (the foreign languages coordinator's angry explanation). At the time I was talking to the affirmative action director, three women had left, all of them after earning tenure. Since that conversation, another woman left before she went up for tenure, but the four men hired since that date are still there. My final argument focused on how the department responded to the three deans that met with us during the chair fights. One of them was a black woman, one a black man, and the third a white woman. Although the men made disparaging comments about the black male dean behind his back, they were very respectful toward him during the meeting. They were less respectful toward the black woman, but several of them, including White, were openly hostile toward the white woman. In fact, it was the treatment of the white female dean that made me realize that the EFL men were more sexist than racist.

During my early years, I never thought about sexism. I was too focused on racism. And since most of my teachers were women, I assumed they had no problems with my gender. Even when I attended Northwestern, where only one of my professors was female, a young woman whom I couldn't stand because she didn't write comments on my papers, I didn't think much about how men and women were treated. I did wonder about that special award for sophomore women but assumed that it was established to encourage women to succeed during a time when it was unusual for them to attend college. That time had passed by 1967, so there were plenty of women in my classes. In fact, both the School of Education and the English Department were dominated by women. I actually felt somewhat sorry for the male students in the School of Education because they were so outnumbered.

However, when I entered graduate school, I noticed a change. There were still more women than men in my classes, but the men seemed to be treated differently by at least some of the professors. Dr. Rose seemed to respect most of the women, but he could also be condescending, almost paternal toward others. But the "liberal" Dr. Potter was the most sexist. He openly showed his preference for particular men. He wrote articles with them; he called on them more in class and seemed more delighted with whatever they said, no matter how inane. There was this one male student in particular whom Potter just adored. He called his name with great affection. And when his pet talked, Potter always listened intently. On the other hand, when most of the women talked, he seemed impatient, as if he wanted them to shut up so his pet could talk more. During one class meeting, Potter's Pet said something foolish, not because he was stupid, but because we can all mis-read texts or draw illogical conclusions. I don't remember what foolish thing Potter's Pet said, but the rest of the class laughed. And we probably laughed louder than we would have if any other student had made the foolish comment because Potter's Pet was so understandably (given Potter's adoration) full of himself. In fact, we might not have laughed at all if a student with less self-esteem had made the mistake. When the laughter ended, Potter asked, "Pet, how many articles have you published?" Potter's Pet gave the number while Potter looked around the room at the rest of us, as if to say, "You assholes haven't published anything." Then he said regretfully, "Well, you were wrong this time."

Okay, now, that little defense of Potter's Pet and silent put-down of the rest of us was too much for me, and not because I was thinking about sexism, but because I had been a high school teacher and had studied to be a teacher, which is something Potter clearly had not done. So the next time I was in his office, I had to explain the self-fulfilling prophecy to him. He was telling the rest of us that we were not as smart as his pet, and since he believed that, nothing that we said or did would seem as smart to him. And even worse, if we believed him (and I didn't), we might not perform as well as Potter's Pet because we were living down to the low expectations of Potter. I had that conference with Potter before I realized that his favorite students were always men. Had

I noticed that, I might have said something about his inability to recognize that women might have something intelligent to say.

There was one funny sexist incident involving the generally kind Dr. Research and me. It was one of those upsetting at the time incidents that later became a funny story as often happened in my life. Research's class met on Monday, and one of those Mondays was a holiday (probably Veterans' Day). Because the class met only once a week, Research did not want to observe the holiday, so he asked the class to meet at his house (the university was closed). Since I lived on campus and didn't have a car, I was annoyed that Research was asking me to try to find a way to his house off campus. Of course, when I complained, several too helpful classmates offered me a ride, so I rode with two male students who lived near the campus. We were the first to arrive at Research's house, which was up in the hills of some expensive town like Westwood or Brentwood, anyway near UCLA. After greeting us and offering us a drink, Research said, "Miss Sisney, you look like a hostess. Will you cut the cheese?" Oh, no, he didn't!

Although I didn't actually put my hands on my hips and move my head around, I certainly let Research know he had made a terrible mistake. I said angrily, "I didn't come to graduate school to cut cheese." I was about to say something else about Research's needing to hire a maid or ask his white wife to cut his cheese when I caught one of my male classmate's eyes, saw that he looked worried, and shut my mouth. But I was furious for several minutes until another woman arrived, a blonde, blue-eyed woman. Research, who either didn't learn his lesson or wanted me to realize that he was sexist, not racist, said to her, "Miss Blonde, you look like a hostess; will you cut the cheese?" Miss Blonde happily cut the cheese, and I felt better. I knew that Research shouldn't have asked either one of us women to cut the cheese, but I preferred (and still prefer) a white man who is sexist to one who is racist.

I never saw any of the white female students' letters of recommendation, so I don't know if they were as tepid as mine or if some of those women managed to score stronger recommendations. But I seriously doubt that any USC woman received letters as glowing as those provided for Student Screwer. And I remember one of the professors bemoaning the fact that he could no longer contact his pals at other schools and find his favorite students jobs. I knew he was mourning the loss of the old boys' network, and I have a feeling the female students would not have been included in that network.

There were only two tenured women, both relatively mature, at USC when I started there, but that was two more than I found at Tufts. The year before I arrived, the poet Denise Levertov had left, apparently during some kind of departmental upheaval I'm happy I missed. She may have been tenured, but the other three women who were there when I arrived were not. During the 1979-80 academic year, there were five women in the department, counting another thirty-year-old woman who was hired the same year that I was and me. The other three women were also in their thirties. I'm not sure why there were no older, tenured women in the department. But I checked the Tufts website recently and found that two of those original women are still there, and both have been chair of the department, so whatever was going on during the late seventies, things must have changed.

The two Tufts professors did something that none of the Cal Poly English women faculty could, become the chair of the department. When we finally selected a female chair, she was a French professor who had spent several years being mentored by White and Non White, and still some department members wanted to kick the foreign languages faculty out of the department rather than let this usually diplomatic, not at all threatening woman become the chair.

When I came to Cal Poly, there were seven women in the EFL department, all of them tenured. Five of these women, including a Mexican-American Spanish professor, were full professors. Another tenured woman, ironically another poet, Virginia Adair, had just retired. Two more women were hired after me, so by 1983, there were ten women in a department of around thirty-five faculty. We hired three more men before the men started retiring, and we started hiring more women. Since some of those women left, either moving out of the department into administration, retiring, or moving to another school, by 1997 we still had only eleven women in the department, but the number of men had shrunk to the point that women had become a more significant numerical force. And with more men retiring and a few more women hired (we also hired four men during this period), at some point in the early 21st century the number of women in the department surpassed the number of men. By that time, we had a female chair.

As these numerical changes occurred, some of the men felt threatened. I had spent many years being the only woman (not to mention the only black) on various department committees. I also remember several important committees, including one elected to select the next chair, with no women on them, yet when a chair, Gray, realized that the RTP committee might, for the first time, be majority female, he nominated a man to serve. Fortunately, the department voted for the two female nominees, who joined another female and two men on the committee. The graduate committee attracted Gray's attention because it was heavily female. In fact, at one point there were only two men on the committee, and when one of the two took a sabbatical leave, the other one said urgently that we needed to select a replacement. I suggested several females, but this man said that we needed a man. When I looked at him with astonishment and asked why, he suddenly decided that we didn't need another committee member after all. The man was clearly uncomfortable being the only man on a committee even for a quarter.

However, no man worried more about female dominance than Gray, who attended the graduate committee meetings when he was chair of the department just so he could monitor and disrupt our activities. Once, before he became chair, he asked me in a composition committee if the fact that there were more women than men among the lecturers meant, according to affirmative action rules, that we had to recruit more male lecturers. Now I assumed that this was Gray's sly way of taking a shot at affirmative action, so I gave him a "thanks for that softball; now watch me knock it out of the park" look and said, "No, Gray; the

fact that we have more women in all of the powerless positions-
-students, staff, and lecturers--while both the chair, the assistant
chair, and most of the committee chairs are men means that we
need to work harder to recruit women for the tenure track and to
encourage women to chair some of these important committees."
Gray's face told me that he knew he lost that battle, and I'm sure
my face told him that I knew I won.

A few years later, Gray became department chair, and during his first department meeting, he used power point to profile
the department. As part of that profile, he counted the men and
women in the department. By counting lecturers and staff, as
well as tenured and tenure-track faculty, he made it look as if the
department were dominated by women. When I raised my hand
and asked what the count was for tenured and tenure track only,
he waved me off with a quick, quiet, "Oh, that's another number."
After the meeting, the Spanish professor who helped overthrow
White teased me about trying to start trouble. I wasn't really trying to start trouble; I was actually curious to know how different
the male-female ratio was when we counted only the tenured/
tenure-track faculty.

Of course, it didn't occur to me until much later to wonder
why Gray felt the need to count the women and men in the first
place. If he had counted us by race, I certainly would have asked
him what the point was, but my discrimination radar was still
(and this was 1995) not as sensitive to sexism as it was to racism.
Ten years earlier, when I had a conversation with that Spanish
professor, my sexism radar was almost inoperable. During our
pre-coup lunch date, I was suggesting candidates for chair. I

mentioned a smart, slightly older woman who later became a close friend but was then just an acquaintance. When I mentioned her name, Spanish Professor, who was a friendly, seemingly nice man, although a bit high strung, said that she would be a terrible choice. When I asked him why, he said that she was a bitch. Now if I had suggested Other Black as a possible candidate and Spanish Professor had rejected her, calling her a nigger, I would have probably cursed him out and complained to the chair, the dean, the president, and the chancellor, maybe even the governor of California. But when the white man called the white woman a bitch, the black woman just said something like, "Really? Why? What did she do?"

I don't remember what Spanish Professor said, but I soon figured out what the white woman did to be called a bitch. She was a smart, competent woman who didn't take crap from the men. By that definition, I was also a bitch. And this bitch joined with that bitch and a third bitch, my officemate, Kentuckian's Wife, to disrupt Spanish Professor's coup. He and Number 1 Linguist were not only determined to overthrow White but also to prevent Non White, White's assistant chair, from becoming the new chair. Their plan was to elect a committee that would weed out undesirable candidates (like Non White) before letting the department vote on the ones they pre-selected. Most of us did not know that was the plan when the chair selection committee was elected.

Three women, including one very aggressive but hard-working and competent black woman, were nominated for the committee. We all lost. I think there may have been one man who received fewer votes than the three women, but we lost pretty badly. I may have had fewer votes than the two white women, but the difference was minor. No woman won. The department was concerned that the foreign languages program be represented on the committee (and they were, by a man), but no one (except the bitches) seemed troubled that women were not represented.

As the chair battle unfolded over the next few weeks, there were three distinct parties fighting. First, there was the establishment group, consisting of White, Non White, and other English professors, including the other two women who lost the chair committee nomination; then there were the rebels, made up of Number 1 Linguist, Spanish Professor, the other foreign languages professors, a few outsider English professors, and the other two nonwhite women (Other and the Mexican American Spanish professor). Finally, there were the three independent women, the bitches. Since it was clear that Smart Woman had no chance of becoming chair (one man told me in a matter-of-fact, so-what voice that the other men wouldn't vote for her), we had less to lose than the other two groups. So the establishment group wisely hid behind us and let us take out the rebels so that they ended up getting exactly what they didn't want—Non White as the new chair. After the black female dean came to the department, the all-male committee was dissolved, we took a vote, and Non White won. Had the rebels been a little smarter, they would have joined forces with the independent women and maybe gotten their choice for chair, Superfly, or perhaps we could have compromised and chosen a candidate that we all could accept, Charlie Blank, for instance.

Interestingly, my vote was cast for Blank. Since my candidate was no longer in the race and since I was so disgusted by all that happened, including the decision to deny the lecturers, whose fate was more affected by the chair selection than mine or any other tenured/tenure track faculty would be, a voice or a vote, I gave my vote to a representative lecturer. I walked across the hall to what was then the lecturers' one office, found a sensible lecturer sitting there, told her what my plan was, and gave her my ballot. She thought carefully about how to cast her vote because she recognized that she was voting not just for herself but for all lecturers. She voted for Blank; I took the ballot from her, and without looking at it, walked it to the department office and dropped it in the ballot box. I found out years later from a friend of the lecturer representative how she voted. Giving her that vote was one of my smartest moves. It wasn't really a power play, more like an act of civil disobedience. But I'm proud that I did it.

At some point during this first chair fight (at least for me, apparently there was some kind of chair coup between my first and second year as a lecturer, but I didn't know or care anything about it), I started to realize why the English Department was an especially difficult place for women to work. Although I recognize that my perspective might be slightly skewed because most of my pre-English Department work took place on a military base (Fort Sheridan), in an investment department (Northwestern), and in the Black House, where my boss was a black man, I don't think I'm too off-base in believing that there are more wimps per square male in English Departments than in just about any other workplace on earth. Anyone looking for macho men in the university should not come to the English Department; they should try p.e, business, or maybe engineering.

On the other hand, women my age or older (and at that point, I was the youngest woman in the department) had to be strong and tough to deal with the old boys' network, or the men who were upset about the loss of that network, and earn the Ph.D. When we were making our way through graduate schools, most of the graduate faculty were men, and some of those men were like Potter, who believed female students should be quiet so men could talk, and a few might have been like Research, who thought all women looked like hostesses who should cut cheese at parties. One of the Cal Poly female faculty members' husbands once commented that the women in our department had bigger balls than the men. Obviously, anatomically that would be impossible, but figuratively, it often seemed true. Certainly, during that first chair fight, the women were the ones taking it to the rebellious men while the other men hid behind our skirts and pantsuits.

There were some funny scenes during those battles. At one point, the rebels brought in their one tough woman, the Mexican American Spanish professor (she usually attended meetings only when they were scheduled on days that she taught), to take on the three independent women. It wasn't a fair fight because there were three of us against her one, but none of the men on her side helped her. They just sat back and let us go at it. Some of the men, who weren't as involved in the fight, were amused as were the establishment men, who were happy to see the female rebel losing a battle, but her allies just sat there, looking impotent.

After the meeting that the black female dean attended, the chair of the selection committee, who had been mouthing off during the meeting because he was personal friends with the dean and obviously thought she would protect him, had made it back to his office without encountering any of the angry women, but then he wanted to go home or to class. Instead of walking past my office, which became the main battle station for the independent women and their establishment allies, he tried to sneak out the back way. Unfortunately for him, Kentuckian's Wife was standing in the doorway of our office and started loud-talking him. She said something like, "Oh, he's scared now that Mama Yolanda [the dean] isn't here to protect him." I jumped up from my desk to stand in the hallway and laugh at the coward as he slithered down the hall toward the back stairway. We didn't care that we were acting like high school bullies. These men were pathetic, and we wanted them to know that we knew it.

Of course, not all of the men were wimps. There were surprisingly, given the level of education and the subject that they taught, a couple of cave men types known for crude jokes and suspected of sleeping with students. They were in many ways less obnoxious than the wimps, but one of them, jive-talking Superfly, had a temper. So he tried to intimidate the women by glaring at us and stomping around the hallway in his cowboy boots. But, of course, glaring at me, a black woman from Kentucky, is like drawing a water pistol on Annie Oakley. I've been told by students and many others that I look mean even when I'm just concentrating hard. Superfly's office was right next to mine, and during the height of the battle and for a year after his crew lost, he stomped down the hall, stopped at his door, and glared at me. Depending on my mood, I either returned the glare or laughed in his face. Just before the end of the first year of Non White's reign as chair, I saw Superfly walking toward his car in the faculty parking lot. I was in my car, and when he reached the lane I was in, I had to stop and wait for him to move out of the way. As I was sitting there, waiting, I thought, "For $2.50 I'd run over this sucker." At that moment, Superfly turned and looked at me. He stopped dead in his tracks and stared, then waved timidly. In response, I threw up my left hand in a gesture that today would be read as "talk to the hand." I think he read my thoughts because from that day on, Superfly dropped his badass walk and glare and became friendly again.

There were other strong men in the department who didn't need to intimidate the women. There were a few officer and gentleman types, men who had fought in World War II, Korea, or Vietnam. They usually either ignored the women or protected particular women. At worse, they were patronizing, and in the case of the World War II veterans, a bit paternal. Then there were some men who had developed a backbone and some moral and mental courage the same way we women had, through life experiences. These men could be our strong allies when they were on our side or worthy opponents when they opposed us. But the rest of the males were wimps, and unfortunately, too often the wimps ran or tried to run the department.

When these wimps were angry, they didn't stomp around the department and glare. Instead they used whatever little power they had from the administrative positions they held to retaliate against perceived enemies. I could always tell when one of the wimps had gone after me because they became nervous and worried looking when they saw me. I passed Non White's office one day, spoke, and noticed that he looked scared. I thought, "Okay, what has this jerk done to me now?" To figure it out, I had to remember what position he held. He was the department scheduler, so I turned on the computer, checked my schedule, and found that he had shafted me with a schedule that he knew I didn't like. Of course, I made him change it, which he surely knew I would. I wasn't even sure why Non White decided to mess with me that quarter. I hadn't had any problems with him. Finally, I figured out that he was upset because I had been feuding with Gray. Obviously, the wimps stuck together better than the black women did.

Gray, who initially appeared to be a really sweet, kind man, was the wimpiest of the wimps and therefore the worst bully. Ironically, he was, for more years than I want to remember, my closest male friend in the department. In fact, if Gray had been straight, and I had been into white men, we probably would have been a couple, but our romantic relationship would have ended a lot sooner than our close friendship did. We were proof that opposites attract, at least initially. Gray was not only the most mealy-mouthed, mousy man (I once described him as pathologically non-confrontational) that I have ever encountered, he also spoke and wrote in a formal, almost too standard English. He taught 19th Century British Literature and often sounded as if he were still living during that period and in that country (although he didn't have the British accent).

Needless to say, I was nothing like Gray, but we had one thing in common when I was still a lecturer at Cal Poly. We both rode the bus. Gray could drive, but his car was very old, and I guess he just liked riding the bus. Since he was witty and charming when we met at the bus stop, we became good friends when I joined the full-time faculty. We went to dinner and the movies together, sometimes with another single woman, a linguist. She usually drove when we were a threesome. But once I bought my new car, Gray and I used my car, which he usually drove because he was the better driver.

Our friendship survived the tension that developed during "the race" when he was the chair of the RTP committee. But there were early signs of trouble. When I joined the full-time faculty, Gray was the graduate coordinator. I was on many other committees, but not that one. Since I was doing quite a bit of work with graduate students, I volunteered to replace Superfly on the committee when he won a grant that took him off campus for a year. I don't remember exactly what Gray said when I approached him about serving on the committee, but I could tell he was troubled by my request. However, instead of telling me that I couldn't be on the committee and explaining why, he sent Non White to deal with me. Non White said something vague about people being territorial, and I said, "That's fine. I just thought I would make a good member of the committee since I'm writing so many exam questions and directing so many graduate independent studies" (extra work for which there was no compensation).

I knew that Gray and Non White weren't telling me the whole story, so I tried to figure out what was going on. When I looked at the list of graduate committee members, I noticed that they were all tenured professors, so I assumed that was the problem. The two wimps didn't want to admit that junior faculty members couldn't serve on the graduate committee because I recently said I liked that our department was less hierarchal than other English departments where I had studied and worked. I specifically mentioned my teaching graduate classes as evidence of their more equitable treatment of junior faculty. But then Kentuckian's Wife arrived and was immediately assigned to the graduate committee, so I was again confused. Finally, I figured out that Gray just didn't like my volunteering to be on a committee; he thought I was being pushy, and he didn't like pushy people; he especially didn't like pushy women.

The other suspicious <u>incident happened off campus. Gray</u> and I discussed seeing a movie. I wanted to see <u>Fatal Attraction,</u> which features Glenn Close terrorizing a meek-looking Michael Douglas. In that movie, Michael is eventually saved by Anne Archer, his sweet-looking wife. Gray didn't want to see that movie; instead he wanted to see <u>Blue Velvet</u>, which features an ether-sniffing Dennis Hopper sexually terrorizing an often nude Isabella Rosselini. I didn't really want to see that movie, so we ended up not going to the movies together. When I later saw <u>Blue Velvet</u> on cable, I started to wonder about my friend Gray. Why would he want to see that movie with me? The movies that we usually saw together were musicals like <u>Fame</u> and <u>Flashdance</u> or dramedies directed by Woody Allen or Spike Lee. Why this sick movie about a man torturing a woman? I thought even then that his choice of movies had something to do with his being such a meek man, scared of strong women.

A few years later, when I came face-to-face with the dark side (or rather the white side) of Gray, I again thought about that movie choice. As too often happened in our department, the battle between us started over the selection of the chair. We were selecting a chair to replace Non White, who was completing his four-year term, and the only candidate this time was Superfly. I was the chair of the totally unnecessary chair search committee, with Gray and the male German professor as the other committee members. Gray and I had been informally discussing whether the department should take a vote. He thought we shouldn't since there was only one candidate, but I thought we should let Superfly know whether the department fully supported his candidacy or whether there were people who didn't want him to be chair. The German professor was neutral on the topic at first. But Gray lobbied him, and soon the two white men were on the same side. Well, I had seen this movie before. I would serve on a committee, lending it my doubly affirmative gender and race, but then would be outvoted by the white men. Because I was known to be outspoken, any decisions made by a committee with me on it was seen as representing the voices of nonwhites and women.

As Gray knew, but the German professor probably didn't, I was especially vulnerable during this period because my not quite 62 year old mother had recently been beaten and raped by the son of her next door neighbor and had moved in with me literally overnight. So I was adjusting to losing the solitude that I had enjoyed for so many years while trying to help my mother heal from a horrifying experience. After snapping at Gray about how tired I was of being used to put the affirmative action seal of approval on these committees while always being outvoted, I decided that this little chair drama was not worth wasting my energy or nerves on, given the situation at home, so I would go along with the men.

We had a meeting in my office, where we each stated our views on why we should or should not let the department members vote, and then we voted. It was two to one, of course. "Okay," I said, calmly moving on, "let's talk about what procedures we will use to let the department members have a voice" (We eventually decided to let people write letters of support or criticism to the dean if they wished). But Gray wanted to continue to discuss the vote. I didn't have anything else to say on the topic, so I asked the other two members if they wanted to add anything. They didn't, so I again tried to move on. At this point, Gray abruptly stood up, went quickly to my office door, which was open, closed it, and came back to stand menacingly over me, while hissing, "What are you up to?" I was astonished. First of all, I wasn't up to anything except trying to complete the chair selection process with minimum drama and stress. But more important, I had never seen Gray even look angry; now he was acting aggressive at a time when he certainly should have known I was emotionally fragile. Initially, I tried to figure out what he was talking about, but when he, in a totally uncharacteristically hostile tone, insisted that I was up to something, I shocked all three of us by suddenly bursting into tears.

Gray immediately returned to his old mousy "I'm the nicest guy on earth" personality, which infuriated me, but the German professor's response was even more peculiar. He first compared me to his wife, suggesting that we were both at an age (early forties) when women became very emotional. Then when I told him that Gray knew that something awful had recently happened to my mother, and I felt he was taking advantage of my weakened emotional state, he started describing atrocities he witnessed during World War II when he was a child living in Germany. Fortunately, my sick sense of humor kicked in at that point. I was sitting there blubbering like a weak kitten, Gray was standing over me, patting my back and cooing some nonsense that made him sound like a character in a sentimental play, while our foreign languages colleague was droning on in his German accent about horrible things that had happened in another country before I was born. Thinking that we all three probably needed to be taken to the nearest mental health facility for observation and diagnosis, I quickly stopped crying and ushered them out of my office.

I also ushered Gray out of my life at that point. Our friendship ended during that emotional scene, and we simply became friendly professional colleagues. But having drawn blood or actually tears, Gray was emboldened. And about a year after he wanted to know what I was up to, he became aggressive toward me again. This time he was defending another department member, a tall white woman who was slightly older and more senior in the department than I. She and I were engaged in a fairly minor dispute at the end of one department meeting. This dispute didn't even rise to the level of a skirmish. We were discussing how many composition classes various faculty members taught (at this point, she was not teaching any classes while trying to dictate what other people should teach). That minor dispute eventually ended with the establishment of the "fair share of composition" rule.

I noticed that when I was talking with the tall woman, Gray was standing nearby, but he was not part of the dispute. So when he was waiting for me in the parking lot a day or two later while I talked to a tutor, I just assumed that he was being collegial and wanted to walk to the department with me. At one point, I tried to signal to him that he shouldn't wait, but he ignored my gesture. When my parking lot conference with the tutor ended, Gray and I started walking toward our building, and he immediately began aggressively attacking me for my comments to Tall Woman. I couldn't believe it. He was in my face over my dispute with another woman? When I realized that this mousy man was again being aggressive toward me, I bellowed: "GRAY, DON'T YOU SAY ANOTHER WORD TO ME!!" I'm sure that everyone within the sound of my voice, stopped and looked to see what was happening, but I was looking at Gray, who turned and practically ran toward the Student Union. I didn't see his face in the department for the rest of that day.

But this second verbal assault sent me to my computer to write still more letters. Not only did the parking lot attack, as I called it, mark the second time that this pathologically non aggressive man was aggressive toward me, but it also marked the second time that Tall Woman created problems between one of the wimps and me. During the first year of Non White's reign as chair, one of the lecturers teaching in the basic writing skills program was pregnant. She needed the money, so she didn't take the whole quarter off. Instead I assigned her to teach lab classes that I thought could be easily covered by substitute teachers. Unlike the situation I would have faced if I had taken Ben's composition class, the people substituting in the pregnant lecturer's labs would not have to grade essays. Just before she left for her maternity leave, I compiled a list of collegial lecturers and four tenured faculty members (counting me) who I thought might agree to substitute teach the labs. We needed either four people to cover each lab or a team of people to cover specific days. I was prepared to take one lab; my former student and future officemate, Lindy O, who was teaching the course version of one lab, took that lab. And another lecturer took two days of the lab for her class; she couldn't handle Fridays. One tenured faculty member, the friendly colleague who discussed computers in my graduate seminar, was willing to cover the fourth lab. So we just needed someone or a group of people to handle the Fridays for the one lab. But because I had included her name on this list of what I called "The Friends of Suzanne," Tall Woman went to Non White, complaining that I was intimidating the lecturers and suggesting that the department could be sued. Now remember that when I was a non-tenured faculty member, I had been asked by Non White to take over Ben's class, and he had used the RTP process to pressure me. But I was intimidating lecturers by asking a whole group of them if a few of them were willing to volunteer to cover easy to teach labs? I had chosen the four tenured faculty members (Charlie Blank was the fourth one) because they were composition/rhetoric specialists and because they had released time (unlike me when I was pressured to take a fourth class). Tall Woman was even then not teaching any classes. After some ugly moments between Non White and me, I sent out a second letter, telling everyone that it was illegal for us to ask them to teach extra units without pay, so we would have to let the administrators find substitutes for the labs. The result was that the department had to pay lecturers, including Lindy O, who would have done it free, to cover those labs. Friendly Colleague, who is Mexican American, and I were certainly not covering a lab free while the white woman who wasn't teaching at all walked around acting as if she had been mistreated because she was asked to volunteer to help cover classes for another woman. By the way, the lecturers appreciated the fact that some tenured faculty might be willing to join with them to help a lecturer. It was the kind of thing that had been done in the past to help tenured faculty who were ill, and somehow it didn't seem illegal then.

I set both Tall Woman and Gray straight in my letters, calling Tall Woman on her use of men to fight her battles and telling Gray that I never saw him be even mildly aggressive toward anyone else in the department. I mentioned that I had seen other men in the department verbally attack him, and he never returned fire. In fact, I even defended him a couple of times. I chose not to involve the chair or the dean in this little dispute and was able to move past it fairly quickly. What helped me forget my pain was seeing a 5' tall Latino male Spanish professor verbally smack down the 5'11" Gray in our next department meeting. Gray was trying to prove to me that he would take on a man by asking Superfly, who was the chair, a series of tough questions. Of course, he was asking them in his usual soft-spoken, mild-mannered way instead of in the hostile tone he had used with me. Still Superfly was becoming rattled until Tiny Spanish Professor snarled at Gray, saying something like, "Shut up, Gray! I'm sick of you." Gray didn't say another word, and I was delighted. It was one of my favorite moments in a department meeting.

I may have moved past that incident too fast, however, because a few years later, in what was definitely one of my most foolish decisions, I agreed to be Gray's assistant chair. I still have trouble figuring out why that happened, but it is no surprise that our attempt to work together ended badly. It started with my trying to recruit Gray to be the assistant chair when Charlie Blank resigned as chair. I was hoping that Jerry would be chair because he was really good with people although not as good with details. Gray had been Non White's assistant chair and seemed to enjoy writing reports and doing other tasks that I assumed Jerry would not want to do. Gray reacted tepidly to my suggestion, but he didn't reject the idea. Unfortunately, Jerry, who was planning to retire soon, was not interested in being chair. At that point, Non White again spoke for Gray, telling me that Gray was hurt that no one had asked him to be chair. Of course, Gray could have just volunteered to be chair as Superfly had, but being a pathetic wimp, he wanted to be asked. Since I opened my big mouth and asked him to be assistant chair, which I guess hurt his little feelings, I felt obligated to ask him if he wanted to be chair. Ten years earlier I wouldn't have felt that way, but after fifteen years at Cal Poly (and thirty-four years in white institutions), I could be made to believe that I needed to make a white man who had verbally attacked me when I was most vulnerable feel better. So I asked Gray if he wanted to be chair, and after pretending to think about it, he said that he would do it for the department, and then I nominated him to be chair in a department meeting.

I guess the fact that I nominated him to be chair put me at the top of his list of candidates for assistant chair. When he came to my office to ask me if I would be the assistant chair, the conversation went something like this:

GRAY: I would like you to be my assistant chair if you would be kind enough to accept the job.

ME: (shocked) Why?

GRAY: (hesitant and nervous) Well, we work well together. We get along.

ME: (even more shocked) No we don't. We've had several run-ins.

GRAY: (sighs and looks hurt)

ME: Of course, I've had run-ins with everyone. (not really true, but he looked so pitiful)

GRAY: You don't let people push you around. You know how to take care of yourself. No one will bother you. (also not true, although they were usually worried when they messed with me)

ME: Oh, so you want me to be your enforcer.

GRAY: (laughing) Well, I wouldn't put it that way.

ME: You want me to tell people that they'd better do what you say or they'll hear from me.

GRAY: (still laughing) That would be helpful.

ME: Okay, I can do that.

I'll admit I liked the idea of being Gray's bodyguard/enforcer. I felt he was finally admitting to me and himself that I was the stronger person, the one with the bigger balls. What I didn't think about was that I wouldn't want to enforce Gray's agenda when I didn't support it. And Gray and I were not always on the same side of issues. I also forgot how much I disliked being an administrator. I had resigned as basic writing skills coordinator so I could teach more classes, and now I would be back to teaching only one class per quarter and going to many meetings, which I hated. But most important, I forgot or refused to admit that Gray would be a disaster as chair, and working with him would probably drive me crazy.

The problems started almost immediately. Gray agreed that as assistant chair I could have the same four-day schedule (with Fridays off) that he had when he was Non White's assistant. However, after agreeing to what I'm sure he saw as a demand, he promptly, in his last duties as department scheduler, scheduled me for a composition class that met on Monday, Wednesday, and Friday. So, of course, I had to change my schedule, taking a later than I liked Tuesday/Thursday composition class. Then during the summer, he had been so officious in his dealings with the secretaries that they had all turned on him, and by the time I arrived in the fall, he was scared to ask them to do anything. So he often came to my office with his papers so I could help him sort and organize them. In other words, I had become a well-paid secretary or file clerk, and I'm convinced if I had continued to be his assistant, he would have turned me into a maid. But before that happened, he insulted me by telling me that he couldn't let me have a key to the meeting/copy room that was near my office because the key to that room also opened the department office. I was the assistant chair, but I couldn't have a key to the department office? I, of course, had a flashback to Dr. Bigot at USC and wondered if Gray thought I would steal the computers if he gave me the key. Finally, I received the key, but the insults just kept coming. He couldn't share any confidential information with me because, of course, I might tell the wrong people. Why was I assistant chair, again? Oh, yeah, so I could be his thug.

The main problem with Gray as chair is that he thought that the position would empower him. But he had been in the department for more than twenty years, and everyone, including the secretaries, knew that he was a weak, timid mouse. Besides, the chair of an academic department is not like other bosses or supervisors. With the possible exception of secretaries and student assistants, the chair can't really fire anyone, and he or she is often caught between a pushy, micro-managing college dean or university president and rebellious department members. In fact, if the chair becomes too drunk with power, the department members, especially in our dysfunctional department, will fire his ass. So Gray was a weak man in a powerless position, wanting to believe, and wanting everyone else to believe, that he was suddenly powerful.

In the meantime, I had made myself sick. I was sick partly because I was so disgusted with myself for agreeing to work with, or really for, this wimp. But I had also eaten badly for many years, and my bad habits finally ruined my digestive system. Starting in the fall of 1995, I had so much trouble trying to eat and digest food that I lost eighty pounds in less than a year. When I saw that my health was deteriorating, I decided that my first step toward recovery would be to resign as assistant chair. I would finish the year but let Gray know I was leaving, early enough for him to find a replacement. I decided to blame my health for the resignation and not tell him all the reasons why he and I could not work together. I wanted to tell him that he needed a student assistant, not an assistant chair, but I didn't. I simply said that I had a stress-related illness and thought being in the classroom would be less stressful for me.

Apparently, Gray worried that he would be blamed for my resignation. He clearly was also concerned that I might collect released time for the rest of the year (I told him I was resigning early in Winter Quarter) and do no work. So he decided to force me to leave the position in Spring Quarter. A day after our cordial discussion of my resignation, when I made it clear that I was really not well and when my illness was visible in my changing physique, he came into my office late in the afternoon on the pretense of asking me to do a last-minute task. I had also made it clear during our meeting that I needed to eliminate stress, so, of course, he knew that I would not want to rush home to complete a last-minute job. I noticed that his hand was shaking, but I just assumed that he was nervous about asking me to do something; usually I assigned myself tasks by volunteering to handle whatever we found that needed to be done when we were sorting his papers. When I told him that I was grading papers for my class and couldn't handle the job that night, he kept talking and eventually shouted angrily at me. Then I knew why he was shaking. He had planned to piss me off. He knew that his raised voice would enrage me. As soon as I exploded, he tried to rush me over to the dean's office, I assumed so that he could show her that I was a crazy black woman, and that's why we couldn't get along. But I told him that I would talk to the dean when I calmed down. His response was, "That will be bad for the department." When he couldn't explain why my talking to the dean after I was calm was worse for the department than my talking to her in a state of rage, bordering on hysteria, I advised him to get his ass out of my office. He took my advice.

Before I went to the dean, Gray and I had another meeting. But this time I knew what his agenda was. As he tried to push my buttons, making comments that he thought would anger me or cause me to cry, I calmly pushed his. He was one of those whites who hated to hear any discussion of race, so when he asked me about my mental state, knowing that his attempt to suggest that I was crazy would anger me, I started talking about all of the black people on campus who had died. Three black men, one of them my age, had recently died while still in their forties. I told him that I understood how working with white folks could send black people to an early grave. We went back and forth like that for several minutes until he finally said in a sentence that I will never forget and in a tone that made me want to knock him out: "I want you back in the classroom." Was I supposed to say, "Yes, Master," to that command. I responded, "I could tell you where I want you, but I won't" and left the room. Soon I had written another letter, copying in the dean and the union representative. But I was finished with him, finished with the assistant chair position, and happy to return to the classroom.

I had one more encounter with Gray, however, before I went home for the summer. I had to meet with him, the dean, and Other Black in my role as chair of the RTP committee. It was their final attempt to put a negative evaluation in Other Black's file. That meeting was probably Other Black's and my finest hour as a defense team. We were not intimidated; we would not be moved. But after we all settled on putting the positive evaluation written by one of the white male members of the RTP committee into Other Black's personnel file, the two white folks insisted that I leave the dean's office because there was some confidential information that needed to be discussed. Other Black said that she didn't mind if I heard whatever they had to say about her, but Gray refused to discuss this "confidential" information with me in the room. I knew what was going on, of course. He didn't like the two against two set up. He wanted to attack Other Black without my being there to defend her. Other Black claimed that as soon as I left, Gray attacked her viciously, saying that he wanted her out of his department. Other Black is not the most reliable source, but I believe her description of this attack because it sounds very much like his tone during our last confrontation. When I asked what the dean said while he was attacking her, Other Black claimed that she said mildly, "Now, Gray, calm down."

During the summer my health continued to deteriorate, and I lost so much weight that by the time school started in the fall, I was thinner than I was when I graduated from high school. The response of most people to my greatly reduced frame, even when they didn't know me when I was larger, was compassion and concern. When I went to the optometrist's office to have my new glasses adjusted to fit my thinner face, for instance, two women who looked to be at least a decade older than I stood up and tried to give me one of their seats. I guess they thought I might faint. When Ben, who obviously is not the most tactful person in the world, first saw me in the fall, he started to walk by without speaking, then recognizing my voice, stopped, stared, and asked if I were anorexic. Still, he looked very concerned about my health. Here is how Gray responded: He saw me enter the auditorium for the beginning of the year College of Arts meeting, rushed over to me, and gripped my arm forcefully and tightly. Now, if he had been one of the cave men, I would have thought nothing of his response. I would have just assumed that he was unaware of his strength and maybe didn't even notice my more delicate physique. But Gray had never grabbed my arm before. Clearly his instinctive response to my weakened condition was to show his physical strength. I don't remember what he said in his soft voice, but his strong, tight grip and hard, mean eyes said all that I needed to know. He was responding like a bully, the kind of bully who would enjoy seeing a movie about a crazy man torturing a vulnerable woman.

Gray's short reign (two years) as a power-hungry, bullying chair would soon end, however, because he made the mistake of attacking some of the white female faculty members. He had problems with all four of the nonwhite women on the tenure track, but when he went after the whites, one of them formed a coalition of three other women (I was the only nonwhite member of the group) to document Gray's abuses (what I called his "Uncivil Acts") and to confer with the dean. After conferring separately with each woman and the dean (I brought the Mexican American male union representative with me to prevent the problem that Other Black faced when I left her alone with those two white folks), Gray agreed to several changes in his administration. However, a couple of the changes affected two other guys in the department. Some of the women were bothered by the fact that Student Screwer had become assistant chair three years after his problem with female students. We thought his promotion to a position of responsibility in the department so soon after his demotion for mistreatment of female students showed a lack of respect for women. And I complained that White had created a new position for himself, the literature coordinator, that allowed him to assign courses to the other literature faculty. He was using that position to prevent me from teaching two upper-division undergraduate 20th Century American Literature courses. Gray was willing to sacrifice those two guys, his allies, to hang on to his job.

But something happened during the summer. Probably White told him that he needed to fight the changes. Not having the courage to take on the dean and the four women, Gray resigned as chair, took an unpaid leave in the fall, leaving behind a 19th Century British Literature course that no one else either could or wanted to teach, and flew to Italy. So we were left without a chair or a teacher for a course taken almost solely by English majors. Yet, less than two years later, after he returned to campus with his tail between his legs, the dean gave Gray another position of responsibility, college advisor, that gave him the opportunity once again to torment me. He didn't even wait until he was officially in the position to come after me.

At the time I was serving as advisor not only for graduate and ILE students, but also for undergraduate English majors. I was the only woman and the only nonwhite faculty member in that position at that time. Each spring the department gives out awards to graduating seniors (and graduate students) who have the highest grade point averages. We always have a meeting to discuss how many and which students should receive those awards. During the Spring Quarter, when Gray was being trained by the outgoing college advisor to take her position, I raised a question at the student awards meeting about a black female student who was one of my advisees. She had made an "A" in one of my courses, and I knew that she had a fairly high GPA, so I wondered what it was and how it measured against the GPAs of the students who were going to be recognized at the awards ceremony. White, who was conducting the meeting, told me the student's GPA and commented that he thought she was a really good student. Since her GPA was lower than those of the students receiving the awards, I shrugged and forgot about it. I wasn't going to make the case that we should include a few more students in the ceremony so the black woman could receive an award.

But that same day, a few hours after the meeting, I received a brief letter from Gray in his not yet official capacity as college academic advisor, telling me that I had made a mistake on a petition that I had signed "coincidentally" for that same student.

Now his note about the mistake was polite; I had no reason to be angry at what he said. But it was clear that he was trying to get under my skin. There was no reason, first of all, to write a note. He could have said something to me since we had never stopped speaking to each other, or he could have just corrected the mistake and waited to see if I consistently made it before drawing it to my attention. He was trying to piss me off because he probably thought I was being pushy or maybe trying to play the race card during the department meeting.

I couldn't believe that the dean, who surely knew that I would have to deal with Gray in my various advising positions, would again put him in a position of power, specifically power over me. So I wrote another letter, which ultimately led to the dean, joining with White and Non White, to kill the ILE program, "coincidentally" just as the man who had been the co-coordinator of the program was retiring, and a woman was preparing to take his place. I was livid at first, and then I realized that this vindictive act had freed me. In fact, recognizing the advantage of losing the one nice perk that I had, an advising position that came with released time, was the first time (years before that final department meeting) that I shouted "free at last" after quoting Kris Kristofferson's famous lyric: "Freedom means having nothing left to lose." I could return to the classroom full time, and since I was not interested in earning merit salary pay, I would simply do what I wanted to do as service--advise graduate students, serve on the graduate and basic writing skills committees--and turn down any work I didn't want to do. When White and Non White tried to lure me back onto the released time gravy train (possibly because they were worried that my calm demeanor meant I was planning a lawsuit), I turned down that job. "I just want to teach," I said, the way Garbo might have said that she wanted to be alone.

I shouldn't have been surprised that the dean rewarded Gray while punishing me. Gray's "suck up and beat down" approach to relationships made him popular with administrators. He would never snap at an administrator or question her judgment. I, on the other hand, had a different approach, call it "reach down to raise up and reach up to knock down." I was much more likely to confront an administrator than a lecturer, a member of the staff, or a student. When I wrote the letter to the dean, I didn't use the whining tone of a victim. Instead I probably sounded as if I were scolding her. I didn't ask her if she had lost her mind, but I did let her know that I thought she might need her memory refreshed. And, of course, the fact that I had stood with Other Black against the dean and Gray when they tried to push her out of the department didn't help my cause.

In fact, the dean had shown me at the end of the summer when Gray fled the country that she was not on my side. When Smart Woman, who was one of the three white women who had joined me in complaining about Gray's behavior, called me with what she thought was the good news of his resignation, my red light started blinking. "Let's not celebrate until we find out who's taking his place," I cautioned. It turned out that no one wanted to take his place. Everyone saw the department chair's job as toxic. So the dean came up with the solution of making one department committee (I think it was called "the planning and budget" committee) an executive committee that would run the department. (We soon started calling them "the couch "). But guess who was on this committee? Non White, who had already been chair for four years and assistant chair for eight, White, who had been chair for eight years and assistant chair for two (during Superfly's reign as chair), and Student Screwer, who was the current assistant chair. So two of the men who were supposed to be losing their positions of power—White and Screwer—were now elevated to some kind of super committee that would have more power.

I was sufficiently disturbed by this strange turn of events to call the dean to express my concerns. Despite being against her attempt to fire Other Black, I didn't see the dean as an enemy at that point. I had even told her that I liked the fact that she was a strong woman, not scared of the men. And when the men, especially White, were going after her in the meeting during the summer, I had come to her defense. The dean listened to my concerns, told me to call her if I had more concerns, and then told me to tell Other Black to call if she had any concerns (If I had been thinking clearly, my racist radar would have sounded loudly at that point since Other Black was not part of the coalition of women who had talked to her about their problems with Gray).

I felt better after our conversation, but when I attended the College of Arts meeting a few weeks later, the dean introduced the executive committee and acted as if they had saved the department by agreeing to run it in lieu of a chair. Then she came to our first department meeting of the year and announced that White would be designated the chair, although the committee would make all of the decisions. In other words, White would be the chair again, but this time he could hide all his dirty deeds behind a committee. Well played, white woman! She found out what I didn't want and gave it to me. My only consolation was that some of the foreign languages faculty members were even more pissed than I was.

When I met with the dean, Gray, and Other Black the year before the dean made White the chair, I told her that there were protected people in the university, but those people were definitely not black women. I guess she wanted to show me that I was right. I never expected the dean or any woman with power to defend every woman who came to her whining about some man who did her wrong, nor did I need her to be on my side. However, Gray had problems with seven of the eleven tenured or tenure-track women in the EFL department. One of the four women that he didn't have problems with was, in fact, working primarily in the dean's office. And Other Black is not the only woman who claimed that Gray attacked her in front of the dean. Smart Woman, a more reliable witness, also said that he was verbally abusive toward her while the dean watched. Yet he was rewarded with another position in the college. Of course, inevitably, his bullying became too much, and as people (I assume both men and women) from other departments complained, the dean eventually had to relieve him of his duties. I tried not to look smug when I was told as department scheduler that he needed to be given another class to teach.

The dean's actions show another problem that women face in these often too patriarchal and white institutions. We don't support each other. Too often women, whatever their race, have the same problem with each other that Other Black had with me. They are competitive. I remember discussing the outcome of the vote for the all-male chair search committee with the female linguist who was one of the nominees for the committee and was the female friend who often hung out with Gray and me during the early eighties. I asked her if she had been hurt by the snub. She thought for a minute, and I guess decided to tell the truth. She said that she would have been more upset if I had won, and she hadn't. That seemed amazing to me; it would bother her more to have me win than to have no woman win? I frankly would have preferred that she won and would have understood that they chose her because she was perceived as less aggressive. Having one of the women win would have bothered me less than having an all-male committee.

Kentuckian's Wife was what I call a born-again feminist. Because she came of age in the fifties, she had spent her early adulthood as a Catholic wife and mother of four. I assume that she completed college before she had her children, but she returned to school after the children were teenagers to earn her Ph.D. When I met her, she was a radical Marxist feminist. She was the kind of liberal professor who gives conservatives nightmares because, unlike most of us, she actually <u>was</u> trying to convert students to her way of thinking, and she wasn't above trying to convert colleagues as well. Yet at some point after that first chair fight, she started worrying about why the men seemed to hate her more than they did me.

At first, it didn't occur to me to wonder why she was so worried about the men's preferring me to her. Instead I tried to explain their attitude. I suggested first that they may have thought that she was radicalizing Smart Woman and me. I pointed out that she had joined the faculty after we did, and maybe they wanted to believe that we were "good girls" until she arrived. I didn't mention that they may have assumed she was influencing us instead of the other way around because she was older than we were and much more vocal about her feminism. I also suggested that they probably didn't expect me to fit into the department because of my race (again, I didn't mention age; I could be tactful when I wanted to be), but they expected her to be more traditional and conventional.

But Kentuckian's Wife figured out the real reason why the men preferred me. I had a good sense of humor, and she didn't. So she said to me a few days after the first discussion, "Mary, they don't take you seriously." At that point I was on to Kentuckian's Wife. She wanted me to stop joking and having fun so the men would hate me as much as they did her. That would make her feel better, the way my losing the chair search nomination made my linguist friend feel better. I let Kentuckian's wife know that I knew what she was trying to pull. I gave her one of my "white woman, please" looks and said, "I don't take myself seriously. That has been the key to my survival." She never bothered me about the men again.

Being in the office with Kentuckian's Wife was, however, helpful to me in one way. It made me aware how sexism affected the way students viewed me. When I shared an office with a much older white man, so many students assumed that I was his secretary that I considered putting up a sign under my name plate, saying "Not the Secretary." Because I was young, black, and female, I didn't know which of those identity markers made students assume that I was not a professor, but the older white man's secretary. When I shared the office with the fourteen years older white woman, I knew it was gender because no one ever assumed that I was her secretary. Instead several students assumed that I was the secretary of my white male next door neighbors, Superfly and Tall Texan. Obviously they felt that male faculty members had secretaries while females were more likely to <u>be</u> secretaries.

Students were also more likely to assume that men had Ph.D.'s. Some women (and men) made sure that students knew that they were to be called Doctor. But when I entered the classroom on the first day, I simply wrote my last name on the board and let them pick a title. They could call me "Doctor," "Professor," "Ms.," "Miss," and even "Mrs." I really didn't care, so long as they didn't call me "Mary." When one female student in a composition class, assuming that I was a different kind of woman, complained about female professors who insisted on being called Doctor, I quickly calmed her down by pointing out that men don't usually have to insist. They are automatically called "Doctor." Composition students were especially likely to assume that a female professor did not have the Ph.D. because so many of those classes were taught by female lecturers, who often had only M.A.'s. But even young looking men teaching composition were more likely to be called "Doctor" than older female full professors. Every now and then, especially when I was younger, some slightly older man asked if I were "Miss" or "Mrs." as if there weren't other options. That's when I would channel Sidney Poitier from <u>In the Heat of the Night</u>

("They call me <u>Mister</u> Tibbs"). "I'm <u>Doctor</u> Sisney," I would say sternly, and usually the foolish older man dropped my class.

When former students became lecturers, they often had trouble transitioning from calling their former professors "Doctor" to using first names. I occasionally realized that a former student who had been a lecturer for years was still calling me "Dr. Sisney" and suggested that he or she switch to the more collegial "Mary." When these former students said that they had trouble calling me by my first name, I appreciated that reaction because I saw it as a sign of respect. But I also didn't mind the former students who transitioned smoothly into calling me by my first name because (especially in my early years) they were often my contemporaries, and I'm a fairly informal teacher and person.

However, as I aged, I became suspicious of a certain kind of former student, usually a young white male, who seemed too eager to start "Marying" me, as I called it. One young white male, in particular, got on my last nerve with his need to become my equal. This young man, while fun and sweet, was not a particularly good student. In fact, he is the only thesis writer of the many that I directed who wrote a complete draft of his thesis and couldn't rewrite it well enough to create an acceptable final draft. But I was patient with him when he decided to switch to the exam, using as his main text the Morrison novel, <u>Song of Solomon</u>, which was the focus of the thesis. After he had passed the M.A. exam and was graduating, thanks to my considerable help (to be fair, he thanked me with a nice department store gift card), he was sitting in my office one day just chatting and said, "Now we are colleagues, and I can call you Mary" as if that were the main reason he wanted to earn his M.A. I calmly explained to him that he was not really my colleague (usually I said the opposite to new graduates planning to teach in the department) in the way my former student, Don K, who was a tenured professor, was because he was going to be a lecturer, teaching composition, not a professor teaching the courses that I taught.

You would think Young White Male would take the hint. But he wasn't one of the smarter graduate students. So, when I entered the room where we were having our first department meeting in the fall, Young White Male said quietly, but loudly enough for me to hear, "Hi, Mary." I asked, again in my best Sidney Poitier impression, "Did I give you permission to call me by my first name?" I'm sure that he could tell by my facial expression that I was not teasing, and I was definitely not amused. Unfortunately, a fake looking young white woman, who for some reason had never taken me as a professor, overheard this conversation and clearly decided that I was one of those women who insisted on being called "Doctor." I was not, but I was a woman who insisted on being respected. And, of course, the fact that this white man was young enough to be my son set off my racism radar. I remembered how Mrs. R's children, who were three and six when I first met them, called my mother "Catherine" while both my mother and I called their mother "Mrs. R," even though she was a few years younger than my mother. I knew, even at fourteen, that the white children's use of my mother's first name was wrong and disrespectful. But we were maids in the twentieth century. As a professor in the twenty-first century, I had earned and deserved respect, and no young white man was going to take it away from me because he wanted to pretend we were colleagues.

I remember explaining to Number 1 Linguist once why a woman's work in the department was harder than a man's. We had to work harder to gain respect that men were automatically granted just because of their gender. Number 1 Linguist, who saw himself as something of a mentor to me in my early years in the department, warned me after one early battle I had won that I should avoid most political battles so that I wouldn't be seen as a troublemaker. It seemed like good advice at the time. But later I realized that Number 1 Linguist didn't take his own advice. He was involved in quite a few battles himself, although he sometimes played a behind-the-scenes role. Of course, a man was less likely to be criticized for battling than was a woman. And there was another problem with his advice. Women were more likely to have to fight to be treated fairly, so it was much harder for them to stay out of battles.

In our department, women seemed to have only two paths to follow when dealing with department politics. The easier path was for women to attach themselves to one or more men who could protect them, as Tall Woman did with the wimps. The relationship between these women and their protective men could be romantic or just collegial; sometimes those relationships were scandalous because the romantic partners were married to other people. The other path was for women to fight their own battles, joining the men when they were on the same side, or joining the right men in a battle against the wrong men. Of course, these women were much more likely to anger the men, and if the men were wimps, the women had to deal with their petty retaliations.

The independent fighters were also more likely to be called bitches. I chose the bitch route, and I have no regrets.

CHAPTER SIX
Making Whoopi

I might have had an easier time in the department if I had accepted an offer that Gray made in the early eighties. It was, however, an offer that I had no trouble refusing. For humorous effect, I called it a marriage proposal, but it was more like a business proposition. When I was still in my Pomona apartment and Gray lived in a house he was buying in another part of town, he proposed that we marry, pointing out that it would be a great tax break. My horrified response was, "But, Gray, we would have to live together." And I wondered why the man wanted to attack me whenever I was vulnerable?

But Gray shouldn't have felt hurt by my refusal to consider living with him. I didn't want to live with anyone, male, female, black, white, or gray. In fact, Gray, I suspect prompted by my competitive linguist friend, later made another suggestion. He thought that we two women should buy a house together. Again,

I quickly dismissed that idea. If I couldn't afford to buy a house on my own, something he had done, I preferred living in an apartment.

When I told the competitive linguist about the Gray marriage proposal, she wondered why he didn't approach her with the same offer. I suggested that he knew that she would take his offer and expect to consummate the marriage. He knew I wasn't interested in him as a sexual partner, and I don't think anyone believed that Gray wanted to have sex with a woman. By the time of Gray's proposal, I was only slightly more interested in having sex with a man than he was with a woman. I didn't know it at that point, but I had already (I was in my early thirties) passed my sexual peak. And even when I was at my sexual peak, in my mid to late twenties, I wasn't interested in white men.

During the fifties and early sixties, most people seeing a single female teacher or professor like me assumed that she was fairly chaste, not necessarily a nun, but probably not really hot to trot. After all, the old maid school teacher is a stock character in American literature and culture. Yet students who bothered to think about my life off campus (and I hope most of them didn't) seemed to think I was having hot sex. Some thought I was a lesbian; others thought I was having affairs with one or more of the white male faculty. And still others just wanted to know what I was doing because they knew I was doing something wild. As one black female graduate student put it, they wanted to look under my dress to see what was going on under there.

I assumed that my race was the reason that my mostly non-black students were so fascinated by my non-existent, almost never existed love life. But during my last quarter of teaching at Cal Poly, I discovered that my generation might have also made them assume that I was leading a wild social life. I was teaching Sherman Alexie's story about the only Indian at Woodstock who heard Jimi Hendrix play (the title of the story is longer than that clause) and commenting on Hendrix's version of "The Star-Spangled Banner." I made the point that I had made in earlier classes, when I taught the story, about needing to be high to appreciate Hendrix's rendition of the national anthem. I went on to say that I had never been high. As I continued to discuss the story, I noticed two young women sitting across from me, engaged in a quiet but animated conversation. Since other students had objected to my critique of Hendrix, I thought that they were Hendrix fans and maybe would voice a different opinion. One of them was a fairly bold young woman, so I asked her if she wanted to say something. She said something like, "we can't believe that you went through the sixties without getting high." Oh.

As I thought about what the young lady said, I revised my statement slightly. I may have gotten a little high, not during the sixties, but during the seventies, because I was in the room where pot was being smoked, but unlike Clinton, I may have inhaled without ever smoking. I passed the joint from one person to another, but I didn't take a hit (or whatever the pot smokers call it). I didn't explain that my roommate during my first two or three weeks at USC smoked pot every night to put herself to sleep and that I fell asleep almost as quickly as she did. I also didn't tell them that I went to a party at the home of one of the other young female faculty members at Tufts (this was in 1980) and was slightly amused when she and her husband whipped out a joint and started passing it around. I wondered how the older man who had driven me and his wife, the other thirty-year-old new faculty member, to the party would react. He was a professor at Brandeis. On the ride back to my apartment, I found out that he and his wife were not happy. I was not shocked by the pot smoking because I had been to a few USC graduate student parties where joints were passed. But I agreed with my fellow non-pot smokers that the hostess should have checked with us and not assumed that we would be okay with their engaging in illegal activity.

If any of you readers are still waiting for that other kind of redlight, blues-singing woman to show up and start partying, forget it. I'm not that kind of woman. (And if you are reading this chapter first because it sounded more titillating than the others, shame on you. Go back to the beginning of the book. You might learn something.) I am not, nor have I ever been, Bessie Smith, singing about how some man or woman done me wrong, while drinking bootleg liquor. Nor am I one of those pot-smoking, acid-dropping, booze-drinking, free-loving, rolling-naked-in-the-mud, hippie, yippie, soon-to-be yuppie baby boomers. Although I was twenty the summer of Woodstock, I was nowhere near that field where Jimi Hendrix was playing, either geographically or emotionally. I was having some fun with people my age since that was my first summer working in the Black House, but I was just one summer removed from riding with four middle-aged, relatively conservative black folks to Fort Sheridan, where I worked with people not at all interested in protesting the Vietnam War. In fact, the year before Woodstock, I rode back and forth to my summer job at the military base, listening to those middle-aged black folks commenting on how they either did or did not feel sorry for my mostly white contemporaries being tear gassed by the original Mayor Daley's goons (Despite my four summers working at a military base, I was still sixties enough to have occasionally called cops "pigs" back in the day) during the 1968 Democratic National Convention. One motherly woman felt sorry for the rich white kids because she thought they weren't used to being beaten and gassed like black folks. But the two black men had no sympathy for those rich white punks who needed to get jobs or get drafted so they could learn some respect for themselves and their country. As usual I said nothing, but I sympathized more with the black men's position; let the white youth take a beating for a change. What were they fighting for anyway? And for whom? Certainly not for me. I actually liked Johnson, who was crudely amusing and, more important, responsible for the Youth Opportunity Program and the Civil Rights Act. At that point in my life, I didn't give a shit about peace, love, and understanding. I was too worried about education, security, and equality.

I don't think about my baby boomer identity as often as I do my race and gender, but clearly baby boomers have ruled the world for a long time, and the other generations (like my students) think they know who we are. Oprah Winfrey and Whoopi Goldberg are the two most well-known black female baby boomers. (I don't know who their white male counterparts might be, maybe George W. Bush and Bill Clinton, or Jay Leno and David Letterman, or one of those four and Bruce Springsteen.) Like me, both of them like to read, and certainly they have been extremely successful in the still mostly white entertainment world. When Oprah and I were both overweight, I clearly reminded some people of her. One young woman in a basic writing skills class would stare up at me adoringly as I made some wise woman comment about life and say, "That's what Oprah says." She talked about Oprah so much that when she didn't do well on a reading quiz, I wrote on her paper that she needed to stop watching Oprah and read her texts. Another person, a young man who was clearly not an Oprah fan, taunted me for my robust frame one day by yelling, "Hey, Oprah!" at me as I was walking, or maybe rolling, down the street.

However, even though Oprah has said several times that she sees herself as a teacher, and she and I share southern roots, a dysfunctional family (although her father seemed to be the more responsible parent), and some early years spent living with our maternal grandmothers, I think I have more in common with Whoopi. First of all, Whoopi is the funnier of the two, and I'm an amateur comedian. Also, although I have had periods in my life when I dressed very fashionably (the year I taught high school, for instance), like Whoopi, I'm not nor have I ever been into makeup. And while Oprah is the woman of a thousand hairdos, Whoopi and I have had the same basic hairdo for decades. I don't know when Whoopi started wearing braids, but I switched from a hot combed June Allyson do to an Afro in 1970 and never went back to the hot comb or the perm. During the greasy Jeri curl years of the early eighties, I kept my wild and woolly Afro. It's shorter and neater now, but it's still a natural fro. Our refusal to change our hairstyle with the changing times reflects what I think most separates Whoopi and me from Oprah. Whereas Oprah clearly worries about what people think of her, Whoopi and I are less concerned with public opinion. Oh, yeah, Whoopi does maybe protest a bit too much when she thinks she's not properly respected for having won the Oscar, but she doesn't seem to care what people think of her hair, her clothes, and her language. She also doesn't mind being on the wrong side of an issue, especially when defending a friend, like the seemingly pretty despicable Mel Gibson. In other words, while Oprah is the ultimate insider, following and sometimes even starting fads, Whoopi, like me, is an outsider who wears and says what she wants. When she's sitting with the other four women on "The View," she's the one who seems not to belong. Sherri, the other black woman, like Star before her, seems to fit in with the white women better than Whoopi does.

Whoopi the comedian, for instance, has offended people with her potty mouth. She offended some Democrats during a 2004 fundraising event with her sexual word play on then President Bush's name. Of course, Oprah is not prudish when discussing sex, as someone pointed out when one of the radio bad boys (probably Howard Stern) was criticized for being too crude. "What about Oprah?" several critics asked, "Look at what she talks about on her show." She's just a little more careful than Whoopi. Interestingly, although I too might be a little more careful and less crude than Whoopi, I'm equally willing to have verbal fun with sex. And maybe that's another reason why my students assumed that I was a hot mama off campus. I can spot a phallic symbol from a mile away, and some of my favorite puns are double-entendres. Once one of the male professors, teasing me about something I had done, suggested that I might be black balled. Of course, the Whoopi in me couldn't let that sexual and racial pun pass. Without hesitating, I said, "I've been blackballed before, and I kind of liked it." My male colleague, one of the cave men, loved that joke.

Probably one reason we black female baby boomers can discuss sex so freely, even when at least one of us is not so freely enjoying it, is that we came of age just when censorship rules were being challenged and overturned. I remember reading James Baldwin's <u>Another Country</u> and one of Henry Miller's novels for the dirty parts when I was in high school. And just as I started going to the movies regularly, actors and actresses started taking off their clothes. I was seeing movies like the Oscar winning <u>Midnight Cowboy</u> (before he became a Republican and Angelina Jolie's often estranged father, Jon Voight played a wannabe male prostitute in that movie) and another movie, called I believe "That Cold Day in the Park," starring Sandy Dennis and featuring an unknown male actor who walked around naked. The only nude scene that shocked me was the wrestling scene in the movie version of DH Lawrence's <u>Women in Love</u>. It's one thing to see mostly the rear end of a nude white man walking around; it's another thing to see two frontally nude white men bouncing around and wrestling each other. But I quickly overcame my shock. Women who came of age in the late sixties and early seventies couldn't really afford to be too prudish. And we didn't have to go to the movies to see flesh or hear risqué humor.

Before "Saturday Night Live," there was "Laugh-In" giving television censors fits.

Of course, there were still sexual lines that couldn't be crossed in the sixties and seventies, especially on television. Sexual relations between blacks and whites happened in the movies, but I remember the fuss that was made when the black woman (Lenny Kravitz's mother) and her white husband kissed on "The Jeffersons." And it took years for a same sex kiss to happen. Homosexuality may still be dangerous territory today. Many people, even young people, still feel uneasy when gay sex is discussed. I encountered this problem in my 200-level black literature class when at one point I taught Baldwin's <u>Go Tell It on the Mountain</u>, Walker's <u>The Color Purple</u>, and Naylor's <u>Women of Brewster Place</u>. That was too much gay sex, especially for the young men in the class. As I said to a graduate seminar that I was teaching during Fall Quarter, 2008, the day after California helped elect the first black President and on the same day passed a very anti-gay proposition, "One thing we can say about black people is they are very homophobic."

Probably not so much because of my choice of texts to teach as because of my very husky, Whoopish voice, the missing make-up, and the don't-mess-with-me attitude more associated with men, some people suspected I was gay. I have lots of stories about telephone conversations where people assumed I was a man and then changed their attitude when they discovered I was a woman. In fact, one reason that I know for sure, as Oprah might say, that it is a man's world is the way I'm treated when I talk on the telephone to someone who thinks I'm a man and how that treatment changes when I give my first name and become a woman. I've heard respectful "yes sir's" turn into condescending "dear's" when that happens. But my favorite gender bending conversation happened back in the eighties when a woman tried to sell me some magazines. She kept offering me magazines for which I already had a subscription or that I would never read. I didn't really notice that she was pushing men's magazines in addition to the usual popular ones (Time, Newsweek, People), so I didn't realize that she thought I was a man. Finally, she mentioned Tennis. I said, "Oh, yeah, I really like tennis; I watch it all the time. I'll try that one." When the young lady heard that my name was Mary, she said in a rather nasty tone, "You sound like a tennis player." I knew what she meant. This conversation happened a few months after the then married Billie Jean King admitted to having an affair with a woman.

Actually, what the obviously stupid magazine saleslady didn't know is that my love of tennis started with a brief crush on a man. Back in 1975, I was watching the news and not paying much attention to the sports segment when I caught a glimpse of a handsome black man with a big Afro, who threw up his fist as he walked to the net to shake hands with Jimmy Connors, whom he had just beaten at Wimbledon. The handsome black man was, of course, the late, great Arthur Ashe. By the time I figured out that Arthur wasn't really the badass black militant that I thought he was and that he was pretty much the only black person playing tennis at that point, I was hooked on the game and the many personalities, including the later revealed to be lesbians, Billie Jean and Martina. My crush on Arthur soon turned to respect and admiration, and I frequently talked about him in my graduate classes when we read August Wilson's <u>Fences</u>. I compared him to Jackie Robinson, who is mentioned in the play, pointing out that they both had the appropriate personalities to integrate their sports. I thought of Arthur again recently when Tiger Woods was having his problems with sex. I believe if the dignified, gracious and classy Mr. Ashe had lived and been around to serve as a role model for Tiger, instead of the bullet head, oversexed basketball players that he hung out with (they know who they are), Tiger might have taken a different route.

But I digress. My love of tennis did have something to do with my sexual orientation; if I weren't heterosexual, I wouldn't have noticed Ashe that evening and maybe never would have fallen in love with tennis. Let me do an Oprah here and state clearly that I am straight. I have never been sexually attracted to a woman. In fact, I'd rather sleep with a white man than with a black woman. If Halle Berry came calling, I would send her away. (I don't think Halle will lose any sleep over that snub since she's now finally given up on her father's race and is enjoying the company of white men.) When I talk about good looking black women, I talk about them as women I would like to resemble. I used to, for instance, try to convince people that I looked a bit like Cicely Tyson. Non White finally shut me up by saying that I looked like Cicely in her role as Miss Jane Pittman, the late years. When one "C-" student told me a few years ago that he really wanted an "A" in my class, I said, "I really want to look like Halle Berry, but it's not going to happen."

I think it interesting that the more feminine Oprah has to spend more time denying that she's gay than does the more stereotypically masculine Whoopi. I guess because Whoopi has been seen with more men (including two famous white actors) than Oprah has, and because Oprah is always with and talking about her "best friend" Gayle, and doesn't mention her tall, good looking best man Stedman as much, people assume that the two women are having sex, and nothing is happening with the man. But people take their gay/straight cues from all kinds of signs. I once was tagged as gay because of one book. Here's how that happened: Soon after I moved into my townhouse, Kentuckian's Wife was going upstairs to see my new desk. She was walking ahead of me, and at the top of the stairs was a small bookcase. Halfway up the stairs, Kentuckian's Wife suddenly stopped. When I asked her what was wrong, she said, "Oh, nothing," quickly and moved on. But she acted rather strange the rest of the time she was in my home and soon left. In conversations after that visit, she made not so subtle comments about some friend she claimed to have who couldn't reveal his sexual orientation. I didn't connect the friend to me until one day when I was walking up the stairs and noticed the book <u>Rubyfruit Jungle</u> prominently displayed on that small bookcase. Could Kentuckian's Wife be so ignorant as to think that because I was reading a book by a lesbian, I was a lesbian? I read books by white people, but I clearly wasn't white. I read books by men, but I wasn't a man. Could a mature woman with a Ph.D. in literature be that naive about sexual orientation? Well, yes, I think she might have been. She probably saw my having a lesbian's book on my book shelf (I had read that book, but there are many books on my book shelves that I haven't read), coupled with my close friendship with Gray, who may have been the closeted gay male friend she was talking about, as enough evidence to convict (since she was clearly troubled by what she thought was my newly discovered sexuality) me of being gay.

Hanging out with someone known to be gay is certainly one cue used to determine whether someone of unknown sexual orientation is gay. At some point during the early nineties, I received signals that some people in the department weren't just guessing that I might be gay but were clearly convinced I was. One graduate student interviewed me for a department publication, and when the interview was over, we started talking about my life in Claremont. I told her that I initially didn't see Claremont as a comfortable place for black folks. She responded that the town might not be friendly to blacks, but at least it was a good place for lesbians to live. She made that comment as if she were saying that was good news for me. I reacted as if she meant it was good news for her. When we each realized that we incorrectly thought the other was gay, the student appeared uncomfortable and said something about her sister and the feminist bookstore down the street from where we were sitting. Unlike Kentuckian's Wife, this woman clearly thought I was an out-of-the-closet lesbian as I certainly would have been had I been gay because, of course, another reason people don't suspect Whoopi of being secretly gay is that they know she wouldn't keep her sexual orientation a secret since she doesn't need to be seen as "normal." She doesn't care what people say. Neither do I, although I don't appreciate nasty smear campaigns.

225

When I realized that some long-term colleagues seemed suddenly to believe I was gay, I tried to think of a reason for this change of view. I hadn't changed my style, and I wasn't hanging out with a lesbian at that point. Then I remembered my graduate school friend from Boston who told me, just before she left USC, stopping first at a mental hospital and then transferring to the folklore department at UCLA, that she "used to be queer." She was still queer, but she hadn't been with anyone during the time I knew her. Once I remembered my friendship with her, I knew who had been spreading rumors that I was gay--Student Screwer. It didn't take me long to confirm my theory by introducing the topic of gay people in front of Screwer and one of the colleagues who had thrown out some "it's too bad that gay people can't be out of the closet" hints at me. It's too bad that white folks can't hide their embarrassment because they both showed me through their facial expressions that they had been discussing my sexual orientation.

Student Screwer didn't really know my Boston friend because he had just arrived on campus when she had her breakdown and left early in the fall semester. Yet he clearly knew gossip about her because he and his more outgoing friend put out an underground newspaper, making fun of many of their fellow graduate students and a few faculty members (they weren't fools, so they didn't go after me), and Boston Friend was one of the people satirized. I always saw him as the shy follower in the two or three-man gang of merry pranksters. But I probably inadvertently called him on doing something that foreshadowed his deviant sexual behavior at Cal Poly.

I have this witchlike ability to say something as a joke or as a casual comment and either make it come true or expose a truth. I have predicted earthquakes, caused a tree to fall on the Claremont Colleges campus, and identified extramarital affairs with this skill. When I was living in the apartment on Adams and Hoover, I received an obscene phone call. I found the call more amusing than upsetting. The creep asked me lewd questions, and I gave him smart aleck answers, then hung up. When I told one of my female friends about the call, I said that the voice was kind of proper and cultured, and the guy sounded like one of the graduate students. I didn't actually believe it was one of my classmates, although I should have suspected something since this jerk clearly knew I was a woman (despite my voice), and only my first initial was in the telephone book. The next day when I saw Screwer and another male graduate student I decided to have some fun. The other male student was one of Potter's favorites, and he seemed a little strange to me, more likely to make an obscene phone call, I thought, than Screwer, who just seemed shy. So I approached them and decided to question Screwer about the call but to watch Potter's Favorite just in case he was the graduate-student sounding caller. I said, "Hey, Student, I got an obscene phone call last night. Was it you?" Screwer looked very nervous, but Potter's Favorite seemed calm and slightly amused. He said something like, "You are so rude."

I still didn't guess that Screwer might be my obscene phone caller; I just assumed that he was embarrassed by my question. Even when years later, Screwer started harassing me on the phone, calling and not saying anything, because he was upset that I bluntly told him to his face that I didn't think he should go up for promotion at the same time as Kentuckian's Wife, who had been in the department several years longer than he had, I didn't connect him to the obscene phone call. In fact, when his continued harassment of me and the fact that he clearly was calling me from the airport (I could hear airport noises in the background) as soon as he arrived back in town after his father's funeral creeped me out enough for me to call the police, I dismissed the policeman's suggestion that he just wanted to hear my voice. (The policeman may have liked my husky voice, which some people view as sexy.) I said, "No, this is a professional dispute; it's not sexual."

Then we had a meeting to view a video on AIDS that Gray wanted the department to consider presenting in our freshman composition classes. The tape included sexually explicit language and featured black supermodel Beverly Johnson. I hadn't seen the video yet, and I'm not sure if Screwer had, but we all knew that it contained sexual language. When I walked into the room, Screwer looked at me and turned beet red. Eww! I finally realized that this white jerk saw me as a sexual object, and then I remembered the obscene phone call and his reaction when I, witchlike, asked him if he was the caller. I think I know the answer. Yes, he was.

By the time of the deep blush, I knew that Screwer was a sexual freak. A friend of mine told me that she and Screwer had sex several times in his office. What made the story even more shocking to me is that my friend, who was married, was pregnant with her second child at the time. These office sexual liaisons happened during the middle of the day while people were walking around the department and talking in the hallway. They also happened in the old building where Screwer shared an office with another man. But even if he had been the only occupant of the office, others, like the secretaries, the janitor, and the department chair, had keys. Obviously, the seemingly quiet and passive Screwer liked to live (and screw) dangerously.

My friend was an EFL composition lecturer when she had the affair, and she and Screwer were around the same age. But later he went after younger women who were students. He still, however, enjoyed sex in his office, which in the new building happened to be next door to mine. Talking to his student lovers about these affairs (the students exposed him when he secretly married, and they found out), I wondered how Screwer had the energy to have so much sex and still teach his classes and grade papers. I was (at around 44) a few years older than he, but not that much older. The students named some drug that he was taking, and when I looked blank and asked what it was, they looked at me as if I were the most innocent middle-aged woman they had ever seen.

At times it seemed I was the only innocent person in the EFL department. Everybody seemed to be having irresponsible sex with someone inappropriate. Before Screwer even arrived at Cal Poly, my linguist friend had a sexual fling with a student fifteen years younger than she was. He wasn't her student, but he was mine, and she used information about me to woo him. He came back from one of their "dates" and told me everything he had found out about my private life. When I first arrived on campus, I was told about Superfly's hot tub and how he invited people to his house and then wanted them to cavort nude in the tub with him. Because of that interesting gossip, I never went to Superfly's annual New Year's party or to anything else at his house. He was said to have an open marriage and was rumored to sleep with students. But I saw him as the victim when he suddenly became enamored of a Mormon woman (a graduate student) with six children; she talked about the man with the hot tub in one of my classes before she met him. Less than a year after that conversation, Superfly was constantly talking about her, then he was cleaning off Tall Texan's desk so that she could sit there (Superfly had too much computer equipment on his desk), sharing their office as a lecturer, then he was trying to ensure that she had composition classes by firing some of the senior lecturers, and finally, in a new low even for the EFL department, he tried to make her his assistant chair. Eventually, he divorced his wife of about thirty years and married the Mormon woman.

The future Mrs. Superfly, who had been one of my favorite students before she committed adultery (her weak-looking first husband apparently became forceful, possibly even violent, when he discovered the affair), made the mistake of trying to sweet talk me after her fall from grace. I had just defended the lecturers in a department meeting when she approached me in the hallway to thank me for my help. Earlier in my career, before I had been embedded in white institutions for so long, I would probably have just bluntly said that I was not defending her. But after years of whitewashing, I had become slightly more subtle (or devious) in my takedowns. I listened to her comments, gave her a long look, and then said, "Unlike some people, I have a sense of shame." She knew what I was saying, and showing that she might have had, if not a sense of shame, at least some pride, never approached me again. Soon she left the department.

Because of my innocence, I often came off as judgmental when discussing department affairs. I remember having a conversation with a female friend about the bad behavior of one of the cave men when this friend said that another man, who was one of the many wimps, had also been known to come on to women. When I asked for details, she said, "Oh, you know how it is when you go out drinking with men." "No, I don't," I snapped, "I have never gone out drinking with men." The woman saw that I did not approve of such behavior and quickly dropped the subject.

I probably should have revised that statement the way I revised my never been high statement. I had been at tables with men who were drinking, either at a party or at lunch or dinner. I simply didn't drink with them. And, because of my experiences with an alcoholic father, if the men drank too much or their behavior changed in some way, I threw up a wall and moved away from them as quickly as possible.

I should not have been that shocked by the sexual escapades of the members of the EFL department after my experiences with my white female friends in graduate school. I don't know what Screwer was doing back then, but Boston Friend and I probably got less action than any other female graduate student, and I was going through my sexual peak at that time. I had one friend whose boyfriend committed suicide shortly before I arrived on campus. Like Tennessee Williams' Blanche DuBois, she responded to death by briefly becoming a nymphomaniac. I remember her bragging to me one time that she was proud of herself because she did not have sex with a man on their first date. Another sweet-looking, blonde friend of mine, a woman who looked so much more like a Mary than I did that people were always switching our names, figured out that I was more Southern Baptist prude than Bessie Smith and convinced me that she wasn't having sex with her boyfriend or even letting him cop a feel. I felt sorry for the poor white man and suggested she should at least let him feel her boobs. Then she switched boyfriends and moved in with the second one, finally admitting that she was having sex with the first guy the whole time. And at some point, she seemed to be juggling both boyfriends, even though the first boyfriend had a new girlfriend. I was at a party where both couples were hanging out and when my friend jumped up and dirty danced with boyfriend #1 while boyfriend #2 and boyfriend #1's girlfriend looked on, I commented that they should be happy that they were all white because black people didn't play like that. Someone would have been hurt in the black world.

Graduate school marked the first time I interacted with white friends outside of the classroom. I'd had white "schoolyard" friends since junior high but never saw them off campus. As I observed the sexual behavior of my white friends, I was surprised to see that they seemed sexually more promiscuous than my black friends. Now I knew black girls (two Henderson friends, for instance) who became mothers as teenagers, and there were a couple of shotgun weddings or seven month babies among black couples at Northwestern. But most of my educated black female friends were more sexually conservative than the white women I met in graduate school.

I certainly was more sexually conservative than all but maybe one of my white friends. Like Norma Rae, the character played by Sally Field, I had more trouble with white men than with black men but not for the reasons she mentioned. Norma was having trouble with the white men in her personal life, not the black men at the mill where she worked. I had trouble with the white men at work, not the black men in my personal life. As soon as a black man looked as if he was thinking about giving me trouble, I made sure that he hit the road, Jack, and never came back.

In fact, if this book were about my love life instead of my life in white institutions, it would have ended after about ten pages. If race is my primary identity, sexual orientation is so far down the list of identity markers that it doesn't even make the top ten. Before "heterosexual" I would list black, woman, baby boomer, Southern, born working class, currently middle class, daughter, recently retired English professor, sister, aunt, friend, Democrat, lapsed Southern Baptist, reality television watcher, Toyota Corolla driver, and recently retired tennis fan. I would list my sexual orientation ahead of my blood type, but then I don't even remember my blood type.

Of course, if I were gay, my sexual orientation would be higher on that list of identifiers, probably second after race. Being a heterosexual with a low sex drive in a culture that sometimes seems obsessed with sex can help me understand what it might be like to be white in a racist society. I can afford to be blind to sexual cues the way whites can afford to be colorblind. Clearly if I had been more in touch with my inner Jezebel, I would have recognized what was going on between Screwer and me before the blush. And as I've thought about the creepy geography teacher in light of what I now know about child-molesting priests, preachers, and teachers, I'm wondering if I misread him. I assumed that he was unnerved by me because he saw me as some kind of subhuman with cooties. I suspected that he didn't want to touch me because he thought I might infect him with my blackness or turn into an animal and tear off his face. But maybe he thought touching me would unleash the animal in him. Maybe instead of seeing the bony, dark-skinned twelve-year-old girl as a monkey or a spider, he saw her as a yummy chocolate Lolita.

Certainly, with the exception of my black peeping Tom neighbor, I have attracted more white perverts than black ones. My first close encounter with a white man suffering from jungle fever happened in Evanston when I was sixteen. I was walking home from school, which was just three blocks from my home, when a white guy driving a late model American car (probably a Chevy or a Pontiac) stopped and asked me for directions to Main Street. Although I had lived in Evanston for over a year by that time, I had never been to Main Street, so I told him that I didn't know where it was. Undeterred, this fairly nice looking, calm guy, who I assumed was an insurance salesman since I didn't know any other reason why he'd be driving around our all-black neighborhood, looking for streets, asked if I knew where Lake Street was. Well, of course, I did since Lake Street was within walking distance of where I stood and was also the street where my cousin lived with his "maid," wife, and children. I started to give directions when the man sweetly asked me to go with him to show him the street. Still naively not recognizing his motives, I reassured him that he could find it easily and started again to give the directions, pointing toward the street, when he said that he wouldn't hurt me. That's when the alarm bells rang, but I didn't become frightened; I simply woke up to what he was trying to pull. Did he think I was a fool? I was in high school; I wasn't stupid enough to get into a car with a strange white man. I drew a deep breath, huffed and puffed, and said, "I know that you are not going to hurt me because I'm not getting in your damn car!" The white man drove off, and because I wasn't frightened, I didn't do what I should have done, try to take down his license number and call the police. I didn't even report the incident to my parents because I thought my mother, the drama queen, would become unhinged, maybe not let me walk the three blocks to school by myself.

My next close encounter with a white pervert happened during my college years when I was in one of the downtown Evanston movie theaters, watching a not very entertaining or well-acted movie, based loosely on Harriet Beecher Stowe's <u>Uncle Tom's Cabin</u>. For some reason, singer Dionne Warwick, who usually didn't act, played Cassie. During a semi-nude bathing scene when Ms. Warwick's back was revealed, I felt what I thought were the toes of the person sitting immediately behind me. Mildly annoyed, I kind of moved up in my seat to give that person room so that his or her bare toes wouldn't be touching me. However, a few seconds later, I felt the "toes" again, but this time they seemed to be probing my back side. I turned around to see what the hell was wrong with this rude person when a white man with long brown hair jumped up and rushed out of the theatre. Realizing that the toes were actually fingers, and that this jerk had been pawing me, I snorted and went back to watching the boring movie.

About a year later, when I was still in college, I was riding the bus on my way home when I looked out the window and saw a dumpy looking white man, carrying some clothes that seemed to be from the cleaners. The white man and I made eye contact, and then he started running toward the next corner. I assumed that he had just realized that the bus passing him was the one he wanted to catch. I had a habit of sitting in the back of the bus, not to recreate my Southern Jim Crow experience, but because I didn't like to share my seat. I sat near the back door, put my books on the side of the seat by the aisle, and stared out the window, hoping that all new passengers would find somewhere else to sit. The strategy usually worked because the Evanston buses were not that crowded. So imagine my surprise when I heard an "excuse me" and looked up to find the dumpy looking white man waiting for me to remove my books and let him take the seat beside me. I gave him a sullen, "you're not welcome here" look while I picked up my books and set them in my lap with my hands on top of them. As the bus ride continued, the dumpy guy leaned his hand carrying the clothes over me and my seat. Just as I was about to tell him to move his clothes because I didn't want them hanging over me, I felt his hand on mine. When I moved my hand and started to look at him, he quickly jumped up and exited the bus at the next corner. That asshole had run, caught the bus, and paid the quarter or whatever it cost just to paw me.

The white men in Southern California were willing to pay more for a piece of me. When I was living in the Adams and

Hoover apartment, a white man who saw me crossing the street came and knocked on the door to offer me money for sex. A few years later when I was living in my apartment in Pomona, I was walking up Holt Boulevard toward the nearest supermarket when a white man going in the opposite direction, made a U turn, drove up beside me, and offered to pay for my services. I suggested that he might want to move on before I called the police. When I told this story to my students, supporting Baldwin's claim in <u>Another Country</u> that black women are seen as sex objects more frequently than are white women, one student pointed out that Holt is a known hang out for prostitutes. Well, I hadn't seen any prostitutes around that section of Holt, but I was certainly not dressed like a prostitute, nor was I acting like one. Back in those days, when I was still fairly slim and not yet driving, I walked very fast as if I were rushing to put out a fire. A prostitute would have been sauntering down the street, trying to attract the attention of male drivers. I guess some white men thought that any black woman, even a conservatively dressed (although my pants might have been a bit tight since I had begun to put on weight), make up free, fast walking black woman was willing to sell herself for the right price.

These close encounters with white sexual perverts, plus my experience with the creepy geography teacher, the first white man with whom I had any kind of personal contact, undoubtedly had a lot to do with my lack of interest in white males as sexual partners. But my rejection of them is probably more the result of my being born and raised in the South during the last years of Jim Crow. Even black female baby boomers born in the North are less likely to be interested in white men than are the Gen X black women (Whoopi is a high-profile exception). And, of course, especially for a black woman who spent her entire professional career in white institutions and in a major (English) that doesn't attract that many black men (Henry Louis Gates can't be everywhere), that means the male pickings have been slim.

I can count on one hand and have one or two free fingers left the number of love connections I have made during my life. In fact, if I count the peeping Tom and Screwer with his obscene phone call, I've had more experiences with perverts than with boyfriends. My play boyfriend in Henderson mainly just played the role of study partner and friend. We were paired as boyfriend and girlfriend by the adults because we were both smart, and, fortunately, he was tall. I towered over all of the other boys in my elementary school classes. I don't remember that Play Boyfriend and I ever kissed, but we attended each others' birthday parties (I had only two, but he had one almost every year) and danced together. The only dates that we had were study dates, going to the park to collect insects or meeting to study.

Interestingly, we met again when I moved to Cambridge. After graduating from one of the public Kentucky universities, he moved North and worked in a student services office (financial aid, admissions) at Harvard. We met and had dinner at each others' apartments, but nothing interesting happened. He had been overweight when we were children, but he was a slim adult while still tall. A bony child, I had filled out some but was not yet heavy, so we were both just right when we reconnected. Still there was no chemistry. I wondered whether he was gay since there was no mention of a female in his life, and he probably wondered the same thing about me. We were both thirty, had never married, and neither of us talked about boyfriends or girlfriends.

I don't know if he was actually gay, but Play Boyfriend was definitely anal. He had neat files of all of his old school pictures, report cards, and notes; they were filed alphabetically or chronologically so he could immediately find whatever document he wanted to show me. He also had a neater apartment than I did, and he was the better cook. I thought it was funny that he cooked spaghetti while I prepared a more stereotypically masculine (and expensive) meal of steaks and baked potatoes. Ironically, he now (after earning the MBA at Harvard) is apparently working at Tufts.

My relationship with my childhood play boyfriend lasted longer than any of my mature relationships. My first summer at Fort Sheridan, I was placed in the same office as a young black man who had just graduated from ETHS. Because we were both the only black and the only young people in that office, of course, we hung out together, eating lunch at the cafeteria. All of the middle-aged people assumed that we were boyfriend and girlfriend, but we were not. I never saw or heard from him again after we left that job. When I returned to school that year, I did have a boyfriend, but he lasted for only about two weeks. We met in French class, where he wanted to hold hands, but I was too busy taking notes. Besides, I suspected that he was just trying to pass French. I was doing well in the subject, and he wasn't. We broke up because all of the hand holding cramped my note taking style, and he had never heard of a girlfriend who didn't at least want to hold hands. Our only discussion of sex occurred when I told him about the white pervert who tried to lure me into his car.

Both in high school and college, I was too busy studying and "overachieving" to be bothered with boys. I also wasn't eager to start dating because I didn't want to have to deal with my melodramatic mother, who would have turned a movie date into an elopement. I had seen how overwrought she could become when my brother stayed out too late or seemed too interested in a girl, so I thought it easier to wait until I was an adult with my own space before I explored the opposite sex. But even my mother thought I should go to the prom. She lined up a date for me, the one year younger son of her fellow Northwestern maid and around-the-corner neighbor. The guy was nice looking and tall enough, but I wasn't interested. I think I spent prom weekend making money babysitting while reading a really good novel.

During the year I taught at ETHS, I came close to having a boyfriend. I wasn't really that attracted to the guy. He was a bit short for my taste (I admit to a height fetish, but that's probably because I became tall early, being taller than my older brother for several years), but he listened patiently to my rants about my problems with the Michael School English Department. I think he might have been the only other black teacher in that school; I believe he taught biology, but it could have been history or social science. We ate lunch together and flirted a bit. One of the few times I held my tongue with a man happened when this little guy looked at me and said, "I bet you can love a man to death." I managed not to laugh in his face, nor did I say what I was thinking: "If by love a man to death, you mean pick up this textbook and beat you over the head with it until you die, yeah, I can do that." Still I was ready to make a date with him; I would meet him somewhere so I could keep him away from my mother as long as possible. But before we could hook up, I walked out of the supermarket near my home one Saturday and saw walking toward me my little future boyfriend with three tiny children who looked remarkably like him. Could they be his siblings? I spoke to him and looked significantly at the children, assuming that he would explain who they were. But he just said "hello" breezily and went into the store. When we saw each other at school that Monday, I asked if those were his children. He said they were. "Are you married?" I asked. "Yeah," he answered belligerently, as if my question were stupid. When I asked why he, a married man, was trying to hook up with me, this little jerk pointed out that I shouldn't be so picky since I wasn't getting any younger. I don't think I had yet turned twenty-three when he basically called me old. Needless to say, that little adventure didn't make me want to rush into another relationship, and I certainly wasn't worried about being too old to find a man.

Based on my early experiences at USC, I didn't need to worry. At twenty-three, I was probably looking about as good as I was going to look. The first few years of graduate school, I still had all of the clothes I bought during my one year of teaching, and I had put on enough weight so that my too skinny legs had become "great gams," long and surprisingly shapely. This period was toward the end of the mini skirt/hot pants period, and I was still wearing some of those outfits, so I caught the attention of quite a few men. But my first catch was the brother of two women who worked in the bookstore. They weren't looking for a hot babe, but a nice woman who would not break their younger brother's heart. He had been left at the altar by some no good woman and was on the rebound. I liked Little Brother (he was vertically challenged, of course; I seemed to attract the short ones), but he was boring. Worse, he wanted me to entertain him, and I was taking three classes and an independent study. I didn't have time to entertain Little Brother. Then he started making nesting noises. We'd had about three dates, one of which was to Universal Studios, with a female friend I met in the dorm tagging along, and numerous boring telephone conversations when he started talking about marriage. No, thanks, Little Brother. He was soon history.

Shortly after I dumped Little Brother, I attracted the attention of some kooky guy, sitting in front of the main campus library playing a guitar. Now here's the problem with me; I'm not smart about choosing men. Since USC was in a relatively dangerous neighborhood, I would never have even talked to a man, much less given him my telephone number, if I had met him off campus. But let that man walk two or three blocks and approach me on campus, and I was listening to his lies, telling him my business, and giving him my telephone number. This guy turned out to be a pathological liar, the first of two that I met on campus. This one I dumped fairly early because his lies were so obvious, but the second one, whom I met several years later, actually became a major hook up. By the time I figured out he wasn't really a USC student and may not have even been from Nigeria, as he claimed, although he did have an accent, so he was certainly from somewhere outside the United States, we'd seen Annie Hall, he'd been in my apartment, been into other things that he should never have gotten into, and I had trouble dumping him. In fact, he's the only man that didn't immediately hit the road when I made it clear that I was through with him.

I should have realized that Nigeria would be harder to dump because he outsmarted me (admittedly not hard to do) when I tried to avoid giving him my telephone number. After my problems with the first pathological liar, a wiser woman than I told me to tell the next man who asked for my number to give me his number instead. She said that I could then call him if I decided I wanted to be bothered with him, or I could just file the number in the trash. But Mr. Nigeria made up some excuse (changing phone numbers or something) to avoid giving me his number, so I just gave in and told him mine. I had barely made it to my apartment when the telephone rang, and it was Nigeria. I teased him about checking to see if I had given him the right number, but he pretended he just wanted to talk to me some more. Yeah, right.

When I made it clear that I was no longer interested in seeing him, Nigeria initially continued to call me and even followed me around campus. I was working at the American Language Institute that summer, tutoring foreign (mostly Middle Eastern) students. Nigeria showed up at my job looking for me; I had already left, but the man, an ESL instructor, who told me about him looked concerned. Apparently, Nigeria acted as if he didn't believe the man when he said that I wasn't there. A day or two later, I was walking with a friend, and suddenly I spotted Nigeria, sitting in the same place where he had been sitting when we first met. I told my friend to ignore him, and we just walked on by, although she started talking about how cute he was, loudly enough for him to hear. But the next time he called me, I let him know that I'd had enough of his nonsense. I channeled every mean black woman I had ever known, used my badass attitude and my loudest baritone voice to assure him that I did not want to see or hear from him again. After I shouted in his ear loudly enough to burst an eardrum and then slammed the telephone down into the receiver, picked it up and slammed it down again, he never called me again, nor did I see him on campus again. Maybe he went to UCLA, Cal State L.A., or Occidental to pick up a nice college girl.

I realized after that close encounter with a potential stalker, however, that I had to be more careful about letting unknown men into my life. Fortunately, my sexual peak had been reached and passed just about the time I was having fun with Nigeria, so I was never tempted to give some strange black man my telephone number again. When I was still living in my apartment in Pomona, I received an interesting telephone call one night, where a man, who at least sounded black, tried to convince me that some friend of mine had given him my telephone number so he and I could date. I was initially intrigued and wanted to know who the friend was. His story was somewhat believable since I had an unlisted telephone number at that point, and he knew my name and that I was an English professor, but he refused to tell me the name of the friend, although he said it was a woman. I first tried guessing, listing a few friends who seemed the type to want to find me a man, but when he wouldn't tell me who this friend was, I told him that any friend of mine would know that I had better sense than to make a date with a man I had never met, sent by some unnamed friend. I hung up, and he didn't call back.

I actually suspected this one nosy staff person who worked in another department. She may have been trying to see if she could find out if I were dating, but if she were behind that little stunt, she found out that I don't appreciate people trying to make a fool out of me.

There were a few more come ons from strange black men in malls and supermarkets, but I was never tempted to give any of them the time of day. Once my mentor, Number 1 Linguist, tried to facilitate a hookup with a tall, good-looking black man that he and I saw eating in the faculty/staff cafeteria at Cal Poly. I think he was a textbook salesman, or maybe he was a financial planner, helping people invest for retirement. I'm fairly certain that he wasn't on the staff at Cal Poly. Anyway, he wasn't interested in me; he may have been married, but he probably thought a black woman who sent an overly cheerful, preppy-looking white man to make a love connection for her was lame. I don't blame him.

So that's the story of my love life. It basically ended when I turned thirty and left USC. For all of those Cal Poly students who were wondering: nothing was going on under my dress except the pantyhose that my millennial students criticized me for wearing; apparently, pantyhose went out of style at the end of the twentieth century. No one lit my fire in the eighties. I had no sexual healing during the nineties (although I could have used some when my digestive system broke down). And I had zero action during the zeroes. I can't say that I couldn't get any satisfaction during these years because, until my digestive system broke, I ate lots of chocolate and was very satisfied. The great advantage of getting satisfaction from eating chocolate, of course, is that it can be done alone (I know that sex can be done alone, but most people prefer a partner), but I even briefly belonged to a chocolate club. Two of my former students and I met in my office and ate brownies and candy. Unlike people having sex, we had good conversations while enjoying our chocolate.

Of course, like anything that gives us pleasure, eating chocolate has negative side effects; too much chocolate can be bad for one's health and figure. Just before I became ill, during my Oprah lookalike days, I weighed just over 200 pounds. Because I truly am big-boned, I probably looked like I weighed 180, but I was clearly overweight. When I heard about the women who gained weight as a protective device to avoid sex, I wondered if that's what I was doing. It is certainly true that I attracted the perverts when I had a better figure, but I wasn't really that troubled by their sexual advances, probably because I wasn't that focused on my sexuality. I liked being heavy because it made me feel and look tougher. As I explained to one of my friends after I shrank back down to my high school weight, I want people to get out of the way, to hug the walls, when I walk down the hallway. Because I was skinny and kind of wimpy as a child, I associated thinness with weakness, and I wanted to be strong. I didn't mind being sexy, but I preferred being tough and scary.

I'm not sure why my sex drive is so low. Maybe it had something to do with my weak, ineffectual father figures or my chaotic early life. I used to joke that it was my maternal grandmother's fault, not because she confused up and down when she told me what to do with my shorts, but because she used the term "pocketbook" to refer to a woman's private parts. Since a purse is also a pocketbook, and I was trained from the time I started carrying a purse in fifth grade to keep it with me (my mother still is very protective of my purse, telling me to keep it zippered, and picking it up when I briefly set it on the floor, and I'm always teased by friends and colleagues because I keep my purse with me at parties), I would naturally protect that other pocketbook. But it's probably genetic. My maternal grandmother had several siblings (two brothers and a sister) who never married, and four of my five female first cousins on that side of the family never married (although one had a child). I also have two second cousins, my grandmother's great granddaughters, who are now in their fifties and have never married. One of them had a boyfriend years ago, but the other one apparently never did. We Barnetts, or at least some of us, are just not that into sex.

And I think that low sex drive is an asset, especially for a teacher. Given the number of teachers, most of them heterosexual and a surprising number of them women, who have taken advantage of their positions by having sex with their underage students, it's clear that all other things being equal, a woman or man who is not that into sex will be a better teacher. I find it interesting that most of these women who have had sex with their students have been fairly innocent looking white women, many of them blondes. Of course, it's possible that the media focus on only the blonde women who have sex with their students the way they focus on only missing blondes or good looking brunettes, but I doubt it. If a dark-skinned black woman had sex with a blonde elementary school student, gave birth to two children by him, and then after spending time in jail, married him, she probably would have been lynched. Although I chose secondary education instead of primary or elementary school because in my younger days I had little rapport and less patience with small children, I know that I would have been a better elementary school teacher than sweet-looking Mary Kay Letourneau BECAUSE I WOULD NOT HAVE SEX WITH ANY OF MY STUDENTS!

I don't really see the downside to having a low sex drive. If I didn't enjoy solitude and wanted to be married, I guess it would be a problem unless I could find a man with an equally low sex drive. But I would probably do what many other spouses have done, just lie there and wait for it to be over, or I'd have headaches. The lawyer Lisa Bloom was recently on television, selling a book, and she claimed that sex made women smarter. Obviously, that's not true. Women and men act stupider when they are having or trying to have sex. (Lisa is probably just trying to drum up business for her mother, Gloria Allred, who, in a spectacular example of how far people can fall, has become the go-to lawyer for women who have been sexually involved with prominent men.) If I thought that having sex would make me less tense, I'd be looking for a man, but I know too many sexually active women who are more high strung than I am, so clearly having sex is not the answer. If I become too tense, I might try yoga. If I thought that having sex would improve my disposition, I might also consider hooking up with some not too vigorous old fellow, but again, I've seen no evidence that women having sex are kinder, more patient, or more compassionate. Back in the eighties, we were joking at one of our department lunches about women's having sex to improve their skin. That was around the time that

Number 1 Linguist tried to play Cupid for me; my skin was bad during that period, so I thought a little sexual activity might improve my looks. But when I became ill and so had to drink more water while eating less chocolate and greasy fried food, my skin "miraculously" cleared to the point that a much younger black woman asked for my secret. Dr. Oz and a few others have argued that having sex helps us live longer. I'm not buying it. Remember the Delaney sisters, who lived to be over one hundred and outlived all their siblings? They weren't exactly nymphomaniacs.

In fact, it seems that sexual activity causes more problems than it cures. Long before AIDS, there were all kinds of venereal diseases that sexual partners could catch from each other. And we wouldn't have to argue so much about abortion and contraception if everyone, especially teenagers, had less sex. And then there are all of the sex scandals that we could avoid if more people were like me. As I'm writing this chapter, Weinergate has erupted, John Edwards has been indicted for having sex in 2007 while running for President and while his wife was fighting stage four cancer; his indictment came "coincidentally" shortly after it was revealed that the former governor of California had a love child, now thirteen, with his maid, and a high-ranking French politician was accused of raping a maid in a New York City hotel. Meanwhile, locally, a choir director of a church that I pass whenever I travel from Claremont to Chino has been arrested for having sex with a fifteen-year-old girl, the Chino School District is being sued by a young girl whose middle-aged male teacher had sex with her, while a thirty-something female teacher's aide (with four children) in a Palmdale middle school had sex with a thirteen-year-old boy. And my very religious mother and one of her equally religious friends have been talking on the telephone about Bishop Eddie Long, who apparently paid millions of dollars to men who accused him of having sex with them. At one point during the nineties, a sexual scandal broke every summer. One summer it was Woody Allen sleeping with his common law stepdaughter (they are now, I guess, happily married); another summer it was Michael Jackson and his first underage male accuser, and then OJ turned into Othello and took his Bronco ride through the streets of L.A.

Sex can also cause problems in the workplace, especially when it mixes with politics. Number 1 Linguist lived with and finally married the department secretary, a sweet, soft-spoken woman who would probably never have been involved in department politics if she had not been living with one of the faculty members. But whenever Number 1 was on one side of an issue and the chair, for whom the department secretary works most directly, was on the other, it caused tension for her. And after one contentious department meeting during that first chair fight, Tall Woman went back to her office and started crying because people were attacking her very, very good friend, apparently with benefits (I never saw them have sex and neither confessed to me about having a sexual relationship, but no one thought that their friendship was platonic), White. I've been upset when I felt that friends or colleagues were being attacked, but I've cried only when I was under attack. In fact, the only person who brought me to tears during a department conflict was my good friend <u>without</u> benefits, Gray. One male department member, hearing about one of my battles with Gray, described our relationship as sounding like husband and wife. I suspect that if Gray had been my husband or lover, I would have actually tried to knock him out and not just thought about it. Fortunately, the one married couple in our department, Renaissance and his wife, who is a rhetoric specialist, were never on opposite sides of a political battle. If they had been, they probably would have divorced.

Given the many problems caused by too much sexual activity, it seems to me that we would all be better off if we stopped pushing sex and started deemphasizing it. I'm not endorsing the phony chastity programs, led sometimes by young people who've already lost their virginity (Yes, I'm referring to Bristol Palin). I mean let's stop selling sexual appetite enhancers and start pushing sexual appetite suppressors. Why do we need Viagra and whatever drug they're now trying to sell to women? Why do people who don't want to have sex or can't have sex need it? Clearly, people can live without having sex; it's not required for life, like food and water. I can't eat fried chicken anymore, so when I have to eat, I just eat baked chicken. I've given up lots of food (pizza, barbecue) that I used to eat regularly. Why can't my fellow baby boomers give up sex? If the men can't get it up, let it stay down. If the women aren't hot and wet, let them stay cold and dry. On the other hand, for those people who are oversexed, wouldn't a nice drug be helpful?

Don't misunderstand me; I'm not arguing that people shouldn't have sex. People who enjoy sex should have it with willing partners the same way that people who like to drink alcohol should drink. But some people are alcoholics, and apparently some people are sex addicts, and those people need a drug to curb their appetites. And if there are some Tiger types whose sexual fires burn so bright that they can't successfully do their jobs without a great deal of sexual activity, then they need to find a partner with the same needs, probably not marry, or have an open marriage. They might also try this new sex suppressor drug that I hope will be on the market soon or maybe chocolate (Overweight people can play golf since it doesn't require running).

People believe they must have sex because they've all been brainwashed to accept that there is only one pathway to happiness. But if we look around, we can see that most people aren't following the husband, wife, and two children path, and even when they do choose that path, how often do they find happiness? My original family unit consisted of a married heterosexual couple with two children; in my family the boy child was born first, which seems ideal. We also even briefly had the white house; ours didn't have the picket fence, but it had some lovely evergreen shrubs in the front yard and all of those fruit trees in the back yard. But we weren't happy because my father was a drunk, and my mother was an obsessively clean drama queen who never should have had children. Today we can find in our culture and on our television screens all kinds of families, one married couple with nineteen children "and counting," one unmarried couple (Brad and Angelina) with six children, three of them adopted and from different races than the parents; there are single parents with children, gay parents with children, married couples without children. And I assume that all of those people are trying to be happy.

In one of her recent "Behind the Scenes with Oprah" episodes, Oprah discussed with her staff a show (I didn't see the actual show) about women who were still virgins at what they thought was a too old age (They all seemed to be in their thirties). Oprah initially raised the question of why being a mature virgin was a problem, but she was quickly convinced by three or four women on her staff that yes, indeed, it was a problem. The discussion reminded me of a friend who became obsessed with losing her virginity before she turned thirty. I don't think she was especially eager to have sex; she just didn't want to be a thirty-year-old virgin. I suspect that Whoopi would not have been so easily convinced by these female staffers, not because she's less into sex than Oprah, but because she's less willing to fall in line and follow the norm. Whoopi seems not to accept the one life fits all argument that silences people like Oprah. Certainly, I don't accept that argument. Those relatively young women seemed to feel bad about being virgins only because society told them that they should have sex before they were too old. Well, not so long ago, society told women that they should have sex only when they were married, so were the women who had sex outside of marriage during the nineteen fifties freaks?

I believe that women who don't need to have sex are probably the luckiest women in the world. They can live happily without sex just as they can live happily without taking drugs, drinking alcohol, or jumping out of airplanes. Not everyone needs to be thrilled. I certainly don't. When B.B. King or Aretha Franklin sings, "the thrill is gone," I say, "good riddance." And although they took different redlight paths from me during their early years, having done drugs and been with inappropriate men (well, even I've hung out with a few Mr. Wrongs), I think that Oprah and Whoopi would agree with me at this point in their lives. After all, Oprah has been with the same almost too appropriately named (steady man? steadfast man?) man for twenty years, and Whoopi, after two or three marriages and two high-profile relationships with white men, has joined me in enjoying solitude.

CHAPTER SEVEN
Not a Motherless Child

If I'm Whoopi, then my mother is Diahann Carroll. She even has the high cheekbones and the lovely soprano voice. In fact, during her younger years, she was a church soloist. Can you imagine Whoopi and Diahann living together as mother and daughter? I can't even imagine them as mother and daughter in a movie. Diahann is a very proper fashionista. Even when she dressed down in the movie Claudine, where she played a maid, she looked dignified and classy. Although my mother is not above wearing rollers under her straw hat in downtown Claremont, she also is fashionable. The people at her mostly white church have asked her if she ever worked as a model (yeah, there were so many black models back in the nineteen forties) as they've admired her matching suits, hats, gloves, shoes, and purses. She may have the same name as the new princess, Catherine Elizabeth, but she dresses like the old Queen, who is, in fact, only two years older than Queen Catherine.

A regular watcher of "The View," my mother complains about Whoopi's wardrobe and/or her hair at least once a week. She'll say, "Why doesn't she get those plaits out of her face?" Or if she and I are in different parts of the house at 10:00 a.m. (typical black folks, we have five televisions), she'll ask me when we meet for lunch at 11:00, "Did you see that old thing Whoopi was wearing?" If I watched the show (I often don't), I will say, "No, I was paying more attention to what she was saying."

Whoopi isn't the only black woman on television whose style is criticized by my mother. She also complains about Oprah ("That dress is too tight; it makes her butt look big"; "She has good hair; why does she wear those old wigs?"), Oprah's best friend Gayle ("Her hair looks awful; why do black women wear that red hair?"), Michelle Obama ("She should wear suits when she's with the Queen") and the 11:00 a.m. ABC news anchor Leslie Sykes (She likes her suits but finds the red wig annoying). No black woman is safe from the one-woman "Ms. Blackwell" fashion police.

And, of course, her daughter is not safe from her critiques either. Only recently, since my hair has become more salt than pepper, has she given up trying to convince me to switch to a more attractive (in her view) hairdo. Whenever she saw a black woman wearing a new hairstyle (well, as long as it didn't involve bleach and braids), she suggested that I would look pretty with my hair like that. She also gives me unsolicited fashion advice. When she moved in with me in 1990, she checked what I was wearing to work every day and either approved or suggested changes. It took me years to break her of that habit, and even now, when I'm going to some rare social event, she wants to see what I'm wearing. She's learned to keep her mouth shut if she doesn't approve of my outfit, but her silence speaks volumes. When she looks me up and down and says, "hmmm," I know that I have not met her high standards for what to wear to someone's retirement, 80th birthday, or 45th wedding anniversary party (Most of my friends and colleagues are older than I am).

So how did Diahann and Whoopi end up living together? It all started in 1971. If I could redo one year of my life, it would probably be 1971-72, the year I taught at ETHS and continued to live with my parents. When most people talk about a lost year or having regrets about something they did in their past that has affected their present, they are usually referring to bad behavior, the kind of behavior that many of my contemporaries engaged in back in the sixties and seventies. But my problem in 1971-72 was that I behaved too well. While I battled those white folks in the Michael School English Department, I paid rent to my parents ($60.00 a month, an appropriate amount for a room and bath at that time), buying my own and my mother's food during the week (Dexter ate leftovers, neckbones, and other country food while we enjoyed lamb chops, steaks, and pork chops; they bought food for Saturday and Sunday dinner), and even installing my own telephone and paying that bill. During that year, I never entertained a man in my room, never came home drunk or high, and stayed out late (past midnight) maybe twice. I didn't even play my record player or television loudly. I was, in other words, the perfect boarder.

To make matters worse, shortly after I moved to L.A. in September, my brother, who was living and working on the North side of Chicago, separated from his first wife (now known as "that white woman") and moved back in with my parents. When I returned home for Christmas break, I found a lock on the telephone because my brother was making too many unpaid for calls to Chicago, signs in the upstairs bathroom, telling him to wash out the tub and pick up his wet towels, and my mother was complaining constantly about what a pain he was. His behavior made mine seem ideal. I was seen as the world's best boarder, thanks to the man I renamed Pigpen.

If I could redo that year, I would either move out before I started paying rent or behave more like my brother. Or maybe I would bring in a few inappropriate men, perhaps commit adultery with the little teacher. Maybe, if his wife had come looking for me with a knife one Saturday night, my parents wouldn't have wanted to follow me to L.A. But my reward for being a responsible, mature adult and a thoughtful boarder was to have my parents decide that they wanted to live with me until death did us part. Because at 22 I had my head on straight and my feet on the ground, my parents decided that I should be their caretaker when they grew old.

And since Dexter was already in his fifties when he and my mother married, he was growing old even before I left for L.A. During his years as a Pullman porter, he often worked the Chicago to L.A. route, so he knew the L.A. area fairly well and liked how the warm weather felt on his arthritic hips. He also had a sister and a half-brother living in San Fernando. In fact, he stayed with his sister when he worked the L.A. route. So, shortly after retiring as the chauffeur for a bank president, Dexter convinced my mother to relocate to San Fernando. And in January, 1976, they arrived in the area and immediately added stress to my life.

When they arrived, the repossessed house they bought during a quick trip to L.A. in October or November was not yet ready for occupancy, so they briefly moved in with Dexter's sister whose house was two blocks down the street from theirs. But my mother had problems with the sister's husband, so she came to stay in my one bedroom apartment. Then, when I spent her 48th birthday with her (in February) in their newly decorated (and furnished mostly with the same old furniture that came from Kentucky) house, she fainted and because her insurance had not yet been transferred from Illinois, I had to ride in an ambulance with her from a hospital in or near San Fernando to the County Hospital in L.A. I didn't sleep at all that night and at daybreak found myself in a strange neighborhood, catching the bus back to my apartment.

After things settled down a bit, I saw how having my parents in the same area could cramp my style. Before the "family and friends" plans for both landline telephones and cellphones, there were other plans for frequent callers, and my mother signed up for one that allowed her to call L.A. as often as she wanted. She usually called me every evening around eight p.m. Since I had been living on my own for several years by the time they moved to California, I expected to come and go when I pleased without accounting for my whereabouts. One freedom that I enjoyed was spontaneously joining classmates for dinner after a grueling graduate seminar. We often went to The Original Pantry, a downtown restaurant known mainly for its meat, or to one of the nearby fast food restaurants. I don't remember the first time that I indulged in one of those spontaneous post seminar dinners after my parents came to town; it may have been before the fainting spell. But soon after I returned to my apartment that evening, the phone rang, and when I answered it, my frantic mother told me that she was about to come to my apartment to look for my body. In fact, the only reason she wasn't already there was that she couldn't drive the freeway, and Dexter refused to bring her. From that day on, whenever I joined my classmates for an after class dinner, I had to find a public telephone (if only there had been cellphones back then) and call my mother to tell her where I was and when I would be home. Of course, my graduate school friends teased me, and I didn't blame them. What made her behavior especially annoying is that she didn't have the excuse of being really old. She was forty-eight, which was the approximate age of one of my female classmates.

Despite these inconveniences, I had been on my own long enough to appreciate having my parents living closer to me, and I actually enjoyed having Dexter, the calm good driver, around more than I did my nervous, barely able to drive mother. Not only did he not mind driving back and forth between L.A. and San Fernando so that I could visit them, but he could keep my mother out of my business by refusing to drive her to my apartment every time she had one of her overprotective, hysterical mama fits. I also appreciated that he recognized that it was inappropriate to continue to call me, a college graduate in her late twenties, by my childhood nickname, "Sister." The once annoying Dexter became my hero when he, without prompting, switched to calling me "Mary" as soon as he arrived in the L.A. area.

Still I blamed him for the "let's all live together" campaign that my mother started waging immediately after the fainting spell. After all, it was Dexter who wanted to move to Southern California. My mother, who had found a job that she loved, ironically working as a security guard at ETHS, came reluctantly. And, of course, since Dexter thought it was appropriate to take control of the money of a teenager that he barely knew and certainly hadn't supported, it would make sense that he would think nothing of trying to take over that young lady's life when she was old enough to take care of herself.

But years later after Dexter had died and my mother renewed her "let's live together" campaign, I rethought my original conclusions. My mother was not the type to be easily influenced by someone else. She not only didn't let Dexter take my money or her money, she also didn't follow his lead and become a spendthrift. Instead she taught him how to manage money, how to pay his bills on time, and occasionally even save. So why would she buy into his theory that they had a right to take over her daughter's life, to move in with her or have her move in with them so that she could take care of them?

I remembered that when I was twenty and my father's older brother died, my mother and I went to the funeral in Henderson, where we met my brother, who was at the time (1969) a Second Lieutenant in the army. My mother proudly reported to several people that my brother had paid for her to come to the funeral.

Although she and I came down on the bus together, I took a week's vacation (I was at my Black House job at that point) to visit my Henderson relatives while she returned home. When I spent the night with some of my Sisney relatives, they wondered why my brother had to pay for my mother's bus ticket. Didn't she have a job? Well, yeah, she did. Didn't her second husband have a job? Well, yeah, he did. I couldn't really explain why my mother didn't pay for her own bus ticket. I paid for mine. She clearly had enough money; I guess she just didn't want to spend it on a trip to her now former brother in-law's (no matter how nice and supportive he had been) funeral and thought my brother should take care of it since the dead man was his uncle. A few years after that trip, my mother was talking to my brother's first wife, "that white woman," and said that the only thing that she wanted her two children to do for her was to give her a trip to Europe. The white woman looked at her strangely and said that she hoped to go to Europe herself. I don't know about the white woman, but my mother never made it to Europe. Still, I understood the white woman's look. Why would my mother want her children to pay for her trip to Europe? Why didn't she just hope that her children would be happy, healthy, and successful? Wouldn't that be enough of a gift for a mother?

As I thought about my mother's expectations for her adult children, I formulated what I call the "chicken parts" theory of parenting. Richard Wright's anecdote in Black Boy about the greedy preacher who looked as if he would eat all the fried chicken and Amy Tan's story, "Best Quality," in her novel Joy Luck Club, helped me to formulate this theory. Tan's story focuses on a Chinese New Year's crab dinner and makes the point (as she does several times in the book) that the way the Chinese mother shows her love for her children is to give them the best food. Well, my mother had a different approach to feeding her children. When we ate fried chicken, she took what my brother and I perceived to be the best pieces, the breast and the wing, while my father (when he was at home) ate the thighs, my brother had a drumstick and back, and I was given the other drumstick and the neck. Now I don't know who would think the neck was a good piece of chicken. Certainly I didn't. I was the youngest and the thinnest, so maybe that's why I was assigned the neck instead of the slightly more desirable back. But I'm not sure why my father ate thighs while my mother ate breasts. He was older and bigger than my mother, but she made the most money and did the most work, cleaning the house, usually cooking, washing, and ironing, while he just cut the grass. It seemed to me as a child that my mother was given the best food because she was the most valuable person in the house.

Now here's how the "chicken parts" theory of parenting works. If parents put their children first when the children are small, let them have the best food, the best crabs, the best parts of the chicken, then they will continue to put their adult children first. My mother and I criticized the woman who lived across the street from me in my townhouse community because we felt she let her adult (or "grown" as my mother called them) children rule her. The mother, a teacher, seemed to do all of the work in the house, she drove an old car while her oldest son drove a new one, and after we had moved out of the neighborhood, we learned that her married daughter had moved back home, bringing her new baby and husband with her. My mother and I tsked tsked and talked about what a fool this mother was. But she was probably just continuing the pattern of giving her children the best parts of life. On the other hand, since my mother had taken the best chicken parts for herself, she wanted to continue that pattern when her children were adults. Her youngest child was given leftover chicken parts, and so she was expected to have a leftover life.

But there was one problem for my mother. I didn't always live with her, so I knew that there was another way to eat chicken and also another, better way to live my life. During the brief time that I lived with my Sisney relatives in 1962, I was allowed to pick what parts of the chicken I wanted to eat. And, of course, I ate the breasts and wings as I always did, even when I lived with my mother and father, whenever there was a special event like the Sunday School picnic. And when I lived with my mother's mother, I decided what I wanted to eat and when I wanted to eat it. Maybe if I had stayed with my mother throughout my childhood, I would have accepted her plans for me as my lot in life, but after my two years of living as "Queen of the World," I thought too much of myself to accept someone else's leftovers.

It might seem harsh for me to say that my mother wanted me to live a leftover life just because she hoped we could live together, but she was clearly counting on me not to marry so that she and Dexter would have a comfortable place to stay. I don't know about Dexter, but my mother did not want to live with a son-in-law and grandchildren. During the early months of her campaign, she constantly talked about a woman named Betty

Jean, who, according to my mother, said that she was not going to marry until <u>her</u> mother died. Keep in mind that when my mother was incessantly telling this story as an example of what a wonderful person Betty Jean was, I was 27, and my mother was 48. And if I said something like, "Betty Jean sounds like a fool," or, "I'm not Betty Jean," my mother either talked about how mean I was, started to cry, or both.

By the time my mother started her campaign, I was about 80% sure that I would not marry, mainly because I loved living alone. And that's what made the live-with-Mary plan so upsetting. My parents knew I enjoyed solitude; in fact, they counted on my enjoyment of being alone to keep me unmarried so that they could live with me and prevent me from being alone. What's worse, whereas children go to school (usually by the age of three these days) and most husbands work out of the house (some, like Pullman porters and airline pilots, even work out of town), old, retired people (and my parents weren't "hey, let's go on a cruise" type of old people) are at home more than any other relatives. So I was supposed not to marry, not have children of my own, who might take care of me when I grew old and feeble, so that I could take care of one parent whom I didn't even meet until I was fifteen and with whom I lived for only eight years and another parent who supported me financially throughout my childhood but with whom I also did not live during key growth years. And, oh, if I decided to marry and have children, I should wait until my mother died. My mother is now 83, and I'm 62. If that's not a leftover life, I don't know what is.

Despite her drama queen personality, my mother and I had a fairly easy relationship once we reunited during my teen years. I usually can focus on only one enemy at a time, and my new "show me the money" stepfather was the bad guy during those years. I was also, of course, the opposite of a teenage rebel. Even an over-protective, overly strict mother can't find much fault with a young woman who just studies, goes to work, and minds her business. I had one rather pushy female friend who liked sleepovers, but I rarely socialized with other girls outside of school, so my mother really had no reason to complain about me.

However, when she started her "let's live together" campaign, two events from my past replayed in my head. One was so trau-matic that even now it's not funny to me; the other was somewhat funny even at the time, but it was also rather chilling. The first event happened when I was in fifth grade; I was ten years old. My brother and I were what are now called "latch key" children. My mother left for work about an hour before we left for school and arrived home about an hour after we did. For some reason, I, the younger child, was in charge of the key. Maybe my brother had been in charge of it first and didn't keep up with it well, so I was assigned to be the key keeper. Or maybe my mother decided that keeping the key was something a girl should do. At any rate, I had that responsibility when I was in fifth grade. Like most children and adults who spend a lot of time thinking and daydreaming, I was, and still am, absent-minded. So, of course, I occasionally misplaced the key or forgot to take it with me to school.

One day when I left the key at home, my brother and I were waiting outside after school when my mother walked up the street and saw us. She immediately started yelling, asking me what happened to the key. I had to use the bathroom, so after she opened the door with her key, I rushed in and took care of that business, then started frantically looking for the key. When it wasn't in the places I thought it would be, I became more frantic because my mother was screaming at me like a maniac. She insisted that I go back to school to look for the key and that I look for it as I walked toward the school. I knew I hadn't taken the key to school, but I was happy to leave the house and her screaming. I was walking slowly toward the school, taking the alleys, when I thought I heard my mother's voice. I assumed I was just remembering screams from the house, but when I turned around, I saw her following me, screaming as she came down the alley. I walked faster, entered the school, looked around my desk, knowing that I wouldn't find the key, and then just waited for her to come into the classroom and see that the key wasn't there. After she looked all around the desk and probably hit me a few times, we walked back home, and even though we were walking side by side, she screamed at me all the way back home.

My mother's soprano voice may have been lovely when she was singing, but it was also very loud. As an adult, I have entertained friends and occasionally my students by recounting how she used to wake up her cousin, who lived a few doors down and across the street from us when we lived in the projects, by standing at our door and yelling her name, "Lorene! Lorene! Wake up!" When we moved, Lorene had to buy a telephone so that my mother could still make sure she was awake, but a man who lived in our old neighborhood told my mother that he started oversleeping after she left because he had counted on her to wake him up along with Lorene. She was like a rooster. So as she screamed at me on our way back from school, people came to their back doors to see what was happening. We eventually found the key at home where I knew it was (and I soon had a purse in which to carry the key), but that scene was one of the most horrific of my childhood, probably worse than anything that happened during my father's drunken antics.

As a result of my mother's behavior, to this day when I lose something, I have to fight to control my emotions. I tend to become both tense and angry. And it's harder to find anything in that condition. I especially have trouble with keys. I lived in two consecutive apartments, the Adams and Hoover one and the one in Cambridge, that had security locks that were locked from the inside with a key. Because the door of the Adams and Hoover apartment was next to a window, I didn't want to leave the key in the lock, so I tried to remember to keep it in a specific section of my purse. But, of course, being a future absent-minded professor, I sometimes misplaced it and rushed around my apartment looking for that damned key. It was especially bad when I had to be somewhere and couldn't find the key to let myself out of the apartment, and once I had food delivered and couldn't find the key when the delivery man arrived. Fortunately, I was a regular customer and (despite my poverty) a good tipper, so he waited patiently and even made suggestions about where to look. Shortly after I moved to the Cambridge apartment, I couldn't locate the key when the man coming to deliver my new television arrived, so I had to yell to him from the window of my second floor apartment to wait while I rushed around looking for that damned key. I eventually figured out that I should leave the key in the lock since the Cambridge apartment opened into a hallway, and there was no window next to the lock.

I knew even as a child that my mother's screaming at me over a lost key was unfair and borderline insane. I knew that she was wrong, first of all, because probably the same year that I forgot the key and couldn't immediately find it, my parents had one Sunday locked themselves (and my brother and me) out of the house by forgetting the key. I don't remember either one of them yelling at the other. If adults can be forgetful without being punished or called names in a voice loud enough to wake the dead, why couldn't children? I knew that children should not be held to a higher standard of conduct than adults. And I also knew that I was the kind of child who didn't need to be screamed at or whipped. I didn't start fights (well, except when I was called "nigger"), didn't steal (well, except for a few pieces of candy and a spoonful of ice cream here and there, but it was always my brother's idea), didn't curse (well, maybe I mouthed "shit" a few times, but that was my mother's favorite word), didn't talk back (although I certainly thought back), didn't do anything that would cause the wrath of the average adult. The fact that my grandmother, who was probably even stricter than my mother, which is why she evicted my brother in the middle of the night, loved living with me and never even raised her voice at me, shows what an easy-to-raise child I was. And, of course, back in those days, elementary school teachers whipped students. I received two licks in my hand with a ruler once from the fifth grade teacher when the whole class was punished for talking too loud when she was out of the room, but I was probably the least whipped child at Alves Street School. I was an abnormally quiet and docile child.

Still, I was screamed at and occasionally whipped by my mother for forgetting keys, forgetting something when I went to the store, or for clumsily breaking something. Is it any wonder that I love being an adult and that I didn't want to spend my adult years living with my mother? I especially enjoy being an adult when I make mistakes that could cause maternal screams. When I was living in the Pomona apartment, a friend of mine from graduate school visited me. Because she was slightly better with machines and technology than I was (all of my friends are), she put a new ribbon in my typewriter while I served her a glass of 7Up. When I put the glass of soda on the table just as she hit the return key on the typewriter to see if it worked, the typewriter carriage knocked the glass over, spilling 7Up on the table and the carpet below it. My friend, whose mother was a high-strung screamer like mine, froze and looked at me with frightened eyes; I gave her the same look. When we both realized that we were adults, and that I was not her mean mother and she was not mine, we started laughing hysterically. We were so relieved not to be yelled at by our mothers that we spent the rest of the evening entertaining each other with tales of our mean mothers. This woman was an inch or two taller and a year older than I was, so it really amused me that some part of her, like some part of me, was still scared of her mother.

I was once teasing one of my black students when she looked as if she would cry over her midterm grade. I looked at her sternly and said, "If you start crying, I'll give you something to cry about." Another black woman standing nearby groaned and said that my comment gave her chills. She had heard her mother make that comment many times. I said, "Where do you think I got it from? My mother said the same thing." Although my tall, terrified-of-her-mother friend is white, it seems that black mothers are generally more terrifying than white ones. Recently, the comedian Bill Maher, commenting on a controversy involving black comedian Tracy Morgan (it involved homophobia, and Bill might have pointed out how homophobic black men can be), noted that black comedians can joke about (physical) child abuse while white comedians can't. He mentioned specifically Bill Cosby, and I know exactly what he means. Cosby has joked about how black mothers show their love by hollering at, threatening, and beating their children. Well, I don't find that behavior funny.

Instead I enjoy tales of white women who let their children run wild and free. My friend and former student, Suzanne, the impending birth of whose second child led to the writing lab battle between Tall Woman and me, entertained me once by describing how her older child drew on one of her walls. Worried about the child's safety, I asked what she did. Thinking that I meant what she did about the wall, Suzanne, who is an amateur artist, said, "Oh, I just left it there for a few days; it was kind of interesting." That casual attitude cracked me up; my mother would have beaten the crap out of my brother and me if we had drawn on her walls. She still brags about how she kept her house spotless while raising two children. We were trained not to sit on certain chairs (we have a whole room of furniture in our house today that is meant to be seen and not sat on) and to jump over certain light-colored floor rugs. Draw on a wall? I don't think so.

Another easygoing white mother whose boys gone wild tales I've enjoyed is the woman the Spanish Professor called a bitch, my friend Smart Woman. I remember riding the elevator with her and her younger son before I knew either of them very well. I was already on the elevator when the younger son jumped on and hit the button that would close the door on his mother. I cringed, waiting for her to slap the little guy or at least scream at him, but she just laughed and said in a teasing voice something like "you little devil." When I told her years later how surprised I was by her reaction, she described other scenes involving that rather hyperactive son. She occasionally used a stern tone with him, as she did when he somehow started the car, and she had to run, jump in, and brake really fast to avoid a disaster, but she never screamed. The sons of Smart Woman and Suzanne may have been little terrors when they were growing up, but they are all doing quite well as adults. Suzanne's boys, who are Obamas (previously known as mulattos), both went to excellent colleges. The older boy, who drew on the wall, earned his B.A. from Pomona College and his M.A. from Princeton. He's currently working for the city of Newark. The younger son graduated from Swarthmore and is a musician. Smart Woman's oldest son is a successful lawyer, and the formerly hyperactive younger son has a Ph.D. in chemistry (his father is also a chemist) from Duke. Even better, he's married to a fellow Duke Ph.D., a very tall, part black, part Asian woman. He has done well indeed.

When I talk to my mother about these white women and their sons, I argue that the mothers' allowing their boys to be boys helped them grow into successful men. I believe that my success came in spite of, not because of, the harsh treatment I received as a child. While overcoming poverty, racism, alcoholism, and divorce at a young age made me stronger, being browbeaten by a high-strung mother made me weaker, vulnerable to bullies like Gray. When I lose control of my emotions now, I know that it's not just because I am my mother's child in the genetic sense, having inherited some of her high-strung emotions and tension, but because I was her child, raised in the tension-filled environment she created.

The second event that played in my mind when my mother tried to convince me that I should live with her and Dexter was less traumatic than the lost-key episode, but still made me determined to hold on to my privacy. It happened during that lost year of teaching at ETHS and paying rent to my parents. One night I was talking on my private telephone to one of my black Northwestern friends. This woman, who was attending graduate school on the East Coast, occasionally called me, or I called her, to chat. I'm not sure who called whom that night, possibly she called me, which alerted my mother that I was talking on the telephone. At any rate, I was having a pleasant conversation in a quiet voice because I assumed both of my parents were asleep when I thought I heard something in the hallway. I stepped to the door of my upstairs bedroom and found my mother sitting on the stairs, listening to my conversation. My first reaction was to laugh because what I was talking about wasn't that interesting.

But the more I thought about her spying on me, the more annoying and even creepy her behavior seemed. Why would she want to eavesdrop on my conversation? What was she trying to find out about me?

Those two memories kept me in my L.A. apartment and my parents in their San Fernando home as I completed my dissertation and taught at both USC and Cal Poly. Gradually, my mother stopped pushing her "let's live together" program and started focusing on my need to find a permanent job before (as she put it) I was too old. During this period, I came to appreciate that she was not interested in my academic achievements when I was younger. After a few weeks of having her ask me every day if I had finished another chapter of my dissertation, I had to lay down the law. She was not to mention my dissertation; if I wanted to discuss it, I would talk to her about it. I would let her know when I finished, not a chapter, but the whole damn thing.

When I finally finished my dissertation and landed a job in the Boston area, my parents were so happy that I had a job and (they hoped) could make more money that they didn't seem to care that I was moving even farther away from them than I was when they lived in Evanston and I lived in L.A. But before I moved to Boston, I spent a little over two months living with them in their small three-bedroom home. Although there were no major conflicts, the fact that Dexter was at home all of the time (well, except on Sundays when he and my mother went to church) just reminded me why their plan for me was so selfish and cruel. I liked living alone; with seniors in my house I would almost never be alone.

My parents' casual attitude toward my move to Boston was probably also due to their knowledge that I did not expect to live in Boston forever because I hated cold weather. And maybe they assumed that if I changed my mind, they would just follow me to the East Coast, and Dexter would wear many layers of clothing to protect his sore hips. Still they were delighted to learn that I was coming back to Southern California even earlier than I planned. (I had assumed that I would have to be at my first job at least three years before I could find a job in a more comfortable climate.) They even drove out to the Pomona area one Saturday to look for apartments for me. They were looking in Azusa but agreed when I pointed out that I needed an apartment nearer the school since I didn't have a car and couldn't yet drive.

During the Pomona years, there was less pressure from them to cohabit, but as I prepared to buy a house, my mother worried. I realized she counted on my not wanting to live in an apartment forever but not having enough money to buy a home. And she may have tried at least subconsciously to undermine my ability to buy that house. After I taught two summer school classes to earn the down payment for my home, my mother asked if she and Dexter could borrow money to buy a new car. Now they did need a new car in 1985. Their 1972 Pontiac had been back and forth between Illinois and California once when Dexter drove me here and then made the trip from Illinois to California when they moved here in 1976. They also drove it quite frequently for the first six years they were here, often chauffeuring me, before I bought my car in 1982. So I didn't doubt that they really wanted to buy a car. But I asked an important question. If they couldn't save for the down payment on a car when they weren't paying a car note, how could they pay me back by the next summer, when I planned to buy my house, once they were paying a car note? My mother didn't have an answer to that question, and they never bought a new car. Instead, the next summer I bought my townhouse.

My mother's reaction to my purchasing the townhouse reflected her mixed feelings about our living arrangements. On one hand, she was happy, also probably proud, that I was moving into a nicer neighborhood and could afford my own home, but on the other hand, the home that I bought was so small that there was clearly no place in it for her and Dexter. She let her disappointment show at one point when we inspected the townhouse right after I had moved in. I was showing her the ceiling light that was over the kitchen sink, and she began by saying how nice it was, and then she suddenly seemed to grow angry as she talked about how I should thank God that I was able to buy this townhouse. She started a little shout, but it was clearly not a happy shout; it was an angry shout. I could tell that she thought I, who wasn't exactly Ms. Good Housekeeping, didn't deserve a nice brand new townhouse in an upscale neighborhood. She deserved it and couldn't have it because her selfish, ungodly daughter refused to live with her. I let her finish her little sermon and then calmly but snippily said, "Most mothers would be proud that their single daughters could afford to buy a nice home like this, instead of telling them how they should thank God, as if they hadn't worked and sacrificed in order to pay for this townhouse, as if they hadn't lived beneath the poverty line for years so that they could gain an education that would allow them at the relatively mature age of 37 to buy this townhouse. Most mothers would be proud and happy for their daughters." My mother knew she had lost that round, so she hugged me and claimed to be proud.

But I didn't have much time to enjoy my new townhouse before disaster in the form of cancer struck. I moved into my new townhouse on the last day of August, 1986. At the beginning of December that year, my mother called to tell me that Dexter, who had been on crutches for years but by that time mostly used a wheelchair, was in the hospital because his bowels had locked. He was soon discharged but felt sick and was uncharacteristically melancholy during the Christmas holiday (He loved Christmas). About a month into the new year, my mother called to tell me that Dexter was again in the hospital, and it looked as if he might die. The immediate medical crisis, which soon passed, was caused by an endoscopy, which for some reason caused him to have heart problems. But the even worse news was that Dexter had cancer that had started in his prostate and moved to his bones. He lived until May, 1988, but I had to make several emergency runs to their home as his condition twice sent my mother, who has had heart problems since childhood, to the hospital.

At one point during that year, I was asleep in the relatively (for me) early morning hours when I heard the downstairs telephone. Realizing that I had unplugged my upstairs telephone to take a nap the previous evening and had forgotten to reconnect it, I quickly corrected my error. When I answered the telephone, it was my officemate, Kentuckian's Wife, telling me that my mother had called her, crying because she couldn't reach me on the telephone. Kentuckian's Wife had a key to my townhouse, so she told my mother that she would call first and then come to my house to see if I were okay. When I called my mother, she told me that she had hurt her back, helping Dexter, and needed me to come out there to take care of both of them. When I called Kentuckian's Wife back to tell her what was going on, she warned me that I would increasingly receive such calls. She and her husband had been through their own taking care of the old folks dramas in the years before they moved to Southern California.

She was right, of course. But what made the dramas worse for me is that I had been drafted for the job, and I didn't have a husband or adult children to assist me. My parents followed me to Southern California so I could take care of them. At the time of his illness, Dexter had many relatives living in the Chicago area, sisters and brothers, nieces and nephews (My stepbrother died in the early eighties). However, the sister who lived down the street from him when they moved to San Fernando died of cancer about a year and a half after he moved there, and his half-brother had died about two months before he became ill. Worse, his sister's young son had died of meningitis a few years after his mother's death, and that young man's older sister, along with her adult children, moved out of the area. So I was it. My parents had no other close relatives to call.

Of course, they were active church members, and members of black Baptist churches are very helpful when their folks are sick or in trouble. Still, they expect relatives to participate. And all of my parents' church members knew they had a daughter in the area. So I was on call; no matter what was happening in my professional life, I had to rush out to San Fernando when my mother fainted and had to be hospitalized, or when she hurt her back. I think about those days now when I'm more than two years older than she was then, and she acts as if I'm forty or maybe even twenty and dismisses any suggestion that I could become seriously ill.

After Dexter's death and burial in Evanston (where close to a hundred relatives attended the funeral), the drama subsided, but the let's-live-together campaign began again. I hadn't realized until after Dexter's death how fortunate I was to have bought my townhouse before he died. It would have been harder for me to counter my mother's arguments if I had been still living in that increasingly uncomfortable and unsafe Pomona apartment. But since I had been in my new perfect-for-me townhouse not quite two years, I could argue against selling it and buying something bigger so we could live together. My mother tried to convince me that I was the meanest, most selfish person in the world for not wanting to live with her, but I wasn't buying it. As I still tell her today, if I were really mean, she would never have wanted to live with me.

My mother's problem was that she had never lived alone. She married my father when she was eighteen, essentially so she wouldn't have to live with her too strict mother. Both times that my father skipped town, she had two children, and when he left the first time, my brother and I were already nine and seven, not exactly babies. Then, of course, when she left Henderson, she lived with the white folks until she married Dexter. She is also a much more sociable person than her daughter, which is why her mother, who believed children should be quiet, preferred me.

Although she never really liked living alone, my mother was starting to adjust to her single status by 1990. She had a seasonal job with a photographer and traveled around with two other women--her crew--taking pictures at various L.A. area schools. One of her best friends was also a recent widow, and they usually had Sunday dinner together and often shopped in Northridge or North Hollywood. At the end of 1989, she and I went to my brother's home in Atlanta (he and his family moved there from Chicago earlier in the year) for Christmas. When we returned, we spent one night at my townhouse, and the next morning, she was rushing me because she wanted to hurry home to check on her house. I thought it was a good sign that she was so eager to return home. I didn't even mind when she angrily snapped at me because she became nervous when her furnace didn't come on quickly enough. For some reason, she had turned it off completely and was worried that it wouldn't come back on. I asked if she was sure she had turned it on, and she snarled "yes" angrily at me. No problem, I thought, I'm going back to my house, and she will be here in hers. I should have known better than to gloat; I should have known that I would seal my fate. I should have seen the red light ahead.

About a month later, my mother called me around nine or ten on a Thursday night. I remember that it was a time that was not scary; if it had been midnight, I would have been worried. Even though everyone knew I stayed up until three or four in the morning, people usually didn't call after eleven p.m. unless it was bad news. I answered the telephone, assuming it was one of my friends. Even when I heard my mother's voice, I wasn't worried. She often didn't go to bed until around ten during that period. But then I noticed that she sounded scared and shaken. Soon I was shaken as well because my mother told me that a young man had broken into her house, beaten, raped, and robbed her. As we talked, she said that she had called some of her friends, including the other widow who had recently remarried. She also said that she thought the rapist was the son of the woman next door because he looked like another son of that woman's, and she knew that she had a son who had been in jail. She then said in a really pitiful, scared voice, crying, that she couldn't live in her house anymore. I responded in a strong voice that she wouldn't have to, which clearly made her feel better. I wouldn't have her living next door to a rapist, and I knew she wouldn't want to stay in that house even if the rapist lived in Alaska. She would have to move. I told her to stay on the telephone with me until her friends arrived. When the doorbell rang, she started screaming. Of course, that shook me up, but I tried to remain calm and told her to go to the door, and I would stay on the line. I was shaken even more when I heard one of her friends, an equally high- strung woman, screaming when she saw my mother (her face had been badly beaten). The recently married friend, a calmer woman, maybe because she worked in a hospital and her son was a policeman, picked up the telephone and told me to stay at home until the next morning because my mother would be worried about me if I drove to San Fernando at night. She promised that they would stay with her if she were released from the hospital.

The rest of that night and the next day, I felt I was in a nightmare or in a television drama. Usually, I didn't have to go to work on Fridays, but because I was advising students that Friday, I had not only planned to be in my office, but to observe one of the T.A's teaching a basic writing skills class. I called that woman to cancel the observation, briefly explaining what had happened; she told me later that she also felt as if she were on a television crime show. Before I left for San Fernando, I called the one EFL secretary who arrived on campus at 7:30 a.m. to tell her to place a note on my door letting the ILE students know that I wouldn't be there that day. Then I drove to the house of my mother's newly married friend. When I looked in the window and saw my mother, she at first looked okay, so I waved at her and tried to look happy. But once I entered the house and saw the other side of her face, I had to fight back tears because her eye was swollen shut. The rest of the day was spent talking to police, taking my mother to the beauty shop (my mother thought the rapist was trying to drown her, but he was actually just viciously messing up her hair, which she was proud of, by sticking her under the shower; he was also undoubtedly trying to eliminate evidence, being an experienced rapist), taking her to the police station for pictures, and loading my car with her clothes and any other valuables we didn't want to leave behind. We had plenty of help as my mother's retired friends and their husbands walked back and forth from the house to the car, putting in everything my car would hold. We also all shot evil glances at anyone who went in and out of the rented house next door.

As my mother and I were on the freeway heading back to Claremont in Friday evening rush hour traffic, I had to concentrate hard because my head was spinning. I was running on maybe forty minutes of sleep and was probably in a state of shock. Fortunately, she was sleeping in the seat next to me. I didn't really stop to think about what her moving into my home meant for me. My mother was the victim of a terrible crime, and she was an almost 62-year-old widow with a heart condition. I knew I needed to make sure she recovered before I thought about myself. As I drove for about two hours, I kept replaying in my head one scene from the many in that traumatic day. My mother's newly married friend had driven us to the police station for an appointment so my mother could have her bruises and scratches photographed. We were running a little late, so I held my mother's hand and pushed us ahead of other people standing around the reception desk. One man was about to give me attitude, as I probably would have him were the situation reversed, but then that man saw my mother's face, and he immediately stepped back and said, "I'm sorry; go right ahead." He saw what I already knew. My mother needed to be placed ahead of everyone at that moment in her life.

Although I'm not good with sick people, one of the many reasons why I was not an appropriate choice for caretaker of old folks, I turned out to be very good at taking care of a crime victim. First of all, I could put myself in my mother's shoes and understand what she needed and what she couldn't do. I knew she couldn't sleep on my couch bed downstairs, which is where guests usually stayed. So until she bought a bed for what had been my office and became for more than two years her bedroom, I slept on the couch, and she slept in my bedroom. I understood that she would be frightened to walk alone in a new neighborhood but needed to continue walking, so I walked with her for a few days. I also knew that my odd hours were helpful because I could watch the house while she slept. In fact, since my mother always awoke by 4:00 a.m., and I usually didn't go to bed until 3:00 or 3:30, one of us was almost always awake.

I also luckily had helpful social worker type friends who immediately counseled my mother. Smart Woman, who is now a therapist, showed up with food, cookies, and advice. A Cal Poly p.e. professor, who lived in my neighborhood and was my mother's age, found her a Big Sister, a fellow senior crime victim, who could walk with my mother and help her find a new doctor, and most important, help her deal with her fear and anger. And, of course, it helped that I am an amateur comedian, and my mother likes to laugh. We laughed about how she walked around the neighborhood, telling everyone she was my mother, when most of the people didn't know me. "I left the South when I was in my teens; I don't tell everybody my business. These people don't know me from Eve," I told her. She and I went to lunch every Saturday and out to dinner every other Wednesday evening just so that she had something to do, and we laughed at each other and at the people we saw in the restaurants.

Because my mother is a high-strung drama queen, I was surprised at how relatively calmly she handled such a traumatic event. Of course, she had nightmares, but I knew that would happen and knew how to handle them, with a joke and a laugh. And one day when she was walking alone, a man suddenly ran up from behind her, said something, probably "excuse me," and she started screaming. A woman who was coming from the other direction ran quickly up to help her, and both runners were very consoling and comforting when she told them her story. The Claremont folks may be snobs, but they are compassionate snobs. When my mother came home and told me about that incident, we were soon laughing. I told her she probably scared that poor running man even more than he scared her because she was one of the world's loudest screamers.

Bell hooks, who was teaching at Oberlin at the time, happened to be in the area because she had recently given a presentation at Cal Poly. She agreed to the invitation to speak at our school, mainly to earn money, but also because she wanted to see the place where I was teaching. When I told her what happened, explaining why we couldn't meet again before she departed, I mentioned how surprised I was by my mother's relatively calm reaction to such a violent, horrendous crime. Bell, who had seen my mother only twice, most recently at the Cal Poly presentation, which my mother and one of her friends attended, said, "Of course, she has what she wants, all of your attention." I thought bell had made a good point because my mother liked to be the center of attention. But I attributed her almost Zen acceptance of her fate to two other factors. First, she was very religious and found solace in prayer and in talking to her religious friends. But second, and more important, she thought that she was now going to stay with me forever. I felt that my mother believed that if she had to go through that horrible night of torment to convince me that we should live together, it was worth it. As she probably would have put it, "If God wanted me to go through all of that to convince this girl that she needs to live with her mother, then that's okay with me." Bell thought I also had a good point and suggested that I quickly move my mother out of my house because if I waited too long, she might have a stroke or a heart attack when she finally realized that I didn't plan to live with her forever.

But I used a different strategy, which eventually worked. I knew my mother would not be satisfied living with me in my two bedroom townhouse while most of her antique furniture was in storage. I also knew that my mother had enough of a sense of fair play (a trait her daughter inherited) not to try to dominate me in my house. So my plan was to give her as much time as she needed to heal and decide what to do but to refuse to move out of my townhouse.

After she had lived with me for several months, sold her home, and visited my brother in Atlanta and some relatives in Henderson, my mother had healed enough to start seriously lobbying me to sell my place and buy a larger house with her. She looked at a townhouse in my community and one in a nearby neighborhood, but they would have cost most of the money that she made from the sale of her San Fernando home, and she couldn't really afford the association dues, taxes, and utilities since her only income was a tiny Social Security check. She also was clearly not ready to live on her own in the L.A. area. Her let's-live-together campaign was even more intense this time than it had been when Dexter was alive and immediately after he died because she was more desperate. But I was also desperate to hang on to my privacy, so I refused to be guilt tripped into doing something that I did not want and didn't feel obligated to do. So no matter what her arguments, I was ready with counter-arguments. While making my case, I referred to both the past and the future. I subtly (using tactics I learned in white institutions) or directly pointed out that her mother lived in a convalescent home for several years even though she had two daughters and one son. I also pointed out that I had no adult daughters to take care of me when I was old. During one calm conversation, I made her see how selfish her plan was. "Let's say we both live to be the same age as Mother was when she died," I argued. So you and I will live together, and then when you die at 84, I will be 63 with 21 more years to live alone. By then I will have gotten used to living with you, but I will be all alone at the same age that you are now. What will I do?" Her response was: "You can marry." She was obviously still clinging to the Betty Jean plan. But I made her see how ridiculous that comment was, asking if I should have children at 63. Then I hit her with, "Why don't you just admit that you don't care what happens to me as long as you have a comfortable place to spend your old age?" What could she say?

The argument that probably convinced my mother that she could not persuade me to sell my townhouse focused not on the past and the future but on personalities. I pointed out that she was not trying to dominate (I used the phrase "run over") me because we were living in my house. If we bought a house together, I said, you will want to be more in charge of it, right? And she admitted that she would. I then pointed out that as an adult who enjoyed living alone and could support myself, I would be a fool to sell my house and buy one with her so that she could push me around. Interestingly, she didn't really try to deny that she would want to be the boss in our new co-owned house.

Then, as the months passed, my mother started to worry about my health. One day when I left for work, she was sitting in one of the 1950's era gold chairs that she had moved into my living room; when I returned home several hours later, she was sitting in that same chair. Now I knew that my mother had not been sitting in that chair all day. She walked every afternoon, and she had cooked, eaten dinner, and washed the dishes. She probably had also dusted and cleaned something because she cleaned something every day. But she just happened to have been sitting in that chair, both when I left and when I returned home. As I opened the door and saw her sitting there, I greeted her rather coldly and headed straight for the pantry, where I kept my stash of bite size Hershey bars. Watching me as I headed up the stairs with my briefcase in one hand and two or three tiny candy bars clutched in the other, my mother said dryly, "I'm gonna have to move, or you'll be big as this house."

Her first plan was to sign up for the new senior apartments being planned for the south side of town, but when they weren't built fast enough, she went to a second plan. During a few visits to Henderson, she had enjoyed staying with her first cousin and reconnecting with family and old friends. One of her old friends, who had been living in Chicago for many years, had recently returned to Henderson and claimed to be enjoying her stay there. So despite the fact that my father, not her favorite person, had also returned to Henderson, my mother decided to buy one of the new houses being built there. The plan was that she would live in Henderson most of the year and spend the coldest months with me.

When the house was completed, my mother moved back to Henderson in May, 1992. Before she left, she bought me a new Toyota Corolla so she could take my 1988 Corolla (I had given her my 1982 Citation, which was a lemon, when I bought that first Toyota) and to thank me for letting her live with me for more than two years without having to pay rent or utilities. I visited her during Christmas of that year and was impressed with her beautiful one-story new home that cost so much less than what she had made from selling her not quite so lovely home in San Fernando. A few weeks later, my mother visited me for about a month, and then we started a routine of her coming to Claremont in early December and leaving for Henderson near the end of February.

When we started that routine, I would become anxious as December approached, dreading giving up my privacy. But usually, once my mother arrived, I was happy to see her, and we had no problems living together again. After a year or two, I came to appreciate both the time that I spent alone and the two months spent with my mother. I ate better when she was in town because she was a better cook. I also suspended my cleaning service because my mother kept the townhouse spotless. After she moved to Henderson, I discovered that I could no longer tolerate my mess, but since I didn't want to clean as regularly as she did, I had hired people to clean once a month.

By the fourth year, I looked forward to my mother's arrival and dreaded her leaving. There had been a few problems with her travels in December. One year it was snowing in Evansville on the morning she was supposed to leave, so we worried that she would be grounded. Another year, a small plane crashed a few weeks before she was to leave, and those planes were all grounded, so she had to take a bus from Evansville to Chicago. Since she was heading swiftly toward seventy, I knew that it would be more and more difficult for her to travel back and forth between her two homes. It was also troubling that Henderson was so far away and difficult to reach, a point brought home by the grounded small planes. At least Atlanta and Chicago were only one plane ride away, but there were no direct flights from L.A. to Evansville, so if something happened to my mother, and I needed to fly there to see about her, it would be more trouble than a tense, (pre) menopausal woman should have to face. One summer, we discussed my mother's possibly having a pacemaker implanted; I told her that she should do it during the summer when I could stay with her. Because I was her daughter (she also almost never missed work, no matter what was going on in her life), I couldn't or wouldn't leave school in the middle of the quarter if she became ill in Kentucky while I was teaching in California. Then I became ill in California.

Stomach problems run on both sides of my family, and the women seem to be especially vulnerable. I'd had occasional bouts with severe stomach aches throughout my life, and twice in earlier years (during the year that I was teaching at ETHS and when I was studying for the qualifying exams at USC) briefly had trouble swallowing food. But starting in the summer of 1995, I struggled for almost two years with acid reflux and other stomach problems. My mother had been with me during the winter of 1996 and witnessed my problems, but after she left, I initially tried to downplay how much trouble I was still having. However, during the summer, when my condition had not improved, I admitted that I was still rapidly losing weight. My mother decided to come to see about me. I tried to dissuade her, saying that I would not pay for her flight (I purchased her annual December to February tickets), but she said she'd pay for her own flight. Then I said I didn't feel like picking her up at the airport. She said she'd catch a cab. Not being a mother, I had underestimated her need to take care of her not so young child. So I gave in and let her come. She arrived in early August, and when we met at the airport (I was bluffing about not showing up), she became tearful when she saw how much weight I had lost since February.

During the three weeks that my mother, who had worked as a nurse's aide at the Northwestern Health Center and for Homecare organizations, and so is much better at dealing with sick people than is her daughter, stayed with me, accompanying me to doctor's appointments and trying to find food I could eat, I decided that she and I had both mellowed enough that we could maybe live together as equals in a co-owned house. I could give up my privacy if she could give up her need to control and dominate. I'll never forget her response when I told her that I might be ready to live with her around the time I turned fifty. First, she said that she wouldn't be alive when I turned fifty; when I reminded her that I would be fifty in not quite three years and that she would be seventy-one at that point, she said, "Oh." And then her left eye started jumping. I believe that she developed that new nervous tic because she thought that my change of heart about living with her meant that either she or I (probably I) would die soon.

Somehow the almost three years turned into immediately, and soon my mother and I were both trying to sell our homes so we could buy one together. She sold hers first and moved back in with me in November, 1997. After spending another year living together in the townhouse and then seven weeks in a two-bedroom apartment in San Dimas, we finally moved into our new home on Martin Luther King's birthday in 1999, exactly two months before I turned fifty.

Initially, what I saw as my supreme sacrifice seemed to pay off, and my good deed seemed to go unpunished for a change. Although my mother and I got on each other's nerves occasionally, we mostly enjoyed each other's company, and she was more help than trouble. As a still fairly healthy seventy something, she could drive, clean the whole house, do the laundry, do most of the cooking, and take care of the plants and flowers we planted in our tiny yard. She was also a good telephone receptionist, having worked in that capacity at one of the many jobs she held when she moved to San Fernando. I loved to hear her ask in her professional receptionist voice that made her sound vaguely like a Northern white woman, "Who's calling, please?"

During this period of living comfortably with my mother, I started to understand her personality better and realize why she differed from me in so many ways. I had discovered when she was living with me in the early nineties that she was a Southern Belle, Ebony DuBois, as I liked to call her. But I hadn't figured out how she became a Southern Belle. How does a black woman of any era and any class become a Southern Belle and especially how does one who came of age in the South before the Jim Crow period ended pull off such a feat? As I listened to her stories (seniors love to reminiscence), I realized that she had been a child of privilege for the first ten years of her life. Her father, Joe Jackson, had worked for the railroad and had been a good provider, so my maternal grandmother did not have to work. My mother talked about the fur coats her daddy bought for her and her older sister. And she loved to tell the story of how she was crying because she wasn't allowed to eat the free lunches the other black children of the Depression were given at school when one of her teachers told her that she couldn't have the lunches because her father made too much money. I don't think it takes Freud to figure out the significance of her second husband's being a railroad man seventeen years her senior.

Unfortunately, her father died when she was ten or eleven (she always says ten, but if he died in December, 1939, as it says on his ancestry.com records, then she was eleven), and she was soon working for white folks. She and my grandmother (and until she was married, my aunt) received checks from the railroad and/or the World War I veterans pension, but my ambitious mother wanted more money so she could continue to wear beautiful clothes. But those years of living like a little princess in the house that in the thirties probably wasn't so rundown and didn't seem so primitive created the spoiled Southern Belle with whom I live today. Thus, it's not surprising that she, who had her two children at home in a two-room shack, can turn up her nose at renters (the fact that the rapist next door was a renter also contributes to her disdain), or that she could actually boast that she had never lived in an apartment before our exile in San Dimas. (I, who had lived in several apartments, reminded her of that shack and the projects.) Her experience living with a strong, doting father (as well as having a strong maternal grandfather) probably also explains why she has no trouble asking men to help her. Her interactions with various handymen reminds me of the original Southern Belle, Blanche DuBois,' dependence on the kindness of strange men. My mother will ask the plumber installing the sink to change a light bulb, ask the electrician installing the chandelier to see if he can figure out what's wrong with the television, and ask the cable man to see if he can make the CD player work right. She's even better at calling on the services of various male neighbors; in fact, her favorite handyman, because his services are free, is our across-the- courtyard neighbor, Irl, who happens to be the first cousin of the political Hahn (Janice and James) family. Does my mother care? Not at all. If Irl is handy and friendly, which he is, then she thinks he should be her beck-and-call man, no matter who his family members are.

I, of course, benefit from my mother's Southern Belle ways even as I try to protect the various handymen and "poor Irl," as I call him, from her manipulations. I also surprised myself by actually enjoying being in this house with furniture from my childhood. When we discussed what furniture to keep and what to discard, as we planned to join households, my mother wanted me to dump my 1980 bedroom suite and use the 1946 bed I was born in. I hated that idea since my childhood wasn't exactly a Disney movie. Why would I want to relive it every night? So even though

I did dump my old bedroom suite, I bought a new one to replace it. We put the antique bed, with its matching but newer night stand, dresser and chest of drawers, in the guest bedroom. But for some reason, I love showing people that bed and the complete 1959 bedroom suite that my mother has in her room. I guess, as I've grown older, I've learned to appreciate antiques. As Faulkner might say, that furniture endured, which is more than I can say for most of the more expensive, but not well-made, furniture I bought through the years.

Of course, I knew the happy, comfortable times wouldn't last. Old people just grow older, and usually with old age come health problems. So, even as I appreciated that life with my mother was more fun than I expected, my red light blinked. I knew there were difficult days ahead. And those difficult days started in 2003 when my mother was 75. She had managed to avoid having the pacemaker implanted without the dire consequences doctors predicted, but that year she started fainting. And until she finally gave in and accepted the pacemaker in September, 2006, she fainted at least once each year. In fact, she fainted so much in 2006 that I didn't even call 911 the last time it happened.

During that period I became very familiar with emergency rooms. I've been in the emergency room of every hospital within ten miles of our house at least once. During one late-night run to the hospital, my mother wasn't ill enough to warrant immediate attention, so we sat in the waiting room for hours. As I watched the other patients, I saw another reason (besides impatience and love of solitude) why I was lucky not to have children. Most of the people coming to the emergency room late at night or in the early morning hours are either old people or young parents with small children.

Because I inherited some of my maternal grandmother's fear of the seriously ill, my mother's health problems really unnerved me and also reminded me of the downside of being unmarried and without children. There is no lonelier feeling than being stuck in the house alone with an unconscious person, waiting for paramedics. And then when they arrive, at least in Claremont, they come in larger numbers than seem necessary. Often the police arrive first, and then come firemen and paramedics. I'm not one of those women who enjoy being around men in uniform. Maybe because I'm a black woman from the sixties, such men, especially white ones, make me nervous. During one late-night emergency, I counted eight men in my house; only one of them, a Latino, was nonwhite. During another emergency, there were two black men in the crew, one middle-aged, and I kept looking at him when one of the white men asked me questions. The white man would ask me a question, and I would answer him while looking at the middle-aged black man. Finally, the black man pointed at the white man, and I laughed as I looked at him (at last) while answering his question.

My mother's health problems also made some of her other traits more disturbing because they added stress to my already too stressful life. She's a hypochondriac who loves attention, so she's always complaining about her health. Now a healthy hypochondriac or a stoic sick person might be worrisome, but still tolerable. But a sickly hypochondriac is almost unbearable. How can I tell when she's really sick and about to pass out, or she just wants attention, or is just complaining about her health because she has nothing else to do? I tried initially to appeal to her maternal instincts, pointing out that I had a stress-related stomach ailment and having a person pass out is stressful, so when she talked about feeling "fantified," dizzy, or light-headed, it made me nervous. I was gentle about it at first, but then I overheard her laughing to one of her friends, a nurse, about how scared I became when she fainted. I have a good sense of humor, but terrorizing someone who is in her fifties and has strokes on one side of her family and heart attacks on the other does not sound like fun to me. So my next move was to start complaining loudly, laughing sarcastically, or sighing dramatically every time she referenced her health. That strategy didn't work either. She just began her complaint by saying, "I know you don't want me to say anything about my feelings, but . . ." Or she began with, "I said I wasn't going to say anything to you about this, but. . ." Or she asked me questions: "Have you ever had a real sharp pain in the front of your head?" "Have your legs ever felt so weak that you didn't think you could walk?"

When she's not fainting or threatening to faint, my mother can be a troublemaker. She's the unofficial neighborhood cop. She informs all new neighbors, especially the renters, what the rules are and will confront them if they commit violations. And heaven help the child playing ball near our house! My mother's voice may no longer be as shrill and piercing as it was during her church soloist days, but she can still shout loud enough to scare wayward children. She rushed downstairs and confronted them in person when she was in her seventies, but now that she's past eighty and can't move so fast, she just throws open her bedroom window and shouts from there.

The year after she started fainting, my mother had an altercation with a young mother of two who was renting the house next to ours. She and that young woman had initially bonded over their mutual love of a spotless house and clean surroundings. A few months earlier, they worked together (with their hoses) to clean away ashes left on our courtyard by the October, 2003, fire. But my mother is as confrontational as she is friendly, and so it wasn't surprising that she eventually battled this woman. What was surprising was the woman's reaction. She first stuck a letter on our door, chastising my mother and me (she addressed the letter to "neighbors") because she felt my mother, who was old enough to be her grandmother, had been disrespectful toward her. (My mother complained about renters.) I found this letter attached to my door at the end of a day of teaching. As soon as I read the snippy letter, before I prepared my dinner and ate, before I even took off my work clothes, I sat down at my computer and wrote Ms. Disrespected a two-page letter. I didn't say in that letter what I was thinking as I tapped on the keys so fast and so hard that I'm surprised that the keyboard survived. I was thinking, "Does she realize that I'm an English major? Only a fool would write such a snotty letter to a person who teaches writing for a living."

Ms. Disrespected never bothered us again; in fact, she tried not to be outside when we were visible, but she managed to show us what she thought of us in a way that reminded us that we may have been buying our home, that I may have been an English professor who could show her how an angry letter should be written, but we were still, in her opinion, inferior to her. Ms. Disrespected had been a primary school teacher before she had her two children, so she liked to display in her yard cute little signs commemorating the seasons or special holidays. She displayed a bunny rabbit for Easter, for example. A few weeks after our little neighborly feud, Ms. Disrespected put up a new sign. I guess it was supposed to announce the coming summer. At any rate, the sign featured a crow eating watermelon. Her signs usually faced the street, but she turned this one toward our house.

After the racist sign appeared in Ms. Disrespected's yard, I was having lunch with my friend Smart Woman on campus, describing the whole incident, including some of the points that I had made in my letter about my mother's deserving respect from this much younger white woman (I didn't mention race in the letter). At that point in the conversation, I suddenly choked up and had to fight to regain my composure. Smart Woman thought I was upset because of the way the young white woman treated my mother, but I actually was upset first, because I was still having to deal with racism in the twenty-first century, but also because I was dealing with the conflict I always knew living with my mother would bring. Unless the neighbors are outrageous, like the fighting couples in Pomona or the Rolling Stones in L.A., my motto is live and let live. I like just to speak to my neighbors and leave them alone. I don't tell them my business and don't want to know theirs. I also don't care where they park their cars or what their children do as long as they don't inconvenience me. I knew my mother's approach was different, and I knew that the difference would add stress and disturb my peace if we lived together.

Ms. Disrespected's racist sign was the most disturbing example of my having to cope with the aftereffects of my mother's confrontational approach to life in the neighborhood.

Still, once my mother's pacemaker was installed, and she stopped fainting, I was again more happy than not with our living arrangement. I enjoyed telling my classes stories about my live-in senior. When we were reading about Southerners, mothers, or Southern black mothers in my literature classes, I told how people were fooled into believing that my mother was this soft, sweet little woman because she called everyone "honey" or "chile." Or I said my mother put me in my place by calling medical doctors "real doctors," implying that Ph.D. means "phony doctor." Or I jokingly complained that when we saw some crazy-looking and acting, possibly homeless, man walking around Claremont (the city of Ph.D.'s), my mother inevitably said, "He's a professor." And when we read a story about a young man visiting his grandmother in my basic writing classes and discussed what seniors contributed to society, I used my mother as an example to show why seniors were ideal neighborhood watchers. They are at home all day, I would say; they are very nosy, and they don't mind calling the police.

However, as I became increasingly more senior and my retirement date approached, a new tension developed between my mother and me. For decades, probably since I turned forty, I planned to retire no later than sixty, and as that year approached, I was eager to pack up my books and come home. One reason I was eager to retire is that my senior caretaking duties had increased. After she started fainting, my mother no longer drove, so I had to take her to beauty and doctor appointments, as well as to the store. Initially, I drove her to the store and walked up and down the aisles with her, pushing the cart while she selected meat, produce, and can goods, but eventually I just started shopping for her. I also had to take on some of the household chores. She could no longer hand wash the floors, so I did that, and because I was living with Mrs. Clean, I washed the kitchen floor and the hallway from the garage into the house twice a week. Now I was willing to pay Molly Maid or some other cleaning company to clean the house once a week, but I knew that they would not be able to meet my mother's high standards for cleanliness so long as she could see fairly well and move around well enough to clean the house herself. Until she was almost blind or became incapacitated, I had to help her clean the house.

A few years before I took on these extra duties, I became a full-time teacher again, so at a time when most people slow down, I was actually working harder. And because I was mentally and physically slowing down, it took me longer to complete tasks so that I never seemed to have free time. Even during the summer, I seemed rushed as I went to doctor's appointments, had my car serviced, and tried to take care of other professional and personal projects that I didn't have time for during the school year.

Clearly, then, it was time for me to retire. Since my mother always hated to see me return to work in September because it meant that she had to take afternoon walks alone (I walked with her in the morning only during the brief times when I worried about her safety) and had to schedule all appointments on Friday, you would think that she'd be happy for me to retire. Of course, most mothers might be a little disturbed to have a child old enough to retire, but my mother knew that she started having children young, so she had to deal with having great grandchildren and children old enough to retire.

However, about three years before I retired, my mother started a campaign to keep me working. She talked about how stupid it would be for anyone to retire in this bad economy. And she praised people who continued to work into their sixties and even seventies because they wanted to have something to do. She even worried about people going crazy when they retired because they didn't know what to do with themselves. I couldn't figure out why she was on this keep-Mary-working campaign. I knew it wasn't because she didn't want me at home. I'm quiet, and my mother likes company, so it couldn't be that. I decided that she was worried that I would not have enough money when I retired, and that our lifestyle would be affected. After all, she and Dexter had trouble living comfortably on his fixed retirement income (they couldn't afford to buy a new car) even though she worked various temporary jobs. But when I was a few months from retirement, she finally let me know her real fears. She had been reading news stories about how we retiring baby boomers were going to suck up all of the Social Security, so she was worried about her tiny check's disappearing if I retired. I couldn't believe it! She makes less per year than I pay in federal income tax even now that I'm retired. And she wanted me to keep working so she could collect her tiny check? I told her she should be ashamed of herself, trying to force her daughter, who had been preparing for retirement for decades, to keep working just so she could make a few hundred dollars a month. I guess that's how mothers born into the middle class treat their born-into-the-working-class daughters.

Once I finally retired and her Social Security check continued to arrive at the bank, my mother seemed content with my decision. But then I had problems with her behavior. Having spent twenty-nine years on that battlefield called Cal Poly, I looked forward to a peaceful life at home. But my mother was always worrying me about something. She thought the air conditioner made a funny noise and might be breaking down. Or the gardeners didn't properly clean up after themselves. Or one of the neighbors parked in the place where we liked to put our garbage cans and didn't move her car fast enough. As Gilda Radner used to say, it was always something. Several times during my first summer after retirement, I "accidentally" locked my mother out of the house. Even though she couldn't articulate the idea that I was subconsciously trying to lock her out of my life, she knew enough to be vaguely insulted by my absent-minded lockouts.

Then on the night before what I thought would be my new favorite day of the year, the day when classes would start at Cal Poly and I would not have to go back to work, my mother fainted for the first time since the pacemaker was implanted. She had been having problems with diarrhea for a few days, apparently because of a mild case of salmonella and was dehydrated. So instead of celebrating my freedom on the first day of classes, I was at the hospital with my mother. I was frustrated, aggravated, devastated. I even called my brother to complain (since he was also retired) and started crying. Even though I found the whole episode amusing a few weeks later, I still resented the loss of what would be my only first day of freedom. The first day of Winter and Spring Quarters or the first day of my second year in retirement would not be the same.

What made it worse is that this first fainting episode in three years started another series of fainting spells, so I was visiting emergency rooms again during my first quarter of freedom. But just as I became resigned to the fact that my first years of retirement might be full of angst and hospital visits, my mother's health improved, and we both started enjoying my retirement. She enjoyed the fact that I made enough money as a retired person so that I could buy new televisions and appliances without complaining, and she was happy that she didn't have to wait until Fridays or school vacations to make appointments. I was even happier, appreciating times spent sitting in my house, quietly enjoying my freedom, without worrying about her health.

As we've settled into our new existence as two retired old ladies, one senior and one super-senior, as I call us, we're managing to laugh more than we complain or bicker. We make fun of each other and of everybody else. (I recently gave one of my mother's super-senior friends her "laugh for the day" by explaining that my mother was out watering the lemon tree because I didn't know how to do it. "I can water all of the other plants," I said, "but I don't know how to water the tree because I'm only 62.") And we try not to get on each other's nerves. Because I don't like for my mother to tell me when to leave the house for appointments, I won't tell her what time they are. So when she asks, "When are you going to get your taxes fixed?" I'll say, "I'm not telling you because you'll try to tell me when to leave the house, and I'm never late, so I don't need your help." Since she doesn't like for me to remind her that I'm picking up the tab for everything, she'll give me a little extra money (she pays for the cellphone bill because I bought the cellphone so I could call her when I run late) when her tiny check arrives. She also tries not to boss me, which is what prompts me to remind her that since I'm paying all of the bills, I should be at least an equal in our house. And I, of course, almost never feel the need to try to boss or control her.

I like to watch other mother-daughter teams featured in reality shows, Joan and Melissa Rivers on WE, Naomi and Wynonna Judd on OWN, and Chris Jenner and her Kardashian daughters on E to see how they handle conflicts. When I compare those mother-daughter relationships to mine, I'm usually pleased with the one I'm in. When we had two couches in our overstuffed family room, my mother may have convinced me to donate my 1995 couch to the Salvation Army so she could keep her 1972 one, but at least she didn't give away all of my furniture and replace it with furniture that she picked out the way Joan Rivers did when she moved into her daughter's house. And, in fact, I may have won that battle because I refused to dump my couch until she removed the plastic off hers, saying that I wouldn't sit on plastic. I would happily sacrifice another, even newer couch to rid the house of all plastic-covered furniture.

The relationship between Joan and Melissa also makes me appreciate the fact that I've been more successful than my mother. If my overbearing, somewhat domineering, mother had been an English professor and I had worked as a school security guard and a photographer's assistant, we probably could not live together.

The Judds seem closest to my mother and me physically. The mother is the feminine, pretty one, while the daughter seems more butch and is larger. (My mother and I have taken turns being heavier and are about the same size now, but I've always been taller and less feminine.) Mama Judd also had a serious health problem (hepatitis) for several years and seems to have a domineering Southern Belle personality similar to my mother's. So when I watched those two interact as they toured, I was happy that my mother and I never worked together. And when I see how the very meddlesome Mama Jenner tries to control her daughters' careers, I'm equally happy that my mother was not my manager. She's very good at publicizing my achievements, but if she were ever in charge of booking jobs for me, I would have worked myself into an early grave.

I have always been bothered by the celebrity women who don't speak to their mothers for years. Often these are seemingly sweet women, America's Sweethearts, like Meg Ryan and Jennifer Aniston. I wonder what these mothers did to cause their daughters to freeze them out of their lives. Even though I twice put thousands of miles between my mother and me, I never stopped talking to her. We talked on the phone regularly and even occasionally wrote letters. But as I think about our relationship and how I, a fairly strong, even intimidating to some, woman, have had to battle to remain an autonomous adult while sharing a house with my mother, I understand those celebrities. They are probably staying away from their mothers to avoid defeat in battles they know they cannot win.

Not long after my mother moved in with me in 1990, one of my friends at Cal Poly and I were discussing the situation when she made a comment that caused both of us to laugh. She said, "Your mother is never going to leave, Mary, because she's smarter than you are." Her comment was funny because my mother is clearly not as well educated as I am, but mothers generally are smarter than their daughters. And even if they aren't, they have powers that can destroy a weak daughter.

Because I'm definitely not one of America's Sweethearts and because I'm not weak, I can hold my own against my mother. I can stand up to her, fight back, and usually win the arguments. I guess I should thank my years of being educated and educating in white, mostly patriarchal institutions for being able to survive sharing a home with my now quite elderly, but still fierce mother.

CHAPTER EIGHT
You'd Better Think, Think, Think

One of the semi-serious ongoing disputes between my mother and me is what I call the books versus hats debate. My mother complains falsely that I have books all over the house; there are no books downstairs, but I do have books in bookcases in every room upstairs, except hers, and there are two full bookcases in our garage. I complain accurately that she has hats in every upstairs closet, including mine. I usually win this debate by pointing out that my mother never made any money from wearing hats since she was never a model while my books were directly responsible for our living in an upper-middle-class house in an upper-middle-class neighborhood.

My mother also likes to call me lazy, a label which I sometimes embrace and at other times reject. Certainly I am physically lazy, especially compared to my mother, who loves to work. I've told her that I will make a much better super-senior than she is because I don't mind sitting still. In fact, my first complaint about growing older was that I couldn't sit as long without becoming stiff. I'm surprised that I haven't bought my rocking chair yet since I spent my last years at Cal Poly bragging to younger (and a few older) colleagues that I would soon be at home rocking and reading while they still drove the freeways, attended meetings, and graded papers.

But clearly I am not really lazy. A truly lazy person would not have won scholarships and fellowships by overachieving academically. Nor would a lazy person have the kind of attendance record that I had, starting in elementary school. By sixth grade, I had survived all of the childhood diseases now usually prevented by vaccinations--measles, mumps, chicken pox, and whooping cough--as well as tuberculosis and the operation to remove my tonsils and adenoids. So even though I had frequent colds, occasional stomach problems, and later "female" problems, I had perfect attendance from sixth to tenth grade, and I missed only a half day, the last day of school, in tenth grade because I was at Fort Sheridan, applying for a summer job. During my junior year, I missed only one class, the last period, because I had to go to Fort Sheridan to pick up my last check since no one told me to make arrangements for the payroll department to mail it. I missed three days in my senior year because I succumbed to the pressure of applying for college and taking numerous tests and thought I was having heart palpitations (It was probably the beginning of my stress-related digestive problems). But that was it. And that pattern continued through college, graduate school, and at my various teaching positions. A lazy person would have taken more sick days and personal leave days.

A lazy person would probably also have found a better way to survive economically (student loans, for instance) than riding the bus from L.A. to Pomona while teaching three composition classes at two different universities and trying to complete a dissertation. None of my students who marveled when I returned their well-annotated, usually copiously commented on papers, often the next class meeting after they were submitted, or wrote their letters of recommendation the first free weekend that I had, saw me as lazy.

The problem with my kind of hard work is that it doesn't look like work to the uninformed. I don't sweat or huff and puff when I grade papers, read books, or prepare handouts and syllabi. If I'm reading an entertaining book or a well-written paper, I might even smile as I work. Still, even my mother changed her tune a bit about my easy job when she moved in with me and saw me sitting at my desk, grading papers for hours. She admitted that she couldn't sit that long and read that much.

No offense to the people who engage in heavy physical labor, but I believe that my kind of work is ultimately more productive, and I would argue that being physically lazy is much less destructive and dangerous than being mentally lazy. Of course, physical labor and mental labor are not mutually exclusive, and many people enjoy both. In fact, I do some of my best thinking when I wash dishes (unless I'm watching television), dust or vacuum my room, and certainly when I take my daily walk.

Still, I believe we all need to push mental at least as much as we do physical activity. First Lady Michelle Obama wants us to start moving, but I say we also need to start thinking. Our failure to move, to engage in physical activity, can cause health problems and cost the country money in expensive healthcare, but think of the cost of mental inactivity. What has been the cost, for instance, of our inability to think clearly while voting? Two wars, one recession, millions unemployed, and the loss of the middle class.

Not thinking clearly or not being well educated can also be costly for individuals. My maternal grandmother was smart enough to realize that her friendly neighborhood grocer was cheating her when I started shopping for her. She realized that I brought home more money than she did when we bought the same items. That cheating grocer taught both my grandmother and me how important education is. I illustrated the importance of education in my basic writing classes by telling them what happened when I misplaced an airline ticket during my graduate school years. I nervously called the airline and explained my situation. I even had the small folder that the ticket came in so I could give the person on the line the number of the ticket. But this person insisted that I must buy a new ticket. He explained by saying that if I went to the bank and cashed a check for $100.00 and lost the $100.00, the bank would not be responsible for replacing the money. I probably sounded stupid to this jerk because my Southern accent became more pronounced in those days when I was nervous or tense, and people who don't think clearly assume Southerners are stupid. But fortunately, I <u>was</u> thinking clearly, so I told him that his cashed check scenario was a false analogy. I didn't have to explain why; he immediately switched to the information that he gave to smart people: I <u>would</u> have to buy a new ticket, but if no one used the original ticket, I would receive all of my money back, minus a small lost-ticket fee. I know that this guy on the telephone was not some renegade trying to punk me for fun because when I asked the steward on the airplane how long I would have to wait to receive my refund, he started to give me the same false analogy. It seemed to be company policy to try to make money off of fools.

When I told this story to one basic writing class, one of those rebellious students that I always like said that he would have responded by saying, "That's bullshit." That response might have worked since it would show that he was thinking, but it didn't say, "I'm educated, and you can't make a fool out of me," the way the phrase "false analogy" does. Using the right words and summoning the right arguments can help in almost any situation. Another story I told students, usually when we were reading Robert Frost's "Mending Wall" in American literature, involves what I like to call the Wild West land grab. The builders for our new homes in Claremont had created an odd configuration where some homeowners did not have direct access to their land; if they wanted to paint one side of their house, for instance, they would need to go through their neighbors' gates and walk through their yards. When a new supervisor took charge of the development, he changed that plan so that all of the houses had gates, and everyone had access to their land. But there was one problem; we were among the first buyers, and we, along with our next door neighbor, who had control over our land, had already purchased our homes when the changes were made. Unfortunately, the next door neighbor, a plumber, was a slick operator. He had bought his house at a cheaper price than was listed because he demanded that the builders sell him a house for the lowest amount they listed on the billboard advertising the homes. When the builders approached him, saying that they wanted to give us a gate and access to our land, our neighbor insisted on keeping the property the same as it was when he purchased it.

I was vaguely aware that there was some kind of dispute over our having a gate and more land but didn't really care to have more land that needed to be landscaped and maintained. I saw the advantage of having a gate since there was no way out of the backyard without one (we had to walk back up the side yard and through the garage) but didn't really covet more land. Had I been thinking clearly, I would have realized that I was paying taxes for this land that I didn't want and couldn't access and that there might be a situation, like a fire in the front of the house, where I might need to exit the back yard.

Fortunately for me and unfortunately for him, the neighbor was thinking even less clearly. He decided to make sure he kept land that wasn't his by putting a side patio cover on it and by planting trees and flowers against our house. The side patio cover was a violation of association rules, so the builders, who were in charge of the association at that time, demanded that he remove it. At the same time, my mother was bothered by the trees being planted so close to our house and asked him to remove them. He promised that he would but didn't. Eventually (about two years passed, and the builders had left the association), one of the association board members talked to my mother about their problem with the neighbor and reminded her that the land was ours. When I finally realized I was paying taxes on land that he was using, I went to work.

When she heard the land-grab story, one of my cousins said that we would have to hire a lawyer, but she underestimated the power of research and a well-argued, well-written letter. I sent a letter to the builders with copies to city officials. Someone from the city came out to check on the land and sided with us. Soon the patio cover was torn down (our neighbor had moved and was renting the house at that point), and we had our land. Soon after that, my Wild West neighbor decided to sell his house. I learned while conducting my research that if I had not protested his land grab within five years, he would have been allowed to keep our land, and I assume that I would have continued to pay taxes on land that would no longer be mine.

This land-grab episode not only illustrates the value of education and clear thinking, but also explains why ignorance can be blissful, and knowledge can cause pain. I was perfectly happy with the yard that I had and not even that bothered by the missing gate until I realized that I was paying for land used by someone else. Knowing that I had paid taxes for two years while someone else enjoyed the land really made me angry.

Some information might seem too painful to know. Another conversation I had with my basic writing classes was prompted by a story titled "From Mother with Love . . ." The mother in the story is dying, but the father and daughter keep her impending death a secret from her. After the mother dies, the daughter discovers that her mother knew she was dying because the mother, a notorious procrastinator, had bought Christmas presents for everyone. When I asked the students whether they would want to know if they were dying, usually more said they wouldn't want to know than said they would. For many of them, such knowledge would be too painful; they preferred to be ignorantly blissful in their last days.

The best example of blissful ignorance in my life involves driving. I enjoyed being a passenger in a car much more before I learned to drive. I felt nervous when riding in a car as a non-driver only when the driver was nervous. If the driver seemed confident, he or she could speed, tailgate, switch lanes rapidly, and engage in any other reckless driving without troubling me. I remember one wintry Sunday when I was driven home from my job working for the Rs in Highland Park by my stepbrother, John Lee. Being only nineteen, he was a very confident, if somewhat reckless, driver. On this Sunday he was driving slower than usual because the roads were intermittently icy. Just as we turned onto our street, the car hit a patch of ice and went into a 360 degree turn. The turn was slow enough to allow John Lee and me to exchange looks. He looked over at me with glee and said, "Whee, Sistah, this is FUN!" Well, if the driver thought it was fun, who was I to disagree? So I laughed gleefully as the spin ended, and we drove the last block home. I didn't know enough to be frightened.

I'm convinced that ignorant people are happier than the well-informed. When I see people who seem too happy, I assume that they are faking, not too smart, and/or not well-educated. Anyone who knows how complicated and dangerous the world is cannot be truly happy. But, of course, what we don't know can hurt us, so I'm also convinced that those happy people are in for a rude awakening. They will discover one day that they've been cheated or misled, and unless they're fools, they will no longer be happy.

Still, I understand why some people prefer not to know too much and also why they are suspicious of, and even frightened by, people who seem too smart, too in love with knowledge. They call them "snobs" and "elites." This distaste for the intellectual is deeply engrained in our society and our literature. Two of the most despised villains in American literature, for instance, are the scientist Roger Chillingsworth in Nathaniel Hawthorne's nineteenth century novel, The Scarlet Letter, and the un-named Schoolteacher in Toni Morrison's 1987 novel, Beloved. Schoolteacher is violent and cruel, but what disturbs Sethe most about him is his interest in finding out about her and the other slaves. She's suspicious of this desire to collect information about slaves, which he writes in a book with ink that she made. She even believes that Schoolteacher's questions drove the most heroic of the slaves, Sixo, crazy.

No Americans seemed more suspicious and even contemptuous of intellectuals than former President George ("Is our children learning?") W. Bush and his so-called brain, Karl Rove. In the early years of his presidency, Bush, perhaps in defiance of his mother and wife, who supported literacy, bragged about not reading. The fact that he had attended an expensive private secondary school, as well as both Yale and Harvard, apparently without learning to speak Standard English, suggested that he was not joking or lying about his illiteracy. I wasn't sure how he learned to speak nonstandard English since both of his parents went to college, and while his father occasionally had trouble with syntax, both spoke relatively well. Did Bush learn his ungrammatical constructions from his nanny, his maid, his cook, or his chauffeur? It was odd to hear a wealthy white man with an Ivy League education sounding like some of my relatives who didn't even attend high school.

But the seemingly smarter Karl Rove (I liked the insult dog's comment that he thought Bush's brain would be a smaller man) is the one who really demonstrated anti-intellectualism when he was asked in an interview (I believe it was published in <u>The New Yorker</u>) who the Democrats were, and he said, "Ph.D.'s." Now, if Mr. Rove had seemed disappointed or embarrassed when he made that comment, I would understand his response. Who wouldn't be disappointed or ashamed that the most educated people were in the other party? But his comment was clearly meant to put down Democrats. To Mr. Rove, calling the Democrats Ph.D.'s was as good a dig as my calling the Republicans ignorant, greedy bigots.

But here's the good news, or at least it was good news for a few years until the Tea Party emerged. President Bush was such an ineffective President that people started to realize that the President should be smart. My spirits lifted when I heard a man say on a CSPAN call-in show something that I had said almost as soon as Bush was appointed by five conservative Supreme Court justices: The President should have to take a test. And I know Bush's brain received the message because soon Bush was bragging about competing with Rove in a book reading contest and claiming to have read Shakespeare and Camus. Of course, I didn't believe that Bush was reading those challenging authors and would have loved to give him a "No Fool Left Behind" test to see how much he knew about literature, but I enjoyed the fact that people no longer wanted to elect a President with whom they could have a beer but instead wanted one who seemed to know something about the country and the world. They wanted a smart, well-educated President, an intellectual. At the end of 2008, I was thanking Bush for two gifts. He gave us a black President to clean up his mess, and he made us all value education and intellectualism more.

In fact, Bush actually made me embrace my intellectual self. Although I always promoted education and especially reading, my working-class black woman background made me suspicious of people who seemed too eager to flaunt their intelligence. I saw those people as pompous and pretentious. In my writing classes I was hard on jargon and dismissive of academic discourse. While I haven't changed my mind about the need to write clearly so that the average Newsweek or Time reader can understand what we're saying, I now much prefer a person who is flaunting her intelligence to one who is either showing off his stupidity or pretending to be ignorant.

It was, in fact, the celebration and success of the "stupid white man," to quote Michael Moore, that made me start to think about my journey. I saw myself as the anti-Bush and argued that if Bush could be President of the United States and Gropenator Arnold Schwarzenegger could be governor of California, I should be Queen of the Universe, Empress of the Solar System. More than

Arnold and certainly more than Bush, I represented the American Dream. By the time Bush and Arnold were overseeing large budgets and staffs, I was a tenured full professor at Cal Poly, living with my mother in my still new house in my upper-middle-class neighborhood. I arrived at this place, not by taking steroids and showing off my monstrous physique and certainly not by taking advantage of my connections and the low expectations for my debating ability, not to mention the ability of my cohorts to steal an election at the expense of black and Jewish Americans in Florida, but through hard work, discipline, education, and intelligence.

Smart, nonwhite women like me should run the world, not "the stupid white men," I decided. But, of course, I was not interested in being President or governor and so was happy to see an intelligent black man take advantage of the backlash against Bush's stupidity. I contented myself with pointing out the anti-intellectualism in our literature and our culture and focusing even more on encouraging my students to think and to value thinking and thinkers. Instead of making fun of pompous or pretentious intellectuals, I started making fun of overbearing ignoramuses. Showing off one's intelligence might be somewhat annoying, but showing off one's ignorance is extremely obnoxious.

Even before I pushed the intellectual approach, I included a section called "Thinking As You Read" in my basic reader textbook, <u>Growth through Fiction</u>. And I always argued that students need to think ("brainstorm" the composition textbooks call it) before they write; now I wanted them to think before and during every activity--talking, watching television, listening to professors, listening to politicians. If we think, we can learn, and we are less likely to be punked. Since I'm not an intellectual snob, I can still enjoy pop culture, which has shocked one of my old high school friends with whom I recently reconnected. She thinks that a professor should watch only PBS and not waste her time watching silly shows like "Dancing with the Stars." The PBS shows are educational, she argues, while most of the shows that I watch are just a waste of time. But I counter that I'm learning when I watch "Dancing with the Stars." I did not know the difference between the jive, the fox trot, and the quick step until I watched "Dancing with the Stars" and "So You Think You Can Dance." Now I'm practically an expert. And I can tell which couple is about to do the Argentine Tango just by looking at the costumes.

As I see it, garbage-in does not necessarily mean garbage-out. Just as there are some people (yes, I'm talking about G.W. Bush) who refuse to learn, no matter how much educational material they are given, there are others who can learn from what many people see as useless garbage. During my decades of watching tennis, I learned as much about the psychology of an athlete--or at least a tennis player--as I probably know about a writer's psychology. I knew, for instance, that Andre Agassi needed to be the underdog to win his first Grand Slam; I preferred that his opponent be Stephan Edberg or Boris Becker, players he had beaten in other big finals, but when he drew big serving lefty Goran Ivansivec on grass, I was not surprised that he won Wimbledon. A year earlier when he ended up with Jim Courier in the French final after having already lost two Grand Slam finals, the second to the younger, less well-known American, Pete Sampras, I knew he was in big trouble. Anyone who doesn't believe that having to play a younger underdog from the same country is a major handicap just check out Boris Becker versus Michael Stich at Wimbledon in 1991. Becker considered Wimbledon his second home, and Stich was a nervous player who never won another Grand Slam tournament, but against Becker he felt no pressure. He knew that the pressure was on Becker, and so Stich also won his first and only Grand Slam as an underdog at Wimbledon.

Of course, I don't always think so clearly when I'm taking in the garbage of pop culture. For years I was a shameless reader of tabloids. I rarely read the <u>Globe</u> but bought <u>The National Enquirer</u> and <u>The Star</u> almost every week. I knew why I enjoyed reading about the exploits of rich celebrities; it was the same reason I enjoyed nonfiction books about rich murderers (For instance, I read two long books about the woman who killed her rich father so that her daughter could be in the New York ballet). Working for richer than I was white people made me resentful, and books or articles about rich, mostly white people's crimes and misdeeds made me feel better. Of course, I also enjoyed reading positive stories about celebrities whom I liked. I read only the celebrity stories (never the aliens or odd looking people stories) and only stories about celebrities who interested me. I had little sympathy for celebrities who complained about tabloid coverage because most of them were not exactly Garbos. When they had movies, television shows, music, or causes to sell, they were everywhere, talking, singing, exposing their lives. Every job, every career, every life has positives and negatives. Just as English teachers have to grade papers, and high school teachers have to patrol the halls and deal with parents, celebrities have to deal with paparazzi and gossip. That's why they are paid the big bucks and can command attention that many other more sensible and even some better looking people never could attract.

Occasionally, a tabloid went too far, and I boycotted a few weeks or months. When I was still in graduate school, for instance, I was offended when someone from The National Enquirer took a picture of Elvis in his casket. I refused to buy that issue, but it sold out quicker in the USC neighborhood than any other issue, so the publishers didn't miss my cash. I also never liked it when the Enquirer revealed that people were dying; even when, especially when, the celebrity was actually dying, it seemed cold and cruel to announce it. I understood that the problem with the tabloids was not that they lied so much, but that they mixed truths with lies. And they were usually accurate when announcing someone's impending death. Even ignorant people would stop reading the tabloids if everything they said was a lie.

What I didn't think about during my many years of reading the Enquirer was its bias. Clearly some celebrities received more attention than others, but I assumed they sold more papers. If Tom Cruise appeared in the tabloids more than Tom Hanks, it probably meant that Cruise was more popular with tabloid readers. I didn't pay much attention to the politicians covered. The Kennedys were perennial favorites, but I assumed it was because they were American royalty; they had been celebrities for generations, and we all liked to read about them. I didn't notice how seldom Republican politicians appeared as opposed to Democrats, nor did I pay attention to the kind of coverage Democrats received as opposed to Republicans.

Even when the <u>Enquirer</u> exposed Jesse Jackson's love child, "coincidentally" as he was leading the fight to count all the votes in Florida, I didn't recognize what was happening. Only after Bush had been in office about two years did I wonder why the <u>Enquirer</u> reporters still targeted the Clintons and didn't go after the Bush family. After all, the Clintons were not political royalty; in fact, the Bushes had more in common with the Kennedys than the Clintons did. The Bushes had been wealthy and politically powerful for generations, just like the Kennedys. And George Bush, the President, had a colorful past, including a drunk driving arrest, other run-ins with the police, and rumors of drug use. The Bushes were a good looking family; one of the younger members was even a model. Why weren't they covered by the <u>Enquirer</u>?

Once I asked the question, it didn't take me long to review all the Kennedy coverage, the exposes of Gary Hart and Jesse Jackson, coupled with what I noticed about the <u>Enquirer</u> covers during the OJ trial and the Clinton obsession and arrive at an answer. <u>The National Enquirer</u> targeted Democrats and protected Republicans. I never bought another <u>Enquirer.</u> But I continued to monitor their coverage to be sure that my assessment was accurate. Several months after I stopped buying the tabloids, Arnold ran for governor of California in a special election. He had been a favorite target of the <u>Enquirer</u> when he was just a Kennedy in-law, but when he became a Republican candidate for governor, he was suddenly missing from its pages. Women complained in the mainstream media about Arnold's wicked ways, but they didn't appear in the <u>Enquirer</u>. We learned later, through reporting in the <u>Los Angeles Times,</u> that Arnold made a deal with the publishers of the Enquirer to write (or have ghostwritten) a column for one of their fitness publications in exchange for keeping quiet about stories they bought from some of these women. But I wonder if they would have made the deal if Arnold were a Democrat.

As the 2004 election approached, I noticed that Howard Dean, not a sexy guy, made the Enquirer cover. I don't remember what the gossip was now, but it wasn't favorable. Then when he failed to win Iowa and Kerry became the frontrunner for the Democratic nomination, the Senator from Massachusetts was suddenly on the cover with gossip about his exploits with women. But the most interesting development happened after Bush won the election. Once he had won his last election and would no longer run again, Bush became fair game. Now maybe something else happened. Rumor has it that the Clintons became cozy with the publishers of the tabloids to prepare for Hillary's presidential run, so maybe after he won his second term, Bush simply stopped taking their calls, stopped sucking up to them, causing them to turn on him. But to me the sudden interest in Bush looked like a cynical attempt to make the Enquirer look "fair and balanced" when it was clearly trying to help the Republicans win elections.

When ABC's "Nightline" looked at the Enquirer's involvement in the Edwards case, they listed other politicians who had been targeted. The only Republican on that list was Rush Limbaugh. But unless I missed something, Rush is not a politician; he's a radio personality. Unlike Jesse Jackson, who ran for President twice and regularly leads voter registration drives, Rush has been content to just use his big mouth and loud microphone to influence elections. What's interesting is the list of politicians not exposed by the Enquirer. The same year that Edwards was caught by Enquirer reporters meeting his mistress in a hotel, Barbara Walters revealed that decades earlier she'd had an affair with black Republican Senator Ed Brooke. Now that was a juicy scandal! How did The National Enquirer miss that story? Is it likely that no one knew that the first woman national news anchor and the first black Senator since Reconstruction were having an affair? Can you imagine if Katie Couric and Barack Obama were having an affair? The tabloids would be all over that story.

And then there are the love children. The National Enquirer revealed Jesse Jackson's daughter when the child was a toddler, and before Edwards' daughter was born, pictures of his pregnant mistress were published, but we didn't learn that Strom Thurmond had a black daughter until after he had died at the ripe old age of one hundred. And then the daughter, in her seventies at that point, told the story. The Edwards story was interesting because his wife had cancer, and he was supposed to be a devoted family man. The Jackson story was interesting because he's a preacher, and preachers are not supposed to have love children, even if they're not married. But what could be more interesting than a notorious segregationist's having a black daughter? If I didn't know better, I might believe that The National Enquirer was leery of stories involving miscegenation. That would certainly explain their silence on these two stories. But their obsession with the OJ Simpson case and their interest in Tiger Woods' scandal show that they don't mind gossiping about racially mixed couples. The common thread in the missed stories was that the politicians were Republican. I was not reading the Enquirer during recent

Republican sex scandals, but I don't remember seeing Ensign, Sanford, Craig, or Foley on its covers and would be surprised if there were much coverage of those scandals inside the pages. However, I noticed that Democrat Anthony Weiner recently made the cover.

Sarah Palin and Mrs. McCain became targets during the 2008 election, but I assumed that the Enquirer was again trying to portray itself as fair and balanced. They had ruthlessly chased Edwards, so they probably knew that some clear thinkers might make connections to other scandals and discover a pattern. But notice that they didn't go after McCain even though the New York Times claimed earlier in the year that he was having an affair. Tabloid editors and publishers are smart enough to know that most people don't vote based on the behavior of potential first ladies and vice-presidential candidates. So they could dirty the ladies a bit without hurting the Republican candidate's chances.

Probably more than any other professionals, journalists shape how we view the world. Depending on the number of classes (and class sizes) they teach, teachers might shape a few hundred students' minds each year, but then those students move on to other teachers. Preachers can influence their specific congregations and denominations, but given the number of different religions, not to mention atheists and agnostics, their influence is limited. Politicians might reach millions of people with slick advertisements and slogans, but if journalists don't cooperate, if they refuse to carry their messages, the politicians will have trouble being heard. Some politicians, like Sarah Palin and President Obama (and, unfortunately for him and us, Weiner), have started to use the new social media--Twitter, Facebook--to bypass the old media filter. But Palin has also joined what she calls the "lamestream" media, appearing regularly as a commentator on Fox News (of course, she probably doesn't see Fox as mainstream), and whenever he needs to sell the public on his latest bill or power move, Obama holds multiple news conferences.

One of my earliest lessons in how the media can shape opinion involved my second favorite male tennis player (after the original AA, Arthur Ashe), Agassi. A few months after I switched from disliking him as the long-haired, bleach blonde punk who beat fellow baby boomer Jimmy Connors at the 1989 U.S. Open to being a serious fan because I discovered that the black man in his entourage was his agent, meaning that the brother was making a percentage of all of that endorsement money, I started reading a new sports paper, called the National. I was drawn to the paper because it was edited by Frank Deford, who wrote a really touching book about his daughter's death from cystic fibrosis. I also recognized some of the columnists' names because they wrote about tennis. Although I'm not sure how Deford felt about Agassi, the tennis columnists, Mike Lupica and John Feinstein among them, couldn't stand the then twenty-year-old. They took every opportunity to attack him. The attacks were so vicious that I remember one fan wrote a letter, saying something like, "Look, I hate Agassi as much as the next person, but you guys are obsessed." He was responding to an article that was supposed to be about Agassi's former brother-in-law, Pancho Gonzales, who played the game before I was interested in it. The writer kept comparing the much older tennis legend to Agassi to show what a jerk Agassi was. Possibly just so they could take one last dig at Agassi, the staff conducted a poll at the end of the year, asking which athlete was the most obnoxious or the most hated. The twenty-year-old tennis player won in a landslide. But what drew my attention to this poll was that USA Today conducted a similar one, and Agassi didn't even make the list. Clearly, the National readers had been influenced by the constant attacks on Agassi while USA Today readers probably picked an athlete (I think it was a college basketball player) who had been criticized and ridiculed in that paper. (Of course, Agassi had the last laugh since the National was published for only about a year [1990-91] while I'm still reading USA Today.)

Politicians clearly know how important media brainwashing is because they work very hard to spin the media. The Republicans are especially known for their tight messaging. They all repeat the same language ("death panels," "tax and spend") in television interviews. And candidates from both parties are so aware of how influential media commentary on their debate performances is that they have special people assigned to spin the media immediately after the debates. It is hilarious to watch the spinners rush to the microphones to talk about how delighted they are with their candidates' performances and how their candidates clearly won the debate. It's also interesting to watch how the polls change after the commentary. Sometimes one candidate wins in instant polls, and then after the spinners and pundits dissect the performances, another candidate tops the polls. More often, the loser in the debate (according to the pundits) is closer to the winner in the polls taken immediately after the debate, but the gap widens as the commentators discuss all of the many ways the loser lost.

It's easy for someone who is not well educated or does not think critically and/or clearly to be swept along by media hype. I frequently have to calm my mother down when she thinks Obama will lose the 2012 election or that her Social Security checks will be cut because of what a few not well-informed or clear-thinking pundits said on MSNBC or CNN. But well-educated, critical thinkers are not immune to media hype. Since we are all prisoners of our time, place, race, gender, class, religion, political leanings, and sexual orientation, any of us can be blinded by our biases into believing the hype.

Two media-driven scandals that show both how the media can shape, often deliberately, our views, and how my own biases occasionally prevent me from seeing the truth, are the OJ trial and the John Edwards sex scandal. Edwards and OJ on the surface don't seem to have much in common. Both are better looking than most of us and projected a possibly fake nice guy personality, both came from the working class, and both played football in high school. But whereas OJ became a star college and professional football player, Edwards did not make the college team. And whereas Edwards finished college in three years (I don't care what a student's major is or what school he or she attends, a stupid person cannot finish college in three years), was accepted into and completed law school, passed the bar, and became a successful lawyer, OJ did not finish college and showed no signs when he talked of having ever attended USC. Their "crimes" were also very different. OJ was accused of killing two people with a knife while Edwards (who is awaiting trial at this point) is accused of violating Presidential campaign laws.

Although I, a fellow working-class baby boomer, share OJ's race and alma mater (he had, however, left USC before I arrived) and Edwards' Southern roots and child-of-a-mill worker background, I have little in common with these two men. Other than boxing and hunting, football is my least favorite sport, and fair-haired Good Old Boys are not my favorite Americans. I frankly was never interested in OJ until his trial, and John Kerry was my favorite candidate (sorry, Al Sharpton, but I did the vote for the black man thing in 1984 and 1988) during the 2004 election. However, once OJ went on his Bronco ride, I was hooked on his story like everyone else; I followed the trial closely and read most of the books written about him. Similarly, once Edwards was selected to be Kerry's running mate, and I learned more of his story (the lost child, the very smart former English major wife who happened to be my age), I found him more interesting and decided he was the Democrats' Great White Hope to win in 2008. I looked at recent political history and saw that the most recent Democratic winners--Johnson, Carter, Clinton, and even Gore, who actually did win--were all from the South, so I was an Edwards supporter. Even with Hillary Clinton and Barack Obama in the 2008 race, I stuck with the Good Old Boy (although thankfully he was out of the race by the time I voted in California, so I was free to vote for my second choice, Obama) because I wasn't sure that Americans were ready to elect a woman or a mixed race man (Obama or Richardson), but I knew they would elect a Southern white man.

And no Democrat was more Southern (or whiter) than Edwards in 2008.

Of course, National Enquirer was all over both of these stories and gained credibility from its coverage of the two scandals. I was still a frequent reader of the Enquirer during the OJ trial, but for the first time analyzed the coverage, especially the covers, and drew conclusions about how the tabloid operated. When the Edwards' story broke, I no longer read the Enquirer but recognized the pattern of targeting Democrats. I didn't read the story but took only a couple of minutes of checking out the photographs while standing in the line at the supermarket to figure out what apparently most people still don't seem to know: the Enquirer (as the adulterer, his wife, and even his rat fink aide all pointed out) published fake pictures to bring down Edwards.

These two scandals, while very different, illustrate basic principles of media hype. 1) The press tells us only what they want us to know, and there is no such thing as an objective press. 2) Image may not be everything, as Agassi once said in a commercial, but it is very important, and it affects how we respond to people, especially people that we don't really know. 3) Race, gender, and class bias affects how stories are told and received. 4) The more we think and analyze people, events, and stories, the more we realize that no one can really answer the question that Marvin Gaye once asked, "What's going on?" but often our guess is as good as, or better than, the so-called experts'.

My first reaction when I heard that OJ was a suspect in a double murder shows how image affects our judgment. My response was, "OJ Simpson? That's hard to believe. Now Jim Brown I could see killing two people." OJ and Jim Brown were both superstar running backs who had been arrested for domestic violence. But somehow I did not remember that OJ had been accused of beating his wife. Clearly, he and the people around him managed his bad press better than did Jim Brown and his representatives. And, of course, OJ's public demeanor was genial; he was the smiling sports announcer, Hertz endorser, bad actor, best known for his appearances in the comic "Police Squad" movies. Jim Brown was an angry, mean-looking rabble rouser who portrayed tough guys in movies.

My second response showed how the early media hype shaped expectations that may have ultimately undermined the prosecutor's case. When I read, not in the Enquirer, but in the supposedly reputable L.A. Times, about bloody clothes found in either OJ's washer or dryer and blood all over his property, I wondered why he didn't turn himself in and cop a plea to a crime of passion. He clearly was guilty. There was even a woman who claimed to have seen him close to the crime scene, although she was quickly proved to be a pathological liar and media whore, looking to sell her story and gain fame. She reminded me of the crazy people who claimed to have seen Patty Hearst right after most of the SLA members were killed in L.A. When Robert Shapiro asked in the preliminary trial about the bloody clothes, and they turned out not to exist, I started to wonder about OJ's supposed guilt. Clearly, the alleged evidence against him had been overstated, and how the hell did he kill two fit, fairly large, younger-than-he-was adults with a knife?

The preliminary trial happened because the LAPD released tapes of Nicole Brown Simpson's 911 call, which featured OJ shouting and cursing at her while she talked about how he would beat the shit out of her. The tapes were released in response to the outpouring of sympathy that came during and right after the Bronco ride. That response showed how differently celebrities are treated. Most double murder suspects receive sympathy only from close relatives and friends, but just as we all mourn the deaths of such celebrities as John F. Kennedy Junior and Princess Diana, we all felt bad for this famous man we thought we knew. People actually chased the car as it exited the freeway and shouted, "Go, OJ!" as if he were running for one last touchdown.

The LAPD (or the prosecutor), in trying to remind people that OJ was no longer a football player but a murder suspect, went too far, and so the case was taken from the grand jury and given to a judge. During that preliminary trial, I at one point found my class clashing with my race, so that I didn't know whom to support. Police officer Vannatter was on the stand, trying to explain why he was so eager to enter OJ's house without a warrant. Vannatter said something about thinking that OJ had a maid, and Shapiro asked if he didn't think that maids had days off. When Vannatter responded rather nastily, "I don't know, Mr. Shapiro, I don't have a maid," I initially took his side, saying, "Yeah, Shapiro, we don't all have maids," but then my race bias kicked in, and I turned on Vannatter, "OJ has a right to have a maid; he earned that money being knocked down and jumped on by a bunch of oversized athletes." I knew at that point that this trial would be hard on me.

334

My initial reaction to Mark Fuhrman was also interesting. I hadn't liked the other two cops. They were badly dressed and didn't seem to be good witnesses even though they should have been accustomed to testifying. Phil Vannatter appeared too grumpy, and Tom Lange looked bored. But the tall, well-dressed Mr. Fuhrman sounded professional and looked the part of a competent police officer just doing his job. I'll never forget his one line, "When I saw the glove, I knew what I had." He reminded me of the cops on television.

But shortly after the preliminary trial, I read a story in <u>New Yorker</u> about the case and learned that Fuhrman had been to the Simpson house on a domestic violence call a few years before the murders. If that point were made when Fuhrman was on the stand, I missed it. Suddenly, my view of him changed. Instead of a competent cop, trying to investigate a crime and stumbling upon important evidence, he became a racist cop, smart enough to know that an abusive ex-husband was the most likely suspect when his wife was found murdered, and who planted the glove so that he could quickly put OJ's black ass in jail. OJ had killed two white people; a racist like Fuhrman might not mind a black man killing his white wife since she was married to a black man and had his children, but he had killed an innocent white man. Fuhrman wanted him in jail ASAP. I was way ahead of the Dream Team in pushing the racist rogue cop theory and was pleased when they exposed him.

My debates with my colleagues about the planted glove illustrated how blacks and whites could view the trial so differently. When they argued that the cops couldn't have been sure that OJ was in town to commit the murders, I responded, "Excuse me, OJ is a big black guy who was driving a Bentley all over Brentwood that Sunday; the fact that they didn't stop him shows that the cops knew OJ was in town. They probably have a code for famous Negro in expensive car. OJ went golfing early that morning. You find a black man who has driven in a nice neighborhood early in the morning on his way to play golf, and you'll find a black man who has been stopped by the police." White people don't know about black visibility and even after the Rodney King incident, they still didn't understand the crime of Driving While Black. They also had a less skeptical view of cops. They didn't believe that Officer Friendly would plant evidence, so I was happy to remind them of our OJ discussions a few years later when the LAPD evidence planting scandal broke.

I used logic to show why we should assume that the glove was planted. I pointed out that it would be unusual for someone clumsy and not at all athletic like me to drop one piece of evidence at the scene of the crime and a matching piece of evidence on my own property. The odds that OJ Simpson, who made most of his fame and some of his money carrying an object while running fast and dodging other powerful, well-trained athletes who were trying to knock him down and take it away from him, would conveniently drop evidence twice are astronomical (DNA type odds). In fact, the only reason it was at all believable that he killed two fit younger people with a knife without help is that while he was arthritic and almost 47 years old, he was still a well-trained, powerful athlete who could pull off physical feats that the average middle-aged man couldn't.

Although I still believe that Fuhrman planted the glove, I've changed my mind about his motive. Clearly, he was racist, which is probably why, after he left not only the LAPD but L.A., he escaped to an area where there are few nonwhite people. But his behavior after he was exposed as a perjurer suggests that there was a more important motive, the same motive that led the pathological liar to claim that she saw OJ near the crime scene. Mr. Fuhrman wanted to be famous. He delivered his lines so well on the stand because he was ready for his close-up; he was ready to be the television cop. He knew that OJ was the likely murderer and that therefore the case would be big (although probably even Fuhrman didn't realize how big), so when the L.A. cops, Vannatter and Lange, were brought in, he knew that he had to do something to keep himself in the case. When he "found" the glove, he knew what he had all right; he had the glove that he had planted so that he could become the hero cop. The fact that he, the disgraced cop, continued to appear on television, even inserting himself into a case involving a so-called Kennedy cousin (Ethel's nephew), while the other cops only made occasional grumpy appearances during OJ anniversaries proves to me that he was chasing fame.

The case became so big partly because of characters like Fuhrman, Kato Kaelin, and the dream teams of lawyers on both sides. All seemed more than ready for their close-ups. But the media, both tabloid and mainstream, made these previously unknown people stars. For months the <u>Enquirer</u> featured the OJ trial on its cover. The only week that it didn't was when it covered Michael Jackson's marriage to Lisa Marie Presley. In fact, I felt sorry for Michael, who I believe married Lisa partly to counter the child molester publicity, only to see OJ suck up the media attention. Talk about bad timing. As the Enquirer coverage continued, I noticed something interesting about those covers. They featured the dead beautiful blonde white woman much more often than they did OJ. In fact, during the time I studied the covers, the Enquirer never had a cover featuring a single black person (OJ was always with someone else when he appeared) while several times a white person, usually Nicole, appeared alone. Of course, the non-OJ cover included Lisa Marie as well as Michael. Nicole is not the first person to become famous after death. The murdered (in the nineteen fifties) black child Emmett Till has been immortalized by several black writers. But it was odd to see sexy pictures of the murdered mother of two. The media's fascination with her image helped convince those of us who were looking at the case through a racial lens that the trial would not have attracted so much attention if OJ's murdered wife had been black.

As I watched the trial during the summer of 1995, I paid attention to how the television media covered it. In Los Angeles there were half hour summaries of the day's testimony after the national news. I watched the KNBC summary most evenings and was struck by how biased their coverage seemed. They used loaded language; I don't remember the exact words now, but the prosecutors' strategies were called "tricks" when used by the defense. One day I watched OJ's doctor testify; my conclusion, after watching that testimony, was that it had been a good day for the defense. But on KNBC that evening, the reporter Jim Avila presented a very different view, including only details that suggested the prosecutors had won. I was so disturbed by that clearly biased report that I called KNBC to complain and saw how influential one husky voice and bad attitude could be. I ended my rant by asking where black reporter Furnell Chatman was. A few days later, Furnell was reporting on the case, but KNBC was still pro-prosecution.

During the trial, I also watched coverage by both Larry King on CNN and Geraldo Rivera on CNBC. Their approaches were very different. Both often featured dueling lawyers, one (or more) representing the defense and the other(s) representing the prosecution. But while King took no sides, the usually liberal and pro-black Geraldo was so anti-OJ that I thought it might be personal. Both were rumored to be players, and Geraldo had even written a book bragging about women with whom he'd had affairs, so I thought maybe OJ had taken one of Geraldo's women. Geraldo's reaction to the verdict was typical of his biased approach to the trial and remarkably similar to many journalists' recent response to the Casey Anthony verdict. I watched his CNBC show the night we heard that the jury had reached a verdict after deliberating for only a few hours. Geraldo was convinced that the jury would find OJ guilty, and he was ecstatic. He talked smugly about how the jury had rejected the defense's arguments. But when I watched his show the night after the verdict had been announced and OJ was found not guilty, he was incensed that the jury had taken so little time to arrive at that verdict. His response seemed both hypocritical and illogical. Why would he be happy that a jury had taken only a few hours to send a man to prison for life in a circumstantial evidence case that featured all kinds of questions about the reliability of the forensic evidence and the credibility of police officers? There was no confession, no eye witness, no bloody clothing. It would seem to me more logical to assume that if the jury came back that fast after so many months of testimony, they had found reasonable doubt and didn't really need to review all of the evidence.

People who were shocked and angered by the OJ verdict were probably shocked because they were listening to Geraldo and other biased commentators instead of watching the trial. People who watched the trial while thinking critically understood how the jurors could find reasonable doubt. Although I didn't follow the Casey Anthony trial, I'm sure the same point could be made about the almost hysterical reaction to the not guilty of murder verdict. I watched debates between the relatively calm Dan Abrams and the always overheated Nancy Grace on "Good Morning, America" but had no real interest in the trial or the verdict. Still I understood what the jurors and the reasonable commentators were saying. The prosecution has to prove its case, and they didn't. Just because Nancy Grace convicted "Tot Mom," as she called Casey for some strange reason, does not mean that she could be found guilty beyond a reasonable doubt by twelve jurors.

We don't know yet (in 2011) what will happen to John Edwards when his case goes to trial, but I would be surprised if he were found guilty. Mr. Edwards, a lawyer for twenty years, is probably willing to go to trial because he knows a flimsy case when he sees one, and all of the experts say that the government's case is flimsy. Even I can see holes in the case that make me wonder why government lawyers would waste their time and our money trying to turn a politician's bad behavior into a criminal offense. Well, actually, I do see the reason; the Republican federal prosecutor who filed the case has resigned as prosecutor and is now planning to run for U.S. Representative, so he needed a big scalp to launch his campaign. But given that the state's chief witness seems remarkably similar to the pathological liar that claimed to have seen OJ near the crime scene, I wonder if this case might end up being more of a political liability than an asset. In addition to being a liar who sold a book about the scandal, the despicable Mr. Andrew Young (his name is the only good thing he seems to have) also was a participant in the crime. He was the one receiving all the money, the one taking advantage of the scandal to ride on private planes and live in large mansions while hiding Edwards' mistress. That he is a liar is clear; he entered the spotlight as a liar, claiming to be the father of his boss's child. Then during the 2010 case involving a ridiculous dispute over a sex tape (and why would anyone want to keep someone else's sex tape?), Young admitted under oath that he couldn't swear that everything he said in his book was true because he was drunk during some of the events. Okay, now I'm not a lawyer, but I could destroy this guy on the stand. My first question would be about the alleged vasectomy. The authors of Game Change, the best-selling, gossipy book that was published shortly before Young's even more salacious book, claimed that Young had a vasectomy and talked about it to everyone. Refusing to reward his bad behavior by giving him some of my money, I just skimmed Young's book (I would, of course, have read it if I were to cross examine him) in the book store, so I don't know if or how he addressed the vasectomy question in that book, but I know for sure that none of the interviews that I watched discussed a vasectomy. Oprah didn't ask him about it, nor did Joy Behar, Chris Matthews, or Bob Woodruff in the part of the "Nightline" interview that I caught.

Perhaps my OJ education made me aware of how biased and fact-free press coverage can be, but I have been stunned by how sloppy the Edwards scandal coverage has been. The lack of interest in Mr. Young's alleged vasectomy, which certainly casts doubt on his story of being just an innocent father looking for a turtle for his children while that devil Edwards coaxed him into pretending to be his baby's father, is just one example of how the media didn't seem interested in checking out facts. Mr. Young, for instance, grabbed my attention by saying, in an aside when he was discussing what evidence he had, what I already knew, that the <u>Enquirer</u> pictures were fake. I initially skimmed his book to search for any mention of the fake pictures. The passage that I found was brief, but it made the obvious point that John Edwards would not wear work clothes to a fancy Beverly Hills hotel. Young didn't mention that the clothes were also sweat stained. In fact, what made me know that the pictures were fake was the sweat stain analysis. The <u>Enquirer</u> was trying to prove that the hard-to-decipher picture of a white man who might be Edwards, holding a baby in a room, was actually Edwards by pointing out that his blue shirt had a similar sweat stain to the one found on the blue shirt in the clear picture that showed Edwards at some unidentified location, looking blandly happy. Those pictures raised more questions than they answered. Where were the pictures of Edwards trying to dodge the press? Where were the pictures of him escaping into the men's room (which was the story told before the pictures were published)? When and where was the clear picture taken? And why was he sweating in it? And why in hell would the supposedly vain Edwards, a man criticized for his expensive haircuts, wear a sweat-stained work shirt into any hotel? And is it a coincidence that the stained garment is blue? Wasn't there another Southern Democrat, a President, whose sexual scandal was exposed by a stained blue garment, a dress?

I initially saw only the first pictures and didn't pay attention to the <u>Enquirer</u> coverage after that issue. But when "Nightline" covered the tabloid's role in the scandal during its promotion of Young's book in early 2010, some more pictures of Edwards wearing the blue shirt were shown, and I thought I recognized the pose. Probably three years earlier, I had seen pictures of Edwards working in a woman's house; I guess he was trying to make it more energy efficient, but mainly he was trying to look like the working class man that he no longer was. I didn't really notice what he was wearing in those pictures. But I remembered that in one of them, he was looking up at a light bulb; my sense memory suggested it was the same picture that appeared in the <u>Enquirer,</u> as shown briefly in the "Nightline" story. If I'm right, I'm sure others, including some of his staff, not to mention the woman whose house was being repaired, have recognized those pictures, yet I've never heard anyone except Edwards, his wife, and Young say that the pictures were fake.

It's interesting to consider why the <u>Enquirer</u> printed those pictures to frame the guilty Edwards and why so many people seemed to accept the pictures as real. If Edwards were a black man, more people might recognize the bias underlying our acceptance of pictures supposedly featuring a rich man, wearing sweat-stained work clothes in a swanky hotel, but it's a little harder to recognize classism. Edwards is a multimillionaire lawyer, who lived in a very large house and wore work clothes only to pretend that he was like the people whose votes he solicited, but during the 2004 campaign he constantly reminded us that he was the son of mill workers. In fact, he repeated the line so much that he started to joke about it. Obviously, we received the message; we believed that he would wear sweaty work clothes in inappropriate settings because he's from the working class. It's the same reason that people probably bought Young's vicious little story about Edwards asking for a dirty diaper so he could retrieve the baby's DNA to see if she was his child. Why would Edwards ask for a dirty diaper when he could use hair (from a hairbrush) or a spoon used to feed the baby? Those who accepted that story without question clearly saw Edwards as dirt poor instead of filthy rich. I read more than one comment about the players in the scandal being trash, but Edwards was the only person in this story whose family members would fit the socio-economic definition of what snobs call "trash," working class white folks. His wife was an officer's daughter, the mistress had a rich father, and the aide's father was a famous minister.

Some conspiracy theorists believe that the Edwards scandal received so much more attention than some other sex scandals because he was a populist (at least in his second campaign for President), fighting for the poor and the working class. They may be right, and certainly it's disturbing to see how venomously the trial lawyer who fought for a little girl who had her intestines sucked out due to a faulty, easy-to-repair device is attacked as an ambulance chaser and a sleazy guy while the corporate lawyer (or more likely, lawyers) who defended the corporation that made (and didn't repair) the faulty device has not been called names. But there are other reasons why the Edwards case has continued to make news while other randy politicians whose scandals broke within a year of his have been allowed to go quietly about their business. Democrat Eliot Spitzer, who resigned as New York governor only months before Edwards' "Nightline" confession and who briefly had a show on CNN, had to deal with the revelations of a prostitute who serviced him, but his wife said nothing. The wife of Republican Governor Sanford, whose Argentine tango scandal broke about a year after Edwards' confession, wrote a book and briefly went on a book tour, but the mistress didn't talk. The aide of former Republican Senator John Ensign, whose scandal erupted around the same time as Sanford's, talked, mainly because Ensign had an affair with his wife, but the mistress and the wife were quiet. In fact, I don't even know what Mrs. Ensign looks like since she didn't stand silently behind her husband when he confessed. But Edwards' theme song should be "Everybody's talking about me." The mistress, the aide, and the wife all talked. The latter two wrote books, which discussed the affair, and both went on extensive book tours. In fact, all three of them participated in hour-long interviews with Oprah. After that "Nightline" interview, Edwards seemed to be the only person involved in his scandal not talking, although he made a sheepish cameo appearance during his wife's Oprah interview.

And he had another problem--his hair. Although he's older than the other three "disgraced" politicians of the class of 2008-09, he looks quite a bit younger than all of them, mainly because his hair is full and not graying. Edwards' youthful looks and alleged sexiness have probably had the same effect on his story as Nicole Simpson's beautiful blondness had on the OJ story. She made the cover of <u>National Enquirer</u> so frequently, not just because she was a white woman, but also because she was a beautiful, blonde white woman. There has been much discussion of how we focus on certain victims, like Laci Peterson or the missing-for-months Elizabeth Smart, because of their beauty, but I also think that we have focused on certain villains, like Mary Kay Letourneau and Pam Smart, because of their beauty. There's even a book out now suggesting that American student Amanda Knox was tried and convicted for killing her roommate in Italy, at least in part because of her beauty. If Edwards looked like the old-enough-to-be-three-of-his children's-grandfather, fifty-something man that he is, I doubt that people would be so interested in his sex life.

Indeed, from the time I became aware of Edwards, the focus seemed to be on his physical appearance. He was named the sexiest politician by <u>People</u> in the early 2000's, and several times during the 2004 election, his "cuteness" was discussed. I even remember one male entertainment reporter asking First Lady Laura Bush if she thought Edwards was cute, and she said, "Yes, he is cute." There was also much discussion of the physical differences between the Senator and his wife, who was overweight and looked middle aged. Initially, I felt a bit sorry for her since no woman, no matter how smart or successful (and Mrs. Edwards wasn't as successful as was her husband), wants to be seen as too old or fat for her sexy husband. But I now realize that Mrs. Edwards was helped by her physical appearance as much as her husband was hurt by his. She benefited from being compared to two people, her husband and the 2004 Democratic Presidential nominee's wife, Teresa Kerry, who were suspiciously youthful looking, had too much hair that was too well coiffed, and who had accents. Mrs. Edwards, in comparison to those two, looked and sounded ordinary. When she first appeared on Oprah's show, promoting her first book, the billionaire, who probably doesn't know that many soccer moms or car poolers, described the well-educated, wealthy lawyer as the kind of woman with whom we would want to car pool the children. I can't imagine Oprah applying such "plain folks" language to either John Edwards or Teresa Kerry. But, of course, Elizabeth Edwards was not only just as rich as her husband, thanks to his career as a brilliant lawyer, she was actually the one who wanted to build the expensive mansion that she showed off first to Oprah and later to Oprah protégé Nate Berkus.

There is no better representative of a person's benefiting from a less than perfect physique than Oprah. Despite her billions and power, she appears to be everywoman because she's constantly battling her weight. Had she remained a size ten after her first great weight loss, I'm convinced that she wouldn't be as popular (And I would offer Star Jones as exhibit A to prove my case; she wrote about being a diva in 1998, but people didn't mind her full of herself personality until she lost weight). Of course, Oprah also has discussed her problems with sexual molestation, men who didn't love her, and even substance abuse. We like Oprah because we can sometimes feel superior to her. Mrs. Edwards' situation was similar. Despite her wealth and intelligence, we could feel sorry for her because she was seen as not sexy enough for her "cute" husband, and she had suffered other hardships, breast cancer and the death of her son, which she was willing to discuss at length.

Her husband, on the other hand, seemed too good to be true. He had managed to go from the mill village to the U.S. Senate without gaining weight, graying, losing hair, or wrinkling. And he was perpetually smiling. Then to make matters worse, he had this overweight, aging wife, who seemed smarter than he, and who occasionally liked to put him in his place, and still he didn't cheat on her. Is it any wonder that people thought he was phony? Even after it was clear that Mrs. Edwards had not told the whole truth about her marriage, some people still talked about how genuine and sincere she was, but Edwards was seen as a phony even before there was clear evidence that he had lied about cheating on his wife (and what adulterer doesn't?). Like Mitt Romney, who has also (like Edwards) been labeled a Ken doll, Edwards just <u>looked</u> phony.

It's interesting that few people seemed to notice that the son that Mrs. Edwards lost was also her husband's child. I never heard or read any commentary that suggested Edwards might have been throwing his wife under the bus after she became ill to protect his heart. He had already lost someone he loved, so maybe this determinedly sunny man just didn't want to lose another loved one. Maybe he decided to dump her or do something that he thought would make her dump him before she died. The people who excused his behavior usually blamed his wife, pointing out that she let herself go physically or complaining that she castrated him. He also received little sympathy for having lost a race for Vice President on the same day that he discovered (or had confirmed) that his wife had cancer. And I don't remember anyone's pointing out that he had a rare double loss in 2004. He lost the nomination for President and then lost as Vice President. Most losing Vice Presidents (Lieberman in 2000, Palin in 2008, Mondale in 1980) were not running for President in the same year. George H.W. Bush, on the other hand, lost the nomination for President in 1980 but won as Vice President.

Part of the reason we don't feel sympathy for Edwards is his perpetually smiling, too young for his years face. He has the opposite problem of the sad-faced Lieberman and former ticket mate John Kerry, who was famously told by Billy Crystal, "Senator, if you're having a good time, tell your face." Edwards needs to tell his face that he's having and has had a bad time.

But some of the differences in the way the former Senator and his wife were treated during and before this scandal relate more to gender. I would never use the phrase "reverse sexism," but Edwards would probably have received more sympathy for his dead child, sick spouse, and election losses if he had been a woman. Certainly, we feel sorrier for a mother who has lost her child than we do for the father. One way that we can demonstrate discrimination is to imagine what would happen if the person were a different race, or in this case, a different gender. So when

349

we see people criticizing Mrs. Edwards for having temper tantrums during which she cursed out her husband's staff, we can ask if the criticism would be so harsh if her husband had the hot temper. And when some people wonder if she should have spent her last years flying around the country giving speeches instead of staying at home with her young children, we can ask if they would feel the same way if her husband, the father of those young children, continued to pursue his career while battling stage four cancer. Similarly, we should ask if people would have responded as sympathetically to Edwards if he had been the cancer-stricken, less well-known spouse, and she had been the famous candidate. After all, the losing Vice Presidential candidate in the next election cycle was a woman, Sarah Palin. If we had learned, shortly after the 2008 election, that Todd Palin had prostate cancer, would he have received thousands of sympathetic letters and e-mails, or would Sarah have received most of that sympathy? And how would we have responded if Mr. Edwards had revealed in a book that when his son died, he quit his job and sat by the dead son's grave for two years, reading his high school textbooks to him while his wife returned to her job, won a major case, and then became a U.S. Senator? And how would we respond if he had described going into a supermarket, seeing his dead child's favorite soda, then sitting on the floor, screaming and crying while other customers (and this was in North Carolina, not New York) walked around him without offering assistance. Would we call him "dignified and gracious," the "iconic father by the side of the grave," or would we say, "Don't let that crazy man anywhere near the White House. Why didn't he go back to work? Why didn't he go home and take care of his wife and living child?" Finally, could Mr. Edwards have described multiple emotional breakdowns, discussed how his wife took such good care of him, call her his rock, and then write a book called "Resilience"?

John Edwards is, in fact, the perfect media scapegoat. He's a rich (being born poor doesn't help when you're a multimillion-aire who pays $400.00 for haircuts and lives in a huge mansion), good looking, white, male trial lawyer/politician from the South. He has no generic pity cards to play and seems not to know how to play the personal ones that he has (grieving father, husband of a dying woman). His wife, on the other hand, despite her wealth and race, was an almost perfect media darling. She was a victim who could describe her victimization eloquently, both in speech and writing.

Mrs. Edwards also had another advantage over her husband; she was more willing to spin the media. When Edwards fell from grace, he conducted that one ill-advised "Nightline" interview with fellow handsome guy Bob Woodruff (I initially assumed that Team Edwards picked Bob because they thought the audience might be less critical of two cute guys, Ken and his buddy Bob, discussing sex, but I learned later that Bob is a friend of Mrs. Edwards' brother) and then shut up. No matter how much mud was thrown on him, he kept quiet. But when Mrs. Edwards was attacked in two bestsellers, Game Change and Young's The Politician, she fought back with a major media campaign, primarily with help from her friends at People, who loved her so much that they put her on the cover five times in 2010 (the last two times after her death) and for the three large cover photos (that's right; this wife of a disgraced politician was featured in three large <u>People</u> covers in one year; Michelle who? Hillary who? Nancy who?) appeared to use the exact same seemingly airbrushed picture found on the cover of her first book. In the first 2010 <u>People</u> article, Mrs. Edwards' sister described how the woman who had previously been criticized for calling her husband's love child "it" met the child and gave her Christmas presents. In a later article, Mrs. Edwards' adult daughter, Cate, "wrote" a tribute in her mother's style, saying that this woman who had been portrayed in the two books as a cursing, arrogant, possibly insane shrew taught her children grace. Cate's mother also defended herself in an interview with Matt Lauer on "Today" and in an hour-long interview with Larry King.

Mrs. Edwards was not an effective spinner in those two interviews. She kept repeating the love child's name, Quinn, when she talked to Larry and even made the almost absurd claim that she was initially preparing to be the child's stepmother (Months earlier Anderson Cooper had reported that Mrs. Edwards was the reason that her husband had not admitted that he was the father once the DNA test confirmed his paternity, and around the same time she had said in an interview with the same Larry King that she hoped for the sake of the child that her father's identity would be kept secret). But then Larry asked if her children had seen their half-sister, and she smoothly and calmly answered that she was waiting until Quinn was older and could have a memory of meeting her siblings. Almost as soon as those words were out of her mouth, she briefly looked worried, probably because she realized that critical thinkers like me would wonder why she didn't want her own children, who were already old enough to have memories, to enjoy their cute little sister's early years. Luckily for her, Larry didn't challenge her, which is probably why she chose him and not the "View" women for her image repair tour.

Matt Lauer was equally gentle. He kept a straight face when Elizabeth compared herself to Sandra Bullock while I shook my head and laughed. I assumed that the obvious attempt to link herself to the woman who was being called "America's Sweetheart" would backfire since there were so many differences between them. Academy-award winning actress Sandra Bullock was more famous than her husband and was famous before she met and married Jesse James. Mrs. Edwards, who was married much longer than she was famous, was famous only because she was married to a former Senator and failed Presidential and Vice-Presidential candidate. Sandra Bullock received nothing but glowing press in 2010 while Mrs. Edwards had been accused (with evidence) of harassing the Youngs on the telephone, falsely accusing Young of stealing her dead child's sports cards, cursing out and/or trying to fire most of her husband's staff, threatening to take away the staff's healthcare, ridiculing her husband and his parents, and trying to tear off her clothes while screaming and crying at an airport. Most important, Sandra Bullock refused to talk about her cheating husband while Mrs. Edwards couldn't stop talking about hers. In fact, the country had moved on and forgotten about the Edwards sex scandal by 2009 until the arrival of Mrs. Edwards' second book, which devoted only a few pages to the adultery, and her book tour, which focused almost solely on the sex scandal. Given how ridiculous the comparison to America's Sweetheart was, imagine my surprise while watching "Good Morning, America" the morning after the Edwards "Today" interview when I heard a reporter introduce a segment by saying, "Elizabeth Edwards and Sandra Bullock, two strong women" and then spend several minutes pointing out what these completely different women supposedly had in common. Don't ask me what the similarities were because I was too shocked to listen. I guess if I had friends in the media I could promote the myth that I look like Cicely Tyson or Halle Berry.

Perhaps because I'm something of a contrarian (my name is, after all, Mary), the more Mrs. Edwards spun the media, the less I liked her, and the quieter he stayed, the more I liked her husband. Despite (or maybe because of) his working class background, he seemed to be the classiest character in this tawdry soap opera. He was, after all, the one person who admitted behaving badly without pointing the finger at someone else. In the "Nightline" interview, he said, "I'm to blame; it's no one else's fault." And when his wife finally released him to claim his child (probably so that the press could stop attacking her and attack him again), he said, "I was wrong." He didn't say, "I had to deny my child on television or my mentally unstable wife would have killed me or killed herself." He didn't say, "I didn't trust this tramp who pursued me, a known-to-be-married man, when I met her in a bar, so I wanted to provoke her into providing a DNA test so that I could be sure the child was mine, and then when I discovered that Quinn was indeed my daughter, my crazy, controlling wife wouldn't let me tell the world." He just said that <u>he</u> was wrong.

It's hard to decide which of the more privileged, "pathetic" (to use Mrs. Edwards' own word) characters, who publicized what was undoubtedly Edwards' most shameful moment to keep themselves in a spotlight that he created for them, to sell books, to go on television, to pose for sexy pictures in <u>GQ</u> or warm and fuzzy pictures in <u>People,</u> was the most despicable, the trashiest, if you will. Probably I would choose the appropriately named, born-rich mistress, Ms. Hunter, who seems to believe, or wants us to believe, that she saved Edwards by helping him to ruin his political career and to destroy his thirty-year marriage. Her smug performance on Oprah's show probably did more to help Mrs. Edwards' cause than any of the latter's own post-scandal interviews. Compared to Hunter, Mrs. Edwards was indeed a saint.

Of course, these pathetic secondary celebrities could not have grabbed the spotlight if the media had not cooperated with them. So the media might be the most despicable players in this story. During his last interview with Mrs. Edwards, Larry King bragged that he had not interviewed either Hunter or Young, but he had allowed Mrs. Edwards to come on his show several times after the scandal, and they always discussed it. In fact, I had one of those smartest woman in the room moments in 2010 when I read a discussion on either the Daily Beast or more likely the Huffington Post message board about whether Mrs. Edwards posted under the name "Cherubim" (apparently not, unless "Cherubim" is now posting from heaven). One poster thought it wasn't Mrs. Edwards because she wrote about being a Michael Jackson fan after the King of Pop died in June, 2009, and I guess this poster didn't think Elizabeth could be a fan of Michael Jackson. I became even more interested when either that poster or someone else said that Cherubim claimed to be a black woman during her fan-of-Michael-Jackson posts and used nonstandard English. Well, I was intrigued because I happened to know that the day that Michael Jackson died, Elizabeth Edwards was the scheduled guest on King's show. I had been watching his show the evening before and saw the promo for the next day's show, listing Mrs. Edwards as discussing healthcare. Being smarter than the average television viewer, I knew what would happen. This show was scheduled shortly after the Sanford and Ensign scandals broke and several weeks after Mrs. Edwards had completed her book tour (Her second book apparently did not do as well as the first one). It didn't matter whether King contacted her or she contacted him; I knew that she traded a discussion of the sex scandals for a chance to discuss healthcare. And when King finally stopped talking about Jackson's death, and Mrs. Edwards appeared weeks later to participate in an uninspired, totally unenlightening healthcare debate with former Republican governor Tommy Thompson, she did spend two segments (without Thompson) discussing her husband's situation, leaving out the Republicans since their scandals had much shorter shelf lives than her husband's (because their wives, at least at that point, weren't talking). I knew, then, that if Cherubim were Elizabeth, she wasn't posting as a Michael Jackson fan; she was an angry spotlight seeker, smart enough to know that one way to incite a message board attack was to defend the person that she wanted to be attacked. And if she posed as a black woman and played the race card in "defending" the man who one comedian accused of changing from a black man to a white woman, I suspect that she was successful in turning the posters against Michael because he had the nerve to die and bump her off Larry King's show.

Unlike the OJ case, the coverage of the Edwards' sex scandal didn't teach us much. During the OJ trial, we learned about DNA, about police work, collection of evidence, and forensic science, about how trials are conducted, including the importance of jury consultants, about how wide the racial divide between blacks and whites still was in the mid-nineties, and about domestic violence. Those who covered the Edwards' scandal just wanted to tell the same old story of an arrogant, corrupt politician who cheated on either his saintly, cancer-stricken or his shrewish, "ball biting" (as Chris Matthews called her, and he was a fan) wife. I saw no discussion of the effects of fame on a long, supposedly successful marriage that survived the death of a child. How much did the suggestion that Mr. Edwards was too sexy for his wife hurt the marriage? How much did the suggestion that Mrs. Edwards was smarter than her husband hurt the marriage? Did Mr. Edwards, who was used to being the jock, carrying the ball, while his wife led the cheers, resent her movement into the spotlight? Although a few posters on message boards suggested that Mr. Edwards may have been still wounded from the loss of his son, there was no discussion of the different ways that men and women handle grief. Although a few commenters looked at the possibility that the steps taken to have children so late in life might have caused Mrs. Edwards' cancer, there was no serious discussion of wheth-er it's a good idea to have "replacement" children, which surely at some point the children will realize that they are. And there could have been a discussion of whether it is appropriate to use extreme measures, like taking shots, to have children when we should be having grandchildren. Mrs. Edwards was proud that she had an AARP card when she was pregnant with her last child, but I noticed that she said that child, Jack, told her to dye her hair, which grew back a beautiful gray after the first cancer treatment. She also said that Jack asked who would be his children's grandmother; when she told the story, she made it sound as if he were responding to the news that his mother had stage four cancer, and maybe he was. But I wondered if she had taken that comment out of context; what if some big-mouthed first grader, who knew Jack's story because his parents were famous, told him that his mother was around the same age as that child's grandmother? Mrs. Edwards said that she decided to have more children because children made her and her husband happy. But did she think about her children's happiness?

The most important lesson that we might have learned but didn't from the Edwards scandal is how stupid we are about selecting our political leaders. How did this one-term Senator, a lawyer until he was elected Senator, find himself on the fast track to the White House? Why was he on Gore's short list for Vice President? If the answer is, because he was Bill Clinton without the sex scandal, then not only might we have an alternate answer to what Edwards was doing when he opened his hotel room door to Ms. Hunter (maybe he didn't want to be President), but it also shows us why we have so many disappointing leaders. And let me admit that I was an Edwards supporter, not because I was thinking about what kind of President he would be in comparison to

Barack Obama or Hillary Clinton, but because I thought he could win. And when I read the Edwards' books and watched the couple interact on television, I wasn't studying them, trying to figure out how well they would run the country (I assumed that they would have a Bill and Hillary type of two-for-one co-presidency), but to see how many votes they could win. The fact is John Edwards was less experienced in government and politics than either Obama or Palin, but maybe because he was a white man, no one seemed to notice. I thought the North Carolina person who supposedly said he or she would vote for Edwards for Senator because his wife was fat was a fool, but my reasons (he was a smart, successful Southern white man with a smart, English major wife) for planning to vote for him for President were almost equally ridiculous.

If we paid close attention to the OJ and Edwards cases, both could teach us how little we know about celebrities. Even if we read their books, listen to their interviews carefully, and watch their body language, we don't really know these people. What we should know is that we must look behind the curtains, beyond the smoke and mirrors, beneath the surface of things, as Ralph Ellison says in <u>Invisible Man,</u> to find some version of the truth. And we must understand that we might never know the whole truth because there are too many different truths. Your truth is not necessarily my truth. As a Lily Tomlin character once said, "What is reality but a collective hunch?" We are all guessing, but we should at least base our guesses on facts and critical analysis rather than hype and spin.

Of the many positive evaluations and tributes I have received over the years, my favorite came from an anonymous graduate student who wrote in support of my 2004 Graduate Faculty Teaching Award, "She entertains her students with ideas and inspires them with hope." I'm not sure how I inspired students with hope; maybe they felt that if a person as odd as I am could be successful, so could they. But I was delighted to know that I had entertained them with ideas. I hope most of my students at all levels learned that ideas can be entertaining and that thinking can be fun. I'm reminded of a scene in one of my favorite movies, Broadcast News. When one of her bosses tells the Holly Hunter character that it must be wonderful or nice always to feel that she is the smartest person in the room, she looks upset and says, "No, it's awful." Well, yes, sometimes it is frustrating, annoying, and awful when we feel we are the only ones thinking, the only ones with any sense, but mostly it's wonderful to know that we're smarter than the fools who are talking to us and probably trying to make fools out of us.

CHAPTER NINE
To All the Students I've Taught

More than once Oprah has said that she has always considered herself a teacher. Depending on my mood, I either receive that comment with a smile, delighted that such a powerful and wealthy woman would want to have my job, or I snort and say, "Well, yeah, I like to think of myself as a billionaire, but I'm not." Oprah is apparently not the only television personality who wants to be a teacher. I never watched Glen Beck's CNN and Fox shows, but I've seen enough film clips of him at the blackboard to recognize that he is one of those celebrity wannabe teachers. And on MSNBC both Rachel Maddow and Lawrence O'Donnell often seem to be auditioning for my former job. Both like to lecture their audiences, but O'Donnell sounds more like a professor determined to make sure his students remember his main points as he repeats them slowly while

Maddow, with her occasional silly props, sometimes seems more like a junior high school teacher.

But the kind of teacher that these celebrities want to be is not the kind that I was. They are wannabe lecturers, like the men who taught most of the classes that I took at Northwestern. These professors usually stood on a stage, talking to as many as two hundred students. Most of them never answered questions during class, rarely saw a student during office hours, and certainly didn't read exams or assign grades. Those lowly tasks were handled by graduate students. The lecturers have a much easier job than the teachers do because they have complete control over the classroom. It doesn't matter whether they are talking to one student or hundreds, to attentive students or sleepers, they can still deliver their message in the same voice and at the same speed. A good lecturer is dynamic and entertaining, maybe but not necessarily, amusing. He or she has a powerful, expressive voice and a charismatic personality. A bad lecturer is dull, with a too quiet, too grating, and/or too monotonous voice, and no personality. My officemate at Tufts was a fellow Northwestern alumnus (he was four years younger than I and arrived on campus the year I left), so he and I bonded over our mutual disdain for the worst lecturer either of us ever had, a Nabokov specialist who read his notes in a monotone. The tradition at Northwestern was to clap for the lecturers at the end of the quarter. Dr. Dull smugly said, after some of the people clapped while I used my visibility (I was the one dark spot in the class) to demonstrate my disdain by refusing to clap, "It's an old Russian custom to clap for the audience," and then clapped for us. It's the one time that jerk did or said anything interesting, showed any personality.

But there was no reason for Dr. Dull to clap for his audience since we didn't have to do anything except sit there and take notes. Most teachers, however, depend on their audiences as much as comedians do theirs. Maybe that's why Steve Martin said in one of his books that teachers were like entertainers. He was talking about the kind of teacher that I was. Except for the first day of class when I described the course or during my usually briefer preparations for midterms and finals, I did not lecture. I led discussions. Sometimes I placed students in groups so they could discuss among themselves before talking to the class as a whole. In most of my literature classes, students were required to do brief presentations while composition students spent time working in peer-evaluation groups. And for the last approximately fifteen years that I taught graduate literature courses, I used a successful class-discussion format, where students chose specialty topics to focus on throughout the quarter, or at least until the midway point, when I allowed them to sign up for a new topic if they chose. The assigned topics were language, structure, American culture (for American literature courses), religion/Biblical allusions, class/politics, race/gender, and teaching/canon. I guided the students by asking them to consider specific questions or to look for certain elements (the language specialists often had to look for motifs and puns) when they discussed their topics. Clearly, in these classes the students' contributions were as important as mine.

Any teacher who has taught two classes that cover the same material can testify to the importance of not only student participation but also student-teacher and student-student chemistry. That first graduate-level Ethnic Literatures class that I taught was one of my least favorite classes of all time, not because the students didn't participate or because their contributions weren't intelligent or interesting, but because they didn't like each other, some of them didn't like me, and I didn't like some of them. And my least favorite class was, of course, that racists-filled "Language and Human Behavior" class, which also included plenty of talkative, smart students. In fact, I started class late one day (I did everything I could not to teach that class) so that several of my students, graduating seniors, could pick up awards at the annual department luncheon for top students.

The most important students in any class are the aggressive, outspoken ones. They can make or break a class. Usually my favorite classes included at least one student (the more the merrier) who liked to tease and be teased. When I discovered that student, we became a comedy team, entertaining the class and ourselves. The student could be male or female and from any race. But my best comedy partners seemed to be white males. Given how well I worked with white men, often by the end of my career, considerably younger white men, I'm surprised that there hasn't been a salt and pepper version of Elaine May and Mike Nichols.

I also enjoyed classes in which there were what we called at Cal Poly "reentry" women; these were usually women who had married, had children, and returned to school when their children entered elementary school, or in some cases, graduated from high school. When I started my career, many of these women were older than I was. In fact, Lindy O, who eventually became my officemate and is still one of the ladies with whom I lunch, was one of those early, slightly older (not quite two years, although she looks younger, thanks to hair products) reentry women. Whatever their personalities, these women come to class prepared and can usually be counted on to attend regularly and participate enthusiastically. There were fewer "reentry" men at Cal Poly, and that was fine with me because they didn't seem to take me or the classes as seriously as did their female counterparts, and they were also the students most likely to want to know if I was a "Miss" or "Mrs."

Other than overtly racist and/or openly hostile students, the ones who caused me the most problems were the silent, blank-faced seat fillers. Although I had trouble with discipline when I taught high school, as a college professor, I much preferred a rowdy, slightly out of control class to one where no one wanted to talk. I knew that I could crack the whip if I needed to, and students who are talking are at least awake and paying attention to something. The Spring Quarter 096 classes were usually not fun to teach because the students were either lazy and unmotivated, having failed (or made lower than the "C" required to move into freshman composition) 096 twice because they didn't attend class or submit papers, or they were not good writers and readers, who made lower than a "C" in either English 095 in the fall or English 096 in the winter. Some of them were both lazy and weak. I taught the course primarily because I thought I was good at motivating the lazy (mainly through fear) and assisting the weak. I also knew that Spring Quarter 096 students often disappeared, so classes were smaller by the last few weeks, with fewer papers to evaluate and final grades to compute (Hey, we teachers who have to teach three classes and grade papers need to take care of ourselves, especially at the end of a long year). Despite these handicaps, one of my favorite classes of all time was a rowdy Spring Quarter 096 class that I called the Wild Bunch. Because the basic writing classes are small, they often meet in drab, uncomfortable little rooms, and this one met in a room next to the women's restroom on the second floor of the Engineering building. When the class was quietly writing, we could hear the toilet flushing in that restroom, and we all laughed, especially when one of the female students had left class because we assumed she was the one flushing the toilet. We were constantly laughing, but the students also did their work, came to class, and all but one earned a "C" or higher in the course.

On the other hand, English 201 (Introduction to Modern Literature) was one of my favorite classes. It was a general education course, consisting almost exclusively of non-English majors. We read two novels during the quarter, but mostly we read short stories. Some English instructors didn't really like these general education literature courses because the discussions weren't academic enough, but I enjoyed hanging with students who weren't English majors. They usually didn't mind learning a little bit about symbolism, point of view (or as one of my freshmen called it "point of you"), and foreshadowing as long as I allowed them to discuss why they did or did not like certain characters and certain stories. Even though the classes were large (somewhere between twenty-eight and thirty-eight students), discussions were often livelier than those in my smaller upper division English major classes. But one Fall Quarter near the end of my career, I had a deadly dull 201 class, and unfortunately, I taught two sections of the course that quarter. I think most teachers with two sections of a course prefer to teach the duller section first so that repeating the material will be more enjoyable with the second, more lively section. However, I was forced to teach this dull class second, so I would have a lively discussion of Truman Capote's In Cold Blood in the first class, go to the second class, ask the same questions, and hear crickets. It's not clear why there were so many seat fillers in that class. It met at 4:00 p.m. on Monday and Wednesday, but I've had plenty of talkative classes during that period. It was in a large room, seemingly designed for science classes (there were sinks and some kind of lab equipment in the back of the room), but I had taught an enthusiastic and bright English 212 (American literature survey) class in the same room during Spring Quarter of that year. It was just bad chemistry I guess. This dull class made my top five list of least favorite classes.

That deadly dull class had more men than women in it, which I thought might be part of the problem, but a year later I taught a 201 class in which there were twenty-six men and three women. Assuming that the class would hate me and I would hate them, I tried to scare some of the guys out by telling them about the second novel we would read, Amy Tan's Joy Luck Club. "It's about mothers and daughters," I said. "There are not that many male characters, and most of them are villains." One game young man said, "We can't wait!" Well, the boys and I had a great time. They didn't love <u>Joy Luck Club</u>, but it was the last text we read, and by that time they had decided that I was a fun teacher. In fact, I had such a good time with that class and was so pleased with their positive evaluations of me and the course that I found myself missing them the next quarter when I taught my usually favorite 200-level class, black literature. Based on that class and a really outstanding almost all-female (seventeen women and two men) Fall Quarter English 096 course I taught a few years earlier, I decided that I might have enjoyed teaching at an all-male or all-female college.

I enjoyed the black literature classes partly because they were the only classes where I had a significant number of black students. The percentage of blacks to other races in that class ranged from 80 to 90% in the early years to 50 to 60% during the post-<u>Color Purple</u> (that novel and movie seemed to inspire more non-black students to take black literature) years to 30 to 40% during my last few years of teaching when black students were disappearing from campus (They wore t-shirts that showed their population having slipped below a thousand). In all of my other classes, I was more likely to have no black students than to have even 20% of the class be black. Three times during my career, I taught classes in which there were no white students. The first time was at USC when I taught an all-female, all-black, second semester freshman composition class that focused not coincidentally on black women writers. Needless to say, it was my favorite USC class and probably my favorite writing class of all time. The other two times, I was also teaching writing, but they were basic writing classes at Cal Poly. One was the last composition class that I taught, in Spring, 2009; it was a very small 096 class with seven students. I didn't have any problems with them, but they weren't a good class. The other class was a much better group because they were new freshmen, but after I noticed (a couple of weeks into the quarter) that everyone in the room was nonwhite, I forgot about, or at least ignored, the racial composition of the students and just tried to teach them how to write well.

But in black literature, race is the focus of the discussion, so having a racially diverse group of students makes the class more interesting. Also, because there were so few black students and professors at Cal Poly, the black students seemed to relax and enjoy themselves more in that class, even when they were no longer in the majority. The rest of the students either sat back and enjoyed the show or, if they were bolder, took the opportunity to learn as much as they could about black culture, asking the black students and me questions and comparing their cultures to ours. I always assumed that any white student who took black literature taught by a black professor was ready to hear some hard truths about racism, so I didn't sugarcoat my comments but also made sure that no one felt attacked. Occasionally, I acted as if the whole class were black, and the nonblacks seemed to enjoy being honorary members of my race. In the late eighties, when I was still taking breaks during two-hour classes (I later just let classes go ten minutes early), many of my black literature students used the break time to march down from the third floor classroom to the second floor, where there were vending machines, so they could buy snacks to eat during the second half of our discussion. Technically, students were not supposed to eat in class, but

I didn't mind when they made themselves at home, as long as they didn't disturb me or the other students. Unfortunately, some of the eaters were sloppy, leaving candy, chips, or peanut wrappers on the desks or the floor. And even more unfortunately, the linguistics class that came in after us consisted of mostly white women, several of them in their thirties and forties. Now I loved the reentry women, but some of them could be a bit prissy and controlling. They seemed to think that the classrooms were their living rooms. Naturally, these women complained to Number 1 Linguist, who was teaching the class, about my students' leaving behind their trash. When Number 1 brought their complaints to me, I couldn't wait for him to finish talking so that I could say, "Tell your students that we cleaned up their messes for centuries; they can clean up our mess for ten weeks." Number 1 didn't have the nerve to tell his students what I said. But I told my class that was only about 60% black how I told off my colleague and his snooty class. Everyone laughed, even the white students. Of course, I also told them to throw their snack wrappings away and gave a little speech about not making black people look bad.

Although the teacher who leads discussions does not have as much control over how well a class session goes and how much students learn as a lecturer does, her contribution is extremely important. In fact, the teacher is probably still the person who most determines whether a class will succeed. My two least favorite classes would have been less tense, for example, if I had kept my cool and maintained my sense of humor when faced with student racism. If I had handled the older student's critique of Smitherman's book the way I handled Charmer's comments about hearing drums when he saw the black high school students gathered under the clock, maybe I would have enjoyed that class more. And certainly, I could have diffused the tension brought to the Ethnic Literatures of the U.S. graduate seminar if I had joked about the segregated seating arrangements. Even that dull 201 class might have opened up a little more as the quarter progressed if I had not lost my cool one day fairly early in the quarter when I tried what I called my waiting-for-the-bus response to student silence. My students and I would laugh about how long I could wait for an answer. I asked a question and just stood (or sat) there, looking around at the students. Once when I used that technique in an 096 class, a cute black woman finally said plaintively, "We don't know, Miss Sisney." I guess because I hadn't waited for the bus in decades and had grown less patient with age, I couldn't outwait these students and so bawled them out, asking them if they had read the stories, and then telling them how much more talkative my other 201 class was when I asked the same questions. After that outburst, the timid students were even more intimidated by the now angry black woman, and the indifferent students were pissed and became even more silent, but now with a hint of belligerence.

That 201 class got on my nerves because I usually had talkative, stimulating, entertaining classes. Even in tense classes, the discussions were lively, interesting and occasionally loud. I rarely had to use my waiting-for-the-bus strategy. The anonymous graduate students who wrote in support of my 2004 Teaching Award explained how I kept the conversations going: "She pushes beyond the obvious in every discussion." "She engages the class by asking profound and insightful questions." "She encourages participation and motivates students to express their opinions and ideas." But one student (I suspect it was Kyla H, who had observed me having a good time with that Spring Quarter 096 class that I called the Wild Bunch) may have found my strongest asset: "She is funny, and she thinks her students are also funny."

Not all teachers can be funny, but they must have a sense of humor. And they must listen as well as (if not better than) talk. Former graduate student and long-term colleague, Don, K, explained why my classes were so lively in a retirement tribute: "She likes people--make that she likes <u>students</u>--and listens to them. She doesn't make them feel that they are <u>lesser</u>. She cares, then--about students, about texts that matter, about whether students learn to be not only good students but also better readers of and more-careful writers about texts that matter." He then makes the point that is made most often about me as a teacher: "She likes to laugh. She likes to have a good time, and if having a good time learning is even remotely possible and appropriate, then her classes will have a good time learning."

Not only did I want my students to have a good time learning, but I also liked to learn while having a good time. Don is right that I didn't think my students were lesser; certainly I was better educated than almost all of them (I had one graduate student, Maya, who added an English M.A. to her Spanish Ph.D.), but I wasn't necessarily smarter. And if I was smarter about English, then they were smarter about something else--football, computers, engineering, architecture, or whatever their majors were. I enjoyed teaching an advanced composition course, called

"Advanced Professional Writing," because the students were required to write a term project in their fields as their primary assignment. Most of the students were either liberal studies majors, planning to teach elementary school, behavioral scientists, or accounting majors. Although some of the accounting projects were boring, I learned more from them than I did from the other two majors that were closer to my own academic background. I even used information about starting a business that I learned from one accounting student to tell off some of my relatives who had tried to start a business without sufficient capital.

Since I wasn't like my graduate professors, who thought that they didn't need to learn about writers who weren't taught when they were in college, I often learned about new writers from my students. I was introduced to Native American writer Sherman Alexie, for instance, by a bright Asian American student in one of my English 212 classes. He had chosen as his presentation topic the very broad "Other Native American Writers." The only requirement for that topic was that each student choose a Native American writer different from the ones chosen by others on the panel of presenters and that they not choose the one that we were reading--Louise Erdrich. As soon as I heard the title of Alexie's short story collection, <u>The Lone Ranger and Tonto Fistfight in Heaven</u>, I knew that I must read that book. And within a few years, I was teaching it in the graduate Ethnic Literatures of the U.S. seminar and later in my Twentieth Century American Literature undergraduate course, pairing it with a collection of Flannery O'Connor stories, comparing the two writers' humor, their portrayal of grotesque characters, and their focus on the importance of place.

Letting students know that what they have to say is worth hearing is an important part of the teacher's job. I teased, mocked, and sometimes chastised graduate students, especially the women, for being timid when they participated in class discussions. I mimicked their qualifications: "This is probably wrong because I'm just a graduate student, and I don't know what I'm talking about, but maybe . . ." Once when I lost patience with a very bright female student who apologized every time she spoke, she claimed that some of the other graduate professors had made her feel that her comments weren't valuable. I didn't know which of my colleagues had been guilty of lowering her self-esteem, but I'd had professors like them during my academic career. In addition to Potter, who didn't want to hear from women (although he didn't mind listening to a black, husky-voiced woman), there was one fairly personable Austen, Wharton, and James specialist whose comments were so tactless and caustic that I sometimes wondered if he were putting us on. I took him my first semester at USC for a Henry James and Edith Wharton seminar, and I'll never forget his comment on one of my papers on which I received an "A-." Dr. Tactless said, "You didn't say anything new or interesting, but what you said, you said well." There were approximately eight students in the class, and we were all fairly talkative during the first few weeks. But when a student made what I thought was an insightful comment about a text, Dr. Tactless looked at her or him dismissively and said, "So what's your point?" Inevitably, we stopped talking so this class looked and sounded like the Chaucer seminar, with everyone looking at their books or at each other while Dr. Tactless waited impatiently for someone to respond to his questions. Finally, he became annoyed and wanted to know why we weren't talking. Maybe because I was bolder than everyone else, but more likely because I was the Education major who thought I knew how teachers were supposed to act, I helpfully informed him that we stopped talking because when we were talking we thought we had made our point and then he asked us what I point was. To his credit, Dr. Tactless became more tactful after my helpful hint, and especially after another bold woman teased him about his caustic comments on our papers.

I don't think I was ever as tactless as my fellow Edith Wharton fan, but I had to watch my mouth with some students and classes. I tried to gauge which students were bold and which were bashful, which were strong and which were weak, and act accordingly. Generally, I tried to be gentler with the younger students, especially the basic writers, and most especially the Fall Quarter freshmen who were new to college and easily intimidated. Just the way I looked when I walked into the room often scared them. My officemate Lindy O, who was definitely not a basic writer and was in her thirties when she first saw me, described her first impression in her retirement tribute: "You swept dramatically into 5-133 ready to start a new quarter of English 108--frowning, silent, striking fear into the faint hearted. I thought 'Damn this one looks like she means business!'" Yeah, I did mean business when I walked into a classroom on the first day. If a student smiled at me and spoke, I might have nodded and tried to look friendly. And, of course, during the second quarter of a graduate seminar,

I often greeted and chatted with students because I knew almost all of them. But there were fewer jokes that first day because I was laying down the law, telling them what they must do to pass the course and what they must not do (plagiarize, miss classes) if they didn't want to get on my last nerve. But as I set them straight, I paid attention to the students' eyes and faces and if I saw the Fall Quarter freshmen looking scared, I'd lighten the mood with a joke. Unfortunately, I could never bring myself to try the joke that came to me when I was too old and scary looking to use it, "I love the smell of freshmen in the fall." I consoled myself with the theory that most of the freshmen wouldn't recognize the allusion to <u>Apocalypse Now</u>, but I think the line is funny even without the movie reference.

Because they were more mature and should be more sure of themselves academically, I was less careful with graduate students. As I told one graduate seminar, "I use what few maternal instincts I have on the freshmen, so you people have to be tough." I didn't dismiss their comments the way Dr. Tactless did ours but challenged them, and I loved to argue. During one of my last graduate seminars, a student who had taken me the previous quarter and seemed bold enough to take the heat presented "Faulkner and Race." At some point in the presentation, she said she didn't think Faulkner was racist. I didn't even have to say anything; she saw my face and claimed her eye started jumping. She knew that when she finished talking, I would start an argument about Faulkner's racism. But one of the worst moments in a graduate seminar happened in an otherwise outstanding class. Another seemingly bold young woman, a high school teacher, was reading a passage from <u>Song of Solomon</u> when she mispronounced the name of my favorite character--Pilate. She pronounced it the way the exercise Pilates is pronounced. She was about the fifth or sixth person, but the first graduate student, to mispronounce the name that way, so I took that opportunity to complain about students suddenly not knowing how to pronounce this Biblical name because of some stupid exercise program. Then I told the young woman to continue reading, and she mispronounced something else. It wasn't a serious enough mistake for me (not the world's greatest enunciator) to correct her, but the woman sitting next to her helpfully (she thought) whispered the correct pronunciation. At this point, the previously bold woman asked if she could stop reading, and I said in my fake tough voice "No, read on." She started to read on, then stopped, and I realized that she was crying. Oops! Of course, instead of being consoling and apologetic, I looked at the woman next to her and asked, "Is she crying?" and when she nodded "yes," I impatiently called on another woman to finish reading the passage. It was only after the class ended that I felt bad about what happened to the clearly not so bold young woman and wasn't surprised that she soon disappeared.

There were not many tears shed in my classrooms. In fact, I can think of only four other students, all women, who cried during, or in one case, right after, one of my classes. Two of them were older white women who cried in response to discussions of traumas faced by blacks, and the other two were lively, talkative young nonwhite women who cried because they felt they were not living up to my high expectations. The first woman who cried appeared to be in her sixties, which made her older than

377

my mother (I was in my early to mid-thirties at that point). She started crying when I discussed the essays they had written, explicating the Claude McKay sonnet, "If We Must Die." When the students wrote their essays, they did not know the poet's name or when the poem was written. They also, of course, did not know that McKay was black. Many of them thought the poem was about war. When I explained that it was about lynching, the older woman started to cry. Assuming that she was worried about her grade, I reassured the class that I didn't expect them to figure out that the speaker was black and writing about lynching and said that no one had discovered the racial message, but some of them had made "A's." The older woman continued to cry. When I asked if she was okay, she said that she was just upset by the idea of people lynching each other. Many years later, another older white woman, originally from France, started crying when we discussed a passage from Women of Brewster Place that focused on the relationship between a mother and daughter. I was more impatient with her, but another older female student realized that the French lady probably had a daughter and identified with the mother.

One of the nonwhite younger students cried because she had problems talking while the other had problems writing. Interestingly, the first student, an Asian American, was in a writing class. It was a rare under-enrolled Advanced Professional Writing class. I told the students on the first day that the one good thing about the class being so small (nine students) was that they would not be nervous when they presented their term projects at the end of the quarter. I had the class laughing about how nervous some presenters had been in larger classes, shaking visibly and barely speaking above a whisper. I should have kept my mouth shut because I obviously made the students feel they would look foolish if they were nervous presenting to such a small class. The young woman did not look or act like someone who would be nervous during a presentation. She enjoyed talking during class, in her peer group, and in one-on-one conferences with me. But when she stood up to present her topic, something went terribly wrong. She became flustered and started to cry. She tried to hide her tears, so I wasn't sure that she was crying, but I could see that she was having trouble. When it became clear that she was indeed crying, I let her take her seat, and she later presented from her seat as we all sat in a circle. Clearly, there was something about the formal presentation that unnerved her, and my saying at the beginning of the quarter that she shouldn't be nervous didn't help.

The other nonwhite student, a black woman in one of my black literature classes, had no trouble with her presentation to a much larger class. In fact, by the time she took the class, I had moved from standing to sitting in a circle, allowing the presenters to speak from their seats. But occasionally students preferred to stand, sometimes because they were using the board or video equipment, but often because they just liked taking the floor and being in charge of the class for a few minutes. This woman stood, and she was a dynamic and entertaining speaker. However, she was not a good writer, and her midterm grade reflected the writing problems. So when she wrote the final, she choked. She admitted later that she didn't want to disappoint me (At this point I was old enough to be most students' mother or aunt, and some of the black students responded to me as if I were an older relative). I was shocked to see this seemingly tough, strong, young woman crying after all of her classmates had left and understood that she felt embarrassed. I tried to pump up her confidence and gave her a chance to finish the exam during my graduate seminar final the next day. She still didn't do that well, but at least she didn't cry again.

The fact that I saw only five students crying in my classes (a few more cried in my office) during my thirty-three years (thirty-four, counting high school) of teaching, and only one of them was crying because of an immediate interaction with me, suggests that I'm not as scary as I like to think I am. So there weren't many tears, but there was plenty of laughter in my classes. As Don said, we had fun, but as G.W. Bush might ask, "Was my students really learning anything?" They seemed to think so. Quite a few of my composition students said in their evaluations that they learned more about writing in the ten weeks that they spent with me than they did during four years of high school. And one anonymous graduate student, writing in support of my 2000 Graduate Faculty Teaching Award, said that I taught in a manner that made my students feel that they had learned more in one of my classes than they had in all of their undergraduate courses. And their performances on exams and in papers usually indicated that they indeed learned a great deal.

I wasn't always convinced, however, that my students retained what they had learned. In fact, I saw quite a bit of evidence that they didn't. During a brief period in the mid-eighties, I taught both basic writing and freshman composition. Often students in my basic writing classes would also take me for freshman composition. They didn't take me again because they were so crazy about me as a teacher; they were just used to me and were used to having the same teacher all year in high school. I noticed that students who took me twice didn't show as much progress in the second class, probably because I was covering some of the same points (how to develop topics, how to organize effectively and write clearly) in both classes. But more disturbing was the fact that some students who were writing better at the end of the basic writing classes started the freshman composition classes writing as they did before they took me for ten weeks. Even when the break between classes was only the three or four weeks between fall and winter, students dangled modifiers, shifted verb tense, and failed to develop their points as if the ten weeks spent with me were only a dream.

I had a similar experience with some of my literature students. Many English majors who took me for English 212, the American literature survey, also took at least one of the 400-level American literature seminars that I taught. Of course, some students took both classes the same quarter, and a few took them out of sequence, taking the lower level class second. But when they took them in the right order, I more often than not found myself staring at blank faces when I touched on a point covered in the lower-level class; clearly, these students did not remember discussing that point. Occasionally, I asked an especially bright returning student for help in explaining naturalism, which we discussed in 212, using Stephen Crane's "The Open Boat" as the textbook example of a naturalistic story. Usually the student had no memory of the discussion. One student said in defense of his inability to remember, "That was in the spring, five or six months ago." Another student, who took 212 a full year before she took the 400-level course, American Realism, said sweetly, "I don't remember anything about naturalism, but I remember you."

Even the graduate students could sometimes shock me by how little they remembered just a few weeks after they completed a seminar. When there were new students in the second quarter of a two-quarter sequence, I asked one or two of the returning students to summarize in a few minutes what we had learned in the first quarter. I sometimes had to wait a minute or two for some brave student to attempt a summary, and then he or she often needed help remembering exactly what we did learn. I noticed, too, that these students sometimes focused more on what we did than what we learned. They described how we organized discussions, and if there were recurring jokes or arguments, they mentioned them. In other words, they remembered the process of the class more than the content. Returning freshmen and undergraduates had a similar response; the freshmen knew that they had to submit their papers in the student writing guide and knew how to conduct themselves during peer evaluations. The undergraduate literature students knew how to sign up quickly for presentation topics and how to conduct themselves during class and presentations.

Although I was initially troubled by my students' failure to remember the content of my courses, eventually I accepted that learning process was enough. Probably what made me give up on content was a phone call from a former student who was then teaching at a local high school. She was preparing to teach Great Gatsby and remembered that I had said something new and interesting about that novel but couldn't remember what it was. The student had graduated only a few years earlier and had heard my unique Gatsby reading twice, once in the upper division 20th Century American Literature seminar, where I had students comparing passages from Gatsby and James Weldon Johnson's classic African American novel, Autobiography of an Ex-Coloured Man , and once in a Black Fiction graduate seminar where I discussed Johnson's novel and gave a mini-presentation on the Gatsby connection. I was famous--some might say, infamous--for my racial reading of Gatsby. In fact, I had my single best moment as a teacher that didn't involve laughter in one 20th Century American Literature course, where I showed students the similarities between Fitzgerald's and Johnson's passages. Still, this relatively bright former student could not remember what I said, could remember only that it had been new and interesting.

I decided soon after that call that if my students couldn't remember what I said, I would try to make sure they remembered what they needed to do. As Don said, I wanted them to read and write carefully, and I wanted them to think while they read and wrote. In the composition classes, I tried to help those few students who were like the young woman in my black literature class, so fearful and blocked that they couldn't write, find confidence and learn to write with more ease. I used journal writing, where I didn't grade for grammar, punctuation, spelling, organization, and style, to help them "relax and write" (my mantra in the basic writing classes). I also tried to assign topics or help them find topics that interested them so that they would be more engaged when they wrote. Sports usually worked, for instance, for the men. Although I wasn't as into basketball as I was tennis, I was interested enough to be annoyed with Kobe Bryant after he staged his dump Shaq coup and used a story about a base-ball team to take shots at the superstar guard. I asked the class who was more important to the Lakers, the star player, Kobe, or the coach, Phil Jackson. Then I argued with the young men who picked Kobe. At least three different Kobe fans, all males, wrote better than usual essays, defending their favorite player. One young man even made it into freshman composition with a "C," solely because he earned "B's" on both the in-class essay and the revised paper in which he passionately defended the man I called Ball-hogging Kobe.

Most basic writers, however, were not fearful, blocked writers. Instead, many of them wrote too much too fast and failed to edit or rewrite. This sloppy writing became even more of a prob-lem once everyone started e-mailing and texting. Some of them even slipped into texting shorthand; one student actually wrote "u r" for "you are." So my main goal in that class was to teach students to revise and edit. Every paper written outside of class was a revision. The first four papers were revisions of in-class essays, and students were required to submit a (graded) rough draft for the final paper. On the first day of class, students wrote a diagnostic essay that I told them would not be graded, so they should relax and write. They started writing as soon as I finished describing the course, which means that they had at least an hour to complete the essay. Most of them finished in half that time. When the first person finished and was allowed to leave, there was a mad rush to complete the essay by the rest of the class. I could tell that some of them believed that people who finished first were somehow smarter, better writers. Usually the student left writing after everyone else rushed out apologized for being slow. My response was always: "Don't apologize; you're doing what I expect students to do, take their time and write carefully." During the second class meeting, before I returned the usually not well-written or carefully edited essays, I asked students how many of them did some kind of prewriting (an outline, a list of ideas) before they started to write. Only a few raised their hands. Then I asked how many students edited their essays before they handed them to me; again only a few raised their hands, and most of them were lying because I watched them finish their essays and hand them in without looking at them again. Of course, I let the basic writers know that in the future they should use whatever extra time they had when they finished writing to edit. I also let them know that writing was not an Olympic sport; speed should not count. Unfortunately, it did count in college because they had a limited time to write their exams, English essays, and the Graduation Writing Test, but I made it clear that I and all sensible professors preferred good writing to fast writing.

I also used the built-in subjectivity of composition grading to try to force students to take the time to edit when they wrote in class. I let them know that I was harder on editing mistakes made by students who finished early than I was on those made by students who were still writing when it was time for me to leave for my next class or to go home. Clearly, students write at different speeds, and there is nothing wrong with a student's being able to write a competent essay in less than an hour. But I told those students who finished early to take a break, leave the room and go for a walk or use the restroom, and then return to edit their essays. I also left time at the end of class for them to edit their papers before they submitted them. And to be sure that they actually took the time to edit, early in the quarter, I read the first paragraph of each paper and either accepted it or told the student how many errors I found (for example, two punctuation errors and one subject-verb agreement problem) and made him or her sit back down to correct the errors. Believe me, after receiving that treatment the first time, students edited more carefully. Some even sat back down when they realized I was inspecting the papers.

Even during my last year as a professor, I was still trying to improve my writing students' editing. I created special editing checklists for each paper, one focused on punctuation, one on grammar, and one on phrasing and word choice. I had been using a final paper editing checklist for years. Not all students mastered editing, but they all realized that rewriting and editing were very important. And they all left my classroom knowing what my old Fort Sheridan supervisor Ms. Sargeant clearly didn't know; neatness is not as important as correctness. Often, at the beginning of the quarter, students worried about messing up their neatly printed papers with inked-in corrections. By the end, they used their ink pens to revise whole sentences in the "final" drafts.

Of course, I wanted my literature students to write and edit their exams and papers carefully as well, but in those classes the focus was more on reading and analyzing literature. I taught students to look not only for Biblical and literary allusions, but also for cultural and historical references. Students generally have no trouble connecting what they read to personal experience, but I also asked them to make connections to the socio-political world. After the Strom Thurmond love-child scandal, for instance, I connected his story to the behavior of the ex-colored man's father in Johnson's novel. And when the OJ scandal was unfolding, students in my 20th Century American Literature graduate seminar enjoyed making connections between his story and both Richard Wright's <u>Native Son</u> and Theodore Dreiser's <u>American Tragedy.</u>

But occasionally students made connections I couldn't accept, and we could learn from the disconnection. During the second quarter of the 20th Century American Literature sequence, we read William Faulkner's <u>Light in August</u>. At that point, in late January, 1995, OJ's fate had not yet been decided. The trial was still underway. At the point in the novel where the white woman Joanna Burden's body is found, the sheriff says something like, "Find me a nigger, any nigger." He then has the innocent black man who is found beaten by his deputy until the black man tells what he knows. One bright young white woman thought she saw a connection to OJ; she thought OJ was the nigger that the police found when they discovered a dead white woman, his ex-wife, in Brentwood. Several years later when I again taught Faulkner's novel in a graduate seminar, the class laughed when I told them my response to the young woman: "OJ's not a nigger." Well, maybe

I wasn't quite that succinct in my response. But I made it clear to the earlier class that the wealthy and famous OJ was quite different from the poor black man that the sheriff had beaten. OJ was quickly put in handcuffs when he arrived home from Chicago, but he was just as quickly released. Although two white people were found savagely murdered, OJ was allowed to turn himself in, and when he went on the lam and was found by the police, they didn't shoot out his tires, pistol whip him, pepper spray or taser him, and throw his black ass in jail. Instead, they almost casually followed him slowly down the freeway, back to his mansion, allowed him to go to the bathroom and to see his mother (I loved Rosie O'Donnell's impersonation of the big, middle-aged, wife-beating, murder suspect wanting his mama); then they politely escorted him to jail. And, unlike that poor black man, OJ had a dream team of lawyers whose resources matched, if not exceeded, those of the prosecution. OJ's story showed how class and fame can sometimes override race, that green can be a more important color than black and white.

As they examined the writer's allusions, I wanted the students to learn not only about the texts that they were studying but also about the sources. Thus, when I pointed out the many allusions to The Wizard of Oz in Morrison's Beloved, I asked students to take note of both the differences and similarities between the way the slaves acted in each text (and movie). The slaves in the earlier text were freed by Dorothy and her friends while Sethe freed herself. And the slaves in The Wizard of Oz immediately started looking for another master, so they were ready to be slaves again while Sethe preferred killing her children to letting them return to slavery. However, if we look at Sethe more closely, we realize that she became a kind of slave to the young woman who appears to be the ghost of her murdered baby daughter. So Morrison used the earlier text to comment on different kinds of enslavement.

My students and I had fun looking at the way so-called ethnic (meaning nonwhite, as opposed to Irish or Italian) writers like Morrison revised more canonized dominant culture texts. I remember one dynamic graduate class discussion of Native American Linda Hogan's poem "Blessing." The poet parodied the Biblical verse, "Blessed are the meek for they shall inherit the earth," in the following lines: "Blessed are the rich/for they eat meat every night./They have already inherited the earth." As we discussed the poet's version of the verse, I asked students if it was a good or bad thing to inherit the earth, reminding them how Native Americans felt about the earth and possessing property. I also asked them what the bold or arrogant would inherit? Heaven? Hell? And we looked at the difference between inheriting and earning. I think several of us had a different view of the Biblical passage after we discussed the poem. I also used Alexie's story about the Indian listening to Jimi Hendrix at Woodstock to examine "The Star-Spangled Banner." We focused on that last line, "The land of the free and the home of the brave." Of course, both Hendrix and the Native American listening to him might have problems with the first part of that line. Hendrix's ancestors were slaves, and the Native American's ancestors were confined to reservations. Maybe that land was free for them in that they didn't have to buy it, but they weren't free to choose to live anywhere they pleased. Then there is the phrase "home of the brave," which might mean something very different to a Native American. Braves were warriors in Native American culture (thus, the Atlanta Braves), and yes, before it was stolen, America was originally their home. Is it any wonder that the Native American was captivated by Jimi's deconstruction of "The Star-Spangled Banner"?

Although I mostly looked at how nonwhite writers revised the canonized white writers, how Wright revised Dreiser, August Wilson revised Arthur Miller, and both Sandra Cisneros (in House on Mango Street) and Toni Morrison (in Beloved) revised Twain's Huckleberry Finn, my most famous discussion of revision focused on how the canonized white writer, Fitzgerald, revised a text by the less well-known black writer, Johnson (A lyricist, he's probably better known for writing the so-called black National Anthem, "Lift Every Voice"; in an ironic coincidence, Fitzgerald was named after his relative who wrote "The Star-Spangled Banner"). Since Johnson's novel was first published in 1912 and Fitzgerald's in 1925, clearly the black writer's book was the source, and that's why this particular textual dialogue was so interesting. When I taught the books, usually in the 400-level 20th Century American Literature class, I taught the Johnson novel first and then presented my reading of Fitzgerald. I first pointed out the many parallel passages; then I discussed what I thought Fitzgerald was doing.

The two passages that originally caught my attention and eventually led to my unorthodox reading of Fitzgerald's novel described two mysterious rich men, Gatsby and the millionaire. The men had several characteristics in common besides wealth;

they seemed lonely, they formed a special bond with the protago-nists/narrators, Nick Carraway and ex-colored man, they liked to give parties where they introduced new music to their guests, and they were both dead by the end of their respective novels. Gatsby was murdered, and the millionaire committed suicide. There is another similarity that is described in the following passages, the first from Johnson's novel, the second from <u>Great Gatsby</u>:

> The most notable thing that I observed was that the re-serve of the host increased in direct proportion with the hilarity of his guests. I thought that there was something gone wrong which displeased him. I afterwards learned that it was his habitual manner on such occasions. He seemed to take cynical delight in watching and studying others indulging in excess (Johnson, 118).

> I could see nothing sinister about him. I wondered if the fact that he was not drinking helped to set him off from his guests, for it seemed to me that he grew more correct as the fraternal hilarity increased (Fitzgerald, 53).

So both mysterious rich men become more sober and correct, the more drunk and out of control their guests become, and that behavior makes some people uneasy. But notice the similarities between those two passages. Not only are the common words "guests," "seemed," and "increased" included in both passages, but the less common word "hilarity" is used by both writers to describe drunken behavior. I argue that the similarities between those two passages prove beyond a reasonable doubt that Fitzgerald read and was influenced by Johnson's novel. But there are other parallels between the scenes in which the two passages appear. In both scenes the first-person narrator--ex-colored man and Nick--attends a party at the mysterious rich man's home for the first time, and in both scenes the mysterious rich man introduces new music, ragtime in the Johnson passage and jazz in the Fitzgerald passage, to his guests.

If we look only at the similarities between Gatsby and the millionaire, even if we notice the many other similar passages in the two novels, we may miss what I believe Fitzgerald is doing and just assume that he was influenced by the black writer. It certainly is possible that Fitzgerald found and was reading an old edition of Johnson's novel, which was out of print at the time Gatsby was written, and just inadvertently (subconsciously) echoed some of the black writer's passages. But I don't think so. The two characters we need to compare to see what Fitzgerald was really doing are Gatsby and ex-colored man (subsequently, ex). Both left home at seventeen, both changed their names and tried to pass for somebody that they weren't (a white man, a classy rich man), both are college dropouts, both traveled the world with an older rich man (Dan Cody and the millionaire), and, most important, both fell in love with a beautiful, seemingly unattainable, very white woman.

Daisy Buchanan and ex-colored man's white wife are both compared to flowers, both dress in white, and both have captivating voices, which are described in remarkably similar passages:

She was as white as a lily, and she was dressed in white. Indeed she seemed to me the most dazzlingly white thing I had ever seen. But it was not her delicate beauty which attracted me most; it was her voice, a voice which made one wonder how tones of such passionate colour could come from so fragile a body. . . .I contented myself with hovering as near her as politeness would permit; near enough to hear her voice, which in conversation was low, yet thrilling, like the deeper middle tones of a flute (Johnson, 198).

I looked back at my cousin who began to ask questions in her low, thrilling voice. It was the kind of voice that the ear follows up and down as if each speech is an arrangement of notes that will never be played again. Her face was sad and lovely with bright things in it, bright eyes and a bright passionate mouth--but there was an excitement in her voice that men who had cared for her found difficult to forget: a singing compulsion, a whispered "Listen," a promise that she had done gay, exciting things just a while since and that there were gay, exciting things hovering in the next hour (Fitzgerald, 13-14).

These passages have even more words in common than the two that described Gatsby and the millionaire. The repeated words are "low, thrilling, voice," "passionate," and "hovering." Of course, both voices are also described as musical. Still, Fitzgerald could simply be echoing a novel he recently read. There is, however, a major difference between the two women. While both women leave town when they learn of their lovers' "dark" secrets (Gatsby's criminal behavior, ex's race), "Lily" returns, marries the black man, produces a daughter and then dies giving birth to a son while Gatsby is shot by Mr. Wilson, leaving Daisy behind to continue her dysfunctional marriage to Tom. I argue that the different fates of the two American dreamers show that Fitzgerald is revising Johnson's novel. Ex changes his name, moves North, passes for white, is accepted into a wealthy white society, and marries the lily white woman of his dreams, living happily with her until she dies. Gatsby, on the other hand, is never accepted by the old money East Egg society; in fact, even the less classy people at his parties are suspicious of him. Gatsby doesn't get the girl and doesn't even live to tell his own story. Fitzgerald is telling us that Johnson's story of a black man whose origins are unknown showing up and being allowed to marry a beautiful white woman and being accepted into upper class white society is, as Bill Clinton might say, "a fairytale." He even connects race and class through racist Tom Buchanan's comments during his confrontation with Gatsby in the Plaza Hotel:

> "I suppose the latest thing is to sit back and let Mr. Nobody from Nowhere make love to your wife. Well, if that's the idea you can count me out. . . .Nowadays people begin by sneering at family life and family institutions and next they'll throw everything overboard and have intermarriage between black and white" (Fitzgerald, 137).

Of course, in Johnson's novel, ex is Mr. Nobody from Nowhere who is making love, not to someone's wife, but to a wealthy white couple's daughter, and his behavior does lead to intermarriage between black and white.

The death tolls in each novel reflect the revision. In Johnson's novel, the only rich white person who survives contact with ex is his father. The rich widow who flirts with him to make her dark-skinned lover/gigolo jealous is murdered by the black lover; the millionaire jumps to his death after ex leaves him to return to America, and his beautiful white wife dies while giving birth to their son. In contrast, the people who die in Fitzgerald's novel are the working class, or in Gatsby's case, former working class. Daisy kills Myrtle, and Tom tells Wilson that the car that Daisy was driving was Gatsby's, leading Wilson to believe that Gatsby, not Tom, was Myrtle's rich lover, and that he, not Daisy, killed Wilson's wife, causing Wilson to kill Gatsby and then himself. So in Fitzgerald's novel the working-class people who come in contact with the rich are killed, smashed, as Nick says.

When I presented this new reading of Gatsby to my classes, I first helped them find the parallel passages and then asked if they had any ideas about what Fitzgerald might be doing. My students were always stumped; they assumed that the white writer was just copying the black writer, the way white musicians that Johnson wrote about copied black ragtime players. But then I asked questions. Where are the black people in this novel, set in New York during the 1920's, the height of the Harlem Renaissance? I sometimes joked that Fitzgerald's New York was like Woody Allen's; only white people lived there. I pointed out that even in Johnson's novel, set before the Harlem Renaissance, sophisticated whites went to the Club, and the women even dated black men. Surely there would be some blacks at Gatsby's parties. We then looked at the two appearances by blacks and noticed that in both passages the blacks are doing well; the black bucks are riding in a limousine, and the unnamed black man who sees Gatsby's car after it kills Myrtle is well dressed. And in both scenes blacks are associated with death, a pattern that continues in Fitzgerald's later novel, Tender Is the Night, and that seems to support Tom Buchanan's fear that the rise of the colored races will destroy the Nordics. But I really liked to focus them on the appearance of the black man in the second passage; he is described as a pale Negro. I pointed out how odd it was to describe a black person as pale, and then we noticed how often the word "name" is mentioned in that scene. The policeman is trying to learn the black man's name, but we never hear it. At this point in the discussion, a few of the more clever students saw where I was going and beat me to my humorous point: The nameless, light-enough-to-pass-for-white ex has made a cameo appearance in Fitzgerald's novel. Whether or not the pale, well-dressed Negro is ex, he certainly doesn't pass in this novel; Nick recognizes that the pale man is black, thus repudiating the notion that a black man, no matter how light-skinned and successful looking, could pass for white.

As I moved the students toward what I claimed was Fitzgerald's message, I pointed out the many racial and Civil War era puns; several of them appear in the list of people attending Gatsby's parties--Blackbuck, Stonewall Jackson Abrams, Mrs. Ulysses Swett. I also pointed out that Nick calls himself a "bond man," which is a term used by writers such as Johnson (in at least one of his poems) to mean "slave." The book that Gatsby is looking at when he waits for Daisy at Nick's place was written by a British economist named Henry Clay, the same name as the Kentucky Senator who was a major architect of the Missouri Compromise that led to the Fugitive Slave Act. But my favorite racial pun is the name of the country from which Gatsby claims to have received a medal, Monte*negro* (italics mine, of course). The students who were willing to walk with me on the black side really enjoyed that pun, especially when I read the passage describing the Montenegrin people. If I also talked about how Gatsby is never really described (we don't know the color of his hair or eyes, for instance), some students wondered if I was arguing that Gatsby was black. No, I wasn't, but there was a professor teaching in New York who did make that case and even wrote a book about passing, including the novels of both Johnson and Fitzgerald.

When I finished discussing race, I turned to geography. From the time I first read Great Gatsby as a junior in high school, I had been bothered by Nick's claim that Kentucky was in the West. I had just moved from Kentucky; I knew it was in the South. I would make this point to my students, sometimes adding that I went through back doors when I lived in Kentucky just as Tom claimed Gatsby must have done when he met Daisy. I sometimes demonstrated my southern accent by showing that I couldn't pronounce "iron" or pronouncing "towel" or "vowel," which are pronounced the same as "tile" and "vile" (a problem for my basic writers trying to find out when to use "an" versus "a," What's a "vile" sound?) in my native tongue. I then pointed out that

New York is North in black literature, that black writers focus on North and South rather than East and West. And I suggested that Fitzgerald is telling us to pay attention to geography when Gatsby claims to be from the "middle west" and when asked what part says, "San Francisco." He clearly doesn't mean that San Francisco is a city in the middle of the West Coast. We are supposed to see that answer as an example of Gatsby's telling Nick some tall tales about his life. But was Gatsby, who had traveled around the world, so stupid that he didn't know that San Francisco wasn't in the Midwest? I argued that Fitzgerald deliberately made that error to alert his readers that he was having fun with geography.

Finally, I offered my explanation of what I thought Fitzgerald was doing. He was responding to the Post World War I migration of blacks to New York by telling them to go back South. His claim that the main characters weren't suited to the East was really a suggestion that blacks weren't suited to the North, that they needed to return to the South. We read that passage near the end of the novel, where Nick says that Gatsby's dream "was already behind him, somewhere back in that vast obscurity beyond the city, where the dark fields of the republic rolled on under the night" (Fitzgerald, 189). Of course, the dream that Nick claims was "behind" Gatsby was the dream of marrying Daisy. That dream started in Kentucky, the South. When Gatsby tried to fulfill the dream in New York, he was killed. The New York that Nick describes is dangerous and cold, not a good place for Southern blacks to fulfill their dreams.

When I finished my argument, I asked the students if they had any questions. Most just sat astounded; some claimed that they couldn't quite go with me to the final message that Fitzgerald was either consciously or subconsciously telling blacks that they should go back to the South, but they thought everything else made sense. After I'd given them a chance to comment, I usually said something like "Well, now, let's get back to the green light and the American Dream." And we'd laugh about the difference between the usual interpretation of the novel and my racial reading. During the rare times that I taught both novels in my graduate seminars, I would also discuss the importance of an integrated canon, pointing out, for instance, that I didn't notice the death tolls in the two novels until I compared them. I taught <u>Autobiography of an Ex-Coloured Man</u> for more than a decade before I noticed that Johnson killed off all but one of the rich white people who associated with ex, and I didn't notice that Fitzgerald killed the working or middle-class people who fell in love with the rich (Gatsby, Myrtle) or whose world was invaded by the rich (Wilson) until I connected him to Johnson. I also didn't figure out the significance of Fitzgerald's misdirection, calling Kentucky the West, until I thought about Johnson's novel, where ex's movement was between North and South.

It took me several years of teaching the two novels together to refine my alternate reading of <u>Gatsby</u>. Each time I read and taught the book, I found a new racial pun or some other similarity to or interesting difference from Johnson's novel. The students helped me to refine my reading, mainly by telling me when I had gone too far in my attempts to connect the two books and to read race into Fitzgerald's novel. Fairly early in the process, I made the case that both Fitzgerald and Johnson used the word "passing" in interesting ways. I especially focused on the passage where Gatsby and Nick are "passed" by the black bucks in the limousine as they crossed Blackwells (great pun) Island. The "passing" could be moving ahead; these blacks are successful and will thus surpass and cause the death (another kind of "passing") of the whites, as the hearse that passed suggests. But I focused on the kind of "passing" that both Gatsby and ex were doing, pretending to be other than they were. Several classes accepted this argument, but eventually a group of rebellious, fun students in one class started following that word in other texts. I was still teaching Light in August and Song of Solomon as the last two texts in my 456 - 20th Century American Lit class at that point. (I later switched to short stories by Alexie and O'Connor.) And these students kept track of every time Faulkner or Morrison used the word "passing." Finally, I said, "Okay, I'll drop the 'passing' argument," and I did.

Once I refined my reading of the two texts, it was no longer new and fresh to me, but it was still new to the students, and their responses kept me interested. I'll never forget the response of one young woman when she compared the two passages that described the millionaire and Gatsby at their parties. Her jaw dropped, and her eyes gaped. It was the single best moment I've had in a class that didn't involve laughter. I also remember a very smart male student, coming to class, so eager to point out similarities between the two books that he found that he was actually trembling with excitement. And a smart, but somewhat cynical reentry woman, a published poet, walked out of one class, saying, "Well, for once we learned something new."

But not all responses were positive. Some students who had taken me in other classes would just roll their eyes and look amused, a "here she goes again with her crazy ideas" look on their faces. But some became annoyed. One usually quiet student in a graduate seminar leaned forward in his seat and asked belligerently, "Are you saying that Fitzgerald copied Johnson?" I explained that "No, Fitzgerald did more than copy Johnson; he revised him," knowing that if this white male student didn't like the first part of my presentation, he would hate the second part. But at least he was engaged. I never saw a student looking bored, and certainly no one fell asleep when we discussed the Fitzgerald-Johnson connection. Many looked intrigued, excited; some looked amused; some looked angry or annoyed, but they were all engaged, even if they forgot what I said a few years later.

Some students wanted to share my reading with others. Those who were already teaching presented my theories to fellow teachers. At a time when I didn't really know what the Internet was or what it did, one student claimed that he had written about my analysis on the Internet. A few years later, another student copied an article off of the Internet that revealed how another renegade black professor (the New York guy) made the case that Gatsby was black, and we discussed how my argument was different from his. Many students wanted to know if I planned to publish my findings, and depending on how much time we had and how comfortable I felt with the class, I shared some of my adventures with trying to publish an article and having it rejected by two Johnson scholars (one anonymous), who probably were pissed that they didn't find the obvious connections between the two novels. I also complained that the editors of the journal that I submitted the article to were considering publishing it in a special black literature issue even though my article actually focused more on Fitzgerald's novel than on Johnson's. A few graduate students even teased me about stealing my ideas and publishing them under their own names. "Go ahead," I said, "just give me some credit in a footnote."

Although I jokingly expressed bitterness about having my article rejected by the readers for that one professional journal, I really wasn't that eager to publish it because I learned the hard way that what we publish goes on our permanent records. During the early nineties, I published an article titled "The View from the Outside: Black Novels of Manners." In that article I compared novels by Nella Larsen and Jessie Fauset to those by Jane Austen, Edith Wharton, and William Thackeray. I haven't changed my mind about what I said in that part of the article. But I also looked at Gloria Naylor's <u>Linden Hills</u> as a contemporary black novel of manners, showing how she had changed the genre. Well, now I don't buy my own argument. Maybe <u>Linden Hills</u> is an anti-novel of manners, but it has more in common with gothic novels than it does with texts by Austen, Wharton, and Thackeray. Still my argument is out there in the world of Naylor scholarship. It was originally published in a book about the novel of manners, but it now also appears in another book, a collection of articles on Naylor. Interestingly, no one asked me if it was okay to reprint my article. I would have at least tried to revise it, update it, before I agreed to let it appear in a book focused on Naylor.

Of course, in the classroom I could change my arguments, revise and update them from year to year, even quarter to quarter. I also received instant feedback from my never anonymous audience, and I liked the feedback. If I were a professional actress (as opposed to the amateur one that I am), I would want to be on the stage or on a television show filmed in front of an audience so I could hear laughter, see tears, feel the audience's energy. In the classroom, of course, I could also feel the audience's lack of energy, see the yawners, the sleepers, the note passers, the whisperers, and, in the last years, the secret (or so they thought) cellphone or BlackBerry users. I suspect teachers receive more feedback, positive and negative, than entertainers do.

But we are very much like entertainers, as Steve Martin suggests, and not just because we must keep the attention of a sometimes restless audience. We are also as close to celebrities as ordinary people can be. My competitive linguist friend once said that her mother, an elementary school teacher, told her that if she couldn't be a star, she should be a teacher. Like stars, we are often recognized by people we don't remember or never knew. I've been in department stores and heard someone who I assumed was a Cal Poly student whisper, "That's Doctor Sisney." And I'm constantly running into former students. I was eating in a restaurant recently and noticed that the waiter looked familiar. He was a former student, marking the second time I had a former student as a waiter. I've also met my students working as cashiers in supermarkets, movie theaters, and self-serve gas stations; one was a clerk at the Auto Club, and another a teller at a local bank. Five years ago, when my mother was having her pacemaker installed, one of my former students saw me in the waiting room and came in to chat. He was working in the hospital. Just recently, I was in the emergency room of that hospital, again with my mother, and saw that my former student was still there, now working, he said, in the operating room.

I've even found students living in my neighborhoods. When I lived in my townhouse community, I was walking to the mailbox one day when I recognized a student, a woman around my age, who was in my class at that time. "Do you live here?" I asked. She did. She lived on one corner, and I lived next door to the house that was right across the street from hers. We had been practically next door neighbors for almost three years. A few years later, a former graduate student moved into the townhouse in back of mine. He, his wife, and three daughters lived there for two or three years before moving to a home in a nearby neighborhood. My mother and I walked by his house all the time on our summer afternoon strolls. Soon after I started taking my solitary afternoon strolls a few weeks into my first Fall Quarter as a retired person, I walked up a street that's very near mine and saw a man preparing to plant flowers. Before I could register that he was the first person I had ever seen on that street, the man spoke to me, and I realized he was one of my favorite graduate students. I was shocked to learn that he had been living within two blocks of me for seven years and that he had been out of school long enough to have married and produced three cute little boys. Then a few weeks ago, I was walking on the street that has become my regular Tuesday-Thursday route and saw a friendly looking woman emerge from her car. The car was in the driveway of a rather interesting looking house I had admired while on my walks. The woman spoke and asked me if I was Dr. Sisney. I said "yes" and tried to figure out who she was because she looked vaguely familiar. When she identified herself as a student from around 1982, I was shocked. I knew that I didn't remember her face from back then; maybe she had waved at me when I was on my walk. I asked if that was her house and learned that it had originally belonged to her in-laws but had been hers for a few months, so now I walk by that house twice a week, knowing that one of my students lives there.

I think most teachers hope that their students will do well, so we're happy when we learn that they own beautiful homes, have cute children, have earned advanced degrees, and have pursued lucrative and fulfilling careers. I've amused some of my friends by speculating about two politicians who could have been, but probably were not, my students. Hilda Solis, President Obama's Secretary of Labor, graduated from Cal Poly Pomona just as I was returning to campus as a tenure-track faculty member, but she was still a student there when I was a lecturer, so I try to convince myself and others that she could have taken me in one of the two Advanced Professional Writing classes I taught during that time. I certainly hope that she wasn't in that horrible second-quarter freshman composition class that I taught during Winter Quarter, 1979, because I couldn't stand them. On the other hand, I am trying to convince myself that Senator Scott Brown, who was a junior at Tufts the year that I was there, could not possibly have been my student since I taught only freshman composition and black literature. Surely a man who is a Republican and had the nerve to win the seat that Ted Kennedy held for so long could not have been a student in one of those black literature classes.

Probably because of my redlight nature, I can still remember the name of the young man that I only half-jokingly call my least favorite student of all time but cannot remember the names of any of the black women who were in my favorite composition class. Like those women, John L, my least favorite student, was in one of my USC composition classes. Also in that class was a child "genius" who gained fame in the seventies, appearing on Johnny Carson's "The Tonight Show" and in an episode of "The Bionic Woman." The twelve-year old genius, who wrote like a smart child, disappeared after a few weeks, but Mr. L stayed the whole semester. He did not appear to be racist or sexist, was not disrespectful or trifling. He came to every class and worked hard on his papers. Ordinarily, I would love such a student. But he was the worst kind of grade grubber. Mr. L tested out of freshman composition and so took a sophomore-level literature course his freshman year. He earned an "A" in that course, and he took the second semester of freshman composition just so that he could earn an "A." When he earned a "B+" on his first paper, he walked with me toward my next class, politely asking why he hadn't earned an "A." I told him that he shouldn't worry so early about not earning an "A," that he had plenty of time to raise his grade, and was also quickly trying to tell him what to do to improve his writing. Unfortunately, we encountered one of my friends as we were conducting our mobile conference; she was also a T.A. When I told her that I was trying to explain to my student that his "B+" was a good grade for the first paper, my so-called friend said something like, "You got a "B+" from Sisney; you're lucky. She's hard." Thanks, buddy! I was actually not an especially hard grader, but from that moment on, John L was convinced that I was the meanest, hardest teacher at USC, and every time I returned a paper to him that didn't have an "A" on it, he complained. He even went to the department to complain to the T.A. supervisor about me and used the evaluation of a tutor to complain about what a horrible teacher I was, contrasting me to the wonderful teacher that he took his freshman year. I think he earned an "A-" in the class, but it came with a lecture from me. I let him know that he made both of our lives miserable with his obsession with earning an "A." I told him that I should have been able to evaluate his papers without worrying about how he would respond. Instead, when I read his papers, I had to make sure that I wasn't giving him an "A" just to keep him from bothering me or giving him a "B" to show him that I wouldn't be bullied into giving him an "A." Because he was so obsessed with his grade, I became obsessed with it, too.

I suspect that I would have had less trouble with Mr. L if I encountered him later in my career. He probably would have either followed the child genius out of the class (I became a hero among the T.A.'s for scaring her away because she and her mother had tormented the woman who had taught her the first semester), or he would have behaved better. I certainly could have explained the difference between a composition class focused on writing skills and a sophomore-level literature course. I had not taught such a course when I was at USC, but I know now that some of my students who made "A's" in English 201 or English 205 would have earned "B's" in my freshman composition classes. During my years as a senior faculty member, I suspect I could have shown Mr. L the error of his ways so that he would have been less annoying.

Probably the main reason I remember Mr. L so well is that I had few students whom I couldn't stand. I could quickly name my top five least favorite students, starting with John L, and with a little thought come up with the top twenty, but after that I would have trouble. On the other hand, I've had so many favorite students that they probably number in the hundreds at this point. I don't remember many of their names and even some of their faces, but I do remember enjoying discussing literature and writing with them, chatting and joking with them in my office, and in some cases reading their papers, exams, and theses.

I obviously can't list all of my favorite students, especially since I've forgotten so many of their names, but in the tradition of Oprah's "favorite things," I will name a few of them. I placed them in pairs and occasionally triplets because my mind works that way; I probably should have studied comparative literature. In more or less chronological order, they are:

Don K and Jim Jones (I can use his last name because he's changed it for what should be obvious reasons.) - Jim and Don were friends when they were students and are still occasionally in touch. They were the MVPs of my first and still one of my top three favorite graduate seminars. Don taught me an early lesson in not being able to judge a student by his looks. He was waiting for me when I came out of the ladies' restroom one day during my first quarter back at Cal Poly. He wanted to know what books

I was teaching in the Contemporary American Novel graduate seminar scheduled for Winter Quarter. When I listed the titles, he told me that he was planning to take my class. I was not happy. Don was tall and good looking, but he was wearing flip flops, one of those bright-colored, flowered, Hawaiian-looking shirts, and was suspiciously dark for a fair-haired man, suggesting he had spent time at the beach. I went back to my office and told one of my male neighbors (either Tall Texan or Number 1 Linguist) that a beach boy, a surfer dude, was going to take my class. I expected Don to be a George W. Bush type, genial but not very bright. I was, of course, wrong. Don was brilliant. His M.A. exam is still tied (after hundreds) for the best. His performance on the exam was so impressive that I used it as a model for other students until one woman, who was a high school teacher, told me to stop letting students see that exam because it was intimidating. After completing his M.A., Don earned a Ph.D. at one of the Oregon universities and then taught at Temple for a few years before returning to Cal Poly. For the last eighteen years that I was in the department, he was my across-the-hall neighbor, which means he heard more of my blues songs than most people. Of course, because he's one of my former students, he is not a wimp, so he could deal with my redlight, negative personality.

I used to refer to Jim, who was also tall but looked like a hippie with his long, wavy hair, as my favorite student, mainly to annoy Don, but also because Jim was one of my first comedy partners. He was an early Mike Nichols to my Elaine or Billy Crystal to my Whoopi. We earned our biggest laugh during Jim's first class presentation when he told us how he called Ishmael Reed to ask him questions about the novel he was presenting. I couldn't believe that Jim had the nerve to call a famous writer. I had met Reed when he spoke at USC and when he and I socialized with bell hooks and her boyfriend at the 1979 MLA Convention in San Francisco, but I wouldn't have had the nerve to call him on the telephone. Jim said that he began the conversation by asking if the man who answered the phone was Mr. Reed. I interrupted at that point, saying, "And then you said, 'this is Jim Jones.'" Everyone laughed loudly because in 1981 we all remembered the Jim Jones who led the mass suicide and introduced to our culture the phrase "drinking the kool aid." Jim then stopped his presentation on Reed's novel to discuss the effect of having someone else's behavior change the way people viewed his name. It was a great presentation.

Suzanne C, Lindy O, and Linda U - These women were the first to transition from students to friends. While I liked having a friendly, informal relationship with students, I didn't appreciate those who wanted to become my friends while I was still their teacher. I always wondered, especially when the students were white and younger than I was, if they would have tried to befriend me if I had been a reentry classmate. Suzanne, Lindy, and Linda made the transition smoothly. They were friendly but respectful of me as their teacher when they were students but then, maybe because they were contemporaries, were clearly not intimidated by me when we became friends.

Suzanne actually never took a class with me although she sat in on my discussions of Faulkner since she was studying him for her M.A. exam. Instead she was the first of my many

410

independent study students. In fact, she's one of the reasons I was overworked at Cal Poly because I enjoyed our one-on-one discussions so much that I almost always said "yes" when a student approached me to direct an independent study. There were times when I was directing as many as four independent studies in one quarter. Although I enjoyed all but one or two of those independent studies, none was more enjoyable than my first one with Suzanne. I also enjoyed reading her exam, which tied with Don K's for the best ever. But whereas Don's exam was written in a way that the high school teacher found intimidating, she and I agreed that Suzanne's exam was just as good but less riddled with academic discourse.

When she and I became friends, Suzanne made it possible for me to be a mother for an hour or two because, when we had lunch with her little Obamas, the waitresses inevitably assumed that I was their mother. She even provided me with a husband for a few minutes at one of White's holiday parties. I was talking to my officemate's wife, an Asian woman also named Mary, when she told me that she had met my husband. I promptly said, "Oh, really, well introduce him to me because we haven't met yet." I actually had met the only other black person in the room, Suzanne's fiance, the future father of the Obamas, but I was just having fun with Mary, who should have known better than to assume that the only two black people in the room were married, since her husband was white. But my favorite gift from Suzanne was a beautiful original painting of a black woman that she gave me when I moved into my new townhouse. Almost twenty-five years later, it's now hanging in the upstairs hallway of the home that I share with my mother.

Lindy is the only one of the three student/friends who is older than I am. (I'm a few years older than both Suzanne and Linda.) She remembered me as being all business when I marched into my English 108 class on the first day while I remember her as looking like a cheerleader, and I let her know that her name fit my view of her. Her real name was Linda, but she seemed more like a Lindy than Linda U. Of course, as with Don, I was wrong about Lindy. She was much tougher than she looked, which is why we became friends and officemates. I wouldn't share my office with a cheerleader. Lindy was one of several sweet-looking female lecturers who were harder graders and stricter about attendance in class and tutoring sessions than I was; my 096 students and I laughed about how they were scared of me on the first day and then soon learned that I was not as "mean" as their 095 instructors. And, like me, she was not easily intimidated by students. During the early nineties there was a black male Cal Poly student who changed his name from Chico to Ahmed. I had to move him out of his original basic writing class because he called his teacher a bitch; he was, in fact, so scary to most white teachers that Number 1 Linguist lobbied me to encourage him to drop his class. But Lindy had no trouble with Chico/Ahmed when I moved him from the "bitch's" class to hers.

Before she became a tough teacher, however, Lindy was an outstanding student. She was an early example of the conscientious, motivated reentry woman. She was the only student from that English 108 class who bothered to drop by during my finals week office hours to pick up her exam, bringing her two children with her, maybe for protection. Lindy was also the first of my undergraduate students to move into the graduate program. And when she completed her Masters, she showed that we had more in common than toughness. I asked if she wanted me to campaign for her to be named the Best Graduate Student, an honor that I thought she deserved, but Lindy just waved her hand dismissively, saying that she didn't really want to be bothered. Despite the fact that she's a neat freak (like my mother) and thinks I'm messy, we shared a one-person office for twenty years. I said at my retirement dinner, which she hosted, that the Mary and Lindy show had been cancelled, but it hadn't. It had just moved to a new station, the local Hometown Buffet. Lindy and I are now ladies who lunch.

Unlike Lindy and Suzanne, Linda has lived out of the area for many years, so I don't see or hear from her as often. But she has kept in touch with me through e-mails and Christmas letters. She was the quieter of the two Linda's, less likely to volunteer in class, but her papers and exams were always outstanding. She was also a great audience for my humor. We had an especially good time when she last visited me; it was during the period when I was having health problems, but I still entertained Linda with my prediction that I was going to die by the end of 1996 because my alma maters, Northwestern and USC, played each other in the Rose Bowl that year, and the last time Northwestern won the Rose Bowl was 1949, the year I was born. Linda couldn't wait to tease me about still being alive in 1997.

Andre G and Lily K - These two nonwhite, non-English majors might not have known each other, but they shared the qualities of being ambitious, excellent students as well as reliable and effective tutors. Andre was particularly popular with the department secretaries and the supervisor (the nonwhite woman who replaced the surprised-to-be racist white woman) in the writing center. And Lily was an effective role model for the students she was tutoring. She was one of the last of the Humanities majors, who a few years ago notified me that she had earned her Ph.D. in psychology. Although he was a better writer than many English majors, Andre may also have been a psychology major as an undergraduate. When I saw him after he earned his degree, he was working with learning and physically disabled people. I haven't seen Lily since the early nineties, but I appreciated her note telling me of her accomplishments and thanking me for inspiring her. Actually, she and Andre inspired me.

Michaela C and Rachel W - These two English majors were also excellent students and outstanding tutors. Michaela was one of the rare tutors who graduated from tutoring to teaching by becoming a T.A. In fact, she was the T.A. whose class I was planning to observe when my mother was attacked. Rachel probably would have been a T.A. as well if she had not transferred to Scripps, one of the Claremont colleges. She is now a high school counselor, a perfect job for her since she was such a dedicated tutor that I actually had to warn her to set boundaries because students were following her around campus, seeking help outside of the writing center. Both women also became involved with my mama drama in 1990. Michaela, who is almost exactly a year younger than I, played surrogate daughter to my mother one day, taking her to Kaiser Fontana for medical tests when I had to be at work. My mother still refers to her as that "nice girl who went with me to the hospital." Rachel became <u>my</u> surrogate daughter as a joke after I suggested that she would have a better chance of earning a scholarship at Scripps if I were her mother instead of my good friend Nancy. Partly as a tribute to my black and southern roots and partly because of my height advantage over her real mother, I became Rachel's "Big Mama." Because of the family connection, Rachel, Nancy, Great Big Mama, as I jokingly named my mother, and I went out for a mother-daughter lunch, during which we all listened to my mother's stories. Interestingly, Michaela and I reconnected recently, and she inspired me to look up my ancestors on ancestry.com. She had written a book about her Swedish ancestors, called <u>Comeback to Smaland</u>.

Paulette F and Karen Johnson (I have to include Karen's complete last name because there was another Karen J who would make my list of least favorite students) - These two women were among the rarest of students in my career, black graduate students, majoring in English. By my count, there were exactly ten black women and one black man in my many graduate seminars. Toward the end of my career, I had a record three black women in two of my seminars; I thought it was a miracle. But when Karen and Paulette were in my classes, each was the only black student, and both "represented" quite well. Although Paulette earned her B.A. at Cal Poly, I didn't meet her until she was a graduate student. Karen, on the other hand, first took me as a non-English major in the 200-level black literature class. She soon switched to majoring in English, but I didn't see her again until she was a graduate student. She was the other black person in that combative first Ethnic Literatures of the U.S. seminar. Fortunately, Karen was a mature, dignified student who actually kept her composure better than I did during some of the more tense class sessions. After earning her M.A. in English, she attended Howard Law School and is the only one of my former students whom I've seen on television. During one of his OJ shows, Larry King talked to a group of Howard law students, and there was Karen in the group, looking as cool and dignified as she did in my classes.

Paulette has transitioned from one of my best students and best thesis writers to one of my best friends. I refer to her as my e-mail buddy since she's the one person that I e-mail regularly, every other day, in fact. While Karen was cool in class, Paulette was laid way back. I teased her about her low-key contributions to class discussions. She usually began with a "Well" and a sigh then slowly moved to her point. But if she appeared lackadaisical and unconcerned during class, her written work showed another side of her. Her papers were ambitious, creative, and well written. And her thesis, a study of one of Alice Walker's more difficult and weirder novels, The Temple of My Familiar, was the second longest and tied for best of the many theses that I read as either first or second reader.

Judd B and Zak N - These two friends became my neighbors. Judd is the flower-planting guy with the three cute little boys who has lived around the corner and up the street from me for about nine years, and Zak was my next door neighbor in the department for about a decade, being one of several lecturers who occupied

Student Screwer's office once he stopped teaching. Both men were outstanding students who did especially well in their final work as graduate students. Zak wrote an excellent M.A. exam, and Judd's thesis, which focused on Biblical allusions in three of Toni Morrison's novels, was one of the best. Zak, a devoted tennis fan who actually plays and attends local tournaments, and I used to have fun in our offices, discussing our favorite players (he preferred Sampras to Agassi) and sharing funny passages from our basic writers' essays, but Judd provided me with my best moment outside of the classroom. He was approaching my office to confer with me about his thesis when White, who had temporarily moved into an office across the hall from me after he "retired" but was still teaching one quarter a year, saw him and began a conversation. As they exchanged pleasantries, Judd explained that he was coming to talk to me about his thesis. When White asked about the topic, I began to smile as I held my breath, waiting for Judd's answer. White and I had several times engaged in mostly lighthearted debates about the canon. He preferred the Norton Anthology masterworks, meaning mostly white male writers, version of the canon while I supported the Heath Anthology more expanded and diversified canon. When Judd said that he was writing about Biblical Allusions in Toni Morrison's Novels, I couldn't hear White's response (I think he was struck dumb) or see his face, but I pumped my fist and grinned broadly. I wanted to laugh loudly, but Judd was not one of my signifying Billy Crystals, so I had to conduct myself in a dignified manner as we conferred. I waited until I went to the ladies' room after Judd left before indulging in a little victory dance.

Melissa B, Brenda B, and Grace X - These three very bright women were the MVPs of another one of my top three favorite graduate seminars, and in fact starred in four consecutive graduate seminars, all of them outstanding, ending with a Black Fiction seminar in which they gave me a surprise 51st birthday party (I had made the mistake of telling one student I was turning 50 the year before, and she brought me a cake for that class). All three women were excellent class participants, although Brenda didn't kill as many trees bringing in handouts as Melissa and especially Grace did. I encountered Grace first in a 212 class where she clearly did not belong. She was taking the course as part of a requirement for being accepted into the graduate program because her B.A. had been in a major other than English. Her presentation on African American Drama, complete with multiple handouts, was so outstanding that I lectured the class on how they should appreciate what they had just seen and heard and rewarded her with a rare "A+." After that encounter, I was always happy when I saw Grace's name on the roll for one of my graduate seminars.

Melissa made me happy for a different reason; she was one of my rare female comedy partners, Kathy Griffin or Joy Behar to my Whoopi. She was also briefly a fashion consultant, helping me to keep one long, expensive, but irritating, skirt out of my pantyhose. For some reason, maybe because of its length and/ or its soft material, I kept tucking the back of that skirt into my stockings when I went to the ladies' room. Melissa finally suggested that I take it out of my what-to-wear-while-teaching rotation. It took me a few years (and having a male student catch me with part of that stupid skirt tucked in my pantyhose) to take her advice.

All three women wrote excellent M.A. theses. Brenda, a high school teacher, compared Maya Angelou and Toni Morrison, focusing on their paths into the canon. She and I thought it was interesting that Angelou was more popular with high school teachers while Morrison was taught more in college and graduate school. Melissa talked me into directing a thesis on romance novels. Only she could have turned that topic into an excellent, well-researched, and intellectually stimulating thesis. And only she could have talked me into reading and thinking about three romance novels. I probably learned more from her thesis than I did most of the more traditionally academic ones that I read.

But only Grace could have written a thesis that was longer than and as good as Paulette's. Grace, the handout queen, was known for writing overly long, error-free, well-written seminar papers (One paper stretched to 45 pages). Her thesis, which used a metafictional approach to the analysis of Toni Morrison's Paradise and August Wilson's Piano Lesson, followed the same pattern. When I returned the almost two-hundred page draft (remember this was a thesis, not a dissertation) to her with suggestions for minor changes and with maybe ten editing corrections, she seemed embarrassed that she had not written a perfect thesis. Her thesis was, in fact, so good that my former student Don K, the graduate coordinator at the time, considered submitting it for a special award.

These women were also especially grateful students who not only helped plan and host that surprise birthday party, but also thanked me with generous tributes and gifts when they completed their M.A.'s. Melissa was the presenter for my first Graduate Teaching Award, and she read the student tributes with the proper mixture of deference and humor. Grace, who never entered my office without asking if she was disturbing me or if I had time to talk, constantly showered me and her other favorite professors with gifts. But my favorite student gift of all time came from Brenda, who found copies of old <u>Newsweek</u> covers of my two favorite novelists, Faulkner and Morrison, mounted them on a purple background (any student paying a little bit of attention to me could tell that purple was my favorite color), and encased them in a beautiful frame. Those framed covers hung in my office for nine years and now hang in my bedroom over a bookcase that will one day contain all of my Morrison and Faulkner books (I've been too busy to rearrange my bookshelves).

Marianne B and Amy G - These two women were not in the same classes, probably didn't know each other, and are quite different in personality (although they both disliked another female professor as much as they liked me), but they share the three previous women's ability to express their gratitude through generous and thoughtful gift giving. Marianne, a fellow baby boomer, who has become a friend with whom I occasionally lunch, paid tribute to our class discussion of the shoe motif by presenting me with a shoe knickknack. Although she was somehow overlooked when we invited former students and current Mt Sac instructors to my retirement party, she took me to lunch and bought me another lovely present. Her last and best gift came in the form of a character named "Mary Sisney" who appears in her recently published science fiction novel. How many black people appear as characters in science fiction?

Amy, who is at least a generation younger, sent me a surprise basket of fruit and flowers after she learned that I had retired. She had already (the summer before I retired) left a message on my office telephone, thanking me for all that I had taught her, so I named her "the eternally grateful Amy." Interestingly, both of these women encouraged me to write a book when they communicated with me shortly after I retired. Amy thought my book would be funny while Marianne thought I could say something interesting and profound about father-daughter and/or mother-daughter relationships.

Shanyn H and Gina H - I called these two women legendary student/mothers. They were superwomen, performing feats that even amazed this former scholarship girl who almost never missed a class. Gina didn't miss a class during the two quarters that she took me, but I've had many other students with perfect attendance. What set Gina apart from the rest of my students is that she submitted the rough draft (due by the eighth week) for her paper by the second week of class and submitted the final draft (due the tenth week) by the third week. She also finished her M.A. in one year, which meant that she took three or four courses each quarter. And she wrote an outstanding thesis while taking all of those classes. I was her second reader but acted more like her first because (unlike her overwhelmed first reader) I could read her chapters quickly and return them so that she could quickly revise. I enjoyed reading that thesis and the books by the Egyptian writer Nawal El Saadawi that Gina bought for me. She was one of the many students who helped me to expand my own personal canon of writers. Did I mention that she was married and had two small children?

Shanyn was not as driven as Gina. No other student in my many classes was, but her attendance was equally impressive. I noticed her the first day of class because she was pregnant and looked as if she would have the baby before the end of the ten-week quarter. When she saw me looking at her stomach skeptically, she said something like, "Don't worry; this is not my first child. I'll be able to return to class right after the baby is born." I suggested that maybe I could convince the baby to stay put until December, but Shanyn, the experienced pregnant woman, understandably didn't like that idea. The class met on Tuesday and Thursday. When she missed one Thursday and reappeared the following Tuesday, I looked at her hopefully, but she was still pregnant. A couple of weeks later, she missed on Tuesday and showed up on Thursday with the baby. I was astounded. She told me that the baby had been born on Monday. Now I was a conscientious student and an equally conscientious professor. Twice I taught classes when I had such a bad cold that I couldn't talk. I used handouts once and the board the other time. But I would not have shown up in class as either a student or a professor three days after having a baby. The petite Shanyn looked pale and drawn, but she and the baby were there, and she never missed another class. I don't usually talk about my students to people who are not teachers, but I talked about Shanyn to my neighbors, to women in the beauty shop, and to relatives who had never taught but were mothers. Everyone was amazed. In fact, I suspect a few of the mothers thought I was lying.

Dina C and Will W - These two students amazed me with their loyalty. I named them Soul (pun intended) Survivor I and II because they each took me a record six times. Both started taking me as undergraduates. Dina was one of the 20th Century American Literature students who kept track of the word "passing" in <u>Song of Solomon</u> and <u>Light in August</u>. She was such a dynamic student that I suggested she try tutoring (I was still recruiting at that point even though I was no longer the basic writing skills coordinator). Will was the only one of my basic writing students to earn the M.A. in English. Of course, he was misplaced in basic writing and would have been advised to take freshman composition if he had been a student in the eighties when instructors were allowed to override the placement test scores if students were clearly capable of doing well in the more advanced course. Despite his advanced writing skills, Will did not have an attitude about being in the lower level class. He worked hard and probably earned a rare "A" or "A-" as a final grade. Since we met when he was just starting college, it seemed somehow appropriate that Will earned his M.A. the year that I retired. We both attended the 2009 Cal Poly graduation, my last.

It wasn't Will's last graduation, however, because he recently sent me a picture, showing him at his graduation from UC Riverside, where he earned his teaching credential. Since the Soul Survivors are as close to heirs as I will have, I think it's appropriate that they are both teachers. Dina has been teaching at a highly-ranked local high school for more than a decade now, and Will was just hired to teach at the middle school where he student taught. As my heirs, I know, based on their performances in my classes, that they will teach their students to read and write carefully, I hope while having fun.

Joan H, Kyla H, and Kim T - These three women just missed being Soul Survivors since they took five of my classes. Joan is humorously bitter that she wasn't awarded the SS title because she did take six classes with me, but one was a repeat. She had taken the first quarter of the 20th Century American Lit sequence while still an undergraduate and took it again several years later while completing her M.A. When we first met, she was a rare English major taking Advanced Professional Writing. She announced to the class that, unlike most English majors, she was not planning to teach. Well, after taking a few more classes with me, Joan became a T.A. and now teaches composition at Cal Poly and wherever English majors with M.A.'s can find jobs.

Like Joan, Kyla first took me as an undergraduate. She was a quiet student in a relatively quiet American Realism class. But she came out of her shell more in the four graduate seminars that she later took with me. After observing and then guest teaching the Wild Bunch, my favorite Spring Quarter 096 class, Kyla also became a T.A., and I was her faculty mentor (a program that the department tried for one year and then discarded). Soon after Kyla earned her M.A., she called me, somewhat frantic with the news that she had been hired to teach seven composition classes at, I think, three different colleges that fall. When she asked me what she should do, I told her that I didn't know since I had never taught more than three composition classes in one quarter or semester. I think I gave her some tips on how to save time, but mainly I wanted to tell her to drop at least half of those classes. I know she survived that quarter, but I'm not sure she's still teaching. I wouldn't be after teaching seven composition classes in one semester/quarter.

Kim was already a high school teacher when I met her. She took five of my graduate seminars, all of them in American literature, of course. Because she also took four seminars with the other American literature graduate professor, meaning that she took every American literature seminar offered, I named her the American Scholar. I enjoyed her thesis on the African American hero and was amused when I learned that she was drawn to the topic because her boyfriend was black. She claimed that he thought she was writing about him when he saw the title of her thesis. I wondered if she told him that Bigger Thomas, one of the black "heroes" she was analyzing (the other two were Frederick Douglass and Milkman Dead), was a murderer and rapist.

Eric B and Erica R - In addition to the similar names, Eric and Erica, who were in the same Ethnic Literatures of the U.S. sequence, had similar personalities, upbeat and cheerful. In other words, they were very different from their teacher. And like several others, they were grateful students who liked to give gifts. When he completed his M.A, Eric gave me my second favorite gift, a ten-pound box of chocolates, which I must hasten to point out that I shared with students and colleagues. Erica introduced me to Trader Joe's oatmeal cookies and even gave me a gift card so I could buy more. She was the second (Melissa B was first) in a group of very good TESL (Teaching English as a Second

425

Language) students who excelled in my literature seminars (and probably should have been double literature majors). The other two were Jennifer S and Lindsey P. Although Erica seemed to lose interest in teaching and may have been leaning toward editing, I'm sure that she would make an excellent literature and composition instructor.

Eric was never interested in teaching. When he completed his M.A., he entered law school. I have said that of all my many bright, ambitious, and creative students, I pick Eric as most likely to succeed. He was not the brightest, certainly not the hardest worker, or the most conscientious about attendance and promptness, but he was one of the most creative and definitely the most ambitious. He already had some success, having published two books of stories. He and I had a good partnership that led to a series of victories in creative writing contests. I notified him about a contest; then he entered, sponsored by me if a sponsor was required, and won. He won both the poetry and short story contests held by the national College Language Association (CLA), and he won two Cal Poly contests. But what convinced me that Eric would succeed in whatever career he chose was his personality. He was the only student, and possibly the only human, I know who was immune to my evil eye. He would bounce into class late, having misjudged how much time it would take to navigate late afternoon traffic between Pasadena and Pomona. I would fix him with an evil stare, and he would beam at me as if I had just awarded him an "A+" for promptness. And he was one of my favorite Billy Crystals, thick-skinned and always ready to play.

Marcus B and Darrina W - These two undergraduate non-English majors were the MVPs in two of my favorite black literature classes. Marcus was in the first black literature class that I taught after taking a several years break because I had been disappointed by one under-enrolled, badly attending class in the late nineties. Other Black and I had been taking turns teaching the class, and then, after that awful class, I just let her teach it for several years. When she also had problems with a black lit class, I reluctantly took the course back, thinking I would try it one more time. I had so much fun with Marcus and his classmates that Other Black was stuck with 201 until I retired. Marcus also enjoyed the class and took two upper-division English major courses with me. He didn't enjoy them as much and so didn't attend often, but when I entered one of my graduate seminars in African American Novel, there was Marcus, sitting among the graduate students, ready to take the course. I gently (well, at least I tried to be gentle) let him know that he wasn't qualified to take a graduate seminar in English even if he was a senior. But I appreciated Marcus's loyalty. I don't share Woody Allen's (or Groucho Marx's) disdain for people who would have me in their club. If someone has the good taste and good sense to appreciate me, then I will appreciate him (or her) right back. Marcus was clearly a fan, maybe even a groupie, so he deserves to be on my list of favorite students.

Darrina W took only two classes with me, basic writing and my last black literature class, but she made a lasting impression. She is a bold, strong young woman, smart enough to understand that I was complimenting her when I said that I always thought of her (she was probably around 5'1" although she worked as a

security guard on campus) as tall. She had the attitude of a 6'2"
woman. I appreciated that last black literature class because
about 80% of the students had perfect attendance. Darrina had
to miss a couple of times, but when she was there, she was always
engaged in the discussion, asking interesting questions and debating issues. After completing that year at Cal Poly, her second
but my final year, she transferred to Spelman and graduated this
spring. I won't take credit for her decision to move to the historically black women's college since I was not her advisor and only
gave encouragement once she told me of her plans, but I like to
think the black literature class and maybe having a black composition instructor had some influence.

Noelle C, Kelly S, and Adria S - These young women added
color to my last three graduate seminars. Noelle and Adria (who
actually took a total of four seminars with me) also joined another black woman (not one of my favorites) to create the mi-
raculous three- is-almost-a-crowd group of black women in my
last graduate 20th Century American Literature sequence. Kelly is
a member of an equally rare demographic in my graduate classes,
the Asian woman. Maybe because I was ending my career and
therefore looking back quite a bit, each of these women reminded me of my younger self. Noelle, who actually physically resembled my old friend bell hooks certainly more than she did me,
reminded me of my outside-the-box personality. She was the one
more likely to offer an unconventional, controversial reading of a
text. Kelly resembled my scholarship girl self; she was almost as
driven as Gina H. When she showed up in my office right on time
for her weekly, totally unnecessary because she knew the texts

428

really well, preparation for the M.A. exam, I saw myself reading <u>Antony and Cleopatra</u> twice for my Shakespeare class even though I had already studied that play in earlier classes. While not as much of a clown as I was and am, Adria was the funniest of the three. But all of these women were smart and conscientious enough to make me believe that I was leaving the study of literature in good hands. Carry on, ladies!

The students I have listed were not always the best, but they were the most memorable, my favorites for several different reasons. They were on my high honor roll, but I had many other great students, so I would like to name a few more; call them the honorable mentions. In groups and singularly, they are:

The Northwestern students in my student-organized seminar who made me realize that I would be a better college than high school instructor

The USC students in my all-black, all-female composition class who showed me how much fun teaching composition and literature could be

The black Tufts student named David who introduced me to then CBS news anchor Dan Rather as his favorite professor

The Tufts student from Highland Park (Illinois) who became one of my first Billy Crystals

The Celtics fan (still another Tufts student) who taught me most of what I know about the Armenian genocide and who was a good sport when I teased him about the Celtics' loss by crowing, "I have one thing to say--Dr. J."

My first graduate seminar at Cal Poly

Gerri M and John N - my townhouse community neighbors, both of whom were good students

Diana Y - a very bright and amusing student who earned her Ph.D. at UCLA, and when we last talked was (in a semi full circle moment) teaching at USC

Rosemarie M - an excellent student as well as a reliable and effective tutor, who was a member of the short-lived chocolate club

Terri B and Rosaleen M - like Lindy O, two conscientious re-entry students who were also sweet-looking and -sounding composition lecturers who were actually "meaner" than I was

Amy N and Maya A - the first and last of the many thesis writers whom I directed; Amy set the bar high, and Maya, who already had a Ph.D., made my last experience memorable.

Lisa and Jason S, Kim and David M - I have been invited to quite a few of my students' weddings, but except for the wedding of Rachel, who is my surrogate daughter, I attended weddings only when both the bride and the groom were outstanding students. That was the case with both of these couples, which is why I attended their weddings in 1998.

Hansel A and Maria E - These two very different students (Hansel, who matured into a dignified, well-dressed instructor, had been a long-haired, somewhat wild [maybe more Robin Williams] Billy Crystal when he was a student; Maria was quiet and calm) are among several former students (Kim M and Maya are two others) who have tenured or tenure-track positions in the Mt Sac English Department. I'm sure that both are outstanding instructors.

Alexis P - a bright, extremely well-educated woman, who enjoyed being a student as much as I enjoyed teaching; only she could have talked me into directing a thesis on Hemingway. Like Diana Y and Don K, she has earned a Ph.D. in English. Hers is from UC Riverside.

Tim C – a long-suffering high school teacher who wrote the best M.A. response to a Great Gatsby question

The African American Fiction graduate seminar that gave me a surprise birthday party, especially Taiwan A, Cynthia C, and

Chriz Z, who was the only man in that favorite graduate class and who then tried to keep my spirits up when he found himself in a less friendly seminar

Heidi S and Jennifer W - the MVPs, along with Chris Z, of that less friendly (but still bright and lively) group of students; these two high school teachers won a lunch bet with me by joining Alexis P in being (at that point) the only thesis writers who actually did work on their theses during the summer months as so many of them promised they would.

Steve E and Carl F - my two tallest students; Steve is 6'5"; Carl might have been an inch or two taller, but both were also gentlemen (not just too tall but too well-mannered to be Billy Crystals) and very good scholars.

Mike K and Roland R - my favorite reentry men; Mike, a high school teacher, was picking up his second M.A., but Roland, who I believe was a preacher, just wanted to take a few classes.

Lisa S - another loyal and bright student who took five of my classes, two undergraduate and three graduate

Morgan S - a bright and clever woman who helped me to extend my "sick" joke about my black baby boomer husband being killed in Vietnam before I met him by suggesting that if he had survived he would have murdered his big-mouthed, too-aggressive wife

Sarah I and Jennifer O - two smart and amusing women who seem to have some of my spirit; Sarah has the sarcasm, Jennifer the toughness and aggression.

Leo T - a fun student who tried to top Eric B's ten pound box of chocolates by giving me a huge chocolate bar

Jeremy F - my favorite Republican student

Allen C - the blues man, as I called him, who had a too close encounter with Katrina when he was doing research for his thesis, analyzing how August Wilson, Alice Walker, and Walter Mosley were influenced by the blues

The two biology majors who had perfect attendance in that one disappointing black literature class

My favorite 096 class, the Wild Bunch

The three students who talked regularly in that deadly dull 201 class

The almost all-male, lively 201 class

Embert M - the only black male English major (Marcus was game but not qualified) who dared to take a graduate seminar with me; he took the last one that I taught and "represented" quite well.

My last black literature class, who touched me with their near perfect attendance and then saved me from becoming a blubbering idiot by behaving like typical undergraduates just as I was about to start bawling

I could continue naming students and classes for at least another ten pages. After all, I taught for over thirty years. However, I have warned my students that long lists can become boring, so to pay tribute to my many other favorite students, I will use a strategy that I learned from a cute little brother (in both senses of the word). He was at a black awards ceremony, where he and his brothers, members of a group called The Boys, received an award. After his older brothers thanked a fairly long list of people, the youngest brother stepped up to the microphone and said, "To all those people who are going to say tomorrow, 'Man, why didn't you call my name?' thank you." So to all of my former students who have looked in vain for their names on the high honor roll or among the honorable mentions, I say, "If you were not racist, sexist, plagiarizing, trifling, grade-grubbing jerks, or did not in some other way get on my last nerve, I also enjoyed your company, especially if you taught me something and/or made me laugh. Thanks for the memories!"

CHAPTER TEN
The End Is Near

Although I enjoyed my students' company even more as I grew older and more confident in the classroom, I was still more than ready to retire in 2009. Noticing how some of my older colleagues, like Number 1 Linguist, seemed to hesitate when it was time to walk out the door, I thought I might have second thoughts and decide to stay until I was 62 or even 65. But the closer my retirement date came, the more eager I was to leave.

The generation gap helped to push me out the door. I didn't mind growing older, but it bothered me how young my students became. When I first taught at Cal Poly in 1977, I was twenty-eight, and there were at least two or three students in that first class who were my age or older. Even when I was the oldest person in the room in those early years, there was always someone near my age (someone twenty-three or twenty-four). But as the years passed, only the reentry students (people in their thirties or older) were my contemporaries. I would look around for a fellow baby boomer on the first day of class so I could make eye contact with her or him when I inevitably talked about some event that the "conventional" students were too young to remember.

I remember when I first recognized that a generation gap was developing between my students and me. I was making some point about memory when I started to refer to the assassination of John F. Kennedy, an event that everyone my age or older could vividly remember. I said, "Now most of you were too young to . . ." and then I stopped. "Wait a minute," I said, "are there people in this room who weren't born when Kennedy was killed?" My tone as I asked the question was accusatory as if I were disgusted that there could be people in the room who had the nerve to be born after Kennedy was killed. To show how bad the sixties were, one student asked, "The first Kennedy or the one killed in L.A.?" "The President!" I said almost angrily. The students started to answer, "I wasn't." "How many of you weren't born in 1963?" I asked. At least half of the class raised their hands. I shouldn't have been shocked because it was 1984; the class I was teaching was a 200-level literature course, so many of the students were sopho- mores or juniors, meaning that they would be nineteen or twen- ty. But I was shaken. I didn't know if I could talk to people who weren't even born when one of the most important events in my life happened. What did I have in common with these children?

About a year after the Kennedy shocker, I was talking to a ba- sic writing class about how we treat our possessions. Exaggerating slightly, I described how sentimental I felt about my recently discarded typewriter, which I had purchased when I was a sophomore in college. That typewriter had been with me in Evanston, L.A., Cambridge, and finally Pomona. I had typed papers, applications for graduate school and jobs, my dissertation, and numerous course handouts on that typewriter. I then mentioned that I had named my white car, my first, still relatively new car, Lily. At that point, one of the students said that her parents also had names for their cars. I took offense; "I'm not as old as your parents," I snapped and then tried to joke about it (commenting about how grading their papers aged a woman) when I realized I might have hurt the young woman's feelings. But later I thought about my age; I was thirty-six, which meant I was eighteen years older than most of the freshmen. Since my mother was nineteen when my brother was born, and my aunt (her sister) was around seventeen when her first child was born, I knew that it was possible that there were students in my class who had parents my age. That generation gap had just grown wider.

As the years passed, my relationship with the students changed from being like an older sibling or cousin to young aunt to mother to young grandmother. I kept track of the passing years by connecting the major dates in my life and career to the birthdates of the freshmen. So I noticed when the freshmen were born the year (1967) that I graduated from high school, the year (1971) that I graduated from college, the year (1977) that I started teaching at Cal Poly, the year (1980) that I started on the tenure track, ending with the year (1989) that I became a full professor. The last freshmen that I taught were born in 1990. I had been teaching at Cal Poly so long by then that I had run out of career milestones. When I looked at those baby-faced freshmen, I just thought about the fact that I was forty-one in 1990 and that it was the year that my mother first came to live with me. Then I thanked whatever gods that cared about my fate that I would not be around when the freshmen born in 2000 showed up.

In addition to watching students grow younger and younger as the years passed, I had also to deal with rapid changes in technology. When I started teaching at Cal Poly, none of my students had personal computers. I even remember the first student who at least admitted that she had her own computer; she was a re-entry student named Jean. I teased her about this computer she claimed to have and how much easier her life was because she had it. Remember, I was still talking about my typewriter in 1985; I bought my first computer second hand in 1989.

I first encountered a laptop computer in 1996 when one of my students brought his computer to the Advanced Professional Writing class so he and his peer group could work on a collaborative paper. By that time, we all had desktop computers in our offices, the department had developed a computer-based composition program, and many of my colleagues taught composition in computer labs. I never even considered teaching one of those courses. Still, my composition students and I were intrigued by this smaller computer that my student was happy to demonstrate for us.

Now I'll be the first to admit that the computer made my last years of teaching much easier. Instead of having to retype syllabi and keep track of old handouts, I had all of them on file in my computer and could quickly make changes. It was also easier to write multiple letters of recommendation for students seeking jobs and/or entrance into graduate programs once I composed the letters. And composing on the computer is so much easier than trying to compose on a typewriter (a skill I never mastered). I still occasionally hear from students who need me to update a letter so they can apply for teaching positions. It usually takes me just a few minutes to revise the letter, print it, and prepare to send it by mail (I just recently learned how to attach documents on my laptop, but my letters of recommendation files are on my desktop computer).

But then came the Internet and e-mailing. Suddenly, students expected to be able to reach out and touch their instructors 24-7. Uh, I don't think so. Although I frequently visited my professors in their offices when I was a student, I didn't dare call them at home. One USC professor even gave me his phone number and told me to call him to remind him to bring to class a book he wanted me to read, but I was reluctant. He had to reassure me several times that he didn't mind being called at home. I do mind. In fact, one problem I had with the Tufts students was that two of them called my listed phone number, teaching me to keep an unlisted phone number when I moved back to the L.A. area. To prevent students from bothering me at home, I refused to become wired until I retired. I told students that if they e-mailed me after I left my office on Thursday afternoon, they would not receive a response until I returned to my office on Monday afternoon. Still, I occasionally found in my in-box frantic student e-mails, dated on a Sunday night, asking me questions about a paper due on Monday.

Not being on e-mail at home may have prevented me from being bothered by students on weekends and at night, but it also made me busier when I was in my office. Even before e-mail existed, I tried to arrive for my office hours a few minutes early and allow at least fifteen minutes, and preferably a half hour, between the end of office hours and beginning of my classes so I could answer phone messages and read correspondence. But once the e-mail racket started, I found it harder and harder to take care of students I found in my office and respond to the ones who e-mailed me. Once students realized that I responded to e-mails, they assumed that any time they were absent, they could just e-mail me, and I would summarize what happened in class. But if a student missed more than twice, I set him or her straight about the need to come to class and about how I wanted to spend my time when I was in my office.

As the university became more and more wired, we were expected to conduct most of our business online. When I attended a training session one summer day to learn how to post grades online, I remembered coming to a similar session years earlier to learn how to record and take messages for the newly-installed phone system. Since I'd had trouble with the phones, I expected to have trouble posting grades and asked one of the lecturers in the office next door to be ready to come to my aid if I needed help, but I surprisingly had no problems. I also had no problems with retrieving my class lists or dropping and adding students online. But then about a year and a half before I retired, we were required to order our textbooks online. I had been told that one faculty member who was good with computers had taken four hours to order his books. I knew I would not spend that much time ordering books, so I just called the bookstore and had one of the clerks walk me through the process. Basically, she ordered the books for me. I had to order my books online about five times, and I think I completed the process without help once. One time when I was being helped by one of the bookstore clerks, we somehow ended up ordering two different Frost poetry collections and two books that I had used in the past (Song of Solomon and Light in August) but was no longer using. It was a mess; students bought books they didn't need. After ordering my books in Winter, 2009, I happily told the clerk helping me that she wouldn't have to be bothered with me anymore because I was retiring. She told a polite lie about missing me and enjoying our quarterly visits, but I'm sure she hung up the phone and shouted joyfully.

The bookstore clerks were patient with me, but I was not patient when trying unsuccessfully to fill out forms on the computer. My students soon learned that I would not do recommendations on the computer. If I could mail the letter to the university or the place of employment, I wrote it immediately. They could count on me. But if I needed to send it by computer, they should find some other professor to recommend them. And I didn't try any of the computer conversation gimmicks that a few of my colleagues used to spark class discussion. First of all, I didn't need help motivating students to talk, but mostly I refused to be bothered with the computer. I soon started joking about my low tech persona. I told students that I was from the twentieth century, and I would write on my syllabi that my classrooms were "low tech," so they needed to turn off their computers, cellphones, and BlackBerrys when they entered the room. I had to add that line to the syllabus because students' cellphones were playing really bad songs in the middle of my class discussions or during exams and in-class essays. I said to more than one class, "Why doesn't anyone ever have a Motown song on those silly phones? I wouldn't mind the interruption so much if I could hear a decent song."

I disliked the cellphone more than any other new device. It took me a few years of dealing with cellphone users to stop turning around and assuming that the person walking behind me and blabbing into a phone as I walked to my office or to class was not talking to me. And twice I was in a stall in the ladies' room when some woman in the stall next to me started talking on her cellphone. Both times I thought the woman was talking to me. Who the hell would talk on a cellphone while using the toilet? I don't know. I didn't stick around to see who these women were. But I did observe the strange behavior of a perfectly reasonable looking young woman when I was sitting on a bench, trying to meditate and relax between two afternoon classes. The woman came out of the building that I would soon enter, sat down next to me, pulled her phone out of her purse, called someone and told that person that she had just left her 2:00 p.m. class and was about to go to her 4:00 p.m. class and said that she would call the person when she left that class. Now that was just too much for me! As the young lady put her phone back in her purse with a satisfied sigh, I grabbed my purse and briefcase and headed off to my class so I could complain to the basic writers about these twenty-first century people who have to be connected 24/7. I told them about a time not that long ago when people left home in the morning and returned in the evening without talking to their spouses, lovers, or parents during the hours in between. "What are you going to say when you see this loved one in person if you've been talking to him or her all day?" I can't remember what the students said; they probably just laughed at their obviously too-old-to-be-cool professor.

Probably because it's a polytechnic university, the administrators at Cal Poly were very supportive of technology and those who wanted to use it. All of the tenured or tenure- track faculty members had their own computers, and they were constantly being upgraded or replaced. About two years before I retired, we were all given laptop computers, which we could take home with us or to our classrooms, but of course I didn't take advantage of that privilege. There was also plenty of help for those of us who were technologically illiterate. There were workshops, usually scheduled during the summer and offering a stipend to faculty participants, designed to teach faculty how to use the computer in the classroom, to set up websites, to do whatever they wanted to do with these new toys. I didn't attend any of those workshops. And at least in the College of Arts (and I assume in the other colleges) there was a full-time staff person whose job was to help the faculty with computers. I did call on that person for help several times as well as on the staff working at a place called the HelpDesk. If faculty members called that office, a student was dispatched to our offices to solve whatever problems we were having with the computer.

Although I appreciated the help, I was also annoyed that so much money was spent on technology and technological support,

443

at the expense, I thought, of financial support for faculty positions. We were losing faculty to retirement in our department without hiring new faculty. By the time I left the department, there were only two full-time American literature professors (and now there's only one), only one Modern British professor, one nineteenth-century British professor, and no eighteenth-century British professors (For some reason, there had been five at one point). It seemed to me that machines were taking over the university, and I wanted to leave before that takeover was complete.

What made me most eager to pack up my books and purple pens, with which I marked student essays, and go home was my part renegade, part scholarship girl personality. The scholarship girl in me made it hard to do what some senior faculty did, slow down, stop prepping every class, even the ones I could teach in my sleep, stop reading every book again, no matter how many times I'd taught it, stop reading student papers twice when I had time (I never read 200-level papers twice because there were too many students in those classes), stop agreeing to direct so many independent studies and M.A. theses, stop writing so many letters of recommendation so quickly, stop being so diligent when serving on committees or observing junior faculty or lecturers, stop teaching through head colds, laryngitis, and major stomach pain. As I told one sympathetic colleague, if I could just take off without guilt when I was sick or when my mother was sick and had to be hospitalized, maybe I could hang around a little longer, but I was obsessive about being where I was supposed to be when I was supposed to be there. I was well aware that the one major advantage that high school teachers had over college professors was that the high school teacher could call in a substitute. If a college professor is ill and plans to return to campus, classes are cancelled, sometimes for days or even weeks, and my classes generally met only twenty times during the quarter. When I finally took one sick day in 2000 because I was just too ill to drive to campus and try to teach two classes that day, I joked that I was surprised to see the campus was still there when I returned.

While students and colleagues usually appreciate a faculty member's diligence, they also take advantage of it. I told graduate students to allow me at least two weeks to read chapters of their theses and even more time to read their whole theses, but many of them turned in work at the last minute because they knew that they could count on me to read and comment on the theses, sometimes overnight. I had the same problem with letters of recommendation. I think I was asked to write letters of recommendation more frequently than many other faculty members because I again could be counted on to have the letters in by the deadlines. Even if a student asked me to write a letter due in a few days, I complained, told him or her off, and then wrote it. I wrote several letters for one reentry student who had taken only one class with me. When I asked her why she kept "bothering" me (and that was the word I used) and not some of the other faculty she had taken more frequently, she told me that those faculty members were polite but had excuses for not writing letters.

Colleagues were equally quick to ignore my blues singing and take advantage of my scholarship girl personality. I recently came across in my files a surprisingly positive written support of my application for promotion to full professor. I was surprised

445

because it was written by Tall Woman, and I had forgotten that she was at times my ally. In her written support, Tall Woman, the freshman composition coordinator at that time, praised my diligence as a freshman composition committee member. She accurately reported that she could count on me to help her to observe the new lecturers. She described how I made arrangements with the lecturers for classroom visitations, visited the lecturers promptly, met with them after the visit, and then wrote detailed reports of the visits and submitted them to Tall Woman. I was doing what all committee members were supposed to do, but Tall Woman made it clear that my performance was exceptional. I'm not sure if she was signifying about my competition, Charlie, who was also on the freshman composition committee, or just using her evaluation of me to express her frustration with less diligent committee members.

Of course, because I did such a good job when observing my colleagues, I was constantly asked to observe the classrooms of T.A.'s, lecturers, and new faculty members. It was a rare quarter when I wasn't observing at least one faculty member. Once I had a computer, I often wrote a formal letter for the freshman composition or RTP committee and a separate, more informal memo to the colleague whom I was observing. Only in the last year of my career did I finally remove myself from the top of the list of senior faculty to call on for classroom observations. I argued that since I was teaching full time and making less than other full professors, some of whom had administrative released time, I should be excused from doing so much extra work.

As difficult as being a too conscientious faculty member was, being a black female renegade made my career at Cal Poly at least ten times more difficult. In fact, I argue that the black female renegade's time on her job should be counted differently from the white male professor's time. I wouldn't call them dog years, but there are some renegade half years. Being a female probably added six months to each year that I was there, and being black added at least another six months. So for every year I worked at Cal Poly, we should add another renegade year. I taught as a tenure-track/tenured faculty member for twenty-nine years, so that would be fifty-eight renegade years at the job. No wonder I was ready to lay down my weapons and go home. Soldiers don't stay on the battlefield, fighting into their sixties, so why should I?

When I wrote my last post-tenure review, I showed both my scholarship girl and renegade personality. Instead of "forgetting" that I was supposed to submit a post-tenure review or writing a brief perfunctory report, as any sane senior faculty member who thought the process was ridiculous would do, I wrote a four-page, single-spaced report, summarizing all of my activities. I even discussed my strengths and weaknesses as I self-evaluated my teaching effectiveness, research/creative activity, and university/community service. But as I was dutifully completing the report, the renegade in me made me use that opportunity to take shots at the process. For instance, under "university/community service," I listed as my weaknesses, "impatience with bureaucracy, unwillingness and constitutional inability to suck up to the 'proper authorities.'" And then I went into full attack, contrasting the evaluation process at Tufts, which I described as "a small private university, where the teaching load was four courses per year" to the one at Cal Poly, where the full teaching load was nine courses a year. Then came the following paragraph:

> I would like for some of the assessors to assess our evaluation process. How much time is spent by candidates writing these reports, by senior faculty observing candidates and writing reports on their observations, by RTP members writing reports on the reports and discussing and endlessly rewriting the RTP document? And how much are students losing because that time is not being spent preparing classes, grading papers, and advising (not to mention conducting research and writing papers or articles)? And what (if any) correlation is there between the ability to package one's self, to highlight strengths and hide weaknesses, to make a badly written article, published in an obscure journal, sound like a Nobel-prize winning novel, and the ability to teach and advise students effectively?

I wasn't finished. I had attacked the process during my last post-tenure review about five years earlier, so I referred back to that report in my conclusion: "During my last review I expressed a wish that I would be treated like a professional. I have given up on that wish. I now look forward to retirement. I will miss the students and a few of my colleagues, but I will definitely not miss the bullshit."

That's right; I ended a supposedly professional report in which I complained about not being treated like a professional with the unprofessional word "bullshit." And I don't regret the word choice because it perfectly expressed how I felt about the process in which I reluctantly participated. I also have no regrets because it was the last post-tenure review that I wrote even though I stayed at the university another six years. In fact, I think my year was the last time that the dean, who had made the process more arduous since her arrival, requiring each tenured faculty member under review to come in for a conference and writing a report on their report, conducted post-tenure reviews. She didn't have a conference with me that year, and I'm not sure what my fellow professionals under review said or did in conferences or in their reports, but I took credit for killing the post-tenure review in the College of Arts.

I started looking forward to retirement before I wrote that report in 2003. One day in Fall, 1996, the year I was ill and underweight, I was walking toward my office from the parking lot when I started thinking about how long I had been teaching and how much longer I would need to teach. I was walking slower than in my earlier thin days because I was weak from not eating enough. But then I realized that I had been teaching at Cal Poly as a tenure-track faculty member for sixteen years, and that if I retired at sixty as planned, I would have only thirteen more years to teach. I immediately walked faster; knowing that I had passed the halfway point of my career added pep to my step.

Still, when I thought about moving in 1997 and 1998, I looked only at towns close to Cal Poly because I knew that I had more than ten years left to drive back and forth to campus. But then around 2002, I started having moments of premature nostalgia.

They usually happened early in Fall Quarter. As I walked toward the parking lot after my first day of class, I thought, "I won't be doing this much longer." I looked around at the buildings and the rolling hills (I still ignored the horses), soaking it all in, thinking about how long I had been on campus and how much had changed since I arrived in 1977.

Around 2004, five years before my retirement date, I started counting down the years--four more years, three more, two more, one more. Then during the last two years, I counted the quarters and also started taking notice, sometimes aloud, of the last times. We had a contentious contract battle a few years before I retired, and after the contract was accepted by the faculty, I said, "This is my last contract." We had come close to striking twice, so I was happy to know that I could escape into retirement without having to strike. I taught the 20th Century American Literature graduate sequence for the last time in Fall, 2007 and Winter, 2008. I taught my last graduate class (appropriately African American Fiction) and my last new freshmen in Fall, 2008. I also kept track of the last time I taught certain books. I taught Song of Solomon for the last time in Winter, 2009. Finally, I taught my last class on June 4, 2009, the thirty year anniversary of my dissertation defense. The last book I taught was Louise Erdrich's Love Medicine.

Several years before retirement, I worried about that last class. I noticed that I was becoming sentimental with age, and so I worried that I might start crying. I decided that I would not mention that I was teaching my last class. I had never cried in the classroom and didn't want to end my career in tears. I need not have worried; my last class ended with students arguing about religion. I didn't have time to think about its being my last class because I was busily telling them how to prepare for the final and collecting their final papers. However, in Winter Quarter, I came close to crying during my last black literature class. Just before I discussed the final, I closed the book (<u>The Color Purple</u>) and said, "This is my last black literature class, and it's been a worthy last class." Then I congratulated them on their attendance and participation, saying it was unprecedented for such a large 200-level class to have such great attendance. As I talked, I suddenly felt myself choking up. Oh, no! Thank God, the immature 200-level students started begging for a party instead of the final, and I quickly regained my composure as I remembered why I was ready to retire. There was no party, but I did give them the option of writing two essays for the final or just writing one and having it count twice. I think I rewarded them not so much for their attendance but for saving me from crying.

Actually, I should have worried more about gloating than crying. I enjoyed myself so much during my last few years of teaching that it was downright sinful. I got on everybody's nerves, bragging about how I wouldn't be around for whatever torture they would face after June, 2009. What made my joy especially obnoxious is that the department seemed to be under a storm cloud. The new (and only other) American literature professor first lost a baby just before the child was born and then was sent to Afghanistan (he was in the reserves) for a year. Two other male colleagues lost their wives to cancer, and Don K's wife, a fellow renegade who was a composition lecturer in the department, battled breast cancer. All of these personal tragedies darkened my spirits and tied my stomach in knots briefly, but I was soon not so quietly happy again. And then there were institutional tragedies caused by the recession. Lecturers were laid off; we couldn't hire as many new faculty as we needed, and finally the university cancelled summer school. I responded to that last news with the joke: "I knew that this university would fall apart without me." I was amazed and felt slightly guilty that no amount of bad news could destroy my good mood. I, who usually couldn't see the silver lining for the cloud, was walking on air. The more than half empty glass looked full to me.

Indeed, the fact that the campus seemed to be falling apart and that department members were facing so many hardships made me even more anxious to leave. I laughed to myself when I remembered that one faculty member told me I should not retire until the end of our contract so I wouldn't miss some of the good raises that had been negotiated. Well, as I retired, the department members I left behind faced pay cuts in the form of furloughs. In fact, I didn't even receive my last pay raise as an active faculty member because the state did not have enough money. As I said to everyone who would listen, my timing was perfect for a change. I was jumping off the proverbial sinking ship.

I also told everyone who could stand to listen to me gloat that if I enjoyed my retirement as much as I enjoyed retiring, I would be one happy golden girl. So far, I have been a relatively happy golden girl. More than two years since I taught that last class, I have yet to be bored. Not only do I not miss the bullshit, I don't miss my colleagues because I am in touch with the ones I like. I don't even miss the students because I see and hear from them all the time. Some are my friends, some are my neighbors, and some are in my e-mail inbox, asking for letters of recommendation or just checking in to see how I'm doing and to tell me what they're doing.

My outsider status is probably one reason I have transitioned so smoothly into retirement. Unlike Gray, I never saw the EFL department as mine; to me Cal Poly was just the place where I worked. I sometimes called it the plantation and sometimes the battlefield, but it was mainly just that school where I taught. I still am interested enough in the university where some of my friends work to read articles about it in the paper and to skim bulletins that I find in my Cal Poly e-mail inbox, but I don't pay close attention to what I'm skimming unless I recognize the names of faculty or administrators. And I never listen to the President's weekly address, but then I didn't listen to him when I was still an active faculty member.

I have actually been a bit surprised at how quickly and completely I have detached from my former life as a professor. I thought that for the first few years of retirement I would keep track of what was happening at the school and think about what I would be doing if I were still there. But while I have been aware of the beginnings and ends of quarters, and especially the beginning and end of the school year, I don't keep track of what week it is in the quarter and have never thought about what I would be doing during that week if I were still teaching.

Maybe if I had been married to my job, like those two spinster supervisors who were my early negative role models, I would have had more trouble letting go of what was a somewhat tumultuous, but mostly fulfilling, career. But even during my most active professional years, I always had a life off-campus. As soon as I submitted my grades and left campus for the summer, I took my parking decal out of the windshield and retired Dr. Sisney until late September. Occasionally, I administered a summer M.A. exam, advised a student, or attended a meeting, and I came on campus once a month to check my mail (in the later years, e-mail), but I was usually just Mary Sisney from mid-June to late September.

I recently read a book written by Star Jones in 1998; I originally bought it for my mother, but since I started my memoir, I've been reading old memoirs I've found on my bookshelves. Star made an interesting point about her identity. She argued that she saw "lawyer" as her primary identity because she chose it herself. I see her point; no one wants to be defined by others. But Star didn't become a lawyer until she was twenty-four, so who was she until then? And, of course, because people can't tell that she's a lawyer by looking at her and, especially since she didn't practice law for very long, she has to keep reminding people that she's a lawyer, behavior that the "Saturday Night Live" players enjoy parodying.

I have a view different from Star's. Even though I started teaching (my grandmother) in junior high and probably knew I wanted to be a teacher by fifth grade, I still see black female as my primary identity. I was a black female before I began my professional career as a teacher, and I am still a black female now that I am retired. I don't have to announce that identity because it's obvious (well, the black part is anyway; my voice confuses some).

But I haven't allowed others to define what being a black female means for me. If I had let others define me, I would never have earned the Ph.D. and probably would have taught sociology or history, which is what even one of my former students thought I taught (She remembered me but didn't even remember what course she took with me; talk about forgetting the content). I've had people ask me what I did for a living, and when I said I was a teacher, make a not necessarily complimentary comment such as, "Oh, you act like a teacher," or, "I could tell by the way you ordered your food that you were a teacher." Apparently, there's something about my attitude or persona that suggests "teacher." But for me teaching is more what I did than who I am, and that is another reason I've had no trouble letting go of my career.

During my last year of retiring, many people asked me what I would do after I left Cal Poly. My response was "Nothing. That's why I'm retiring. If I wanted to do something, I would stay here and continue teaching." I was partly joking, of course, because I had plenty to do when I retired. I was the sole caretaker of my increasingly more fragile mother (She was 81 when I retired and had stopped driving at 75). Also, I planned to read. At least five years before my retirement date, I started picking out books I would read when retired. And I looked forward to reading the three papers and the many magazines to which I subscribed without waiting until summer or Christmas break.

But my response was also defiant. Most people who innocently asked what I would do while retired were white (I can remember only one black person asking if I planned to travel), and I resented what I saw as the need to keep black women busy.

William Faulkner captured this attitude in his story, "A Rose for Emily," describing the official who passed a law requiring all black women to wear an apron in public. He was writing about a late nineteenth-century Southern racist, but I saw that same kind of racism in the last decade of the twentieth century when my mother moved into my Southern California neighborhood. Twice she had white women approach her (once at the mailbox) and ask if she wanted a job, as a cleaning woman in one case and a caretaker in the other. My mother did not look her age; she could easily have passed for a woman twenty years younger than her sixty-two years. But so what? She was living in a middle-class neighborhood. Why did she have to work? Middle-class, middle-aged white women don't all work. To add insult to injury, my next door neighbor, an elementary school teacher, also named Mary, who was born in Ireland, came to my door one late afternoon to tell me all about her upcoming hysterectomy. When I looked at her, puzzled because we weren't the kind of neighbors who discussed our health problems, she explained that she needed someone to take care of her for a few days or weeks after she returned from the hospital and wanted to hire my mother. Now Mary knew that my mother was in her early sixties and that I, her daughter, was a professor. She didn't care; she saw an industrious, clean black woman and wanted to hire her to be her maid/care-taker. Thanks to my higher education and many years in white institutions, Mary survived to have her operation. I didn't even tell her off; I just pointed out that my mother had her own health problems and was retired. (Then I closed the door and briefly channeled my maternal grandmother, loudly shouting, "Lord, have mercy on these white folks!")

There's something about black people that makes other folks (especially white folks) think that we aren't working hard enough. Ironically, the lazy black person stereotype was most prevalent when blacks did most of the house and field work for whites. In fact, Faulkner makes this point in another text, Sound and Fury, where black servant, Dilsey, climbs up and down stairs, despite her rheumatism, doing all of the work, while her white boss, Mrs. Compson, lies in bed, complaining about being the only one working. More than once I told an EFL colleague that I would not play Dilsey to his or her Mrs. Compson. I would not do all of the work on a committee while my white colleague took all of the credit. And more than once I've had to laugh (to keep from killing) when I've been accused of not working hard enough by a colleague who was hardly working. Just before the ILE program was eliminated, I sat in a meeting with the dean, White, Non White, and two white female colleagues. When the dean asked me to describe my duties as ILE coordinator, I told the truth. I could have lied, claimed to have spent a half hour talking to each student during the advising period or pretended that many of the ILE students came to see me in my office throughout the quarter, and not just during the advising period. I often had students sitting in my office (occasionally an ILE student visited, but they were usually English majors), which was not in the main hallway, so it would have been hard to prove I was lying. But I told the truth, only to be informed that I was not working hard enough for my released time while the two released-time junkies, White and Non White, sat there looking smug. I didn't bother to use the Dilsey-Mrs. Compson analogy since I wasn't sure that the people in the meeting had read the book, but I knew what was happening. I was a black person, so even if I worked twice as hard as White and his nonwhite, nonblack buddy, I was still not working hard enough. (These were, of course, the two men who at one point in my career thought I should teach four courses, three of them composition courses, while Charlie taught two.)

I knew what lazy women looked like. I had seen them up close when I worked in Highland Park during my early teen years. Neither Mrs J, my mother's boss, nor Mrs. R, the woman I served, had a job. Yet they needed us blacks to help take care of their children, make their beds, clean their bathrooms, wash and iron their clothes, and load their dishwashers. I'm not sure what they did with their time. I don't remember seeing Mrs. R, apparently a stewardess before she married, reading a book. The only magazine I remember seeing in the house was <u>Playboy</u>, which I assumed <u>Mr.</u> R read. Several times I saw her in short white dresses, so maybe she played tennis. Still, compared to Mrs. J, who was served breakfast in bed every morning, Mrs. R, who cooked and occasionally even washed the kitchen floor, was a workaholic. When I met Mrs. J, she had two teenage, adopted children (her daughter, who was also named Mary, caused some confusion for Mrs. R's little boy; I had to explain that I was not the one pregnant; it was the one year older white Mary), so my mother wasn't required to babysit. However, she was required not only to cook, clean, wash, and iron, but also to make the family members' beds in the morning and pull back their covers at night. That's right;

those white folks couldn't even pull back the damn covers on their beds. My mother, who still likes to clean and was in her energetic thirties at that time, sometimes had to lie on her bed before she could take off her uniform because she was so tired after a day of working for Mrs. J. Unlike Mrs. Compson, the born-rich Mrs. J didn't pretend to be ill; she was just lazy.

If my race made me defiantly declare that I would do nothing when I retired, my (original) class probably made it easier for me to feel that it was not necessary for me to do anything else; I had already done enough. Remember that I originally planned to be a high school teacher, so I actually exceeded my American dream. I overachieved. In doing so, I became something of a legend in my family. When my nephew was still in college, which he paid for partially with loans, he told me that his father (my brother) mentioned my scholarships almost every time they talked. And recently, Ricardo, my oldest paternal first cousin, who insists on being referred to as Number 1 Cousin (I'm Number 4) instead of the Old One, called to tell me that his grandson had graduated valedictorian from his 90% white high school. Number 1 Cousin claimed that his grandson had taken after me. But I pointed out that I had not graduated valedictorian from my high school. I wasn't even salutatorian, like Number 1 Cousin when he graduated from all-black Douglas High School during the Dark Ages (the fifties). Still, he insisted that his grandson was smart like me.

Actually, my third cousin seems more like some of my white colleagues than he does me. According to his grandfather, my cousin went to a counselor during his freshman year, asked what he had to do to become valedictorian, and then did it. In contrast,

I accepted my placement in basic earth science at ETHS and refused to move out of that class when it was clearly too easy for me. And after a year of living competitively during my junior year at Northwestern, I decided to take four difficult English major courses pass/no pass my senior year rather than pick courses that would help me maintain or improve my high GPA. Similarly, after briefly buying into the race for RTP ranking and losing to Charlie, I opted out during the rematch. And even when I won, I refused to continue to compete, dropping out of the Graduate Teacher Award competition after three victories. I wouldn't even compete for more money, refusing to take part in any of the merit salary competitions.

In contrast, some of my colleagues seemed unable to stop competing. They were like addicts or gamblers who bet on everything. If I told them I started working at fourteen, they said they started at thirteen. If I mentioned that I had taken only one sick day in almost thirty years of teaching, they claimed (falsely because I knew that they had been absent) that they had taken none. If a colleague wrote a book, they wanted to write two. I suspect that one reason many of my colleagues were so much more competitive than I was is that, like my third cousin, they were born to educated parents and grandparents. Earning the Ph.D. in English was not as great an achievement for them as it was for me. Several fathers of my colleagues were in the medical field--doctors, dentists, optometrists--so they were "real" doctors, as my mother might say. Perhaps these "phony" doctors needed to prove something to their fathers. I didn't; my alcoholic father didn't even finish high school; neither did my stepfather.

My parents would have been happy if I had turned that temporary federal government job I had when I was a teenager into a
permanent position. Government workers were held in high es-
teem in my community, so were teachers. Black professors were
almost unheard of when I was in high school and college. I didn't
need to compete with my white colleagues to prove anything to
anybody. I had won when I left USC with my Ph.D. (Rumor had
it that I was only the second black woman to earn a Ph.D. in the
USC English Department, and that was in 1979.)

So I happily packed my three teaching awards, my other gifts
from students, my books, grade books, and purple pens and went
home to do nothing. Well, I said I would do nothing, but in addition to driving my mother to her appointments and taking on
household chores that she could no longer perform, I read. I foolishly subscribed to three new magazines (one weekly and two
monthly) and quickly discovered that I had trouble keeping up
with the seven weekly and three monthly magazines I found in
my mailbox. Soon I had to drop Newsweek. Then I started reading those books I had been putting aside for five years while also
trying to read newly published books I couldn't stop buying. I
had bought a laptop computer and finally was wired at home, so
I checked out web sites and message boards. I even spent several
interesting weeks on ancestry.com, tracing my roots. When I realized I had already read, a few summers earlier, one Philip Roth
novel I was currently reading, I decided to keep a list of books
read so I wouldn't make that mistake again. Of course, once I
started keeping that list, my scholarship girl, goal-setting personality kicked in, and I wanted to read books faster so my list of

books read would be longer. I may not compete with others, but I am still an overachiever.

During my last few years of teaching, I constantly complained about not having enough free time. A professor's schedule is both flexible and rigid. Unless a wimp is in charge of the schedule and trying to mess with us, we can schedule our classes to suit our needs. Some people like to have a packed two-day schedule; others might teach three or four days a week but work mornings or afternoons only. I mostly taught the four-day, afternoons only schedule. However, once a schedule is set for a particular quarter, and the quarter is under way, it cannot be changed. So if I needed to take care of something on a Monday afternoon, I couldn't ask my Monday-Wednesday 4:00 p.m. class to meet at 1:00 p.m. on Tuesday. Professors have to be in their classes on the day and at the time scheduled, or there will be no class. But my complaint about free time focused more on how much time I spent preparing to teach. Unlike some of my colleagues, who worked in their offices, I did my paper grading and class preparation at home. Working at home was more comfortable for me, but in those last years, I seemed always to be working. As my previously sharply focused concentration wavered and my senior care and household chores increased, I found that I literally didn't have time to think. I couldn't wait to have free time.

So imagine my surprise to discover after a few months of retirement that I was following a rigid schedule. I ate breakfast, lunch, and dinner around the same time, which was helpful to my digestive system. And I went to bed and awakened around the same time, which probably also helped my health. But I also worked on my computer at the same time every day and went for my walk at the same time. I even had a regular schedule for e-mailing Paulette, every other day. And if something happened so that I couldn't e-mail at exactly 2 p.m. on the scheduled date, I started my e-mail by explaining why I was "late." When she and I recently had lunch a little later than my usual time (between 11:00 and 11:30), I looked at my watch and said that it was time to go. "Yeah," Paulette teased, "you can't be late reading your book." After a bit more teasing from my so-called friends, I explained that when I said I wanted free time, I meant I wanted to be free to follow my own rigid schedule.

I did find more time to socialize after retiring. Some of the lecturers had been having end- of-the-quarter social events since the eighties. I attended one of the first dinners but then was too busy or too sick of Cal Poly people to spend my breaks having lunch or dinner with colleagues. But after I retired, I attended dinners at the end of both Spring and Winter Quarters. I also went to Smart Woman's forty-fifth wedding anniversary and to the eightieth birthday party of a senior American literature pro-fessor who lives near me. At his party I reconnected with former student Michaela and her husband, who is a former colleague. I also saw Gray there. But the most interesting social event that I attended was the June, 2010, retirement party for Charlie Blank, my Mexican American pal, Friendly Colleague, and a third male colleague. I had mostly enjoyed my retirement party, which both Charlie and Friendly Colleague attended, the year before, so I thought I'd support my newly retired colleagues. I'd always liked Friendly Colleague, and once Charlie and I were no longer forced to compete, we were usually friendly allies. I started referring to him (behind his back) as my fraternal twin since we were hired the same year and were the same age. I even felt a little guilty about leaving him behind, so I was pleased that he was quickly following me off the sinking ship. What surprised me about that second retirement party was how happy I was to see my old colleagues, even White and Non White. I had always resisted the suggestion that department members were like family and was especially annoyed when the men compared me to their wives. But I realized that after working with them for almost thirty years, some of these people were like cousins, maybe second cousins who we want to see once every two or three years at the family reunion, catch up on their families (White's son is the same age as Lily, my first car, so I was always interested in him), wave a fond farewell, and then forget about until the next reunion.

As the beginning of the second year of my retirement approached, I had settled into my rigid routine and looked forward to celebrating my second classes-starting-without-me day. Despite my mother's fainting spell the previous year, I assumed that the third week of September, when classes began at Cal Poly, would be my favorite week of the year, and that Thursday, the day classes began, would be my favorite day. Then our washer broke the day before classes started, and I realized that I might have to deal with some kind of problem every Wednesday before classes began. At least this time, it was a broken appliance instead of a sick senior. Even when I read the e-mail the next day, announcing sad news about a very familiar name, I didn't realize that the broken appliance was not the red light that would

464

ruin my beginning-of-the-school-year celebration. The chair of the department announced that my old frenemy, my last chance at marriage, Gray, had died. She said that she would report the details when she learned more. She never did.

It had been so long since Gray and I were close friends, or even angry combatants, that my feelings were only slightly more intense when I read that sad news than when I learned about the death of less familiar colleagues. There was a shock of surprise, a wistful moment of sadness, and a few bittersweet memories. I didn't revisit the distant past; I just thought about the last time I had seen him, which was at Senior American's birthday party. He had been sitting next to Mrs. Senior American, who had health problems, and said (I assume jokingly) that he would come over and give me a big hug. I (mostly) jokingly responded that I would knock him out if he tried. He didn't try. As the party continued, I moved to another room and was talking to Michaela, Tall Texan, and some other party guests when Gray sidled up to me and confessed that he felt guilty about having (when he was department chair) forced my old friend Ben into retirement. Ben had recently died, and his wife and son were at the party, so I assumed one or both of them gave Gray the evil eye. I tried to reassure him, telling him that he had eased Ben out, letting him keep his office and promising him he could substitute teach for colleagues who were sick (I was healing but still thin, so Ben, another American literature specialist, watched me carefully during his first year of retirement). I didn't spend much time talking to Gray because he was no longer my friend, and I didn't really notice if he was still around when I left the party. After I read about his death, however, I did note that he was not at the June retirement party and wondered if he had been ill. I also figured out his age by adding twelve years to mine; he was seventy-three. I laughed at myself for thinking Gray had been shortchanged a bit by not making it to eighty. When I was younger, I thought that people who lived past seventy should be grateful.

I probably didn't spend more than thirty minutes thinking about Gray that Thursday, but when I checked my Cal Poly inbox on Friday (at 2 p.m.), I found an e-mail from my former office-mate, Lindy, trying to arrange a lunch date for Saturday because she had something to tell me. I knew that she assumed I hadn't received the news of Gray's death since I was no longer on the department's automatic mailing list. I let her know that I couldn't make the lunch date but already knew about Gray. I thought about him a few more minutes and then went back to following my rigid schedule. But that evening as I was multitasking, skimming the local newspaper while watching television, a headline caught my eye. It read "Elderly Pomona Man Found Dead." Ordinarily, that headline would not capture my attention, and I might have skipped the story, but because Gray was an elderly man who lived in Pomona, I read it. And what I read freaked me out. The unnamed elderly man, who was 73 and lived on the same street as Gray, was believed to have committed suicide, and his body was found in the burning guest house, which was behind the main house. Gray had apparently killed himself and tried to cremate his body.

Being an out-of-the-box renegade, I have never followed the so-called five stages of grief. I've been surprised and shocked by the death of a friend or family member, but I have never felt the need to deny it. I'm a realist, a redlight woman. But this time I went into denial. The story didn't give the address for the dead elderly man but listed the block. I actually went upstairs, found my address book, and checked Gray's address as if it were possible that two 73-year-old men would die on the same street in Pomona on the same day. When I confirmed what I surely must have already known, that Gray lived in the same block as the suicide, I cried as hard as I did when he hissed at me in my office. Gray had done it again, made me cry.

My next stage was not anger (that came later); it was panic. Gray killed himself the day before classes began. He had been retired a few years longer than I had. Did he know something that I didn't? I looked forward to the start of school because I was happy to be retired. I knew that reading new books as soon as they were published and (more or less) keeping up with my many magazines would grow old soon. But is it possible that I would some day soon actually miss being at Cal Poly? In three or four years, would the first day of classes at Cal Poly make me sad? I knew I wouldn't kill myself, but I didn't want to spend my golden years wishing I could go back to work.

Being a practicing intellectual, I next tried to analyze Gray, figure him out. He had hinted that he was HIV positive and had lost many friends to AIDS during the eighties and early nineties. Was he ill with AIDS or cancer? Had he maybe been diagnosed with Alzheimer's, like another retired colleague? I thought about our conversation at the party. He confessed feeling guilty about how he treated Ben. Was he trying to say something else to me?

Did he feel guilty about how he treated me? That question made me feel sympathetic toward Gray, so I moved away from it quickly. The burning-the-body move bothered me too, but I assumed that he was either trying to hide the fact that he had committed suicide, maybe so his relatives could collect insurance money, or prevent his body from decaying and smelling. By attempting to self-cremate, maybe he was just being tidy, even considerate.

The problem with being retired, as I'm sure Gray knew, is that there is more time to think. If I had been reading 096 diagnostic essays that weekend and preparing to teach the graduate 20th Century American Literature sequence, I wouldn't have had so much time to worry about what led Gray to his sorry end. But because I was no longer working, I spent several days worrying about what happened to him or rather what he did to himself. Then I moved to the final two stages for me--anger and dismissal. What moved me to the anger stage were two tributes, written by Tall Woman and Non White on the Cal Poly website. I don't remember what Non White said; it was fairly straightforward, although I didn't really agree with it. But Tall Woman wrote some cliché, semi-lyrical nonsense about how Gray loved the small things in life, water, trees, flowers, whatever. Oh, really, Tall Woman, well, if he loved small things so much, why didn't he stick around to enjoy them? Then I consoled myself with the thought that Gray would have stuck around if he had treated me better and remained my friend. Gray had a sense of humor, and I'm funny. If he had been around someone he could laugh with, be real with, instead of hanging with those phony baloneys who were writing ridiculous tributes after he was gone, maybe he wouldn't have killed himself. Then I dismissed Gray, put him out of my mind. I decided that it didn't matter why he killed himself; he was clearly a wimp, a punk. As he lived, so he died, a coward. There would be no more tears for Gray!

Gray's demise may, however, have pushed me toward writing this memoir. I realized as I tried to understand his motives for suicide how little I knew about him. What was Gray's story? I noticed that I had more trouble with white men born in what I called the tween (people born in the thirties and early forties) generation than I did with men from the so-called greatest (World War II) generation or with my fellow baby boomers. I suspected that it was because the white male baby boomers came of age as the world was changing, so they knew that they would not have the privileges that earlier white men had enjoyed while the World War II white men enjoyed some of those privileges during their younger adult years and maybe didn't mind if the younger men had a harder time. But when the tweens came of age in the fifties, they believed that they would be kings of the world, only to see the world change just as they were preparing to ascend to the throne. Of course, a successful black woman represented that changing world as much as anyone, which is why the tweens had problems with me, and in the case of White and Gray, with the Latinas in the department, with whom they were never even friendly.

But if his generation explains why Gray was so bothered by affirmative action and the success of nonwhite women, it doesn't fully explain why he had so much trouble with strong women of all races. Was his mother like mine, verbally or maybe physically abusive? Were his elementary school teachers like my fourth grade teacher, mean-to-the-bone women? Or was he maybe a spoiled rotten, greenlight little brat who expected all women to treat him like a prince?

As I thought about Gray's story, I also reconsidered my own. Since the George W. Bush years, I had been telling my story in a single compound sentence: "I left my illiterate maternal grandmother's house at fifteen, and at thirty I had a Ph.D. in English." But that sentence didn't reveal the hard work, the struggles, the oppression, the anger, the joy, the tears, and the laughter I experienced before and after I earned the Ph.D. In fact, earning the Ph.D. was closer to the beginning of my journey and certainly not the end, as that sentence suggests.

Probably what most moved me to write my memoir, though, were e-mail conversations with former student Paulette, my former high school friend, and a former graduate school friend. While I entertained Paulette with stories of my difficult childhood, I told my friends from high school and graduate school about my years teaching at Cal Poly. And I discussed politics and pop culture with all of them. Then for some reason, one day in early February, I started thinking about my redlight/greenlight philosophy, and the title of this memoir came to me. Once I have a title, I am ready to write. So about nineteen months after I bought my laptop computer, I found the word processing application and started to write.

Now when people ask me what I'm doing, I tell them I'm writing my memoir, which usually shuts them up, especially if they think they might appear in it. When I started writing, I said that I might have a draft completed in two or three years. But I am writing this sentence a little more than seven months after I wrote the first sentence. Soon I'll be doing "nothing" again because I have now told my story.

EPILOGUE
If You Don't Know Me By Now

R etirement parties are like funerals. Since they represent the end of our careers, the people attending the parties pay tribute to us by summarizing our professional lives. As with eulogies, people's comments in these tributes usually say more about them than they do about the person being honored. Some people tell funny stories; others are sentimental. Lindy, the hostess for my retirement party (I refused to accept a department-organized party), asked the English professors and former students who were invited to write their tributes. Two people, my friend, Smart Woman, and a favorite student, Joan H, decided to use the first letters of my name to capture my personality. Smart Woman titled her tribute "There's Something About Mary":

Marvellous sense of humor.
Acidic memos.

473

Rueful observations about others' foibles--and her own.
Youthful outlook--and appearance.

Singlemindedness in getting the job done.
Insight into people, literature, and life.
Sincerity in friendship, and in all she says and does.
Novelty of approach--in thinking, in teaching, in living.
Empathy for others.
Yin and Yang--a balance of opposites and a completeness
greater than all the above.

While Smart Woman focused on what she saw as my personal
attributes, my student, Joan H, described my actions:

Delivers
Retorts

Swiftly,
Insightfully, and
Succinctly while
Noticeably
Eyeballing
You

It's interesting that Joan used the title Dr. instead of my first
name. She was no longer my student and is only a few years younger than I am, but like many reentry women, she had trouble transitioning from "Dr." to the more familiar "Mary." Smart Woman's

focus on my youthfulness reminds me of a comment I made to her more than a decade ago. Since I'm seven years younger than she is and since she keeps forgetting that fact, Smart Woman has several times called me a "stripling" after learning my age. The last time she said it, I retorted, probably "while noticeably eye-balling" her, "When I'm seventy, you'll still be calling me a strip-ling." In a few years, we'll see if I was right.

Both of these women noticed my "acidic" nature since the noun "retorts" does not usually describe sweet remarks. And they both used the "I" in my name to give me credit for being in-sightful, which I hope I am. Others at the party pointed out how I championed the underdog, how I was opinionated and didn't mind sharing my opinions and, of course, how I was funny and liked to laugh. Charlie wrote that he would miss hearing laugh-ter from my open door and inadvertently made me laugh with the following innocent comment: "I know you'd be looking at me rather strangely if I ever asked you your shoe size, but I can definitely say that no matter what the size, they'll be impossible to fill!" Of course, my shoe size is 11 ½ narrow, so if Charlie had asked about it, I wouldn't have thought his question was strange; I would have assumed that he noticed that my feet were unusually long and narrow. And he's right that my shoes will be impossible to fill unless the American literature job search committee (they will finally try to fill my shoes in 2012) finds a six feet tall, very skinny woman to fill them. Friendly Colleague made me laugh with his story of how I had kept him awake at a graduation cer-emony years earlier by reporting the latest gossip to him and the people sitting near us. But the intimidatingly eloquent Don K best captured my loud blackness or black loudness in his description of how the department would change with my departure: "Here it will be less lively, blander--whiter, she'd say. Quieter, too, most likely, which could be horrible: in the face of injustice, Mary was not slow to speak up. She was not afraid to make herself heard."

While I was amused and touched by the retirement tributes, none really surprised me. I agreed with most of the characterizations. But I was surprised, maybe a little shocked, by the reaction of Senior American to an attempted friendly gesture about seven months earlier. Shortly after Obama's election, my mother and I had dropped by his home for a few minutes of celebration. After he retired, Senior American and I complained bitterly in e-mail and supermarket parking lot conversations about the Bush administration, and he was one of several liberal colleagues whom I called on the historic night of the election. The somewhat theatrical Senior called me back, singing "Happy Days Are Here Again," and we agreed to meet with my mother and his wife, both named Catherine, to gloat and kiss the bad days goodbye (or so we thought). When we were leaving his house, I held up my fist, planning to fist bump Senior. I had been fist bumping for days by then; every liberal neighbor and colleague that I saw immediately after the election had been fist bumped by me. But I should have known better than to try that hand jive with Senior American. Years earlier, when he and I had teamed for a departmental political victory, I had tried to high five him, and he had no idea what to do with his hands. So when I held up my fist, Senior American bent his head down, apparently thinking I wanted to punch him in the head. I had to say, "No, Senior, fist bump." The Catherines joined in, and we bumped fists all around. Then I left Senior's house, laughing to myself.

I'm not sure why Senior American thought I wanted to celebrate the election of the first black President by punching a kind, liberal white man with whom I'd had no conflict (and who was old enough to be my father) in the head. If I were into head punching, I would have been punching heads after the election in 2004. I would have punched my favorite Republican student, Jeremy F, gently in the head and then found a few less likable Republicans to punch harder. I appreciate that Senior was willing to let me punch him, but I hope his response says more about him than it does about me. I am a fighter, but I'm not brutal. At least I don't think I am, at least not physically.

Several of my friends and colleagues have complimented me on my self-awareness. As Smart Woman's tribute suggests, they believe that I am as insightful about my own personality traits (positive and negative) as I am about others. However, I was surprised by some of what I discovered about myself as I reviewed my life. I always believed, for instance, that I had developed my warrior-woman spirit during that trial-by-fire year in the ETHS Michael School English Department. I saw myself as somewhat passive, almost timid, before I was forced to fight for myself. But I had punched racist Alice and threatened her mother when I was fourteen. Even at twelve, when that old substitute teacher made his racist comments, I had made some noise and tried to rally the other three black female twelve-year-olds to protest his remarks. I silently defied that old white counselor when I was a student at ETHS and was more vocal in my defiance of Dexter when he tried to take my money. And, of course, I took on the two spinster supervisors at my office jobs. So I was always a warrior; I just found the right weapons when I was a high school teacher, the same weapons that Richard Wright found when he read H.L. Mencken--words.

I also used to think that my big mouth and "acidic" memos and letters caused more problems for me than they solved. I righted some wrongs with those memos, but I also often made myself a target for the wimps' (and their allies, like the white female dean) retaliation. However, I have noticed that I am now less bothered by past wrongs that I at least tried to right than I am by those I silently suffered. Even though I am annoyed that I allowed myself to buy into the RTP race, I am pleased that I fought back when I was unfairly ranked second. If I had not written the protest memo, detailing how unfairly I had been treated, and had not discussed my grievances with the Vice President of Faculty Affairs, a friendly white woman, I would have been even more bitter and alienated during the rest of my time in the department. Even in my personal life, my big mouth probably helped more than it hurt family relations. One member of my extended family, one of Dexter's many nephews, had a stepfather who spent some of the young man's hard-earned money. That now middle-aged nephew not only refuses to see his stepfather, he won't even talk to his elderly mother because he resents her for not protecting him. Because I never gave Dexter my money, he and I had a warm, occasionally even affectionate, relationship when he followed me to Southern California.

As I have with all of the texts I studied and taught, I noticed patterns, motifs in my life. I have already mentioned that I have lived in mostly college and border towns. But I noticed also that certain locations keep recurring in my life. I haven't met that many people from Illinois or Massachusetts in California, but I keep running into people from Kentucky. It actually started in Evanston, where I not only encountered Fake Guy at ETHS, but also two young black women, one a teacher and one a counselor, who were from small Kentucky towns not that far from Henderson. Then we briefly had a boarder from Evansville, Indiana, which is Henderson's across-the-border sister city. At USC I met Gloria Watkins (bell hooks) from Hopkinsville, Kentucky, a town near Henderson. Since we've lived in Claremont, my mother and I have met two other black people who were born in Kentucky, and, at her integrated church, she met an older white woman who was originally from Evansville. Of course, my second officemate's husband, the staredown champion, was also from Kentucky.

Similarly, I kept encountering people associated with Northwestern at the other universities where I studied and taught. My American literature professor at USC, Dr. Potter, was a Northwestern alumnus, as was my officemate at Tufts. And when I arrived at Cal Poly, I found a woman who had actually been in one class with me at Northwestern. She's a year older, but soon after meeting, we realized that we had been in the same Nineteenth Century British Novel class; I was a junior, and she was a senior when we took the class. Possibly because of our Wildcat connection, she and I became close friends. She now lives in Atlanta, but we still exchange birthday and Christmas cards. Even one of my favorite students, Kyla H, briefly attended Northwestern before transferring to Cal Poly Pomona. I think she played softball for the Wildcats.

Names have also recurred in my life. Although my father, brother, and nephew are all named Richard, the most common male name in my family is William. Two of my three uncles were named William--my mother's half-brother, Uncle Willie, and my father's second brother, Uncle William B. My stepfather also had two brothers (one half) named William, one called Bill and the other called W.C. And I have at least two first cousins and one second cousin named William. Uncle Willie's son and grandson share his name. And my maternal aunt's second son (now deceased) was named William Henry. If Uncle William B. has a namesake son or grandson (I have trouble keeping track of his three sons' names since they all have nicknames, like Sputnik), that would be another Cousin William. The most popular family female name was mine--Mary. My paternal grandmother and aunt were both named Mary. My aunt's married name was Harvey, and her mother-in-law, whose backyard was adjacent to my aunt's backyard, was also Mary Harvey. So during the brief time that I lived with my aunt and grandmother, there were two Mary Sisneys and two Mary Harveys living within a few yards of each other. On my mother's side, I had a second cousin named Mary Lou, and her daughter was Mary Ella. Of course, The name Mary was popular when I was a child, at least in Henderson. In fact, there were actually five Marys, counting me, in one of my eighth grade classes. One of the other Marys' last name was Frances, which is my middle name.

Although I never had a friend named Mary, other names have recurred among my friends. During the late sixties and early seventies, I went through a Hellenic period. The black dean's second secretary was named Helen, and since she was only a few years older than I, we became friends during the time we worked together. Then, of course, my only friend in the Michael English Department at ETHS was named Helen, and one of my first friends at USC was an older woman named Helen. Later at USC, I had three friends named Gloria (two black and one white). Next came a brief Elizabethan period. My best friend at Tufts was named Elizabeth, and for a while my best female friend in the English Department at Cal Poly was also named Elizabeth. Maybe I was drawn to some of these women because they had the same names as earlier friends. I am, after all, a creature of habit.

Because of my love of structure, I really appreciated that I taught exactly thirty years after I earned my Ph.D. I was at Cal Poly only twenty-nine tenure-track years and a total of thirty-one years, counting my years as a lecturer. But I taught thirty post-Ph.D. years, starting when I was thirty. I like that kind of symmetry, and I realized several months after I started writing this memoir that there was something symmetrical about my choosing to write in 2011. I noticed that there were quite a few anniversaries being celebrated throughout the year. This year was the 50th anniversary of Kennedy's inauguration, the 50th anniversary of the Freedom Rides, the 50th anniversary of the first black President's birth, and the 150th anniversary of the beginning of the Civil War. Then I realized that this year was also the

50th anniversary of my entrance into white institutions and the 40th anniversary of my graduation from Northwestern. And it was the 21st anniversary of the brutal rape that led to my mother's moving in with me, which means I am now the age that she was when we first started living together. Maybe that was why I was subconsciously moved to write my memoir.

A memoir is, of course, a book of memories. It is not an autobiography. And something else that I learned about myself as I wrote is that my memory is no longer as sharp as it once was. In the past I have dazzled and even intimidated teachers, students, colleagues, and friends with my accurate memory. I could learn students' names rapidly; I could remember page numbers for passages, which drove competitive male students crazy (One even cited fake page numbers in a futile attempt to compete with me). Of course, as I grew older, especially during and after menopause, I had to rely more on tricks to help me keep track of students' names and page numbers. Still, my memory was sharper than the average middle-aged woman's. But as I reviewed my life, I was shocked by how much I had forgotten. I thought I would never forget the details of my battle with the Michael School English Department members, but now I remember little of what was said in the confrontational meeting or the meeting with the superintendent. In fact, I don't even remember the names of the superintendent and the black assistant superintendent.

My memory also may be inaccurate at times. For instance, I believed I heard about the black student occupation of the bursar's office at Northwestern on the news, but my mother claims she told me about it when she came home from work. She heard about it from one of the white students in the freshman dorm where she worked. I decided to stick with my memory of that event. I could check details, such as exactly when the occupation took place, but I decided to write what I remembered rather than what I researched or what someone else told me.

Before I decided to write just what I remembered, I called my brother to see if he had a more accurate memory of when my father left for Baltimore. Since he's almost two years older, I assumed he could remember more about our early childhood than I could. As we talked about the past, my brother started telling me a story about our second cousin (the one with the maid), who put him to work cleaning white folks' houses but took most of the money. I told my brother that I would not include that story because I was writing about my life. I said that if he wanted to tell about Second Cousin's taking his money, he should write his own memoir. Of course, my brother's memoir would be quite different from mine, not just because he is a man who finished only one year of college, spent time in the military, married twice, has three children, and four grandchildren, but also because his childhood experiences were different from mine. How different was revealed in another conversation we had. We were talking about our mother, and he said that he couldn't get over how much she looked like her mother now that she is older. I agreed with him but then realized that he was saying it with dismay while I was happily agreeing. In my brother's memoir, my maternal grandmother would be a villain; in my memoir she's a hero.

Everyone has a story to tell. That point is made in one of the most eloquent literary passages that I have read. It appears in an otherwise mediocre James Baldwin story called "Sonny's Blues." I taught the story in my 201 classes for decades because it was the only Baldwin story found in the anthologies that I used. In the climactic passage near the end of the story, the first person narrator is watching his brother Sonny playing the blues with band members, including a man named Creole, when he says,

> Creole began to tell us what the blues were all about. They were not about anything very new. He and his boys up there were keeping it new, at the risk of ruin, destruction, madness, and death, in order to find new ways to make us listen. For, while the tale of how we suffer, and how we are delighted, and how we may triumph is never new, it always must be heard. There isn't any other tale to tell, it's the only light we've got in all this darkness. (In Going to Meet the Man, p. 121)

If we ignore the conventional use of "light" and "darkness" (Baldwin was a prisoner of his time and religion), we can see this passage as not only a celebration of the blues but also of memoirs. Our tales of how we suffered and how we are delighted should be told and not only heard but also read. I'm sure that Gray had an interesting tale to tell, and so does my brother. But this is my tale of suffering and triumph; this is my blues song. This is my story, and I'm sticking to it.

APPENDIX

THE RACE

Affirmative Action and Negative Reaction

A black woman (call her Evelyn Ashford) and a white man (call him Charlie Blank) were preparing to race. Mr. White, the principal official at the race, came over to Evelyn and handed her two five-pound weights. "Carry these when you run, Evelyn," he said crisply.

"Uh, Mr. White?" Won't these slow me down?" asked Evelyn.

"Trust me, Evelyn, I know how to run a good race," said Mr. White.

"Is Charlie going to carry weights?" wondered Evelyn.

"Don't worry about Charlie," said Mr. White, "you just run your race."

A few minutes later as Evelyn was running in place and lifting her weights, she noticed that Mr. White was placing hurdles in her lane. She trotted up to him.

"What are you doing, Mr. White?"

"Oh, Evelyn, I'm going to have you jump hurdles as you run. You'll look really good."

"But, Mr. White, won't that slow me down?"

"Now, Evelyn, I told you, I know how to run a race."

"Is Charlie Blank going to be jumping hurdles?"

Mr. White became testy. "Evelyn! I told you to stop worrying about Charlie!" As the race was about to begin, the two competitors took their places at the starting line.

Mr. White marched up to Evelyn and whispered, "Step back two feet."

"Say what!?" said Evelyn.

"Step back!"

"But, Mr. White."

"Now, Evelyn."

Evelyn stepped back two feet.

Mr. White walked up to Charlie and whispered, "Run as fast as you can."

The race began. Ready, set, go. Evelyn and Charlie ran. They ran the one hundred yard dash. Carrying weights, jumping hurdles, sweating, and gasping for breath, Evelyn ran hard and fast.

Running smoothly, breathing deeply, hardly breaking a sweat, Charlie ran fast and easy.

They crossed the finish line almost at the same time. It was hard to tell who won.

Mr. Gray, another race official, ran up to Evelyn. "What a great race, Evelyn! Congratulations!"

Gasping and holding her side, Evelyn sputtered, "Did I win?"

"You ran really fast. I'm so proud of you," said Mr. Gray.

"But who won?" asked Evelyn.

"Oh, Evelyn, who won is not important," said Mr. Gray. "Just be happy that you ran a great race."

"But it's a race. And what counts in a race is who won. So who won?"

"Well," sighed Mr. Gray, "you ran really well, but Charlie edged you."

"Wait a minute," said Evelyn, her breath coming back quickly, "I started two feet behind him, carried five-pound weights, and jumped hurdles. If he just edged me with all of his advantages, then I should have won."

"Now, Evelyn," snapped Mr. Gray, "if you had any problems with the way the race was being run, you should have complained earlier. It's too late now. Charlie won, and that's that."

"Wait a minute, didn't you see Mr. White . . . " Evelyn looked around. "Hey, where's Mr. White?"

"Oh, he had to leave town," explained Mr. Gray. "He asked me to handle the ceremony."

"You know," said Evelyn, suddenly feeling really tired, "Charlie is white, you're white, Mr. White is white, and all of the other officials are white. This was clearly a racist race."

"Why, Evelyn!" cried Mr. Gray, stunned and horrified. "How could you say such a thing? You know that I'm not racist! I didn't even notice that you were black."

Evelyn gave up. "Where's my ribbon?" she mumbled.

Glad to see her coming to her senses, Mr. Gray smiled and handed her a red ribbon.

"Congratulations!"

"For coming in second in a two-person race?" snorted Evelyn.
"You ran a beautiful race," beamed Mr. Gray.
Defeated, but still in the race, Evelyn left the track.

Written in 1989

Author's Note

Since I happily completed my memoir in September, 2011, and went on the less happy journey of trying to find a publisher for it (advice to future memoir writers: before you start writing, either sleep with a celebrity or "star" in a reality program), several events have happened that require comment. First, there have been many more sex scandals in the last year, most of them involving teachers and coaches. The most disturbing scandal was, of course, the Jerry Sandusky case. That case and the others make my comments in Chapter Six about teachers and sex seem even more relevant today. Clearly, we need more teachers (and coaches) who aren't that into sex.

Also during this period, there were new developments in the two cases that I discussed in Chapter Eight. OJ prosecutor Chris Darden has just announced almost seventeen years after the not guilty verdict that the now deceased Johnny Corcoran tampered with the bloody glove, which is why it didn't fit and the jury could acquit. His "revelation" so many years after the trial sounds like the sour grapes of a sore loser to me. Stay classy, Chris, while you be-smirch the reputation of a dead man. Perhaps Chris spoke out be-cause a book was recently published arguing that OJ's oldest son killed Nicole Simpson and Ron Goldman. Since I haven't read the book, I won't comment on that theory. But I have several comments on the developments in the Edwards case. First, I'm pleased that my prediction that Edwards would not be found guilty was cor-rect. Since (unlike the OJ trial) his trial was not televised, I had to rely on the always unreliable media for my information, so I still don't know (and probably never will know) the whole story. But the most shocking information revealed was that Andrew Young and his wife spent most of the money donated by two of Edwards' rich friends to build an expensive house. It also became clear that it took some creative interpretation of campaign finance laws to des-ignate as campaign donations money contributed by friends to help Edwards with personal matters while he was running for President. When I heard the prosecution's case, even as filtered through the often biased against Edwards media, I again was shocked that so much tax payer money was wasted trying to prosecute a man who clearly was too smart to violate campaign finance laws.

Still, I enjoyed watching the usual suspects in the media try-ing to bias the jury, which was not sequestered, against Edwards. Immediately after the prosecution rested its weak case, the National Enquirer published a story about how Edwards was yell-ing at his mistress and how she was afraid he might beat her as he did his wife (the apparently false wife-beating story was published in the tabloid in early 2010 and was dismissed even by Andrew

Young as Elizabeth Edwards' attack on her husband from whom she had just separated). The picture on the May 2012 <u>Enquirer</u> cover showed Edwards yelling angrily, probably at some campaign event. Meanwhile Mrs. Edwards' allies at <u>People</u> published two anti-Edwards stories while the trial was still in progress. The first one explained that his adult daughter was accompanying him to court, not because she condoned his behavior, but because she didn't want him to go to jail and leave her younger siblings without a parent. The second one included his mug shots and claimed that he had entertained his mistress in his mansion after promising his wife on her deathbed that he wouldn't.

Of course, as soon as the trial ended, the mistress published a book (which I did not read) and (does this sound familiar?) went on a book promotion tour. Since Oprah no longer has her afternoon show, Ms. Hunter had to settle for Chris Cuomo on "20-20" to conduct her hour-long interview. She also appeared on "The View" and Larry King's old show, now hosted by Piers Morgan. The amount of attention that Ms. Hunter was able to grab and the way the media responded to her book and his courthouse step "God is not finished with me" statement made me change my view of why Edwards still commands so much attention four years after his scandal began. I think now the conspiracy theorists are correct. The corporate media don't want Edwards to rise again because he was "bad," not bad in the evil sense but bad in the Michael Jackson song sense—tough, scary. Edwards made his money fighting corporations and insurance companies, and he was making scary populist noises in the 2008 campaign. When the not-exactly-a-monk Mario Lopez opened the pop culture show "Extra" with the line, "America's most hated couple," and showed pictures of Hunter and Edwards at the same time that Sandusky and his wife were marching in and out of a courthouse in Pennsylvania, where he would soon be found guilty of more than forty counts of child molestation, some of those acts committed in their home with his wife present, I knew that the fixation on Edwards had little to do with his hair, face, and wife.

But my favorite media moment during the Edwards trial came when Jim Avila, the reporter that I called KNBC to criticize during the OJ trial, reappeared. Avila, who is now a national reporter for ABC, started one report during the early days of the trial by saying that Edwards had met Rielle Hunter in a hotel bar and within minutes they were having an affair. First of all, the trial was supposed to be about campaign finance laws, not an affair, and second, while the affair did start the same night that he met her, it took several hours for them to complete the hookup.

Avila's biased reporting on the Edwards trial was one of the many strange media events surrounding this memoir. Another one involved pictures, coffins, and dead singers. In Chapter Eight, I mentioned boycotting the <u>National Enquirer</u> during the seventies because it published a picture of Elvis Presley in his coffin. Earlier this year, when another forty-something musical superstar, Whitney Houston, died in a bathroom in L.A. (Elvis died in a bathroom in Memphis not quite thirty-five years earlier), her open coffin was also published on the tabloid's cover. Meanwhile, several books attracted my attention because of their odd connections to my memoir. I couldn't help but notice that the main male character in the E.L. James' series of novels that apparently

(I haven't read any of them) feature S&M has the same name (although with a different spelling) as my <u>Blue Velvet</u>-loving frenemy. Of course, I originally named him Gray (another name for whites back in the day) in 1989. And speaking of colors (especially "blue"), just as I was finishing my memoir, the writer whose article inspired my title, Joan Didion, published a book (which I did read) titled <u>Blue Nights.</u> Also as I was finishing the memoir, the popular movie <u>The Help</u> was in theaters. I decided to read the novel before seeing the movie and was surprised to discover that the sassy maid Minny complains about the size and quality of the fried chicken pieces she's forced to eat. Interestingly, in Chapter Seven I develop a parenting theory based on the way parents distribute chicken pieces to their children. Also, in Chapters One and Ten, I briefly discuss my (and my mother's) experiences as a live-in maid in the Northern suburb Highland Park, Illinois. Two other not yet released movies, <u>The Great Gatsby</u>, starring Leo DiCaprio, and <u>The Lone Ranger</u>, starring Johnny Depp, connect to my analyses of literary texts (Fitzgerald's novel and a short story collection by Sherman Alexie) in Chapter Nine.

As I noticed all of these strange coincidences, I felt as if I were making things happen in the present by writing about what happened in the past. Could I have caused the Occupy Movement that began in September, 2011, by writing about the Northwestern black student occupation that happened in 1968? But the event that most chillingly connected to my memoir happened this year. One rainy night during early spring, two USC graduate students were murdered in the neighborhood surrounding the campus. In Chapter Three, I discussed how unsafe that area was in the seventies, pointing out that three students had been murdered during the seven years that I lived on or near the campus. Forty years later (I moved to that area in September, 1972), the USC area is apparently still unsafe.

Sadly, several of the people who appear in my memoir have died since I completed it. Actually, the USC professor called Willie Rose died shortly before I began writing, but I learned about his death only after I had written the chapters in which he appears. Then recently the former Cal Poly English and Foreign Languages department chair called Superfly in the memoir died after a long illness. And most shockingly, one of my favorite former students, who was also one of the three e-mail friends who inspired me to write my story, Paulette F, died suddenly of complications from MS.

Paulette's sudden death reminded me of the dangers of being both a witch and a redlight woman. She was my most faithful e-mail friend; we corresponded every other day. But she would disappear for a few days every now and then because she was having trouble with her aging computer or with the Internet connection. So when she disappeared in mid-May, I assumed that she was just having Internet problems. However, when I heard from her after a week, she informed me that her MS symptoms had returned and were much worse; she had been bedridden. She then jokingly asked me if I had used my evil witch powers to make her sick because just before she disappeared we had heatedly debated the appropriateness of saying "Happy Mother's Day" to every woman, whether or not she was a mother (she was for; I was against). I assured her that I would never use my evil powers on a sister. Then I lamented that if she disappeared again, being a redlight woman, I would assume that she was very ill, even at death's door. Paulette sent two or three more e-mails and then disappeared again. I, of course, worried and after more than two weeks without hearing from her, I called to see how she was doing. Just before her mother, with whom she lived (along with a younger sister), answered the phone, I had the redlight thought, "I hope her mother doesn't say she is dead." During our brief conversation, Paulette's mother claimed that her older daughter was on a trip and said that she sometimes went on trips without telling her mother where she was going. I found that information odd but stopped worrying about Paulette. Of course, I now know that I should have been worried and suspicious because Paulette would have dropped me a quick line to let me know she was leaving town or she would have e-mailed me while she was out of town. Anyway, a week after that phone call, I found in my mailbox an envelope with Paulette's sister's name in the return address. The envelope contained a small funeral card for Paulette. That's how I learned that my former student and every-other-day e-mail friend was indeed dead.

So there have been deaths, but there has also been a birth. My brother now has <u>five</u> grandchildren. Between the day that Paulette disappeared from my e-mail inbox and the day that I found her death notice in my mailbox, a beautiful little girl named Kylah Bree Griffin was born. And so the story of pain and pleasure, suffering and triumph continues.

September, 2012